Shelter:
Need and Response

Shelter:
Need and Response

*Housing, Land and Settlement Policies
in Seventeen Third World Nations*

JORGE E. HARDOY
and
DAVID SATTERTHWAITE

*Both of the International Institute for
Environment and Development, London*

JOHN WILEY & SONS
Chichester · New York · Brisbane · Toronto

British Library Cataloguing in Publication Data:

Hardoy, Jorge Enrique
  Shelter, need and response.
  1. Underdeveloped areas—Housing
  I. Title   II. Satterthwaite, David
  301.5'4'091724   HD7391   80-41417

  ISBN 0 471 27919 6

Text set in 10/12 pt Linotron 202 Times, printed and bound in Great Britain at The Pitman Press, Bath

To B.W.J.

Contents

SECTION V COMPARATIVE ANALYSIS

List of Tables

Preface

Although only two authors' names are listed on this book, it was only made possible by the joint efforts of five teams whose members are listed below. The introduction contains a description of how the five institutions collaborated in the project of which this publication is one result. The information on which it is based is drawn largely from national and regional reports prepared by teams from the Institute of Development Studies, University of Mysore in India, the Department of Architecture, University of Khartoum in the Sudan, the Centro de Estudios Urbanos y Regionales in Buenos Aires, Argentina, and the Faculty of Environmental Design, University of Lagos in Nigeria. The national and regional reports that each of these teams has published are listed at the end of each section of this book. We are most grateful to our friends and colleagues within the International Institute for Environment and Development and within these four teams for their help and advice in preparing this book. We are also grateful to Nigel Harris and Michael Hebbert for their comments on Section V, to Ken Wass for preparing the maps and to all at John Wiley for making the publication of this book so easy for us. We alone are responsible for the criticisms, judgements—and errors—the text contains.

We are greatly indebted to the Canadian Government whose generous funding made this book—and the project of which it is part—possible. We are also grateful to the Dutch Government and to the United Nations Centre for Human Settlements (Habitat) for their support of our work.

Jorge E. Hardoy
David Satterthwaite
International Institute for Environment and Development

The Team

1. Arab Countries
Omer M. A. El Agraa
Adil Mustafa Ahmad
Department of Architecture, University of Khartoum, Sudan

2. Asia
R. P. Misra
B. S. Bhooshan
Institute of Development Studies, University of Mysore, India

3. Latin America
Oscar Yujnovsky
Ruben Gazzoli
Beatriz Cuenya
Centro de Estudios Urbanos y Regionales, Buenos Aires, Argentina

4. Sub-Saharan Africa
David Aradeon
Faculty of Environmental Design, Lagos University, Nigeria

N. Gebremedhin
T. Chana
D. Lamba
Mazingira Institute, Nairobi, Kenya

G. Mayao
S. M. Kulaba
Tanzanian Ministry of Lands, Housing and Urban Development

5. International Institute for Environment and Development
Jorge Hardoy
David Runnalls
David Satterthwaite

Introduction

This book summarizes housing, land and settlement policies in seventeen Third World nations and compares and contrasts their effectiveness. Its purpose is twofold. Firstly, it seeks to provide a broad international picture of the current state of settlements and current settlement trends. Secondly, it aims to outline and assess government efforts to tackle such pressing problems as: poor and generally deteriorating urban housing conditions; large portions of the population living in conditions which enormously exacerbate ill-health, endemic disease and social tensions; urban housing markets inhibited by inflated land prices; urban agglomerations growing haphazardly with no effective public control; rising construction and management costs; and whole regions of the national territory largely excluded from economic and social development. These are problems facing virtually every Third World government.

Background

The idea of a major research project to assess housing land and settlement policies came out of Habitat, the United Nations Conference on Human Settlement, held in Vancouver in June 1976. This was the fifth of the international conferences convened by the United Nations to focus world attention on major global issues. It had been preceded by conferences on the Human Environment (Stockholm, 1972), Population (Bucharest, 1974) Food (Rome, 1974) and the Role and Status of Women (Mexico City, 1975).

The idea of a world conference on housing and planning had been discussed for over two decades, when in December 1973 the United Nations General Assembly approved a general framework and budget that launched Habitat. Eighteen months previously, at the Conference on the Human Environment, the Canadian Government had proposed Vancouver as the host city. After a slow start, the Habitat Secretariat began a series of regional meetings in 1975 and requested country reports from each nation. And a preparatory committee with representatives from 56 nations reviewed the draft Conference documents, including draft *Recommendations for National Action* and a *Declaration of Principles*.

At Habitat, representatives from 132 nations approved 64 *Recommendations for National Action*. If implemented, these would require very considerable changes in development strategy for virtually all Third World governments and in aid policies for both multilateral and bilateral aid agencies. For instance, they would demand serious attempts to ensure a more equitable spread of development both among regions and among income groups. They would also demand a much greater commitment to tackling housing and 'human settlement' problems,[1] a commitment noticeably lacking in the 1960s and early 1970s. For the *Recommendations* include: the need for each nation to establish a comprehensive national settlements policy linked to socioeconomic development policy; increased public control of land use; increased support for the construction sector (including the 'informal' sector); priority to the provision of safe drinking water and hygienic disposal of household and human wastes for the whole population; and new institutions at 'national, ministerial and other appropriate levels of government' to formulate and implement the policy with public participation as an indispensable element in this at national, regional and local level.

However, since many of the *Recommendations* involve considerable (and even radical) departures from policies in force in 1976, the question arises: how serious, how real was the commitment made by government representatives at the Conference? In August 1977 the International Institute for Environment and Development began its human settlement programme to assess the work both of national governments and major aid agencies in the light of the Habitat *Recommendations*. This followed on from its work prior to the Conference which included the book *The Home of Man* written by Barbara Ward (the Institute's President until 1980) at the request of the Canadian Government, to stimulate interest in settlement issues. The Institute also organized the Vancouver Symposium at the request of the United Nations Habitat Secretariat to focus both government and non-government representatives' minds on the crucial issues the Conference should address.

The Project

To undertake the assessment of government action in the Third World, the Institute joined with four research institutions, one in each of the major Third World regions. Each of these institutions examined a group of countries in their region. A team from the Department of Architecture, University of Khartoum, studied a group of Arab nations: Egypt, Iraq, Jordan, the Sudan and Tunisia. The Institute of Development Studies, University of Mysore, looked at a group of Asian nations: India, Indonesia, Nepal, the Philippines and Singapore.[2] The Centro de Estudios Urbanos y Regionales, Buenos Aires, covered Latin America: Bolivia, Brazil, Colombia and Mexico, and the Faculty of Environmental Design, University of Lagos, studied a group of SubSaharan nations: Kenya, Nigeria and Tanzania.

Teams visited these seventeen nations in late 1977 and the first half of 1978. National and regional reports were prepared by each team and were published by them in their region. The IIED undertook to coordinate the fieldwork, exchanging and commenting on the information as it was being collected, to prepare background material covering all seventeen nations and to spread the results and conclusions of the project, helped and advised by its colleagues in the collaborating institutes. This book is the final work of this assessment project although the five institutions plan to continue the research and cover other major Third World nations, as well as examining the special problems that confront the very small nations, in a second stage between 1981 and 1983.

The seventeen nations were chosen so they encompassed the widest possible range of size and population, climate and culture, level of social and economic development and degree of urbanization. The seventeen governments have widely differing power and resource bases and thus differing abilities to implement the *Recommendations* they approved at Habitat. The nations combined contain around three-fifths of the Third World's population (excluding China). They also include the most populous nations within each region and many of the nations that played major roles at the Habitat Conference and claim to have been influenced by its *Recommendations*.

A selection of the Habitat *Recommendations for National Action* were judged to be the best way of assessing the depth and extent of each government's commitment to tackling pressing housing, land and settlement problems. This is for two reasons. Firstly, we believe the *Recommendations* provide an outline for a comprehensive policy for any government intent on tackling such problems. And secondly, the *Recommendations* were officially endorsed by representatives of all seventeen national governments. This implies a commitment to follow them up. The comparative analysis in Section V can thus highlight those *recommendations* that have been followed and point to others that have been virtually ignored.

Although this book examines government policies in the light of the Habitat *Recommendations*, it does not seek to measure the Conference's effect. The *Recommendations* reflect policies which had been proposed before preparations for the Conference began in 1974 and already put into practice in certain nations. The *Recommendations* themselves are no more than an amalgamation of ideas; some no doubt influenced by the national policies and experiences the *Recommendations'* drafters regarded as successful. In a few specific instances, the Conference almost certainly was responsible for helping to legitimize new approaches. It may well have given more weight to those factions in national governments (or that influence governments) which are demanding more support for settlement policies. It may have helped hasten the acceptance of a 'basic needs' approach within development planning. But to isolate the impact of the Conference itself as distinct from other influences seeking similar changes is not a task this assessment project sought to fulfil.

The information presented in this volume shows what can be accomplished with well-trained research teams who have knowledge and contacts in the regions within which they operate, but with limited time and resources. Assessments like this are no substitute for in-depth research. But they can become major fact-finding operations that help examine questions and recommendations from which policies can be prepared. After all, it will be a long time before most Third World nations produce the objective information and have the trained manpower for more precise and effective policies, programmes and evaluation procedures.

The book is divided into five sections. Sections I to IV look at housing, land and settlement policies in the seventeen nations grouped by region. Section I looks at Arab nations, Section II at Asia, Section III at Latin America and Section IV at SubSaharan Africa. For each nation there are maps and a background section to give the reader an idea of its physical characteristics, economic base and settlement pattern.

Section V compares and contrasts government action (and non-action). It uses 22 of the 64 *Recommendations for National Action* for this assessment. These 22 are the most specific. Thus, national achievements can be measured against them. They are also the most fundamental. If these were in place, so too would virtually all the others. The assessment does not look in detail at the 'Settlement Planning' *Recommendations* because there is substantial overlap with the 'Settlement Policy' *Recommendations* which are assessed.

In addition, some selectivity was necessary to keep Section V to a manageable length. The *Recommendations* alone (with their preambles and elaborations) take up 80 pages. An assessment of each would have been impossible. For many of them, little or no data exists to assess government efforts. We have not covered the 'Public Participation' *Recommendations*. Although the *Recommendations* themselves are of fundamental importance, we found it impossible to assess government action in response to these for two reasons. Firstly, the concept of 'public participation' and the *Recommendations* which deal with it are vague. There is no general agreement as to what constitutes effective public participation. Thus, there are no agreed criteria on which settlement or housing policy formulation or implementation can be judged for the extent to which they allow 'effective public participation'. Secondly, even if we chose criteria, a comparative analysis of the seventeen nations' popular participation channels and a judgement as to their effectiveness would demand a detailed knowledge of the social and institutional structure of each nation at national, regional and local levels. This was beyond the scope of our national studies. However, the commitment of the various levels of government to meeting their population's basic needs related to shelter at least gives some clue of the extent to which public participation influences government, and an assessment of this commitment (and its effectiveness) is what Section V aims to provide.

Being selective about which *Recommendations* to use and which parts of each to quote inevitably lays us open to the criticism of being biased towards certain aspects. However, we quote the entire central text for each of the *Recommendations* covered. We also feel that anyone reading the *Recommendations* would agree that those we chose were the most specific and appropriate for analysing government action to meet the criteria the *Recommendations* outlined for a settlement policy. These were that the policies 'must facilitate the rapid and continuous improvement in the quality of life of all people, beginning with the satisfaction of the basic needs' with priority given 'to the needs of the most disadvantaged people' (*General Principles*, paragraphs 1 and 2).

Statistics and Definitions

We encountered two major problems in seeking to compare and assess settlement trends and government policies. The first stems from a lack of relevant statistics, the second from a lack of internationally accepted concepts and definitions.

As we shall describe in detail in this volume, only recently have governments become more concerned with the spatial aspects of development policy. Few are even beginning to introduce well-defined objectives related to settlements—and to the spatial distribution of social and economic investments—into development plans. Even fewer are seriously considering what kind of policies and what kind of coordination between the various ministries and regional or local governments and agencies are required to achieve such objectives. The result of such lack of interest in the past has meant that the data required by a settlement policy (or within this a programme to improve housing conditions or basic services provision) has not been collected. This lack of data seriously constrains government efforts in the formulation of plans, their implementation and their evaluation. It also makes an assessment of government action very difficult.

Whenever possible, we use government statistics in this volume. But even the most basic social or economic data was sometimes not available when our teams visited the major housing and planning institutions in each nation. On occasion, it was impossible even to get reliable estimates as to the population of a nation's largest urban centres. Indeed, some nations' official report to the Habitat Conference on their settlement situation did not even give the population of major settlements let alone settlement trends, housing conditions, the spatial distribution of population and of public and private investment and so on. In addition, different sources often give very different figures for the same thing. And figures for the population of a settlement do not make it clear whether the figure is for the urban agglomeration, the city, the metropolitan area or indeed the province or region which has the same name as the city.

The second major problem, the lack of internationally accepted concepts, is perhaps best illustrated by the very different criteria used by the seventeen nations to define what constitutes an 'urban' settlement. For some nations, urban criteria are not related to a minimum population size but to a settlement's function as a local administrative centre or to a certain level of population density, or to certain defined urban characteristics related to commerce or infrastructure. This makes any international comparisons between national urban growth rates or degrees of urbanization somewhat dangerous. For instance, India's urban criteria are that the urban settlement has to have more than 5000 inhabitants, more than three-quarters of which are engaged in non-agricultural occupations, and a density of more than 1000 persons per square kilometre.[3] Using this definition, only an estimated 22 per cent of India's population was urban in 1980. But if Indian settlements were classed as 'urban' if they had a nucleus of 1500 or more inhabitants (as they are in Colombia) or had 2000 or more inhabitants (as they are in Kenya), then more than 40 per cent of India's population would have lived in 'urban' settlements in 1971.[4]

Similarly, Bolivia's population was 32.2 per cent 'urban' in 1976 if urban centres are those with more than 20 000 inhabitants and 42.6 per cent 'urban' if urban centres are those with more than 2000 inhabitants.[5] And Mexico's population would have been 43.3 per cent urban in 1970 if urban centres were those with more than 20 000 inhabitants instead of 59 per cent, a figure based on the urban definition being localities of 2500 or more inhabitants.[6]

The criteria used by each nation to define what constitutes an 'urban' settlement are given in their background sections. We do compare and contrast the seventeen nations' degree of urbanization and growth rates for urban population in Section V because each national urban definition does at least include all its larger settlements. But the major differences in national criteria make these of limited validity.

Another example of the lack of standard concepts and definitions is the use both by the Habitat *Recommendations* and by national development plans of the term 'the informal sector'. Although there is no clear and agreed definition as to what constitutes 'formal' and 'informal' sector activity, for housing construction, it is useful to distinguish between building operations that meet official standards and regulations and those that do not. Thus, throughout the text, the formal construction sector is taken to mean both public and private enterprises constructing buildings that meet official standards and regulations and that are officially approved and, for instance, registered for municipal taxes. The informal construction sector is taken to include all construction activity which does not have such official approval. So the distinction between the two sectors is based only on the houses built. We do not mean to imply that building firms, artisans, labourers and those engaged in self-help construction or improvement only work within one of these sectors. And although the work of these two sectors is closely interrelated, we found the distinction useful in that large portions of the national population in virtually all Third World nations have been housed and continue to be housed in units built in this 'informal', sector. Only rarely are the activities in this sector officially recorded. And despite its major contribution to national housing construction, its efforts are often ignored or even discouraged by governments.

For the Background section, statistics relating to climate, rainfall and population distribution are drawn from the *New Encylopaedia Britannica, 15th edition* (1977). Virtually all other statistics are drawn from the World Bank's *World Development Indicators 1980* and the regional reports on which the sections are based. Information on imports and exports are drawn from *The Economist's Book of Figures* and from *Encyclopaedia Britannica* books of the year. Where statistics are used from other sources, the source is quoted in the notes given at the end of each section.

Inevitably, in a book as wide-ranging as this, there will be errors in interpreting data and incomplete coverage of some aspects. We would welcome any comments, corrections or reactions to this book's contents and hope that demand for it will be sufficient to permit an updated and corrected version at some later point in time.

Notes

1. The term 'human settlement' is understood to include both natural and fabricated elements which together comprise the territorial habitat within which humanity lives, works, raises the family and seeks physical, spiritual and intellectual wellbeing. This is based on the definition given by *Human Settlements: The Environmental Challenge; a Compendium of UN Papers prepared for the Stockholm Conference on the Human Environment*, published by the United Nations Centre for Housing, Building and Planning (1974).
2. The Asian team also looked at policies in China and Japan for comparison with these five Asian nations in its regional report.
3. There are some exceptions to this; see note (3) in Section II.
4. According to 1971 census data, 108.90 million people lived in urban areas, 22.33 million lived in villages with 10 000 or more inhabitants, 32.72 million lived in villages of between 5000 and 10 000 inhabitants and 217.61 million lived in villages of between 1000 and 5000 inhabitants, out of a national population of 548.2 million.
5. United Nations (1977): *Policies on Human Settlements in Bolivia*, Summary of the Report prepared by the mission of the United Nations Habitat and Human Settlements Foundation quoting 1976 census data, page 5.
6. Unikel, Luis (1976). 'El desarrollo urbano de Mexico; diagnostico e implicancias futuras', El Colegio de Mexico quoted in Cuenya B., Gazzoli R., and Yujnovsky, O. (1979), *Assessment of the Vancouver Recommendations for National Action*, (Argentina: CEUR), Table 12, page 53.

SECTION I: ARAB NATIONS

Egypt, Iraq, Jordan, The Sudan and Tunisia

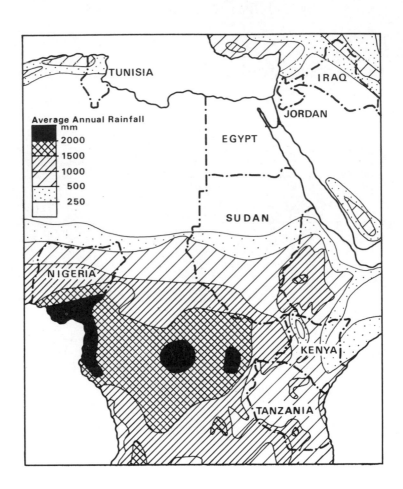

Average Annual Rainfall
mm
2000
1500
1000
500
250

TUNISIA

IRAQ

JORDAN

EGYPT

SUDAN

NIGERIA

KENYA

TANZANIA

Background

Egypt

Located on the north-east corner of the African continent, Egypt encompasses a million square kilometres and had a population of 40 million in 1978. Official projections suggest a population of 66 million by 2000.

Most of Egypt is uninhabited desert. Despite the nation's very considerable size, more than 90 per cent of the population live in the Nile Delta in the North and in a thin strip along the Nile Valley running south–north which cuts the country in two. Average population densities exceed 1000 persons per square kilometre for the Valley and Delta which represent some 3.6 per cent of the national territory. Settlement elsewhere is constrained by lack of water. Since Egypt lies in the North African desert belt, rainfall is very low and falls as one goes south. In Alexandria, annual average rainfall is about 180 mm, in Cairo it is around 100 mm, in Asyut in Central Egypt 7 mm and in Aswan in the south, 1 mm. The climate is thus hot and dry with mild winters in which what little rainfall there is tends to be concentrated. There are three major desert regions: the vast western desert covering more than three-fifths of the nation; the eastern desert between the Nile and the Red Sea covering one-fifth; and the Sinai, to the east bordering on Israel, covering 6 per cent. In the 1966 census, these contained little more than 1 per cent of the national population.

Egypt has one of the world's most ancient urban traditions. Its earliest settlements date from the Fifth Millenium BC while a literate urban society dates from 3000 BC. Throughout its prehistory and history, all major population centres were based on the Nile Valley and Delta with the deserts each side providing some defence against aggressors. After five centuries of relative isolation, Napoleon Bonaparte's brief excursion into Egypt between 1798 and 1800 brought it into the politics of the European colonial world with both Britain and France vying with each other to influence and control the country. The British built a railway from Alexandria to Cairo and then to Suez in the 1850s to improve communications with India. In 1869, the Suez Canal was completed under French direction. The British finally separated Egypt from the Ottoman Empire in 1882 and occupied it until 1922 when a constitutional monarchy was formed. The Arab Republic of Egypt was formed after the Revolution in 1952.

Agriculture remains the most important economic sector. In 1978, half of the labour force were employed in this sector which accounted for 29 per cent of GDP in this same year. It also accounted for around half of all export earnings in 1976, cotton being the major export crop. Annual growth in agricultural production averaged some 3 per cent between 1960 and 1978. The Aswan High Dam (completed in 1970) in the

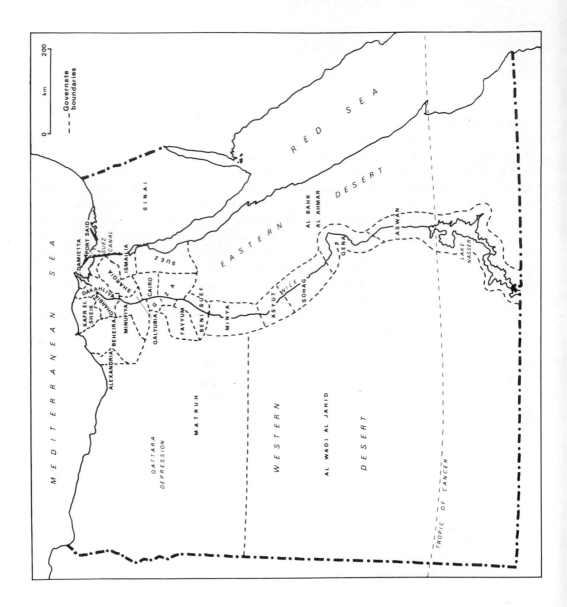

south has allowed perennial irrigation to be considerably extended and the annual flood to be better controlled.[1] However, since almost all agricultural production is concentrated in the Nile Valley and Delta, rural population densities are very high. Egypt has one of the world's highest ratios of rural people to agricultural land with one hectare of land supporting more than six people. Egypt's food production has not kept up with growing demands; 23 per cent of its merchandise imports in 1977 were food. And a report in November 1979 suggested that food imports were growing while food exports were falling.[2]

In 1980, 45 per cent of the population lived in settlements defined by government decree as 'urban'. The term urban does not imply a minimum number of inhabitants and some villages have larger populations than settlements designated as towns. The number of people living in urban settlements has grown relatively slowly in the last decade compared to most other Third World nations, averaging 3 per cent a year between 1970 and 1980. Some two-thirds of the urban population is concentrated in just two cities: Greater Cairo, the capital, by the beginning of the Delta and Alexandria, Egypt's major port on the north coast. An estimate for 1979 put metropolitan Cairo's population at 8.5 million (making it the largest city in Africa)

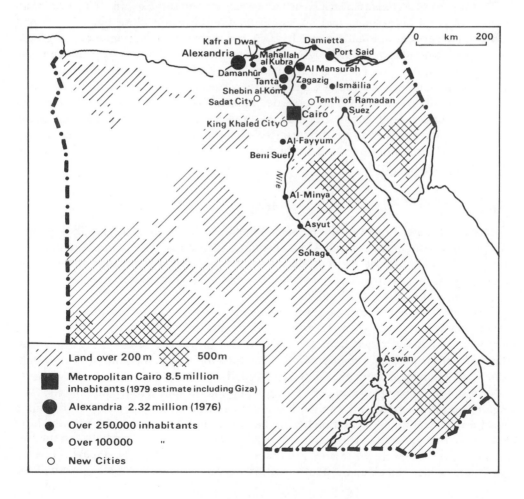

while Alexandria's population was 2.32 million in 1976.[3] These two cities (and the areas around them) have monopolized much of Egypt's rapidly growing industrial sector. In 1978, manufacturing industries produced a quarter of GDP. Spinning and weaving has become the largest manufacturing industry and its products are Egypt's major manufactured export. Other sectors such as food processing, engineering, building materials and chemicals have also developed. So too has the oil industry whose rapid development since 1974 has turned Egypt into an oil exporter. Other important urban areas include Port Said, Ismailia and Suez, all on the Suez canal and Tanta, al-Mansurah and Mahallah al Kubra, all in the Nile Delta. By 1976, according to census data, Suez had 194 000 inhabitants while Port Said had 263 000, Mahallah al Kubrah 293 000 and Tanta 285 000.[4] There are also some major urban centres of over 140 000 inhabitants on the Nile Valley between Cairo and Aswan including Asyut, Fayyum, Minya and Aswan itself. No other urban centres of comparable size exist outside the Nile Valley and Delta. Besides other towns, there are some 4000 villages of various sizes and some 29 000 *Kafr* (hamlets).

Despite considerable economic progress since the 1950s, per capita income remains low, especially when compared to oil-rich Arab states. Per capita GNP was $390 in 1978. Most rural settlements lack basic infrastructure and services. In 1976, more than a third of rural households had no supply of filtered water close by.[5] Health and educational services are inadequate. In 1976, more than half the population aged ten and above was illiterate.[6] Bilharzia and gastrointestinal diseases remain endemic throughout rural areas. There is a comparable lack of basic services in urban areas. Many of the buildings in Greater Cairo are not connected to water supplies, sewage or electricity systems. Housing is overcrowded and traffic congestion severe. Unemployment and underemployment are high in both rural and urban areas and many Egyptians have migrated to neighbouring oil-rich states. Estimates put the percentage of the labour-force working abroad as high as 4 per cent and this includes many skilled or professional Egyptians.

Iraq

Located to the north-west of the Persian/Arabian Gulf, Iraq had 12.2 million people in 1978 on a land area covering 435 000 square kilometres. The national population has grown rapidly in the last two decades with the annual population growth rate averaging 3.3 per cent a year between 1970 and 1978. Projections suggest that the population will be around 23 million in 2000.

Iraq's development through seven millenia of recorded history and settlement development has been strongly influenced by the two rivers, the Tigris and the Euphrates, that run down its centre. These rise in Turkey, cross the Iraqi north-western border and run roughly parallel down to the south, meeting at Al Qurnah, some 140 kilometres from the Gulf. The broad swathe of territory these two river valleys define encompasses most of Iraq's population and major settlements. The region around Baghdad, the capital, has the highest population density. More than a quarter of the national population live in the governate of Baghdad which covers little more than one per cent of the national territory. Apart from the land between the two rivers, the two other major regions are the western desert and the northeast. The four governates which run along the south-western border with Saudi Arabia cover half the

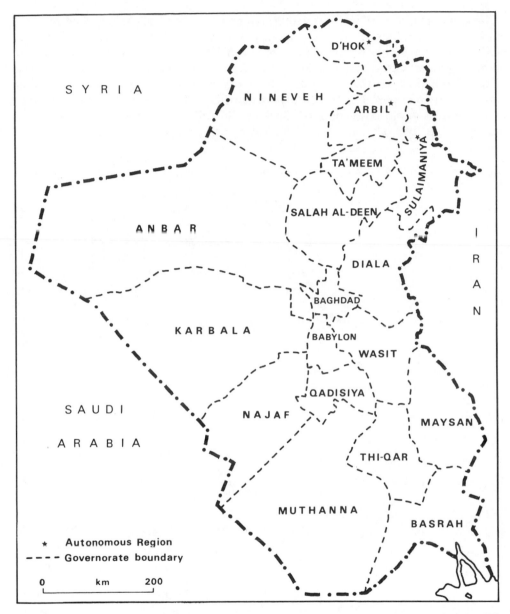

national territory but support little more than 10 per cent of the population. The north-eastern region has areas of relatively high population concentration and is the only place in Iraq where rainfed cultivation is possible. Around one sixth of the national population is in the four north-eastern governates of Ta'meem, Dhok, Arbil and Sulaimaniya.[7]

Much of Iraq is low-lying and has hot arid summers and relatively cool, humid winters. Rainfall is very low for the whole south and west of Iraq and cultivation is only possible with irrigation. In the northeast, average annual rainfall is of the order of 400 to 600 mm and may reach 800 mm or more on the higher mountains.

Mesopotamia, most of which is within Iraq's present border, contained perhaps the earliest recorded, literate urban community. Within Mesopotamia, which means 'the land between the rivers', remains of Nineveh (the Assyrian city), Uruk (one of Sumer's greatest cities) and Babylon can be found. Mesopotamia was under the rule of the Ottomans from the sixteenth to the early twentieth century. Iraq became an independent state in 1932, after fifteen years of British rule which had begun when British forces took possession of Baghdad in 1917. The present republic was established in 1958, after the monarchy was overthrown.

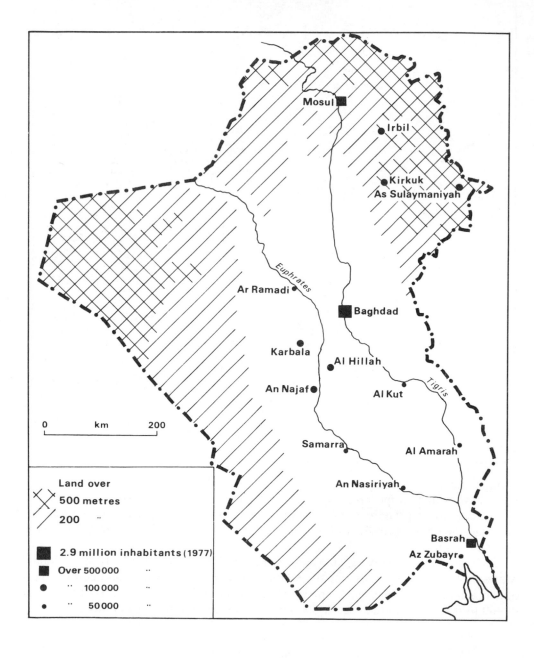

Oil is the most important natural resource. In 1973, Iraq became the first nation in the Arab world to take over the extraction, refining and marketing of its own oil. Oil is extracted both to the south (close to Kuwait's and Iran's oil-producing zones) and to the north/north east. In 1977, oil exports accounted for 99 per cent of merchandise exports. But the agricultural sector remains important. In 1978, 42 per cent of the labour force worked in this sector and dates are the major agricultural export. Up to a quarter of Iraq is cultivable, although much of this potential remains unexploited. Problems of flooding and salination and the lack of agreement with Syria and Turkey over water allocations for the Euphrates have hampered the expansion of cultivated land. The 1975–9 Five Year Plan shows a marked increase in investments in the agricultural sector.

Unlike Egypt, where most major settlements are confined to the Nile Valley and Delta, Iraq has a more dispersed settlement pattern made possible by the Tigris and the Euphrates and tributaries, and by sufficient rainfall for crop production in the north-east. There is a fairly even spread of settlements (and major cities) throughout these areas. The 1977 census showed that 63.7 per cent of Iraqis lived in urban areas (the official definition for urban population being those living within municipality council boundaries). The three major cities—Mosul in the north, Baghdad in the centre, Basrah in the south—contain over half the urban population. In 1977, Baghdad's population was 2.9 million. While accurate figures for the population of Basrah and Mosul are not available, both now exceed half a million.[8] The area in and around the city of Baghdad contains a large proportion of the nation's industry and most of its financial services. Mosul is also a major industrial centre with its growth stimulated by the development of oil fields nearby. Basrah is a major port and also has important oilfields nearby. So too does Kirkuk, at the foot of the mountains which mark the nation's north-east border. Manufacturing industries have grown rapidly since 1960 although their contribution to GDP remains very low due to the dominance of oil which accounts for more than half the GDP. In addition, the heavy industrial sector is being developed, particularly in the Basrah region with oil refineries, petrochemicals, iron and steel and construction receiving priority.[9]

The government's ambitious development plans to develop alternative sources of revenue for the time when oil production begins to decrease have been hampered by a lack of labour. Many trained Iraqis have at various times emigrated in response to political instability or to unsatisfactory living conditions. In 1974, a government estimate suggested there were 10 000 trained Iraqis living with their families in Western Europe and the United States. Since then, a government committee has sought to encourage these people to return.

For rural communities, their scatter over huge areas has hindered the spread of basic services and infrastructure. In general, rural inhabitants have benefited far less than their urban counterparts in rising oil revenues. One response has been rapid rural-to-urban migration. Most existing dwelling units, especially those in rural areas, do not conform to even minimum health standards. In 1978, life expectancy was only 55 years, very low for a nation with a per capita income of $1860 at that time.

Jordan

Located in the Middle East with Israel to the west, Saudi Arabia and Iraq to the east and Syria to the north, the Hashemite Kingdom of Jordan covers some 96 000 square kilometres; 5879 of these are on the Jordan river's West Bank and have been occupied by Israel since 1967. By the end of 1976, the East Bank's population was estimated to be more than 2 miliion while the Arab population of the West Bank was some 700 000.[10] In 1978, Jordan's crude birth-rate was one of the world's highest. Projections suggest that the population in 2000 will be double that of 1976.

The country can be divided into four geographic regions running north–south. To the east is desert which covers four-fifths of the East Bank. The East Bank's uplands mark the desert's end and these contain most of Jordan's major settlements. The Valley of Jordan, a rift valley 100 kilometres long and between 5 and 10 kilometres wide, runs from Lake Tiberius beyond the northern border in Israel to the Dead Sea and contains Jordan's richest agricultural land. To its west are the occupied West Bank uplands. Most of the East Bank's population is concentrated in the northwest which includes the Jordan Valley, the capital Amman and major cities Zerqa (some 25 kilometres northeast of Amman) and Irbid (close to the northern border). The whole country has low rainfall, decreasing from an annual average of some 400 mm in the northwest and uplands of the East Bank to 100 mm in the south. The climate varies from Mediterranean in the west to desert type in the east.

Several settlements in Jordan have histories dating back thousands of years. Jericho, on the West Bank, is the site of one the world's oldest continuous

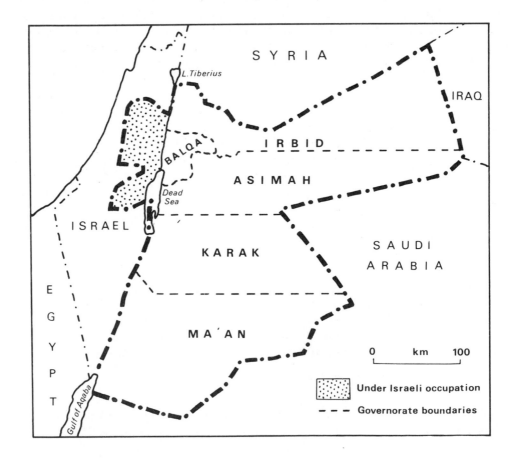

formerly known as the Blue Nile and Khartoum provinces,[14] one-third of the population lives on less than a tenth of the national territory. To the south of the Sudan—where annual rainfall is highest reaching an average 1500 mm in the extreme south—around a fifth of the population lives.

For many millenia, the Sudan has been one of the major points of contact between North and SubSaharan Africa. Stable urban settlements some 2500 years old have been found close to the junction of the Blue and White Niles. Northern Sudan is predominantly Muslim with an Arabic cultural heritage and Arabic as the official language. Southern Sudan's population is predominantly Black African, with many tribes each speaking their own language. For much of the nineteenth century, the Sudan was under the rule of Ottoman Egypt's viceroyalty. A Mahdist revolution in 1885 overthrew this regime but the British, who had invaded Egypt in 1882, finally invaded the Sudan too. The 1899 Condominium Agreement gave the Sudan separate political status from Egypt but with joint British–Egyptian rule. The northern and southern regions were administered separately with much of the development in the colonial period concentrated in the northern and central, predominantly Muslim regions. With independence in 1956, southern fears of northern domination led to a protracted civil war which finally ended in 1972 with a ceasefire and partial autonomy to the south.

Agriculture is the basc of the Sudan's economy. In 1978, 79 per cent of the labour force worked in this sector—many on subsistence farms or, as with the Dinka people, primarily as pastoralists. Around 11 per cent of the population were nomads in 1973. The Sudan is one of the world's major producers of extra long staple cotton, and this accounted for half of all export earnings in 1976, with peanuts and gum arabic also major exports. Most of the important commercial farmlands are between the White Nile and the Atbarah rivers, to the south and east of the three-town capital, Khartoum–Khartoum North–Omdurman which is at the junction of the White and Blue Niles. The Gezira scheme with its Managil extension covers more than 800 000 hectares and is the major cotton-producing area. The Kenana sugar scheme, located between the Blue and White Niles like the Gezira, is a more recent development. The Rahad scheme's first stage which will cover more than 100 000 hectares draws its water from the Blue Nile. These and other major irrigation developments have given the Sudan a rapid growth rate in agricultural production which averaged 6.5 per cent a year in the mid-1970s. Much of the public and private investment has been concentrated in this region over many years and it has been increasing its share of the national population as in-migration adds to natural population increases. Despite these intensive agricultural developments, there still remains considerable scope for further extending the area under cultivation.

Elsewhere, there is also very considerable potential for expanding cultivated land-area. For instance, large areas in the South are suited to growing a wide range of tropical crops. At present, most of the arable and pastoral activities here are at subsistence level. For the whole of the Sudan, total cultivated area represents less than 3 per cent of land area while 13 or more per cent is potentially cultivatable. Water availability remains one of the major constraints, especially in the northern and central regions. However, constructing the Jonglei Canal[15] will boost water-flow in the White Nile and indeed for the whole Nile right up to Lake Nasser in Egypt. There are also vast forest resources in the south, as yet underutilized. And the Sudan is

settlements. Amman has remains of fortified settlements dating back to the fourth millenium BC. Jordan gained independence in 1946 after more than 20 years under a British mandate as Transjordan. A large portion of the population are refugees displaced by regional wars. In East Jordan, there are around three Palestinians to every Jordanian. In 1977, there were 663 773 refugees registered with the United Nations Relief and Works Agency in East Jordan (roughly a third of the total population) 172 102 of whom lived in refugee camps. On the West Bank, there were more than 300 000 registered refugees, more than a third of the total population.

Lack of water constrains agricultural development. More than 90 per cent of Jordan's cultivated land has to rely on limited and irregular rainfall and there is little possibility of extending the area under rainfed cultivation. The Jordan Valley covering around 1 per cent of the national territory is the major agricultural region since it contains most of the irrigated lands. After serious disruptions to both production and settlements between 1967 and 1971, this area has enjoyed priority for government investments both in irrigation and in settlement development. The aim is to double the 1973 population and to use this area's produce to reduce Jordan's very considerable trade deficit. It already accounts for a large portion of Jordan's agricultural exports. Oranges and vegetables were the major agricultural exports in 1975.

Mining and industry have developed rapidly since 1960, apart from disruptions in

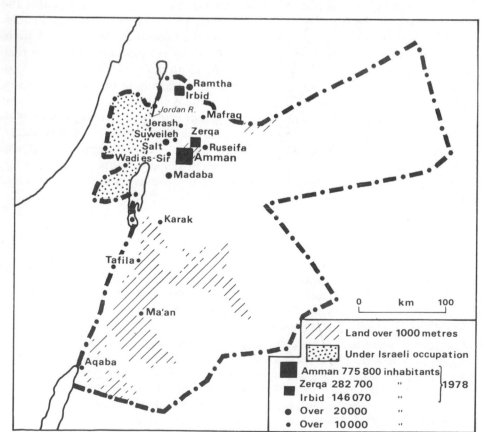

Land over 1000 metres

Under Israeli occupation

Amman 775 800 inhabitants
Zerqa 282 700 "
Irbid 146 070 "   1978
Over 20000 "
Over 10000 "

the late 1960s due to the June 1967 War. Their growth helped push per capita GNP to $1050 in 1978. Industrial production is heavily concentrated in Amman and in the region surrounding it. In 1978, Amman had an estimated 775 800 inhabitants, around half the nation's urban population and more than a third of the East Bank's total population. Amman region (which includes Zerqa) had more than a million inhabitants, 60 per cent of the East Bank's population on 4 per cent of its land. The region's dominant position as the nation's industrial and commercial centre has been due to the fact that it contained the basic infrastructure industry needed as well as having abundant labour and representing the nation's major consumer market. Zerqa had some 282 700 inhabitants in 1978 while Irbid had around 146 070. No other city had more than 100 000 and 13 other towns had more than 10 000 inhabitants in a 1975 census.[11] Aqaba to the south on the Gulf of Aqaba which leads to the Red Sea is Jordan's only port. The port facilities have been modernized since independence and this is the point of export for Jordan's most valuable export, phosphates. With a population of 15 900 in 1975, this town is likely to grow rapidly as exports shipped through it grow and industries develop there. According to a census in 1975, 68.3 per cent of the East Bank's population lived in population centres with more than 7500 inhabitants.

Phosphate production has increased rapidly from 709 000 tonnes in 1972 to 1.5 million in 1975. It accounted for around two-fifths of Jordan's export earnings in 1976. The target for production capacity for 1980 was 7 million tonnes.[12] Despite this and the rapid growth of industry (and of GDP) since 1948, the value of merchandise imports was more than five times that of merchandise exports in 1978. Food remains one of Jordan's major imports. In the mid-1970s, imports accounted for more than half the national consumption of cereals and animal products.

Housing and basic services deficits are growing, especially in the Amman region. And a serious manpower shortage hinders development efforts. The large army draws on people much needed in the nation's development programme. Many Jordanians, especially those with skills, have emigrated to oil-rich Gulf states. Estimates suggest that 150 000 or more Jordanians live and work abroad.[13] And current development plans' concentration on economic growth means inadequate support for extending basic services to the whole population, especially to those living in small towns and rural areas outside the Jordan Valley.

The Sudan

The Sudan is the largest African nation with some 2.5 million square kilometres, stretching from Egypt in the north down to Uganda, Kenya and Zaire in the south. With a population of 17.4 million in 1978, it is also one of the more sparsely populated Third World nations. Projections suggest its population will reach more than 30 million by the end of the century.

The tropical climate is rarely moderated by altitude since a vast, low plain covers virtually all the interior. The Red Sea Hills and the Ethiopian Highlands run close to the eastern border while there are also mountain ranges to the extreme west and south. As in Egypt, the Nile divides the nation as it runs from south to north and has played a major role in the Sudan's history and in the development of its economy and settlement pattern. The White Nile coming across the southern border from Lake

Victoria runs through the massive swamp area known as the Sudd before joining the Blue Nile in Central Sudan and then the Atbarah river further north. Both the Blue Nile and the Atbarah rise in the Ethiopian Highlands.

Water availability has been a major factor in determining where agricultural and settlement development has been possible. The amount of rainfall, its reliability and the length of the rainy season all tend to increase going from north to south. For much of the northern quarter of the Sudan, the land is desert or semi-desert and virtually uninhabited. Most of this area's agricultural activity is concentrated close to the Nile. For the broad central region, encompassing around half the Sudan, annual average rainfall goes from 200 mm in the north to 800 mm in the south. In the west of this region, shifting agriculture is common, while in the centre and east virtually all the nation's commercial crop production is concentrated on irrigated land. In the area

21

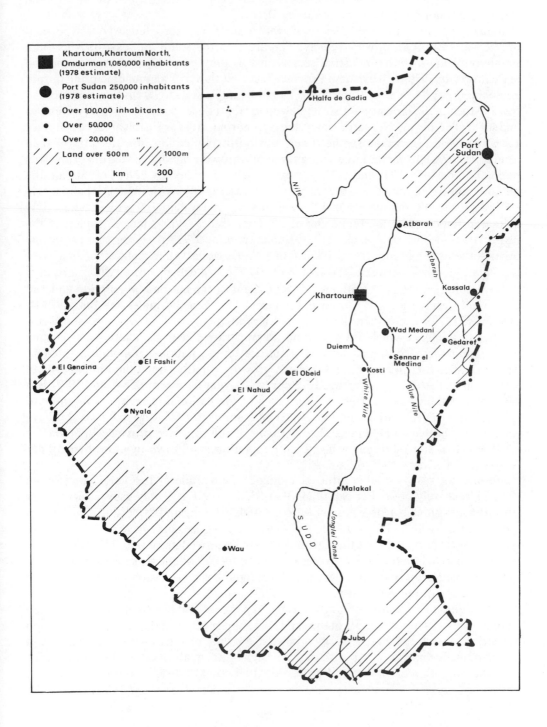

Khartoum, Khartoum North, Omdurman 1,050,000 inhabitants (1978 estimate)

Port Sudan 250,000 inhabitants (1978 estimate)

Over 100,000 inhabitants

Over 50,000 "

Over 20,000 "

Land over 500 m   1000 m

0   km   300

Halfa de Gadia

Port Sudan

Atbarah

Kassala

Khartoum

Wad Medani

Gedaref

Duiem

Sennar el Medina

Kosti

El Genaina

El Fashir

El Obeid

El Nahud

Nyala

Nile

Atbarah

White Nile

Blue Nile

Malakal

SUDD

Jonglei Canal

Wau

Juba

believed to be rich in mineral resources (including oil) although much of the national territory has not been adequately surveyed.

Industry's contribution to GDP is small; with mining, it represented just over 8 per cent in 1973–4.[16] But it is growing rapidly. The areas to the south and east of Khartoum monopolize most of the industrial sector, just as they have most of the commercial agriculture. In 1970–1, Khartoum Province had two-thirds of all manufacturing output while the then provinces of Blue Nile to its south and Kassala to its east had much of the rest.[17] Much of the industry is associated with local produce so such industries as textiles and sugar are growing. Not surprisingly, the larger urban areas are in this area too. Greater Khartoum (which encompasses the three towns) with a population estimated at more than a million in 1978 is by far the largest urban area. It is growing rapidly, having quadrupled its population between 1955 and 1973, and may reach 2.5 million by 1990. Port Sudan, the nation's only major outlet to to the sea has also grown rapidly. With 135 000 inhabitants in 1973, its estimated population in 1978 was quarter of a million, its growth boosted by increased imports and the reopening of the Suez Canal. Wad Medani, capital of the prosperous Gezira Province, had 112 000 inhabitants in 1973. Apart from these, only one other settlement had more than 100 000 in 1973 (Kassala) while eight others had over 50 000 and ten had between 20 000 and 50 000. The 22 urban centres with more than 20 000 inhabitants in 1973 contained 12.8 per cent of the national population and had an annual average growth rate of 6.9 per cent between the mid-1960s and 1973–4. However, the official urban definition is for settlements of 5000 or more and a few smaller settlements which are important administrative centres. There were 68 such centres and these contained around a quarter of the national population in 1980. These smaller settlements have also been growing rapidly, since the annual growth rate for urban settlements averaged 7.2 per cent a year between 1955–6 and 1973. But towns are still few and far between for much of the national territory. Only three of the 22 urban centres with more than 20 000 inhabitants in 1973 were in the six southern provinces. On that same date, only 9 per cent of the southern provinces' population lived in urban areas, although this urban population had grown by more than 10 per cent a year between 1955–6 and 1973.[18]

Despite its vast and underutilized biological and mineral resources, the Sudan remains relatively poor. Per capita GNP at $320 in 1978 has only grown very slowly since 1960. With such a large nation, the costs of developing and exploiting its resources are usually very high. For instance, the southern provinces may have the climate and soil to grow export crops but these would have to be moved more than 1500 kilometres to Port Sudan to be exported. Most rural settlements lack adequate safe water supplies, sanitation and good roads. Primary health care and basic sanitation is not available to large portions of the population.

By the mid-1970s, adult literacy was only 20 per cent and less than half the children were at primary school. People in the capital are better off in all these respects although the city suffers from unnecessarily sprawled growth, serious traffic congestion and major housing shortages. As with many African and Arab nations, there is concern over the migration of skilled and professional labour to oil-rich nations.

Tunisia

Tunisia is a comparatively small nation with a total area of 164 150 square kilometres located on the southern Mediterranean coast between two huge neighbours, Libya to the southeast, Algeria to the west. Its population was 6 million in 1978 and had grown comparatively slowly in the previous two decades, averaging 2 per cent a year between 1960 and 1978.[19]

Its climate, vegetation and development are inevitably linked to its position on the Mediterranean. The Mediterranean climate is characterized by mild rainy winters and hot dry summers, although average temperatures rise and rainfall drops as one goes south or inland. The northern region is mountainous, fertile and well watered with annual rainfall averaging 500 to 1000 mm or more annually. This region contains much of Tunisia's best agricultural and forest land, although production does suffer from very considerable annual fluctuations in rainfall. Below it, on the coast, is the Sahil region, a major olive-growing area. This and the northern region contain most

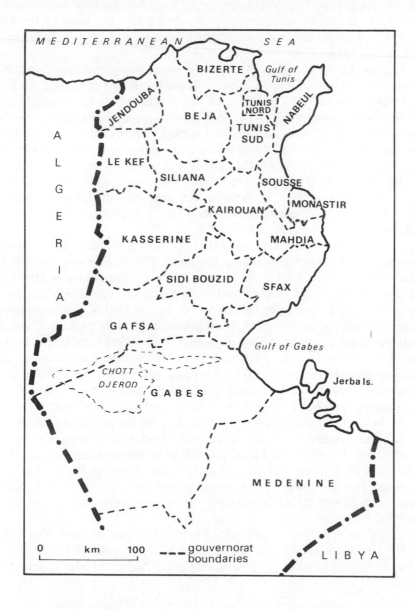

of the major urban areas and much of the national population. Some three-fifths of the population live in the ten governates that stretch for much of the north and east coast although these encompass little more than a fifth of the national territory. The semi-arid central region, also known as the Steppes region, and the south of the country are only sparsely populated. The two most southern governates contain around one-tenth of the national population on more than half the national territory.

Tunisia's history and urban traditions date back thousands of years. Carthage, now in the city of Tunis's suburbs, was a major city when the Mediterranean was dominated first by the Greeks and then by the Romans. The valley of the Medjerda river which flows into the Gulf of Tunis, was once a major granary for the Roman Empire. It is still Tunisia's richest grain-producing area. Many of Tunisia's towns have mosques and traditional Islamic centres dating back hundreds or even more than a thousand years. In the sixteenth century, it came under the sway of the Ottoman Empire and then in the late nineteenth century, under the French. It finally gained independence in 1956.

According to the 1975 census, 47.5 per cent of the population lived in urban settlements, these being defined as those with the status of a commune. In 1978, 155 such communes existed.[20] 35 per cent of the population lived in small, generally isolated rural settlements while 17 per cent lived in isolated dwellings. The Tunisian economy is largely based on agriculture and mining. Wheat, fruit, olives and wine are major agricultural products with olive oil being the major agricultural export. In 1978, 45 per cent of the workforce was in the agricultural sector. In the mining sector, crude oil and phosphates are the major products, accounting for 42 and 20 per cent of exports respectively in 1975. Oil deposits are exploited in the south and in Sfax governate and there is a possibility that the Gulf of Gabes could become a major producing area.

Industry has been developing steadily since independence, based mainly on processing agricultural, fish and mining products. The mining and industrial sector employed 24 per cent of the workforce in 1978 and accounted for nearly a third of GDP. Tunis, Bizerte, Sfax, Gabes and Sousse, all on the coast, are the major industrial centres. The concentration of urban and industrial development on the coast helps explain the general drift of migration from west to east. Tourism, also centred on the coast, is a major economic sector. With 1200 kilometres of beach, easy access from Europe and a rich architectural and historical heritage, Tunisia attracted more than a million vistors in 1975. Together with remittances from Tunisians working abroad (principally in France and Libya), this provides valuable foreign exchange earnings and helps offset a large balance of payments' deficit.

Tunis, to the north, is the nation's capital and by far its largest city. In 1977, it was reported to have a million inhabitants in its metropolitan area. Sfax, a major port for central and southern regions, had some 260 000 in its metropolitan area on that same date while Sousse, also on the east coast between Tunis and Sfax, had 150 000. Besides these, Tunisian towns can be classified into three groups with roughly 40 in each: those with 10 000–70 000 inhabitants; those with 5000–10 000; and those with less than 5000.[21]

Considerable progress has been made over the last two decades. Growth in per capita GNP has averaged 4.8 per cent a year between 1960 and 1978. Per capita income was $950 by the end of this period, one of the highest in Africa. Education has

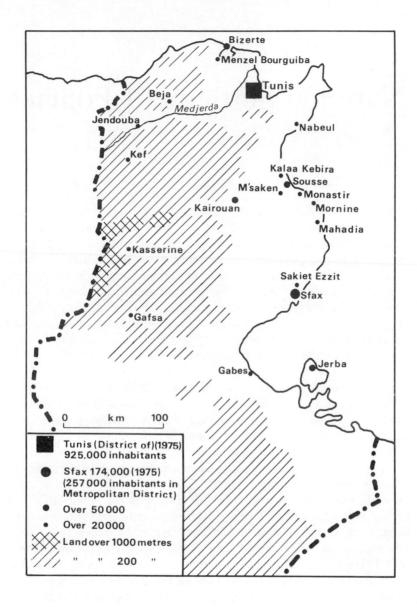

received priority in government spending; universal primary education has been achieved while adult literacy has risen sharply since 1960. However, unemployment is high and basic services and infrastructure often lacking. Problems of drinking water, sewage and drainage exist even in the capital. Squatters abound in all major cities, and the formal sector is unable to keep up with need. The provision of services and infrastructure in rural areas lags well behind that in urban areas. Over half the nation's doctors and 39 per cent all hospital beds were reported to be in Tunis in the mid-1970s even though the city contained less than a fifth of the national population. Clearly, it is difficult to reach the rural population that live in isolated houses, scattered over large distances.

National Settlement Policies

Egypt

Only in the mid-1970s did it become apparent to government that socioeconomic development policies needed a clear and explicit spatial framework if mounting economic, demographic and social problems were to be addressed. Much of the Nile Valley and Delta is overcrowded and virtually all cultivable land in this region is already cultivated. There was considerable underemployment in rural areas. Meanwhile, Cairo and other cities were overcongested and could not generate jobs fast enough to employ their active labour-force. Egypt's Five-Year Plan 1978–82 projects the country's needs up to 2000 and, with various publications from the Ministry of Housing and Reconstruction, outlines a long-term spatial strategy to steer future growth in population and urbanization away from overcongested rural and urban areas.

Rural population is projected to grow from some 22.4 million to 33 million between 1978 and 2000 while urban population will grow from 17.6 million to 33 million in this same period. These projections assume that both population growth and rural-to-urban migration will be checked. Then settlement policy seeks to steer this growth to 'normal' and 'virgin' areas while 'saturated' areas are to receive no net population increase and 'overcongested' areas are to have a net population decrease. Port Said, at the northern end of the Suez Canal, Cairo and Giza have been designated 'overcongested'. For Cairo, several new satellite cities are being built. Sadat City, between Cairo and Alexandria, Tenth of Ramadan, between Cairo and Ismailia and King Khaled City, to the southwest of Cairo, are to be major industrial cities all between 50 and 65 kilometres from Cairo's centre. Other new towns close to Cairo include May Fifteen City, Al-Ubur, October Six and Salam.[22] A new city, Ameriya, is also being built 60 kilometres to the west of Alexandria. For Port Said, the aim is to develop land reclaimed from the adjoining lake. Areas such as the Delta provinces of Minufiya and Gharbia have been designated 'saturated' with no more room for population growth. The third category, 'normal', allows for some increase in population over time and Alexandria, the Canal Zone and al-Fayyum, some 100 kilometres south of Cairo on the Nile, are all in this category. By 2000, the Canal Zone's population should have increased by 2 million people and construction is already well under way around the towns of Suez and Ismailia. Other 'normal' areas are to absorb a further 9 million people by 2000.

The 'virgin areas' are hardly populated at present. These include the Red Sea coast, the Sinai, the New Valley in the south of the Western desert, and this desert's northern coast with Mirsa Matruh as its centre. At present population densities here are very low, typically between 0.2 and 0.4 persons per square kilometre. Current plans suggest that the Red Sea Coast may have 3.5 million people by 2000 while the area around Mirsa Matruh will have 3 million, the Sinai 1.5 million and the New Valley 6.5 million. This will bring population densities in the newly developed areas to around 150 persons per square kilometre. Each development zone is intended to have a diversified economic base. For instance, the New Valley is to have about 2 million *feddans* (840 000 hectares) of land irrigated from ground water wells and from Lake Nasser. The area is also rich in phosphates and other mineral resources. The northern coast around Mirsa Matruh is to have tourism, industry, expanded port facilities and agriculture as its economic base. There are plans to divert sea-water to the Qattara Depression, using the very considerable drop to generate electricity in hydroelectric installations to power the region's new industrial plants. The Lake Nasser region is to have fisheries, tourism, irrigation, industry and mineral resources developed.

At present, regional plans are being drawn up for these major development areas. These include masterplans for the Port Said, Suez, and Ismailia areas, the new satellite cities around Cairo and infrastructure facilities in Greater Cairo and Alexandria.

Egypt's settlement policy and its inclusion in development plans with long-term aims reaching to 2000 looks impressive on paper. Indeed, it represents a considerable step forward when one considers that in the late 1960s, settlement policy was almost non-existent. However, the high cost—and the difficulty in actually implementing such an ambitious spatial strategy—suggest that it, like many plans before it, will not actually happen. Egypt already faces major economic problems and has to service massive foreign debts and maintain a large and expensive army. Previous attempts to divert Cairo's population growth to satellite communities have met with little success. Cairo's first masterplan, published in 1958, suggested such a strategy with Cairo's population to be kept to 3.5 million.[23] It has grown by more than 1.5 million since.

There have also been complaints that some of the proposed developments may have not been adequately studied. The reclamation of land from the lake near Port Said, for instance, may have environmental side-effects that are more costly than the gain the development brings. Policy formulation and planning remains very centralized and more consideration should be given to involving the regions, towns and villages in drawing up and modifying plans that affect them.

There is little doubt that Egypt needs an explicit and comprehensive settlements policy of this type to give a clear spatial framework to socioeconomic development policy. The new strategy appears to be the first step. But its effective implementation is the real test of such a policy. And at the same time, attention must be given to many settlements in the Nile Valley and Delta not included in these plans. For these house more than half the population at present and desperately need improved infrastructure, services and development plans themselves.

Iraq

Iraq's National Report to Habitat shows the government taking more interest in spatial and settlement development. Current objectives include increased agricultural production and rural prosperity and improved housing, services and community facilities for the whole population with such benefits better spread among the 18 governates. Agricultural development aims to increase exports and reduce Iraq's reliance on food imports.[24] Such developments are to be complemented with the provision of more housing and community facilities in rural areas in the hope that rural-to-urban migration can be slowed. Although the government acknowledges that rapid urbanization is inevitable, it does seek to stimulate development away from the major urban settlements while striving to limit the growth of already overcongested centres.

The 1970–4 Five-Year Plan was essentially sectoral in nature. The major concentration was on increasing agricultural and industrial production with little consideration of settlement issues. In January 1974, a conference of the Ba'ath Party discussed important settlement issues and suggestions were made as to where action was needed. Since then, settlement issues have become more evident in national development plans. The government announced that it had begun preparing a long-term housing plan that would aim at improving housing conditions throughout the nation. Although the team visiting Iraq was not able to examine the 1976–80 Five-Year Plan or the National Settlement Plan, the Ministry of Planning claims that it now has a national housing strategy for up to 2000 and that more than half of the 300 existing urban settlements have masterplans. In addition, government officials claim that settlements policy is now an integral part of socioeconomic development policy.

Three alternatives for the spatial development of the three largest urban settlements—Baghdad, Basrah and Mosul—have been discussed. The first is that they should be three poles of urban agglomeration with urban and industrial developments along the Tigris and the Euphrates. The second suggests that Kirkuk be added as another pole of urban agglomeration with a central line of urban and industrial development that allows for the preservation of agricultural land close to the rivers. The third is an increased effort on developing small and medium-sized towns throughout the national territory. Government policy also aims to develop the mountainous region in the north as a tourist centre and to limit urban sprawl in major centres while increasing urban densities by supporting high-rise construction.

Thus, Iraq has gone some way towards including important settlement issues in national development plans. As we shall see in a later section (page 42), the government is attempting a more equitable spread of the benefits of development through expanding health care and education services. There has been some strengthening of planning expertise in the Ministry of Planning (and other ministries). But planning remains very centralised. And for several policy aims, it is not clear how they are to be achieved. For instance, it is unclear what measures will be used to slow population growth in major urban centres and maintain a minimum of population in rural areas. Iraq does not have the problem that continually faces Egypt of rising population pressure on limited amounts of agricultural land. Indeed, Iraq's untapped agricultural potential is very considerable. Thus, a more widely based rural development strategy as part of a national settlement policy would not run into problems with land shortages.

Jordan

No national settlement policy has been formulated in Jordan. However, successive development plans have shown more interest in spatial considerations and both Jordan's National Report to Habitat and the 1976–80 Five-Year Plan show preliminary steps being taken towards a settlements policy.

National economic planning dates from the early 1960s when the Jordan Development Board formulated the 1962–7 Five-Year Plan.[25] Just before Habitat, the Three-Year

Plan covering 1973–5 was essentially sectoral in nature, its major emphasis being on expanding the industrial sector and agricultural production. However, one of the Plan's objectives was a better distribution of industrial plants throughout the nation and efforts have been made to develop industries around mineral resources and increase the land area under cultivation. In some new developments, the Housing Corporation built housing units as part of these new developments. For instance, 30 houses were planned in el-Hasa as part of the phosphate mining complex in that area and a phosphoric acid plant in Aqaba will have a housing settlement for 200 families built by the Housing Corporation.

The Jordan Valley received special attention after the Jordan Valley Commission was formed in 1973. This is the nation's most productive agricultural region with sufficient water to produce up to four crops a year. The settlements in this region were devastated by the fighting in 1967–71, and most of its population left the area. By 1975, many farmers had returned and the population exceeded 70 000. The Commission has considerable authority to plan the Valley's development and to coordinate the activities of the various government departments in implementing the plan. The Valley Development Plan prepared in 1973 envisages expanding irrigated area by 300 per cent, doubling population to 150 000, raising living standards for all inhabitants and creating 32 well-planned and serviced agricultural villages. These villages are to be sited on land ill-suited for agriculture along a line at the base of the eastern valley, and aim to provide valley inhabitants with essential infrastructure and services. Three larger settlements will be developed as the main administrative and commercial centres.[26] In the 1976–80 Five-Year Plan, expanding irrigation in the Jordan Valley and the neighbouring Southern Ghors received high priority.

The Amman region also receives special attention. The High Level Policy Committee including the Prime Minister, the Ministers of Finance and Labour, the Mayor of Amman and the head of the National Planning Council aims to tackle the Amman region's problems. These stem from the very rapid growth of the city from 25 000 in 1948 to more than 750 000 in 1978 and the special problem of refugees who still hope to return to their homelands. There are 150 000 or more people living on unauthorized sites. Neither housing nor infrastructure and basic service provision have been able to keep up with this growth.

The Five-Year Plan 1976–80 remained essentially sectoral in nature. Priority is given to mining and industry and the infrastructure (water, electricity and transportation) that supports their development. The Plan does include a considerable expansion in public housing construction through the Housing Corporation including major housing projects in Aqaba to support its rapid development and housing in mining areas.

Spatial considerations do receive more emphasis, even if the overriding emphasis is on economic growth. The high level committee formulating development policy for Amman may extend its efforts to the whole nation. A regional plan is being prepared for the north, and the Aqaba region is to have a special commission similar to that for the Jordan Valley to oversee its development. The 1976–80 Plan urges the preparation of masterplans for towns and villages based on comprehensive regional plans. Special industrial zones are to be set up in Zerqa, Irbid, Aqaba and other centres as well as Amman, no doubt in the hope that industrial investment will not remain so heavily concentrated in the Amman region. But although special incentives are being used to encourage investment in certain industrial sectors, these incentives are not being used to promote the Plan's wider spatial goals.

The Plan also talks of enacting 'appropriate legislation to prescribe the areas of Amman and Zerqa within a green belt aiming at checking their abnormal growth',[27] and possibly establishing satellite cities to reduce population pressures on the big cities, especially Zerqa and Amman. As we shall see in later sections on Jordan's land and housing policies pages 35 and 43, the Plan proposes various measures to increase public control of urban land use. Even if it is too early to be able to judge these new initiatives, at least they show the government giving more thought to important spatial considerations. And it seems likely that the various regional development efforts and plans may be combined into a more comprehensive settlement policy that covers the whole nation.

The Sudan

The Sudan does not have anything that approaches a national settlement policy. But more attention is being given to spatial and settlement planning in the Six-Year Plan of Economic and Social Development 1977–8 to 1982–3.

Under colonial rule, the agricultural export sector was developed with foreign investment, producing a small modernized 'enclave' in and close to Khartoum and leaving the vast majority of the population in subsistence activities. Since independence, the public sector has played a greater role in both agriculture and industry with increasing reliance on economic planning to guide development programmes. Virtually all major economic enterprises are owned or controlled by the government. Both the Ten-Year Plan for the 1960s and the Five-Year Plan 1970–1 to 1974–5 were sectoral in nature and gave agricultural and industrial development top priority. Housing, settlement planning and basic service provision received low priority, especially in the Five-Year Plan; and both public and private investment continued to be concentrated in what were Blue Nile, Kassala and Khartoum provinces.[14] In both plans, agriculture received top priority in the allocation of public funds.

The main objectives of the current Six-Year Plan is also to expand 'the productive sector'—agriculture and industry. However, the intention is to spread this development to help more backward areas develop and help check migration to urban areas. Housing and settlement planning get more attention than in previous plans. Towns are to have masterplans to control and direct their development. A new physical planning law is being formulated to bring together, update and supplement previous planning legislation. This seeks to decentralize settlement planning and implementation to the regional level, to work along the same lines as the local government system that was decentralized in the early 1970s. The country is divided into eighteen provinces. The six southern provinces make up the southern region which has partial self-government and its own capital at Juba. In addition, the Plan states that new economic developments should include consideration of settlements and housing that such developments will inevitably involve. And the Plan pays special attention to improving transport infrastructure and communications.

The emphasis given to the productive sector in a very poor nation is understandable, especially since the Sudan has a large foreign debt and continual balance-of-payments problems. The authorities do recognize that settlement policy should be a major part of socioeconomic development policy, even if this has yet to happen. But there should be a comprehensive and explicit settlement policy that covers both rural and urban areas as a framework within which socioeconomic development planning operates, even if comparatively few resources can be given to investment in settlements. The new law on physical planning, if passed, should improve the formulation and implementation of plans. If provincial-level governments have more say both in the content of plans and are in charge of implementing them, then the plans should better understand the needs and realities of each region. And it is important that rural areas and nomadic people get more attention within national development plans. The current plan gives priority to urban considerations when the majority of the population—and most of the poorest Sudanese—live in rural areas.

Tunisia

The government has been giving more attention and financial support to settlement policies during the 1970s and to forming or consolidating the institutional base an effective settlement policy demands. National development plans have given more support to housing construction, as will be examined in detail in the later section on Tunisia's shelter policies (page 47). And there is evidence of a national settlement policy emerging, even if the 1977–81 Fifth Plan did not explicitly state it.

This emerging policy is evident in a number of initiatives designed to decentralize both social and economic investment. In the past, such investment has been concentrated in the coastal area or close to it, most particularly in and around Tunis. By the end of 1978, masterplans had been prepared for virtually all urban centres with the regulatory powers of such plans strengthened.[28] A new land agency for residential developments, the Agence Foncière d'Habitation, has acquired land in advance of need in or close to existing urban centres and by developing and then selling it, helped residential developments conform to local plans. In 1975, central government cancelled all municipal debts and efforts are being made to strengthen local governments' funding base.

In addition, major investment programmes by various agencies are seeking to improve infrastructure and services in smaller settlements and in regions largely excluded from such developments in the past. The agencies responsible for water supply (the Société Nationale de l'Exploitation et de la Distribution de l'Eau) and for sewage systems (Office Nationale d'Assainissement) both aim to greatly expand the number of settlements served by efficient water supply and sewage systems over the next decade, including most secondary towns. This increased spread of social investment is being complemented by other attempts to encourage investment away from the major economic centres. A new fund (FOPRODI) was set up in 1973 to encourage the establishment and development of small- and medium-sized industries in smaller settlements.[29] And in addition to the land agency for residential developments, agencies for tourism and for industry were also set up to acquire and develop sites to attract commercial investments and help promote such developments in settlements or regions largely bypassed by such investments in the past. Finally, government investment in universities, colleges and hospitals are to be directed away from the Tunis region which has usually monopolized such investments in the past.

In rural areas, development programmes at the district level have been strengthened with the number of districts (*gouvernorats*) covering the nation recently increased from thirteen to eighteen. In its publicly supported rural housing programme, the government has been promoting the regrouping of rural populations into villages around mosques, schools and other community centres. Only through such regroupings in rural areas where dwellings are often scattered over large areas can basic services be provided. Tunisia's rural housing programme has provided heavily subsidized housing units as an incentive to encourage rural households to move into more densely populated settlements.

Land

Egypt

All agricultural land in Egypt is owned by private individuals or groups. Most urban land is also privately owned. All other land which is mostly desert and represents about 96 per cent of the country is owned by the state.

The present Five-Year Plan (1978–82) aims to consolidate tiny rural holdings so the farmer receives between 10 and 20 *feddans* (4.2–8.4 hectares) depending on the family size and the income the land generates. The government's ability in the past to lower maximum individual holdings to 200 *feddans* (1952), 100 (1961) and then 50 (1969) shows the force of public control in more fairly distributing Egypt's most basic resource, agricultural land. The reform brought considerable improvement to rural life. Just before the reform in 1952, little more than 2000 landowners possessed a fifth of all agricultural land while 2.8 million peasant proprietors owned less than 1 *feddan* and 1.5 million families were landless.[30] Expropriated land was distributed among agricultural labourers, tenants and small farmers with preference to those who already worked the land. Limits were set on the rents and sharecropping arrangements landlords could demand from tenants. Overall, the whole programme raised rural incomes and got rid of the largest estates. It also benefited agricultural production since crop yields have risen steadily since the 1950s. However, redistributed farmland only represents about a tenth of all farmland and the division between poor, land-hungry peasants and a privileged minority of medium and large landowners still remains. Land-reform ceilings were always higher for family rather than individual units which has allowed large landholdings to remain. And many of the landless peasants have not benefited from the land reform programme. The new development schemes outlined in Egypt's National Settlement Policies include as a major component the opening up of new agricultural lands to reduce high population densities and high underemployment in the rural areas of the Valley and Delta.

In urban areas, public authorities have the right of expropriation for community or national purpose (with compensation). But there is no effective legal framework which gives public authorities the power to enforce zoning and land use controls. Private owners continue to subdivide their land as they please with no official permits. Indeed, in doing so, they meet much of the demand for sites on which housing for lower income groups is built. But this means that urban areas are growing haphazardly, basic infrastructure and services are not provided to new communities on the periphery and urban growth is encroaching on Egypt's very limited agricultural land base. One estimate put the yearly loss of agricultural land to urban growth as high as 40 000 *feddans* (16 800 hectares).

There are no controls on land speculation. In urban areas, land prices rose 20 to 50 per cent annually between 1973 and 1975,[31] although such rapid annual rises have probably not been sustained. Urban land, however, still represents a valuable speculative investment. The present system of urban land taxation is based on the annual rental value of the property on the land. Since rent controls keep rents low, the public authorities do not gain as much as they should from these taxes. Many urban properties built on illegally occupied land or on illegal subdivisions do not pay property tax because they are illegal. But this deprives the public authorities of revenue they need to expand urban infrastructure and services. And since there is no tax on the land itself, vacant urban land is not taxed at all. Government policy has been to sell publicly developed land at cost, but speculators can acquire this land and simply leave it undeveloped. According to a report published in 1977,[32] three-quarters or more of the lots in New Maadi and half the plots in Nasr City (both in Greater Cairo) remained undeveloped. Finally, there is no tax on speculative profits made from land transactions, although there is a transfer fee for reregistering a property, based on between 3 and 7 per cent of the sale price.

Public land use controls (and the legislative base these demand) are much needed. A Comprehensive Planning Law, first presented to the People's Assembly in 1973, has been under discussion for many years and, by 1979, still had not become law. This law would demand the preparation of urban and rural masterplans to ensure specific projects and local development programmes conformed with city or area-wide plans. It would also give governates and local authorities more power to control subdivisions and protect agricultural land. Apart from this, a 2 per cent annual tax on vacant urban land has been proposed but this, too, has not been implemented so far.

Iraq

In rural areas, there are various forms of land tenure within different kinds of farming operation. In state and collective farms, land ownership is public. In cooperative farms, land ownership rights are partly private and partly public. The farmer cultivates his own plot but cannot subdivide, sell, rent or mortgage it. There are also private plots. A major land reform in 1958 broke up the large estates[33] but the needed complementary phase of land redistribution and the expansion of extension services and other supports to the farmers was not well organized. This was partly due to a period of political instability with different factions favouring different agrarian reforms. The communists, for instance, favoured collectivization for the land the state owned or had expropriated. Such uncertainties hindered production increases. And a lot of potentially cultivable land remains fallow or underutilized. Approximately one-quarter of Iraq is cultivable; half of this is in the rainfed areas in the north and the other half in the Tigris–Euphrates river system where irrigation is needed. Although around three-quarters of this is cultivated in any one year, less than half is actually used while the rest remains fallow. Today, the government recognizes that the nationalization of all agricultural land with farmers employed simply as paid labourers would be counterproductive. The various forms of land ownership are seen as compromises between 'socialist' and 'traditionalist' forms of land tenure.

In urban areas, much of the land is privately owned. The government is planning to acquire more control over its use and tenure. Baghdad and other major cities are suffering from speculative land markets with prices rising rapidly.

The public authorities have the power to appropriate private property in the public interest. They also have the right to appropriate one-quarter of a property without compensation if it can be proved that its value has appreciated as a direct consequence of public works such as street widening or the construction of a public square. Both holders of long-lease land from the state and real estate owners are taxed; the former at 1 per cent of the land value every year, the latter at 1 per cent of the annual revenue with a progressive surtax as income from real estate rises. There is also a 1 per cent annual tax on the assessed value of vacant land. None of these have been very effective at controlling land speculation or recapturing unearned increment in land values.

The government has sold urban land well below its value to encourage housing construction. The land is usually sold to housing cooperatives who then distribute it as plots to their members who amortize their debts over 25 years. For instance, the Municipality of Baghdad in cooperation with the Ministry of Housing subdivided and distributed some 65 000 plots of land to housing cooperatives between 1964 and 1968. The price for the land was only a fraction of its market value.[34]

Although it is not easy to halt soaring land prices following rapid urbanization rates and the general rise in incomes, a more comprehensive and effective land policy is needed if the urban governments are to tackle mounting housing and infrastructure deficits.

Jordan

Only 5.7 per cent of East Jordan's area is defined as cultivable, 93 per cent of which is rainfed. According to Jordan's *National Report* to Habitat,[35] there is little possibility of expanding the land area that can be cultivated under rainfed conditions since more than 90 per cent of the East Bank receives less than 200 mm annual average rainfall. One of the 1976–80 Plan's major aims is to expand the area under irrigation with much of this effort centred in and around the Jordan Valley. The importance of this region to the nation's agricultural production (and especially its agricultural exports) and the untapped potential led to the setting up of the Jordan Valley Commission. Under the Commission, existing landowners were allowed to retain up to 20 hectares while previously landless tenant farmers were provided with 4–5 hectare holdings. The land reform programme is being carried out in conjunction with the construction of irrigation infrastructure. While the public authorities develop and maintain the irrigation system (as well as other public projects and the provision of basic services to farmers), the actual farms are owned and operated by individuals.

In urban areas, private land ownership predominates. Land prices in Amman have risen very rapidly, the price no doubt being inflated by the rapid influx of refugees. There is also widespread speculation. An estimated 40 per cent or more of the land within Amman's municipal boundaries is not developed. The government or local municipalities can acquire land needed for public purpose. An expert committee with representatives from the private landowner, the municipality and the Ministry of Finance, assesses compensation. The 1965 Town Planning Act introduced the concept of zoning. Today, all major urban centres have development plans with zoning and with public approval needed for all subdivisions and development proposals.

There is as yet no effective control of land speculation. There is a tax on the purchase price of land. In Amman, these amount to 8 per cent of the purchase price, 6 per cent from the buyer and 2 per cent from the seller. The planning authorities are entitled to one-quarter of any holding without payment to build roads and other public works. And the municipality or local government can impose a betterment tax on real estate whose value increases as a result of neighbouring public developments.[36]

The 1976–80 Five-Year Plan contains several recommendations of relevance to the urban land market. These include the reassessment of rental values on lands and buildings and the levy of a progressive tax that will prompt construction on vacant plots within municipal boundaries. They also include the imposition of a tax on capital gains made in land and real estate transactions, and an increase in the proportion of a private landholding the municipal government can acquire free for public developments to 35 per cent. These are among several proposals designed to increase municipalities' funding base, or lower development costs.

In an attempt to stimulate housing production, state land is to be placed at the disposal of the Housing Corporation (whose activities are discussed more fully later, page 43) either for use in public housing projects or for sale to individuals or housing cooperatives at low prices provided that the 'development occur within a maximum period of 18 months from the date of sale and that the maximum area per unit not exceed 120 square metres'.[37] Meanwhile, licence fees for individual houses with an area exceeding 200 square metres are to be raised. Thus, as with National Settlement Policy, the 1976–80 Plan contains several policy proposals that, if implemented effectively, could increase public control of land use and reduce speculation while increasing municipal revenue sources. But it may well take a more comprehensive urban land policy to ensure that the cost and supply of serviced urban land keeps pace with local housing needs.

The Sudan

Virtually all land is publicly owned. Agricultural land is leased to individual households or rented out in large developments such as the Gezira or Rahad irrigation schemes. Urban land is leased, after being classified as first, second or third class, depending on the standard and durability of the proposed building.

In rural areas, the potential for expanding the land under cultivation is very considerable although expensive in many cases since irrigation is needed. However, public ownership of land with farming by individual households on rented plots can overcome many of the problems associated with Third World rural land ownership patterns. In the Gezira, tenant farmers work individual plots with the Gezira Board supervising the cultivation, processing and marketing of the cotton and water distribution. Proceeds from the crop are split between tenants, central government and the Board. Although tenants are unhappy about the amount central government takes, such a system protects tenants against exploitative landlords and against the control of water resources for irrigation by a small élite of farmers. It also protects against increasing fragmentation of landholdings.

In urban areas, closed auctions have been used for the past two decades to dispose of land for housing, using a point system which reflects family size and other factors to govern who gets the plots. Citizens pay a nominal price for the land plus the cost of servicing it. The type and standard of services and infrastructure supplied to the plot depend on its classification. Third-class areas get roads, drainage, water and electricity with one asphalt road to the settlement centre. Second-class areas get all roads asphalted, covered drainage and public sewage as well. First-class areas get all these plus trees and paved footpaths. The higher the classification, the larger the plot sizes and the longer the leases, third-class areas getting 40-year leases, second-class areas 70-year leases and first-class areas 80-year leases. There are also plots designated as fourth-class with no building standards demanded. The proposed Physical Planning Law should put the various laws and directives concerning land into a single comprehensive law.

The force of public control over land-use gives public authorities the possibility of implementing new masterplans and ensuring, for instance, that settlements do not expand haphazardly over valuable agricultural land and do not create unnecessarily sprawled urban patterns. They also allow the authorities to acquire land needed for public works and other public developments. This has proved valuable in dealing with squatter settlements that have grown up on the periphery of major towns. Government policy is generally to classify these as third-class areas whenever possible, grant the squatters legal leases and provide them with the appropriate services and infrastructure. This policy has generally worked well. However, plans to renew old cores of towns have been promised for a long time in many settlements. But no action has been taken. And the promise of such action in the future has frozen private investment in maintenance and upgrading and public investment in infrastructure and services. So conditions have deteriorated. Classifying land in different classes with different plot sizes, standards of construction and quality of infrastructure and services has been criticized for it implies social stratification. Also, the size of first class plots—they can be over 1000 square metres[38]—encourages urban sprawl. However, the lower standards demanded in second and third-class housing does mean that 'legal' housing is not beyond the reach of lower income groups and that land prices and official standards are not a constant constraint, inhibiting construction in the informal sector. And in fourth-class areas, no standards are set although the units built there are legal.

Tunisia

Private land ownership seems to exist widely both in rural and urban areas. In rural areas, at independence, much of the best farmland was owned or farmed by a few thousand colonial families. Elsewhere land was held both under traditional Islamic tenures of *mulk, miri* and *habous*[39] and as collective tribal land. The colonial occupation not only concentrated the best land under the control of a few landowners; it also vastly expanded the amount of peasants with no land and no work. At first, the new national government promoted private ownership of agricultural holdings, leaving colonial holdings as they were and transferring ownership of *habous* land and collectively owned land to individuals. The 1962–71 Ten-Year Plan devoted some two-fifths of all investment to the agricultural sector with a strong stress on cooperatives to actually farm the land. In 1964, remaining colonial farms were expropriated and for the next five years, increasing reliance was placed on cooperative–collective units. Russell King noted that 'by far the most important mode of agricultural production was the *unité*; although in theory a cooperative, in practice it was virtually a state farm.'[40] Then early in 1969, all land was nationalized. However,

September 1969 saw a major reversal of this with the announcement that private holdings could be withdrawn from cooperatives. Within a year, *unités* covered less than 5 per cent of cultivated land, most of this being on former colonial land. The move to cooperative farming was seen as a way of managing the changeover from colonial owners in the short term and of promoting increased production with social justice in the long term. Some commentators suggest that the disruption to agricultural production it caused was due to the inability of government to provide competent farm management on the new farms; others that the model itself is unworkable. Since 1970, agricultural production has grown rapidly, its growth rate averaging 5.6 per cent a year between 1970 and 1978. Today, the agricultural sector has both cooperative and private farms on large, modernized holdings and small peasant holdings. The 1977–81 Five-Year Plan seeks to speed up the land registration process and a new rural land law is being prepared to bring together all previous rural land legislation into one comprehensive law.

Various initiatives during the 1970s show the Tunisian government's resolve to back an expanded housing programme with more effective urban land use control and public control over the land market. During the Fourth Plan (1973–6), the regulatory powers of municipal masterplans were strengthened. As we noted earlier, land agencies for acquiring and developing land for industrial, residential, and tourist developments were set up. The Agence Foncière d'Habitation, the land agency for residential developments, buys undeveloped land in or close to urban areas (by expropriation if necessary), develops it and sells it without subsidy to private developers. The land it acquires, subdivides and services are usually used for relatively expensive houses (so called 'economic' and 'standing' units) and most of its activities have been concentrated in the Tunis region in recent years. Thus, it can help ensure that the private sector housing developments are built according to local plans (for it works within local municipal guidelines) and by the size of its operation, help to keep land costs down by its ability to offer large quantities of land to developers at very competitive rates.

The Société Nationale de la Tunisie (SNIT) is the public housing corporation in charge of 'social-interest' housing projects (in other words, projects designed for lower-income groups). This corporation uses state land where possible to keep unit costs down although within municipal boundaries, it usually has to expropriate needed land.

Tunisian urban land policy also seeks to carefully protect valuable agricultural land from urban encroachment and preserve archaeological sites. However, as in most Third World nations, the informal construction sector provides a significant proportion of the lower-income groups' housing units in urban areas, usually on land subdivided without authorization or on illegally occupied sites. In 1976, an estimate suggested that one-fifth of the Tunis district's housing stock had been produced by this sector.[41]

Shelter, Infrastructure and Services

Egypt

In 1975, the quantitative housing deficit was put at more than 1.5 million in urban areas and 110 000 in rural areas.[42] In Cairo alone, the housing deficit was put at 750 000 units.[43] An estimated million people are squatting in the City of the Dead.[44] Overcrowding, lack of basic services such as sewage connections and piped water and deteriorating housing stock characterize many parts of Cairo. In addition, on the urban periphery, illegal, unplanned subdivisions and villages overrun by the expanding urban agglomeration lack basic services too. In rural areas, the actual housing deficit is less serious but the quality of the housing and the lack of basic infrastructure and services mean that gastrointestinal diseases and bilharzia remain endemic. Although urban areas are also ill-served, rural areas are generally worse off.

Public housing construction—usually 5 storey walk-ups—has been policy for many years. These are built by the national government or by governates' housing authorities. The Cairo governate built 38 757 units between 1955 and 1975.[45] These have been let at heavily subsidized rents and seem to have gone mainly to middle and lower-middle income groups, many of whom were government employees. Government plans for 1977 aimed at the construction of 10 000 units in reconstruction zones in the Suez Canal region and 24 000 elsewhere. These plans contain a new emphasis on reaching lower income groups and the 1977 housing programme sets aside 70 per cent of the public housing for lower income groups. The government estimated that 66 000 units would be built by the private sector in this same year including 22 000 through housing cooperatives and 16 000 through foreign investors. The General Authority of Building and Housing Cooperatives provides housing cooperatives with subsidized loans; in 1976, their loans only charged 3 per cent annual interest.[46]

However, actual urban needs probably grow by more than 150 000 annually. Even if 1977 targets were met, they would not even cover the increase in need, let alone start to tackle the massive backlog. The shortfall will show itself in increased overcrowding and illegal subdivisions on urban peripheries. Such subdivisions are common practice on the fringes of Egyptian urban areas. One estimate suggests that the informal sector—in this case houses built without permits usually on illegally occupied or subdivided land—accounts for over half the current construction activity in urban areas.[47] A law in 1966 legalized subdivisions and buildings that contravened existing codes and allowed public authorities to provide these with utilities. But although the law established a precedent that allowed this sector to flourish, the public authorities rarely support this sector, guide its development or support the settlements it constructs with basic infrastructure such as drainage, piped water or basic sanitation and basic community facilities such as schools. The result is unplanned and haphazard urban growth, very often at the expense of valuable agricultural land (as was noted under the section on land, page 33). Regulations such as those governing subdivisions continue to make legally sold plots too expensive for lower income groups to afford while the cost of a building permit and the standards it demands also put legal housing construction beyond their means.

Another major constraint on the expansion of urban housing construction is rent control. These controls have been in effect over the last three decades and have inhibited the construction of low- and middle-income housing for rent. They have also discouraged landlords from maintaining, repairing and upgrading their properties.

In the 1970s, there have been new government policies aimed at dealing with these deficiencies. There have been attempts to lessen the gap between controlled rents and market values to stimulate the private rental sector and encourage landlords to maintain their properties better. A new National Housing Fund was set up in 1976 to provide loans for the construction of housing for low-income groups by cooperatives and governates. This was to be funded by national government and by the sale of bonds. Some site and service schemes are now being implemented. The Ministry of Housing and Reconstruction is encouraging public housing tenants to become owners by offering generous terms for the conversion of rents into long-term purchase payments. Through this, they hope to improve maintenance and repair work in public housing estates.

This Ministry sees the government's role in housing taking several complementary directions: subsidizing housing for low income groups; ensuring the continuous availability of building materials; undertaking research that will help lower building costs; selling urban land at cost price; and encouraging individuals to save and invest savings in housing.

Despite these new initiatives, there are no signs of urban housing conditions changing, and conditions in Cairo continue to deteriorate. Despite stiff penalties set on the practice of charging tenants or subtenants key money if they wish to rent a housing unit, the practice still continues. And key money payments are rising rapidly as housing shortages increase. Although the public housing programme has benefited thousands of families, when viewed in national terms, it has monopolized government housing funds to provide subsidized housing for only a tiny portion of those in need. Cairo Governate's construction of nearly 39 000 units in the two decades after 1955 sounds impressive until one considers that its population grew by more than 2 million in that period. In 1975, the combined efforts of public and private enterprises in the formal sector was some 61 700 units,[48] less than a half of the growth in need. And as in so many other public housing programmes around the world, there appear to be major problems of maintenance in public housing estates. The government money spent on subsidizing loans to private housing cooperatives may have been better spent providing more loans at less subsidy.

Finally, some critics have suggested that the form of the standard public housing block is inappropriate both to Egypt's climate and to its millenial urban culture. Nor does industrializing the building industry and using complete prefabrication—the policy favoured in the late 1970s—address the root of the housing problem and provide for the lower-income groups' housing needs. It may well be that most urban housing for such groups continues to be provided with little or no government support and guidance and contrary to official regulations.

In rural areas, little has been done to improve housing conditions other than the construction of some model villages. But this can be considered as no more than a token gesture with no substantial benefits except, perhaps, to politicians. The universal provision of water, basic sanitation, electricity, health care centres, and schools should be the priority instead.

Building Industry

The informal sector remains resonsible for virtually all housing construction in rural areas and for a large portion of that in urban areas. It is the government's intention to replace the labour-intensive building industry with partial or complete prefabricated building systems. The government claims that only these can meet the enormous demands for new housing construction, especially in the new development areas. Egypt's building industry has lost a lot of skilled and unskilled labour to neighbouring oil-rich states.

In April 1975, contracts were signed linking ten Egyptian enterprises with ten foreign industrialized building companies.[49] Each of these factories was to start production in the first half of 1977. However, there are good reasons to doubt whether such housing construction techniques are the appropriate solution to Egypt's housing problems. These techniques have a poor record in other countries. Unit costs are high and cannot be expected to compete with labour-intensive *in situ* methods. They will reduce employment generation when unemployment and underemployment are high. And the final product is likely to be even less appropriate for Egypt's climate and culture than the public housing blocks already built.

Iraq

Although there is not much data available on housing conditions and current rates of housing construction, it seems that Iraq's housing industry has fallen behind the needs of its rapidly growing urban population. Shantytowns lacking basic services have sprung up around major cities and central city residential areas are very overcrowded and often in need of repair. In 1977, there were 895 024 urban dwellings including 133 946 mud houses, over 25 000 huts or *sarifas* and over 2000 tents for 1.157 million urban households.[50] According to a United Nations *Report* in 1977,[51] two-thirds of urban dwellers live more than two persons to a room while one-fifth live in dwellings where there are more than four persons per room. This same *Report* stated that only a quarter of Baghdad's residential areas were served by sewers while those beyond Baghdad's municipal boundaries were not connected to the water distribution system. Government estimates suggest that 100 000 units a year will be needed each year for the next 20 years, although no breakdown is given as to how many are needed in rural and urban areas. According to official tables, 41 958 residential buildings were completed by the private sector in 1977 while 56 076 were completed in 1978.[52] No figures were found for the number of residential dwellings completed by the public sector in these two years but they are unlikely to approach the 45 000–55 000 required to keep up with growing needs.

The State Organization for Housing was established in 1966 as the main body responsible for formulating urban housing policies and for distributing public housing units. It also undertakes slum clearance programmes and provides assistance to cooperative societies. In rural areas, the Rural Housing Administration, established in 1974, plans, constructs and supervises rural housing schemes and related facilities. Priority is given to members of cooperative, collective and state farms.

In housing, the government aims to vastly increase the public sector's involvement in housing construction. In the mid-1970s, more than four-fifths of the housing construction was undertaken by the private sector. It also aims to increase total housing production very considerably, utilizing advanced industrial building systems and mass production with multistorey blocks built to increase urban densities. The State Organization for Housing has been establishing factories for industrialized housing in four major cities. In Baghdad and Basrah, factories will have a capacity of 3000 units a year, while in Mosul and Karbala capacity will be 2000 a year. Meanwhile, performance standards for rural and urban housing (and for services) are being developed.

Although the Iraqi government recognizes the scale of the housing problem and the future needs, it has yet to evolve a clear programme with regard to housing construction and infrastructure and service provision for specific settlements and regions by specific dates. It is by no means clear whether present policies supporting industrialized building systems are realistic or effective responses to Iraq's housing problems. The United Nations Report[53] in November 1977 suggested that the industrialized housing units will cost $240 per square metre. This will put them well beyond the reach of most urban households, unless they are very heavily subsidized. New performance standards for rural and urban housing and for services could be a positive step if the standards are not set too high. But no information is available as to how indigenous values and standards embodied in existing Iraqi settlements can be maintained in the shift to prefabricated units. The Arab *Report* points to 'the contrast between the care devoted to the luxurious high technology prestige buildings in Baghdad and the neglect suffered by the debilitated housing within the same neighbourhoods.[54] Current policy suggests that the very considerable amount of government investment in housing will benefit only a small minority while housing conditions for the majority do not improve or even deteriorate. And slum clearance schemes are likely only to increase overcrowding.

The 1976–80 National Development Plan has given strong support to education, social services, sewerage, health and public hygiene. The target for 1980 was universal primary education. And by that date, 'the capacity and efficiency of transportation and communication would be at the level of those in a developed country' while medical services are to be 'brought up to international standards'.[55] The percentage of the population with access to potable water was put at 62 per cent in 1975. However, water supply projects only reached 13 per cent of rural inhabitants and the 1976–80 Plan aimed to increase this fivefold while improving water supply in Baghdad and other cities. In addition, the sewage systems in Baghdad, Basrah and other major cities were to be extended.

Building Industry

Despite rapid expansion in the production of building materials such as cement, in the late 1970s, Iraq's construction industry was facing serious shortages in such materials as bricks, steel and cement, and also in skilled manpower. As we noted earlier (page 41), housing construction was falling further and further behind needs.

The government is increasing its role both in housing construction and in the production and marketing of building materials. The aim is to achieve self-sufficiency in building materials. But the emphasis has been on modernization and industrialization with the goal of creating a fully industrialized building industry. Little progress has been made in developing local materials to provide minimum-standard but low-cost materials for the informal sector that still accounts for much of the urban and rural housing construction. As the Arab Report states, 'the public sector's intention to be in full control of all building activities related to housing is . . . neither commendable nor realistic'.[56]

Jordan

The *National Report* to Habitat states that the housing situation 'has deteriorated continuously due to rapid natural population growth, increasing rural–urban migration and the further complications which resulted from over one million refugees who entered the country in 1948 and 1967'.[57] This report also points to Amman's 'rudimentary physical infrastructure, the poor quality of housing in terms of building materials and construction techniques used, the total inadequacy of utilities available, the high occupancy rate, the physical congestion and the lack of community facilities'. The 1976–80 Plan stated that the average occupancy rate was 2.5 persons per room with six or more persons per room in some low-income housing areas.[58]

Since the mid-1960s, the government has struggled to come to terms with the mounting urban housing deficit and to extend basic services and infrastructure to a larger portion of the population. The *National Report* to Habitat quantified future housing needs based on an annual 3.2 per cent population growth and an average family size of six, and suggested that East Jordan needed an annual average of 12 000 units every year between 1976 and 1985, plus an estimated 2000 a year to replace deteriorating stock and an additional 2000 a year to replace huts and tents. This does not include any attempt to reduce the accumulated deficit.[59]

Up to the mid-1960s, the provision of housing was left entirely in the hands of the private sector. Government involvement in housing began in response to steadily worsening housing conditions when the Housing Corporation was set up in 1965. At the end of 1968 its role was reassessed, since in the previous three years it had given loans to only some 500 civil servants and two small housing cooperatives. After 1968 it began constructing housing, and by 1972 had constructed 950 units. During the Three-Year Plan, 1973–5, it constructed a further 3900, including more than 500 in agricultural projects. More than half of these units were built in the Amman–Zerqa area, many to provide houses for families displaced by the construction of the Amman–Zerqa highway. The Housing Bank provided total or partial funding for some 3500 units in this same period.

The Housing Corporation's target for the Five-Year Plan 1976–80 is 7050 units. Different models will aim to meet the needs of low and middle-income rural and urban households with unit costs (not including infrastructure and services) ranging from JD 1200–2800 ($3733 to $8710 using the 1974 average rate of exchange). To supplement the Corporation's activities, the Housing Bank's activities will also be expanded with loans at preferential rates to be given to low-cost housing projects. The Plan also calls for branch offices to be established throughout the country and for the Bank to be allowed to develop land within municipal boundaries for residential or commercial purposes. Large private and public enterprises will have to promote housing for their employees either through individual loans or through employee housing cooperatives. Low- and middle-income housing projects undertaken by housing cooperatives and the Housing Corporation are to be entitled to benefits from the Encouragement of Investment Law, a law originally set up to encourage private investments in economic development projects through tax exemptions and other incentives. They will also be exempt from customs duties on the imported construction materials they use. Apart from the Housing Corporation's work, the Jordan Valley Authority is the only other body concerned with housing construction. The Authority will be building houses for farmers in the Valley's settlements together with irrigation projects and the provision of basic infrastructure and services. A National Housing Council is given the task of formulating 'a housing policy that takes account of the regional distribution of population and prevents the utilization of agricultural land for housing purposes, within the framework of a national and regional plan for the rational distribution of economic activity within the Kingdom'.[60] With estimates for private investments in housing construction, the Five-Year Plan's housing goal is 31 000 units.

In assessing Jordan's housing policy, one should note the special problems facing the public authorities. As the Arab Report noted, 'one unique problem faced by the Jordanian government is the huge number of Palestinian refugees who refuse to be absorbed in the national housing schemes and prefer to remain in emergency camps and slum areas in the hope of returning some day to their homeland'.[61] But despite increasing government action in the housing field, even if targets are fulfilled they fall far behind growth in need. The Housing Corporation receives much of the public funding devoted to housing and yet its target for five years will meet less than six months' growth in national need. And, as will be discussed in more depth in the next section, the overconcentration on encouraging multistorey housing projects and the use of industrialized building systems may not be the cheapest (or most appropriate) way of increasing housing production and meeting housing needs, especially among the lower-income groups. Experience to date with such techniques has not been encouraging.

Building industry

Jordan's building industry has suffered from a shortage of skilled labour and a limited range of building materials to support a booming construction sector. In urban areas, traditional stone buildings are giving way to buildings made of reinforced concrete. Apart from cement, most building material is imported, at considerable cost to the economy. Foreign firms are striving to import and adapt their various prefabricated systems. The government seem convinced that industrial building systems and multistorey housing projects provide the best response to mounting housing deficits. The 1976–80 Plan recommends that the Housing Bank give priority and special incentives to companies and organizations building multistorey units. The Housing Bank is also instructed to work with the Industrial Development Bank to encourage the development of construction material industries, especially those producing prefabricated components.

As the Arab *Report* points out

> the shift towards reinforced concrete villas from the traditional stone buildings is hardly an aid towards solving the housing problem. Rather than attempting to rationalize traditional methods, the building industry is trying to adapt imported ones. . . . With the gradual replacement of local limestone buildings by concrete framed ones, the dependency on foreign materials is likely to increase. And the increasing reliance on high technology materials will cause decent shelter to drift farther away from the reach of low income groups. The state should seek more realistic ways to decrease this reliance and develop its own materials.[62]

Research efforts are looking at the possibility of developing stabilized earth bricks to lower housing costs.

The Sudan

Shelter, infrastructure and services received low priority in economic development plans throughout the 1960s and 1970s. And the Six-Year Plan of Economic and Social Development 1977–8 to 1982–3 was the first to explicitly state an estimate for the size of the urban housing deficit and the number of units that would be needed in the Plan period. It suggested that 65 000 units were in need of maintenance work, 10 000 needed basic services, and 115 000 needed building to make up for the deficit. And some 40 000 units would be needed annually to keep up with urban growth.

Sudan's *National Report* to the Habitat Conference admitted that the Ten-Year Plan (1961–2 to 1970–1) devoted very little to housing and that even this was 'ineffectively and ungainfully employed'.[63] During this Plan, housing policies concentrated on state-built housing and on serviced urban plot provision, both in urban areas. In addition, some low-cost houses were planned for low-income earners. During the Plan period, no more than 1740 rental houses were built for government officials, and these monopolized a large portion of the funds devoted to housing; 1000 low cost houses were built in Khartoum North and 63 300 plots were disposed of, 23 300 of these with services. The increase in urban housing need for these ten years was put at 136 160, so clearly the government programme was inadequate.

The Five-Year Plan (1970–1–1974–5) gave even less attention to housing in terms of public capital investment. Although it did give more attention to encouraging private investment in housing, the government's Estates Bank which is meant to promote housing construction through its loans only helped build 8000 housing units in the ten years up to 1976. Most of these loans were given to middle- and upper-income households. Moreover, the Bank restricted its activities to the capital.

However, the current Plan does give more attention to housing in urban areas. In phase 1 of a long-term housing plan, up to 1982–3, attention will focus on housing in settlements with more than 20 000 inhabitants; phase 2 will concentrate on improving housing conditions in smaller settlements. The target for 1982–3 is for 53 000 serviced plots for low-income groups, 54 830 for limited-income, and 20 860 units for middle and high-income groups. The total cost of this including services and administration was put at LS 255.5 million which works out (at 1976 exchange rates) at under $700/per plot. Housing construction and settlement planning is to be included in new development schemes such as the Rahad agricultural scheme and the Kenana sugar growing and processing project. A housing improvement programme will aim at reaching 42 000 units in the capital. And the housing loan system has been expanded. The Estates Bank has had its funding base more than doubled and it has recently opened offices in Atbarah and El Obeid. Interest rates for its loans are well below commercial rates. In 1976 interest rates were 5 per cent for lower-income groups and 6 per cent for upper-income groups. Finally, there are plans for some 5000 low-cost houses to be built for limited-income families and a project to encourage private investment in houses for middle- and upper-income groups with a target of 18 000 units.

The government's acceptance that the informal sector—owner builders and small building firms—should play the major role in urban house construction is both sensible and realistic. Thus, the public authorities' major role becomes the supply of serviced land. Each householder can build according to his needs and resources. However, there is a lack of data on housing needs and the quality and quantity of existing housing stock. Housing policy relies on mere estimates. And the current centralization of policy-making for housing, infrastructure and services has led to some misunderstanding as to specific locality's qualitative and quantitative needs. (The proposed physical planning law, if passed and implemented, should remedy this.) Actually providing the basic services usually lags well behind housing construction. And the public authorities have not done enough to develop the housing loans system and to promote more efficient forms of construction. Without such efforts, housing targets are not likely to be met.

In addition, existing housing in rural areas needs vast improvement, especially as regards the provision of basic services. The scatter of rural settlements over vast areas does not make this easy. But overall, for both rural and urban areas, national policies on shelter, infrastructure and services must be within national socioeconomic development plans.

Building Industry

In rural areas houses continue to be built by the people themselves using traditional techniques and materials. The same is true for a large portion of urban housing, especially those built in third and fourth-class areas. Such houses do not conform to government building regulations, which are not enforced in such areas.

The formal building industry that constructs houses to approved standards is handicapped by low levels of development and organization. It has to import many of the materials it uses. And little attempt has been made to develop the local construction or building materials industry. Building materials are very often in short supply, especially if they are imported because of the poor regional road networks. The result is that their price is inflated. The difficulty in obtaining steady supplies of materials such as cement and steel and their high costs inhibits construction activity.

In fact, Sudan does have indigenous resources for a building materials industry. Timber, stone, sand and clay are plentiful, but concentrated in a few regions. Again, lack of well-developed transport links inhibit their development. However, the National Building and Roads Institute is trying to improve the quality and durability of local building materials. One new plant has been constructed to produce mud blocks stabilized with asphalt. These 'asfadobe' bricks may well be produced for less than half the price of burnt bricks, while avoiding the heavy demand for firewood that burnt-brick production demands.

Some of the public authorities are thinking of importing prefabricated construction techniques to speed up housing construction. This seems particularly inappropriate when one considers the Sudan's lack of hard currency to be able to afford such increased import costs and the possible disruption this would cause to employment in the building sector. Moreover, the units such techniques produce are ill-suited to local climate, culture and household incomes. As Anil Agarwal points out in his study of mud brick construction,[64] low-income families in the Sudan will continue to depend on some form of soil construction for several generations and it is their housing and building material needs that the government should address.

Tunisia

Although a survey of Tunisian Shelter policies based on 1975 data commented that urban housing conditions compare favourably with those in other Third World nations, it did point to the fact that around a third of all families in Tunis live in temporary shelters or dwellings with no public utilities and with three to five persons in a single room.[65] In other urban areas, around half the population lived in what were defined as temporary or substandard units; 45 per cent of urban dwellings were not tied into a water supply system while less than half were connected to a sewer system. In rural areas households also lacked access to basic services; only 3 per cent of rural households had piped water (15.6 per cent had a well or cistern) and only 13.1 per cent had a toilet.

The 1970s has seen government support for housing construction increase very considerably. Under the Fourth Plan (1973–6), some 72 500 units were built, three-fifths with state aid. The annual construction rate of some 18 000 units exceeded the target of 17 000 and was a considerable improvement on the rate of 10 000 a year averaged in the previous decade. And it represents more than three units per 1000 inhabitants per year, comparatively high for a Third World nation.

For the Fifth Plan, the annual target is for 25 000 units which represents more than four per 1000 population per year. This is approximately the amount needed to absorb population growth, but does not begin to tackle the substantial backlog in need or make much impression on the replacement of substandard or deteriorating units. If these are included, annual need exceeds 50 000.

During the Fifth Plan, 85 400 units will receive government support; 40 000 of these will be 'rural' while 20 000 will be 'suburban' and 25 400 'economic'.[66] In urban areas, standards range from cheap core units (*evolutif*) to 'economic' units with three or four rooms. Most urban units are fully serviced. Rural units are generally two bedroom units with provision for the houses to be connected to water and sewage systems, once these are installed in rural communities.

Various agencies play major roles in building or financing housing construction. The Société Nationale de la Tunisie (SNIT) is a corporation in charge of 'social-interest' housing. Estimates suggest that it will be responsible for nearly half of all formal sector units constructed during the Fifth Plan. Its role in housing construction has expanded rapidly. In 1971, it was responsible for the construction of 5000 units; in 1977, its programme covered some 18 000 units. The once-centralized agency has now been decentralized into four regional agencies, one each for Tunis, the South, the North and the Central region. SNIT receives a subsidy from the government for every unit built since such subsidies are advanced to reduce the price of all 'social-interest' housing units. In the mid-1970s, the standard subsidy represented some 10 per cent of the cost of a 'suburban' unit and 5 per cent of the cost of an 'economic' unit.

Housing loans for lower-income groups are also subsidized. The central funding institution both for home buyers and for developers is the Caisse Nationale d'Epargne Logement (CNEL), the National Housing and Savings Bank, set up in 1974. This gives loans to households seeking to purchase units including loans for most of the clients in SNIT-backed housing developments. The terms under which loans can be obtained vary with income level. Recently, a new programme, funded by a 2 per cent levy on all employers' payrolls[67] gives low interest loans to lower-income groups. CNEL also lends money to finance construction, SNIT being its major borrower. CNEL gets most of its capital from government funds although it also attracts private savings. Other public institutions, including the Caisse Nationale de Retraites et de Prevoyance Sociale (National Retirement Fund) and the Caisse Nationale de Securité Sociale (National Social Security Fund) and some companies, also give housing loans.[68]

Rural housing units receive the highest government subsidy. The standard subsidy represented around 20 per cent of the unit costs in the mid-1970s. In addition, a further subsidy of nearly 25 per cent of unit cost was given if the unit was produced as part of the national rural development programme, and the government then granted the buyer an interest-free loan over fifteen years to pay off the rest.

Thus, housing policy in Tunisia is both explicit and relatively comprehensive. The government's commitment to improving housing conditions has considerably increased the number of units produced every year. The use of subsidies both to lower-unit costs and to keep housing loans cheap has brought publicly financed housing units within reach of lower-income groups. The commitment of so much of the total housing budget to rural housing is very unusual; it is the only nation among the seventeen to give such financial support to improving rural housing conditions. However, as the Plan itself admits, current housing targets fall well below annual need. The number of houses built and the number of households to benefit from government housing policies could be increased if the level of subsidy per unit was reduced. In 1977, some new directions in housing policy were becoming evident. Firstly, there was a new concentration on slum upgrading in a project in Tunis, rather than slum clearance programmes which had previously done little but further aggravate overcrowding and poor housing conditions. Approximately 45 000 people will benefit from a slum upgrading project in Central Tunis with the provision of water, sewerage, electricity and paved roads.[69] Secondly, it seems that the level of subsidy per unit was being reduced so that government housing funds can reach more people. And thirdly, the first serviced-site projects were being implemented for squatter households displaced by installing infrastructure in the slum upgrading project. Such trends, together with the government's political and financial support for housing and urban land policies, suggest that Tunisia's shelter programme will be one of the most effective among the seventeen nations in the 1980s.

The Fifth Plan also contains ambitious targets for water supply and waste disposal. The agency in charge of water supply (SONEDE) aims to provide two-thirds of the national population (including more than four-fifths of the urban population) with either a fountain or a direct house connection for water. In addition, the agency created in 1975 which is responsible for sewage systems in the nineteen largest urban settlements (ONAS) aims by the late 1980s to construct sewers for all areas now served with water systems.

Building Industry

Little data was available as to the relative contributions of the formal and informal construction sectors to housing production. The fact that housing production in the formal sector is far more rapid than in most Third World nations does lessen the informal sector's contribution although it seems its activities still account for an important portion of urban housing (especially for lower income groups) and for most rural housing.

The rapid expansion in housing construction during the Fourth Plan led to a major crisis in building material availability in the mid-1970s. A shortage of bricks and the inability of domestic cement and steel production to meet growing demands led to rising costs and rapidly increasing imports. Various measures have been taken to ease the bottleneck in building material supplies. New brick, cement, lime and steel plants are being constructed while existing plants are being expanded. Prefabrication of certain components are being encouraged. And the use of industrialized building systems is being considered since this would help overcome the shortage of skilled labour. However, it is not clear whether such systems would help the public authorities reach more households with improved conditions or indeed fit into Tunisia's rich cultural heritage.

Notes

The information in this section is based on the *Assessment of Human Settlements in Arab Countries*, written by our colleagues Omer M. A. El Agraa and Adil Mustafa Ahmad, Sudanese Group for the Assessment of Human Settlements, University of Khartoum, the Sudan. A revised version of this has been published by the University of Khartoum Press in English and Arabic. For statistics for which no source is quoted, the reader should refer to this volume and to the list of general sources in the Introduction.

1. Despite the very considerable benefits the dam brought to Egypt, it has also had some unfortunate side-effects. It has hindered the movement of silt which enriched the Nile Valley and Delta and supported the fishery at its mouth in the Mediterranean. In addition, increased irrigation has not been accompanied by adequate measures to combat bilharzia.
2. *African Business* (1979). *Egypt Survey* (November 1979).
3. Different sources give very different figures for metropolitan Cairo. The figure used is drawn from Europa (1979), *The Middle East and North African 1979–80*, page 320. Alexandria's population is from 1976 census data.
4. United Nations (1979). *Demographic Yearbook 1978*.
5. Preliminary results from the 1976 Census of Population and Housing; Central Agency for Public Mobilization and Statistics, Cairo (April 1977), Table 25.
6. As for (5) but Table 8.

7. Ministry of Planning (1978). *Annual Abstract of Statistics*, Central Statistical Organization, Table 2/2 based on the 1977 census.

8. Different sources give very different figures for Iraq's degree of urbanization and for the population of its major cities. For instance, the *World Development Report 1980* (World Bank) states that 72 per cent of Iraqis lived in urban areas in 1980 which would not be possible if only 63.7 per cent lived in urban areas in 1977 (the census figure). Then government figures from the 1977 census do not list individual city populations but the urban population of each governate. The most recent estimates for Iraqi city populations come from the Economist which put Basrah's population for 1978 at 854 000; Mosul's at 892 000 and Kirkuk's at 600 000. But the figures for Kirkuk and Mosul very considerably exceed the total urban population for the governate they were in for 1977 from the 1977 census. Many statistical sources still give 1965 figures based on the previous census. However, in Table 3, Section V we have used 1974 estimates from Fisher W. B. (1978), *The Middle East*, Methuen which put Mosul's population at 350 000 and Basra's population at 423 000.

9. Fisher W. B. (1978). *The Middle East*, 7th edition, (London: Methuen and Co.) page 390.

10. Most population figures are only rough estimates based on projections from the 1961 census since figures from a more recent census were generally not available.

11. Estimates for Amman, Zerqa and Irbid from Europa (1980), *North Africa and the Middle East*. All other urban statistics from the 1975 DOS Agricultural Census.

12. Jordan, Hashemite Kingdom of (1976). *Five Year Plan 1976–80*, National Planning Council page 60 (export figures) and pages 168 and 181 (phosphate production and phosphate production target figures).

13. Some estimates put the figure a lot higher. An estimate in the *International Herald Tribune's* supplement on Jordan (December 1979) suggested that some 400 000 Jordanian citizens were working in the Gulf.

14. In 1974, the nine provinces which date from colonial times were replaced with eighteen new provinces, twelve in the north and six making up the south.

15. The Jonglei Canal is being built from Bor (rather than Jonglei) to the Sobat river close to Malakal. Although originally planned to run from Jonglei, the new route was chosen because, among other reasons, it no longer cuts through the Dinka's grazing lands.

16. National Planning Commission (1975). Provisional figures from the 1974 *Economic Survey*.

17. El-Hassan, A. M., editor (1976). *An Introduction to the Sudan Economy* (Khartoum: University Press), page 99, Table 10.

18. All urban statistics, estimates and projections are drawn from Agency for International Development (1978), *Sudan Shelter Sector Assessment*, Office of Housing, US AID, Appendix A-1 to A-5.

19. The emigration of Tunisians to work in Europe or other Arab states has helped keep national population growth rates down.

20. Agency for International Development (1979), *Tunisia Shelter Sector Survey*, Office of Housing, US AID, page 59.

21. Tounatki, Bechir (1977). 'Tunisian policy for spatial planning', paper presented at US AID Fourth Conference on Housing in Africa, page 23.

22. Egypt, Arab Republic of (1977). 'Programme of reconstruction and development', Ministry of Housing and Reconstruction and *Egypt Survey*, African Business, November 1979.

23. Egypt, Arab Republic of, and Office of Housing, US AID (1977). *Housing and Community Upgrading for Low Income Egyptians*, Report of the Joint Housing and Community Upgrading Team, page 25.

24. In 1977, 15 per cent of Iraq's merchandise imports was food.

25. This was subsequently modified to become the Seven-Year Programme for Economic Development in 1963.

26. Jordan, Hashemite Kingdom of (1975). *Human Settlements in Jordan: Final National Report submitted to Habitat* (December 1975), page 52.

27. Jordan, Hashemite Kingdom of (1976). *Five Year Plan 1976–80*, National Planning Commission, page 365.

28. Agency for International Development (1979). *Tunisia Shelter Sector Assessment*, Office of Housing, US AID, page 59.

29. Tounatki, Bechir (1977). 'Tunisian policy for spatial planning', paper presented at US AID Fourth Conference on Housing in Africa, page 22.

30. El-Kammash M. M. (1963). 'A note on the system of landownership in Egyptian agriculture 1800–1960', Farm Economist quoted in King, Russell (1977), *Land Reform: A World Survey*, Bells Advanced Economic Geographies, page 380.

31. Egypt, Arab Republic of, with Office of Housing, US AID (1977). *Urban Land Use in Egypt—Appendix*, Report of the Joint Policy Team, page 79.

32. Egypt, Arab Republic of, with Office of Housing, US AID (1977). *Urban Land Use in Egypt*, Report of the Joint Policy Team, page 31.

33. Ceilings were set on landholdings—250 hectares for irrigated land, 500 for rainfed land—and land held under permanent tenure from the state that was not cultivated was expropriated with no compensation. King, Russell (1977). *Land Reform: A World Survey*, Bell's Advanced Economic Geographies, page 392–401.

34. United Nations (1973). *Urban Land Policies and Land-Use Control Measures Volume V, Middle East*, Department of Economic and Social Affairs, ST/ECA/167/Add. 4, page 32.

35. Jordan, Hashemite Kingdom of (1975). *Human Settlements in Jordan—Final Report Submitted to Habitat* (December 1975).

36. United Nations (1973). *Urban Land Policies and Land-Use Control Measures Volume V, Middle East*, Department of Economic and Social Affairs, ST/ECA/167/Add. 4, page 36.

37. Jordan, Hashemite Kingdom of (1976). *Five Year Plan 1976–80*, National Planning Council, page 351.

38. El-Bushra, El-Sayed (1976). *An Atlas of Khartoum Conurbation* (Khartoum: University Press), page 44.

39. *Mulk* is essentially full private ownership; *miri* originally state land and then transferred to individuals; and *habous* is trust land with revenues going to religious or charitable bodies.

40. King, Russell (1977). *Land Reform—A World Survey*. Statistics on Tunisia's Land Reform are drawn from his chapter on Tunisia, pages 413–425.

41. Chabbi, Marched (1976). 'Les systèmes d'Habitat dans le district de Tunis', quoted in *Tunisia Shelter Sector Assessment*, US AID, page 62.

42. Egypt, Arab Republic of (1975). *National Report*, Interim Version, A/CONF.70/NR/52, page 37.

43. Egypt, Arab Republic of with Office of Housing, US AID (1977). *Urban Land Use in Egypt—Appendix*, page 14.

44. So called because it is in a graveyard. Traditionally, tomb houses have room for visitors and many have been converted into permanent houses over time.

45. Ministry of Housing and Reconstruction quoted in Table III–8 *Housing and Community Upgrading for Low Income Egyptians*, report by the Joint Housing and Community Upgrading Team, Ministry of Housing and Reconstruction and Office of Housing, US AID, 1977.

46. Egypt, Arab Republic of, with Office of Housing, US AID (1977). *Summary Report: Housing Finance, Urban Land Use Policy, Housing and Community Upgrading for Low Income Egyptians*, page 10.

47. Egypt, Arab Republic of, and Office of Housing, US AID (1977). *Housing and Community upgrading for Low Income Egyptians*, page 35.

48. Ministry of Housing and Reconstruction Table IV–1 quoted in *Statistical Appendix* of *Immediate Action Proposals for Housing in Egypt*, Joint Housing Team, US AID and Ministry of Housing and Reconstruction (1976).

49. Egypt, Arab Republic of (1977). *Programme of Reconstruction and Development*, Ministry of Housing and Reconstruction (March 1977).

50. Iraq, Republic of (1979). *Annual Abstract of Statistics*, Table 2/12, Distribution of Households (1977), Ministry of Planning.

51. United Nations (1977). *Report of the Joint UNEP/ECWA Mission on Human Settlements Technology in the ECWA Region* (November 1977), page 5.

52. Iraq, Republic of (1979). *Annual Abstract of Statistics*, Table 13/16: Number, area and cost of private sector buildings completed during 1977 and 1978, Ministry of Planning.

53. United Nations (1977). *Report of the Joint UNEP/ECWA Mission on Human Settlements Technology in the ECWA Region* (November 1977), page 6.

52

54. El Agraa, O. M. and Ahmad, A. M. (1979). *Assessment of Human Settlements in Arab Countries*, study sponsored by IIED (London), page 123.
55. Iraq, Arab Republic of (1976). *The National Development Plan 1976–80*.
56. El Agraa, O. M. and Ahmad, A. M. (1979). *Assessment of Human Settlements in Arab Countries*, page 124.
57. Jordan, Hashemite Kingdom of (1975). *Human Settlements in Jordan*, page 18.
58. Jordan, Hashemite Kingdom of (1976). *Five Year Plan 1976–80*, page 349.
59. Jordan, Hashemite Kingdom of (1975). *Human Settlements in Jordan*, page 7.
60. Jordan, Hashemite Kingdom of (1976). *Five Year Plan 1976–80*, page 350.
61. El Agraa, O. M. and Ahmad, A. M. (1979). *Assessment of Human Settlements in Arab Countries*, page 130.
62. El Agraa, O. M. and Ahmad, A. M. (1979). *Assessment of Human Settlements in Arab Countries*, page 129.
63. Sudan, Democratic Republic of (1975). *National Report on Human Settlements*, Department of Housing Services and Engineering Affairs, Ministry of People's Local Government, page 15.
64. Agarwal, Anil (1980). *Mud, Mud; the Use of Indigenous Building Materials in the Third World*, Earthscan Briefing Document.
65. Agency for International Development, USA (1979). *Tunisia Shelter Sector Assessment*, Office of Housing, US AID (January 1979).
66. Ministère d'Équipement (1976). *Plan Quinquennal 1977–81: II—Perspective 1977–81*, Commission Nationale Sectorielle de l'Habitat, de l'Urbanisme et de la Construction, Tunis (April 1976).
67. Fonds de Promotion de Logement Pour les Salaries (Housing Promotion Fund for Wage Earners).
68. Jomaa, Mohamed (1977). 'Housing finance in Tunisia', paper presented at the Fourth Conference on Housing in Africa (Tunis, 1977), sponsored by US AID, page 68 of proceedings.
69. Agency for International Development (1976). *Tunisia: Housing Investment Guaranty*, AID-DLC/P-2205, USA.

SECTION II: ASIA

India, Indonesia, Nepal, The Philippines and Singapore

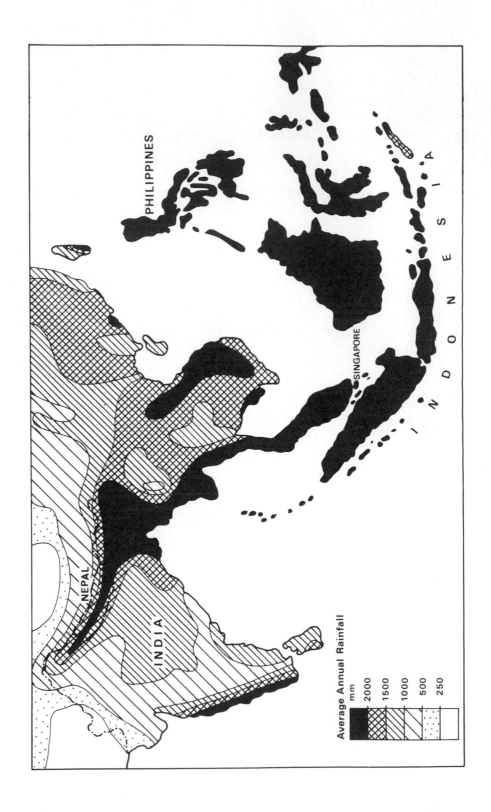

Average Annual Rainfall

| mm |
| 2000 |
| 1500 |
| 1000 |
| 500 |
| 250 |

PHILIPPINES

SINGAPORE

INDONESIA

NEPAL

INDIA

Background

India

By mid-1978, 644 million people lived in India, more than a seventh of the planet's population on one-fiftieth of its land area. Projections suggest the population will be approaching a billion by the year 2000.

India's land surface of more than 3 million square kilometres can be divided into three broad regions: the mountain wall of the Himalayas along its northern borders; the 2400 kilometre-long Indo-Gangetic plain formed by the Indian subcontinent's three great rivers (the Indus, the Ganges and the Brahmaputra); and the Peninsula or Deccan Plateau with coastal plains running up the east and west coasts. With its national territory stretching from the hottest tropical regions to the Himalayan mountains far into the temperate zone, no generalizations are possible about climate and rainfall. Broadly speaking, there are three noticeable seasons—the cold season from November through February, a hot season March to June and a rainy season June to October. Assam to the east and the west coast have high rainfall while the Thar desert running for much of the India–Pakistan border has almost none. The rest of India comes between these two extremes.

The Indian subcontinent's history dates back many millenia with some 5000 years of permanent recorded settlements. Today, India encompasses an enormous variety of cultures, religions and languages—there are fifteen national languages. It also encompasses regions with enormous differences in population density, urbanization and industrial development. National population density is extremely high—some 200 persons per square kilometre by 1978. The most densely populated areas are along the Indo-Gangetic Plain, on the southern tip of the Peninsula and on parts of the Peninsula's coast. The three states that make up much of the Indo-Gangetic Plain—Uttar Pradesh, Bihar and West Bengal—contain more than a third of the national population. Large areas in these states—and in Kerala on the western tip of the Peninsula—have population densities exceeding 400 persons per square kilometre. In the 1971 census, Kerala had 549 persons per square kilometre, while mountainous Sikkim had only 29, and Arunachal Pradesh on the north-east border had only six.

In 1980, 78 per cent of the population lived in rural areas, while in 1978, 74 per cent of the labour force were engaged in agriculture. Despite steady growth in industrial output over the two decades up to 1978, the percentage of the workforce engaged in agriculture on this date was the same as it had been in 1960. And despite steady growth in agricultural production between 1960 and 1979,[1] small farmers and tens of millions of landless labourers have seen little (if any) improvement in their economic position. A comparatively small rural élite has accounted for much of this growth;

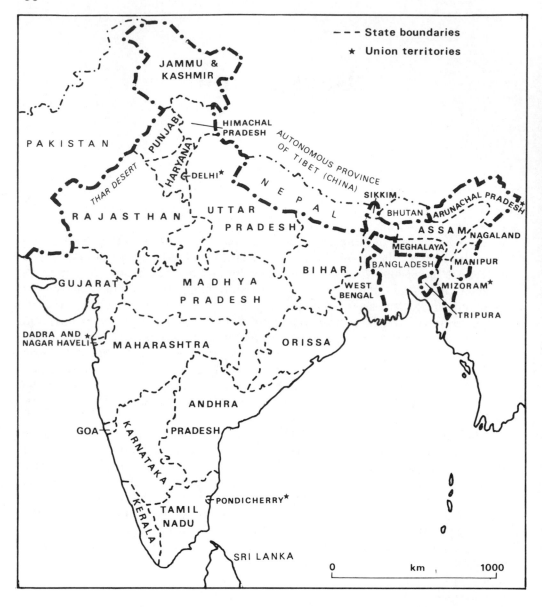

these tend to be farmers with comparatively large holdings and with sufficient capital and water resources to efficiently irrigate their land and purchase the needed machines and inputs to make best use of their high yielding seeds. Land reforms have done little to change the agrarian structure in most states.

Virtually all the rural population live in villages of between 100 and 5000 inhabitants. More than half a million villages are fairly evenly distributed over the country while small towns are comparatively few and far between. In 1971 about half the rural population lived in the larger villages of between 1000 and 5000 inhabitants. Small towns (10 000–50 000 inhabitants) and very small towns (less than 10 000 inhabitants) are mostly market towns with predominantly rural characteristics. The towns of between 5000 and 10 000 inhabitants declined in absolute numbers and in their percentage share of the national population between 1951 and 1961, and again between 1961 and 1971.[2] Their economic base does not seem strong enough to make much impression on the essentially dualistic rural–urban nature of India's settlement pattern and economy.

Despite a predominantly rural population, India, with an urban population of over 150 million, has the fourth largest urban population in the world. By 1980, 22 per cent

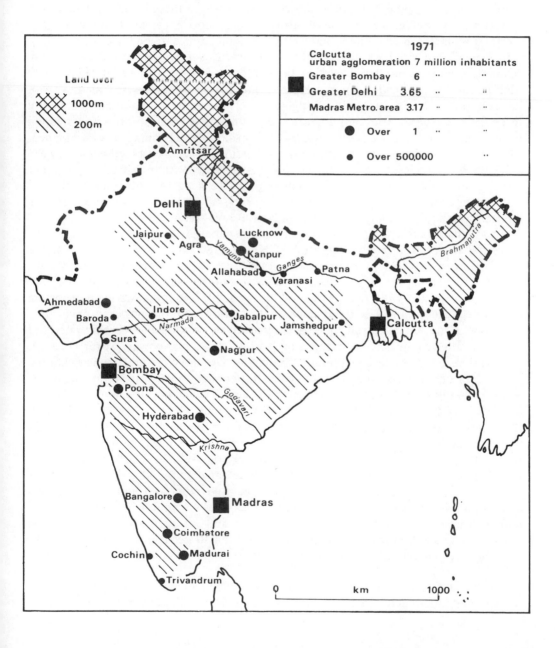

of the population lived in urban areas, that is, in settlements with more than 5000 inhabitants more than 75 per cent of whom are engaged in non-agricultural occupations, and with the density exceeding 1000 persons per square kilometre.[3] By 1981, there were fourteen cities with more than a million inhabitants. Apart from these, in 1971 there were 142 cities with more than 100 000 inhabitants and 221 with between 50 000 and 100 000. And Calcutta's urban agglomeration encompassed 7 million people while Greater Bombay encompassed 6 million and Greater Delhi 3.65 million. Urban population has grown relatively slowly—averaging 3.3 per cent annually between 1960 and 1980.

Industrial development has been drawn to areas where there is easy access to raw materials, fuel sources and industrial infrastructure. Since these are found near or in old metropolitan centres, India's industrial development has tended to concentrate in four states: Maharashtra (with Bombay as its industrial centre) and Gujarat (with Ahmedabad as its industrial centre) on the north-west coast; Tamil Nadu (with Madras) on the Peninsula's south-eastern tip; and West Bengal (with Calcutta) with its eastern border shared with Bangladesh. These states accounted for nearly three-fifths of all industrial output and were among the six richest states in per capita income for 1974–5.[4] There is no evidence of these states lessening this dominance. They monopolized more than half of all state industrial licences issued between 1974 and 1977.[5] Rural migrants tend to flock to states and cities with industrial employment opportunities while urban-to-urban migrants tend to head for cities like Delhi and Bangalore where the employment base is more skill and service-oriented. India's interior continues to receive very little industrial investment.

Although India is often portrayed as a nation characterized by food shortages and industrial backwardness (the per capita GNP of $180 in 1978 remains one of the world's lowest), it now produces a wide range of industrial products. Machinery, textiles and clothing are among its most valuable exports. Sugar, tea and iron ore are also major exports. After a series of good harvests, 1977–9, India was even exporting some wheat and rice in 1979. It has emerged as a major economic power in Asia with a large and powerful industrial base, a comparatively well-developed transport and communications network and a large supply of educated manpower. Nevertheless, it faces serious structural and institutional problems. Despite clear and explicit national planning efforts, the economy has not grown fast enough to keep up with rising needs and expectations. Much of the benefit from the last 30 years' development has gone to a comparatively small élite. In 1967–8, figures for family income distribution showed the richest 10 per cent sharing 35 per cent of total family income while the bottom 20 per cent had less than 5 per cent. Depending on the norms used, between 40 and 60 per cent of the population are below the official poverty line. The Sixth Five-Year Plan (1978–82) added together the number of person-years for which the total labour force is unemployed (that is, including both unemployment and underemployment) and found that it totalled 16.5 million in rural areas and 4.1 million in urban areas. Six million people enter the labour force every year and yet even a rapidly expanding modern industrial sector can absorb little more than 10 per cent of this increase. In fact, only 11 per cent of the labour force worked in industry in 1978, the same as in 1960.

In urban areas, much of the housing is overcrowded and of poor quality while basic services and infrastructure are very inadequate. In 1975, an estimate put 41.7 per cent

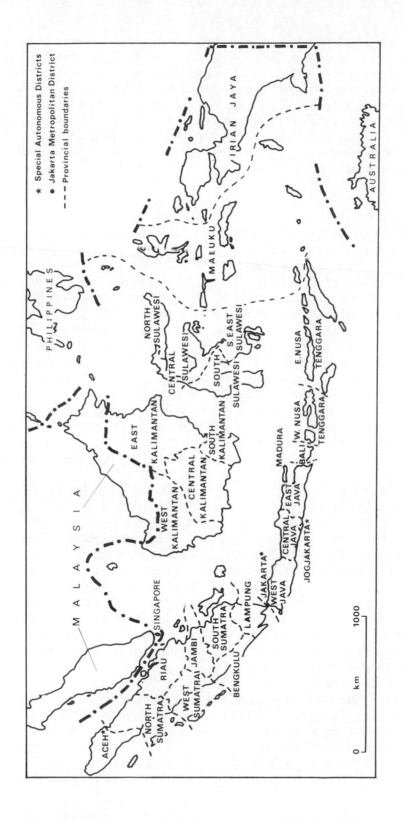

★ Special Autonomous Districts
● Jakarta Metropolitan District
--- Provincial boundaries

of the urban population living in one-room houses with an average of 4.6 persons in each one-room house.[6] In 1975, 64 per cent of the urban population were not connected to a sewage system. And it is estimated that not less than a quarter of the population of every Indian metropolitan centre live in slums and squatter settlements.

A report published in 1975 outlined living conditions in rural areas: 'About 90 per cent of the houses are made of mud concretes or combinations of wood, bamboo and thatched roofs . . . About 41 per cent of India's rural population live in one roomed houses.' Well over 90 per cent of households had no latrines. And 'less than 2 per cent of the villages are served with protected piped water supply'.[7]

Indonesia

The Indonesian archipelago contains some 13 000 islands stretching for more than 5000 kilometres east–west and nearly 1900 kilometres north–south. With a land area of nearly 2 million square kilometres, it is one of the largest Third World nations. With a population of 136 million in 1978 it is already the world's fifth most populous nation. Population projections for 2000 vary between 219 and over 280 million since there is considerable uncertainty as to the rate at which fertility can be reduced.

The main landmasses are Java, Sumatra, Sulawesi and Kalimantan (all part of the Greater Sunda Group) and Irian Jaya (part of New Guinea) while a few smaller islands like Bali and Lombok in the Lesser Sunda Group are major population centres despite their relatively small size. The major islands are characterized by rugged volcanic mountains covered by dense tropical forests that slope down to often swampy coastal plains. Around two-thirds of Indonesia is covered with forest. Its position on the equator and island structure give it high and even temperatures. Most areas receive heavy rainfall throughout the year with a rainy season from December to March. However, from Central Java eastwards, the dry season becomes more pronounced.

Indonesia has a rich history and encompasses many cultures and ethnic groups. Within its many islands, some 250 distinct languages and 300 ethnic groups exist. Remains of early man (*homo erectus*) date back half a million years. In the first century AD, Hindu traders from India were establishing coastal settlements. In the twelfth century, Muslim traders from India and Persia came seeking spices and handicrafts. The nation's abundant natural resources were exploited throughout the colonial period. Indeed, for centuries the country has been famous for spices from the Moluccas, pepper and rubber from Sumatra and teas and coffees from Java. Natural resources remain the nation's main economic base. Primary commodities (including oil) accounted for 98 per cent of all merchandise exports in 1978—crude oil, timber and rubber being the major export earners. Coffee, palm oil, tobacco, tea, sugar and metal ores are also important exports.

Most of the population remains in the traditional agrarian sector. In 1978, 80 per cent of the population lived in rural areas. But the rural population is very unevenly distributed with the major population centres tied to areas of rich volcanic soil and plentiful monsoon rains. More than three-fifths of the national population live on Java which represents only 7 per cent of the land area. Rice and food crops dominate agricultural production in what are among the most densely populated rural areas in the world. In 1971, Java and the neighbouring island of Madura had an average of 569

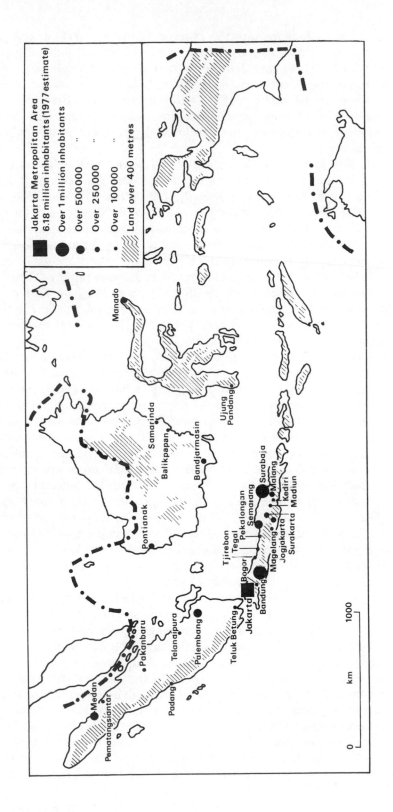

Jakarta Metropolitan Area
6.18 million inhabitants (1977 estimate)

Over 1 million inhabitants

Over 500000   :

Over 250000   :

Over 100000   :

Land over 400 metres

persons per square kilometre with the average exceeding 1000 persons per square kilometre in some farming regions. The islands of Lombok and Bali and parts of Sumatra and Sulawesi also have dense rural populations although they tend to grow cash crops. But average population densities for Sulawesi and Sumatra were around 40 persons per square kilometre in 1971. And Kalimantan and Irian Jaya with nearly half Indonesia's total land area contains one-twentieth of the national population—much of it isolated from development programmes and still engaged in shifting cultivation.

Under Suharto's presidency, the industrial and service sectors have grown rapidly and the economy has been given a more stable basis. The secondary and tertiary sectors account for more than two-thirds of GDP (although much of this will in fact relate to oil and timber production and export). In 1980, 20 per cent of the population lived in urban areas which are defined as municipalities, regency capitals and other places with urban characteristics. While the national rates of urban growth have not been particularly rapid—they averaged 3.8 per cent a year in the 1960s and 3.6 per cent in the 1970s—some of the major centres were growing rapidly. There were over 50 major cities in 1975. Jakarta, the capital, with more than 6 million people in its metropolitan area in 1977 may encompass 16 or more million people by 2000 while Bandung, with 1.2 million and Surabaja with 1.6 million in 1971 are both likely to encompass more than 2.5 million by 1990.[8]

The rural sector, however, has been neglected and expenditure on social services and basic infrastructure has not kept pace with economic growth. Although rice production grew from just under 9 million tonnes in 1965 to nearly 15 million tonnes in 1974, demand grew faster with imports rising to more than a million tonnes in 1973 and 1974. Indonesia has become one of the world's major rice importers. Government programmes to encourage more intensive rice cultivation has tended to benefit the larger and richer farmers, leaving the poorer farmers and the landless behind. Increasing population densities in many of Java's rural areas are exceeding local ecosystems' carrying capacity. Excess population is pushed onto hills or mountain slopes unsuited to crop cultivation and land-hungry people are deforesting land and occupying sites prone to landslides, floods and volcanic eruptions. Most of the rural population lack basic infrastructure and services—and depend on unprotected wells, rivers and ponds for their water. Diseases related to inadequate sanitation and polluted water supplies are among the principal causes of death and disease in rural areas. Life expectancy in 1978 was only 47 years.

In urban areas, although incomes may be higher, infrastructure and service provision is little better and the housing conditions are among the most overcrowded in the world. Squatter settlements are growing rapidly and much of the urban population lack access to safe water supplies and adequate sanitation. Expanding urban areas are encroaching on valuable agricultural land and despite oil wealth, average per capita income in 1978 was only $360. There is little data on income distribution although the distribution of private wealth is generally believed to be less unequal than in, say, the Philippines or in Latin America. H. W. Arndt[9] suggested that the reasons for this lie in the lack of large private landholdings, the fact that few private fortunes accumulated in business survived the era of 'guided democracy' and the fact that most large enterprises are state—(or more recently partly foreign)—owned. However, there is an enormous gap between the small élite of civil

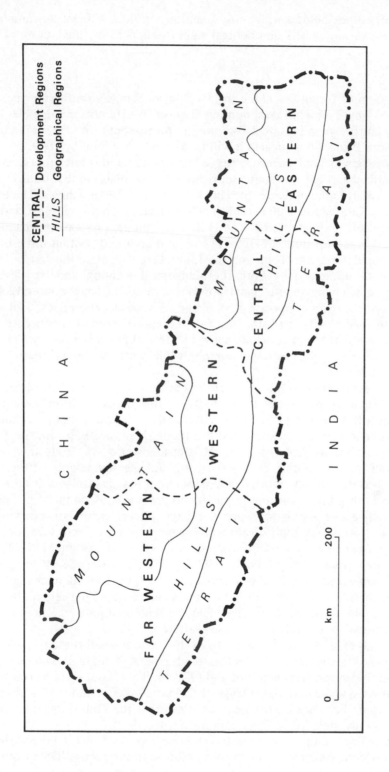

CENTRAL **Development Regions**
HILLS **Geographical Regions**

and military office holders who enjoy sumptuous offices, official cars and houses and the landless rural dwellers and poorest slum dwellers in the big cities.

Nepal

The Kingdom of Nepal lies along the Himalayan Range's southern slopes, between India and China's Tibetan Autonomous Region. It extends for some 800 kilometres east–west and between 140 and 240 kilometres north–south. In 1978, its population was 13.6 million. Projections suggest it will be around 23 million by 2000.

Much of Nepal's land surface is rugged and mountainous terrain. The country has been described as a gigantic staircase, rising from the plains in the south known as the Terai (or Tarai) to the midlands (or Hills) and then to the Himalayas. The Hills region includes the Kathmandu Valley, traditionally the nation's political centre and still today its most densely populated area. The Hills and Mountain regions (which includes the Himalayas) make up three quarters of the land area and contain three-fifths of the national population. The Terai and the Inner Terai[10] contain the rest.

Climate is influenced by both the subtropical location and by elevation—the low-lying Terai having a sub-tropical monsoon climate, the land between 1200 and 2100 metres having a warm temperate climate and then, as elevation rises, cool temperate, alpine and finally arctic climate. Much of the annual rainfall is concentrated in the monsoon period between mid-June and mid-September with the eastern and southern regions receiving higher average rainfalls while western and northern regions are somewhat drier.

For the second half of the nineteenth century and the first half of the twentieth century, Nepali politics were dominated by prime ministers from the Rana family, backed by the British Raj in India. Essentially a feudal military regime with the monarch reduced to a powerless and essentially honorary position, the Ranas kept Nepal almost totally isolated from the outside world. In 1951, this regime was overthrown by a revolution led by the King and the sovereignty of the crown was restored. But even today, much of the population remains isolated from Kathmandu and from both politics and development programmes. Around 90 per cent of the economically active population work in the agricultural sector. Most depend on small subsistence farms for their livelihood, usually farming land they do not own. Productivity per hectare is low but despite this, agricultural production still accounted for more than three-fifths of GDP in 1977. In 1971, there were 28 446 villages grouped into 3915 *panchayats* (the local government unit). If urban settlements are only those with more than 20 000 inhabitants, then on this same date, 97 per cent of the population was rural. In the Terai, clustered and nucleated settlements are common, while further north the population tends to be more scattered.

The virtual eradication of malaria from the Terai opened these fertile and usually forested plains on the Indian border to a steady stream of migrants who cleared the land for agricultural crops. Between 1961 and 1971, the Terai's population grew by around a third compared to the national average of 22.8 per cent. The major area from where the migrants came becomes clear when one notes that the Hills and Mountain regions' population only grew by 12.7 per cent in this decade.[11]

Mounting population pressure in the Hills has led to serious ecological degradation and soil erosion. As farming households struggle to produce sufficient food for their

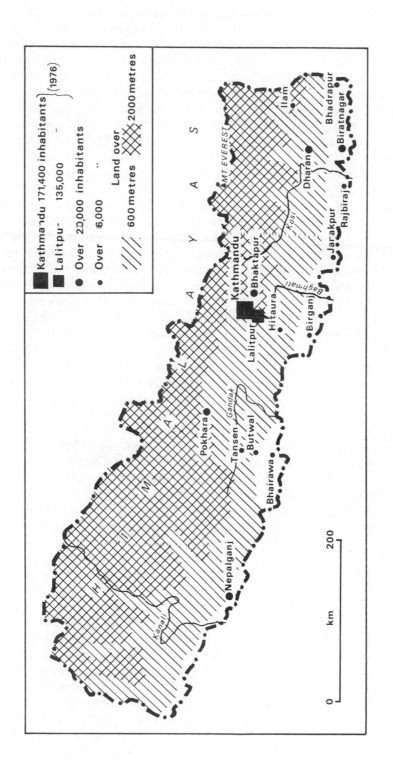

yearly needs, pastures are overstocked and overgrazed, trees needed to combat soil erosion are cut down for fodder and fuelwood and slopes unsuited to crop cultivation are cleared of natural cover. Flood incidence in rivers coming from the Hills has increased in recent years. Erosion caused by human activity is now reckoned to account for half of all soil erosion. River beds in some Terai rivers have been visibly rising year by year. Indeed, topsoil washing down into India is said to be Nepal's most valuable—if unpaid-for—export. While the Terai is relatively prosperous and produces a food surplus every year, life in the Hills and for the few scattered communities in the mountains is becoming more difficult. Even though the Hills and Mountain regions contain three quarters of Nepal's land area, they only have around one third of the cultivable land and have to support three fifths of the national population. More than a quarter of the region is under snow or Alpine meadow. Transport links are usually no more than footpaths which seriously hampers development programmes and the movement of food and other goods into the region. Many of the economically active population in this region have to migrate every year to work for a few months in the Terai or in India to supplement the meagre returns they get from their farm.

The Kathmandu Valley's population also grew faster than the national average between 1961 and 1971. It contains three major urban settlements—Kathmandu itself, Lalitpur (also known as Patan) and Bhaktapur (also known as Bhadgaon). Kathmandu and Lalitpur were Nepal's only settlements with more than 100 000 people in the mid-1970s. In 1976, estimates put Kathmandu's population at 171 400. Lalitpur, with an estimated 135 000 inhabitants in 1976, was only separated from Kathmandu by the river Baghmati while Bhaktapur, some 14 kilometres away, had 84 000 in that same year.[12] The Kathmandu Valley urban agglomeration which includes these three settlements had over 400 000 inhabitants in 1976. There were thirteen other towns in 1971, the definition of an 'urban' settlement being based on its administrative, educational or trade functions and not on its population size. Five of these were in the Hills, seven were in the Central and Eastern Terai and one was in the Western Terai. All had populations exceeding 6000 in 1971 while all but 4 had populations exceeding 10 000. By 1980, 5 per cent of Nepalis lived in urban settlements.

In 1971, only six settlements in Nepal had more than three-quarters of their labour force working on non-agricultural activities. Nepal's modern industrial sector is tiny and concentrates on processing agricultural products and on exports. Much of the modern industrial sector is owned or controlled by the government. And most of the large industrial units are either in Kathmandu or near the Indian border between Birganj and Biratnagar. Small scale and cottage industries producing primarily for local consumption still account for a considerable proportion of total manufacturing output.

Although deposits of oil, gas and various mineral resources have been found, it remains unclear whether these are worth exploiting. Indeed, Nepal's major natural resource is its vast hydropower potential, although at present the domestic economy itself has no need for massive hydropower projects and lacks the capital to construct them. However, hydropower capacity is being expanded to meet growing domestic demand and micro-hydro units are being installed in more isolated areas.

Most of Nepal's trade is somewhat inevitably with India. Contact with its huge southern neighbour has always played an important role in its history and in the development of many of its major settlements which grew up at strategic points along traditional trade routes. Attempts to increase trade links with other nations are constrained by its geographic isolation and the obvious difficulties in establishing major trade links with China over the Himalayas.

Per capita GNP remains among the lowest in the world. It only reached $120 in 1978, having grown by an average of 0.2 per cent a year between 1960 and 1978. Most of the population exist on the margin between subsistence and destitution. Despite land reforms in 1964, a study in 1973 found 17.6 per cent of the agricultural households with 71.5 per cent of the land.[13] The fact that most communities in the Hills and Mountains are only accessible by foot has hindered the spread of basic services and infrastructure. Only 6 per cent of the rural population is reckoned to have access to a safe water source and many villagers have to walk several hours each day to collect their water supplies. There is an enormous shortage of trained staff—especially teachers, agricultural and forestry extension staff and medical staff. Life expectancy remains very low at 43 years (in 1978). Adult literacy also remains low at 19 per cent in 1975, although this is a considerable improvement over the 2 per cent literacy in 1950 that resulted from the Rana regime's opposition to public education.

Urban problems are relatively minor since such a small proportion of the population live in them. Urban growth has been comparatively slow and so there are no rapidly expanding squatter settlements. But the housing stock is old and often in very poor condition. Little new housing is being built. Only one quarter of the urban population had piped water supplied to their houses in 1971 (although recent efforts to extend piped water and sewage to more urban households may have increased this coverage quite considerably).

The Philippines

The Philippines archipelago contain more than 7000 islands stretching for 1850 kilometres off the Asian continent's southeast coast. The total land area adds up to some 300 000 square kilometres, and in 1978 the population had reached 45.6 million. Projections suggest that it will reach 84 million by the end of the century.

The main islands fall into four groups. To the north is Luzon and Mindoro, Luzon being the largest island in the archipelago with more than half the nation's population and its capital, Manila. The other three are the Visayan group in the centre with quarter of the national population; Mindanao to the south with more than a fifth of the population; and, to the west, sparsely populated Palawan. The larger islands have rugged mountains dominating their central area with most of the population living on coastal plains. The islands are volcanic in origin and are subject to earthquakes and frequent typhoons. The Philippines has a tropical climate with distinct dry and rainy seasons, and the islands sustain a rich and varied flora and fauna with around two-fifths of the land surface still covered by forests.

The Filipino culture is a complex mixture of Chinese, Malay and other early settlers with more recent Spanish and American migrants and influences. The country was under Spanish rule for more than three centuries—it is named after Philip II of Spain whose reign in the second half of the sixteenth century marks the peak of Spanish territorial control. In the nineteenth century, commercial agriculture developed rapidly to meet demand in Europe for sugar and abaca (hemp). Then under American dominance during the first half of the twentieth century, the United States became the main market for agricultural exports (especially sugar). An élite of large Filipino

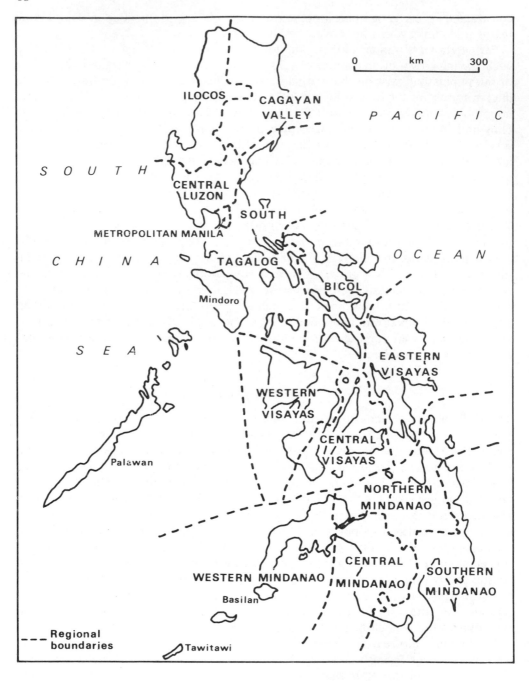

landowners benefited enormously while the free flow of American industrial goods hindered local industrial development. Today, agricultural produce remains the largest export—sugar, coconut oil and copra accounted for more than a third of export earnings in 1976 while their production and processing provides a large proportion of the labour force with an income. However, the production of rice, one of the Filipino's staple foods, has grown rapidly. Nearly half the nation's farmland grows rice and the Philippines is now self-sufficient in it. In addition, corn, abaca, tobacco, fruits and vegetables are grown both for local consumption and for export.

The Philippines also has rich deposits of many minerals and valuable timber resources. Copper ore and timber are both major exports. Since primary products make up such an important portion of total exports (three-quarters of merchandise exports in 1978), the economy has been hit by primary commodity price fluctuations. A large balance-of-payments surplus in 1973 has turned into a major deficit with oil price rises and falling commodity prices. However, the industrial sector has grown rapidly and accounted for 35 per cent of GDP in 1978 (while manufacturing accounted for 25 per cent). Much of this growth and development has been in and around Manila. A paper in 1979 stated that metropolitan Manila alone produces one third of the nation's GNP, handles 70 per cent of all imports and contains 60 per cent of all manufacturing establishments.[14]

There is only very limited information on the type and spread of rural settlements. The lowlands contain small and usually isolated farming settlements, while in the south fishing communities live on floating villages. The scatter of small settlements over large areas and poor transport and communication links with the more sparsely populated islands makes service and infrastructure improvements difficult. There is considerable internal migration not only to major urban centres but also to new frontiers—for instance to Palawan and to the Mindanao group (both to the main island and to smaller islands such as Tawitawi and Basilan).

In 1980, 36 per cent of the population was living in urban areas (a settlement is urban if it is a chartered city or municipality with a population density exceeding 1000 persons per square kilometre). There were 60 chartered cities in 1970. If the 'urban' population was only those people living in settlements of more than 20 000 inhabitants, then in 1970 the percentage of the national population living in urban areas would have been around 20 rather than 31.7, the official figure. Luzon is the most urbanized island due to the concentration of urban activities around Manila. The Manila Bay Metropolitan Area with a population estimated at more than 7 million in 1980[15] encompasses Manila itself with more than 1.5 million people, Quezon City with more than a million and the cities of Caloocan and Pasay each with more than a quarter of a million.[16] Metropolitan Manila doubled its population in the 1960s although a large portion of the growth was accommodated in squatter settlements whose population grew from 283 000 in 1963 to an official estimate of 1.2 million in 1975.[17] The Visayan group is also comparatively urbanized with major cities at Cebu (418 517 inhabitants in 1975), Iloilo (247 956) and Bacolod (196 492). Mindanao island has major cities at Davao (515 520 inhabitants in 1975) and Zamboanga (240 066).[18]

With a per capita GNP of $510 in 1978, the Philippines is classified by the World Bank as a 'middle income nation'. Growth in per capita GNP averaged 2.6 per cent a year between 1960 and 1978. However, the nation's wealth is distributed very unevenly. The top fifth of families enjoyed more than half the national income in 1971 while the bottom third received less than 10 per cent and the bottom tenth received little more than 1 per cent.[19] In that same year, average rural income was half that of urban areas. According to a report in 1979,[20] real wages had dropped by around a third since the imposition of martial law in 1972 and the Ministry of Labour had

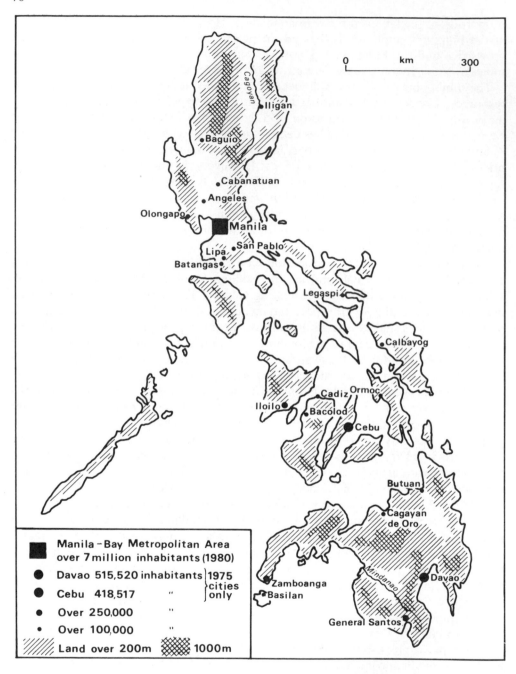

km

0   300

Cagayan

Iligan

Baguio

Cabanatuan

Angeles

Olongapo

Manila

Lipa San Pablo

Batangas

Legaspi

Calbayog

Cadiz Ormoc

Iloilo Bacolod

Cebu

Butuan

Cagayan
de Oro

Mindanao

Zamboanga Davao

Basilan

General Santos

■ Manila – Bay Metropolitan Area
  over 7 million inhabitants (1980)

● Davao 515,520 inhabitants 1975
                              cities
● Cebu 418,517   "   only

● Over 250,000   "

• Over 100,000   "

▨ Land over 200m ▩ 1000m

admitted that in 1977, nearly 90 per cent of rural and urban workers barely earned enough to meet subsistence needs. Basic services are lacking for most of the population and housing conditions are very poor. Slums, squatter settlements, inadequate water supply and sanitation, haphazard land use and industrial pollution characterize urban areas while makeshift housing, poverty and underdevelopment characterize rural areas. In 1970, nearly half the urban population and all but 11 per cent of the rural population lacked access to piped water. Three-quarters of the rural population and more than a quarter of the urban population had access only to an open pit or to no toilet facilities at all.[21] However, educational levels are comparatively high, due to successful consolidation of the school system established by the Americans in the late 1920s. Adult literacy had reached 87 per cent by 1975 while virtually every child goes to primary school.

Singapore

The Republic of Singapore consists of a small island with some 50 islets located off the southern tip of Malaysia and joined to the mainland by a road and rail causeway. Despite a land area of just over 600 square kilometres, Singapore's population had reached 2.3 million by 1978. Projections suggest that its population will reach 3 million by 2000.

Much of the main island is low-lying; nearly two-thirds is less than 15 metres while the highest peak is under 200 metres within a block of rugged terrain in the island's centre. Soils are generally infertile although rainfall is plentiful and reasonably constant. Since much of the island is so low and either cleared for agriculture or built up, many locations are subject to flooding. Despite being very close to the equator, the maritime location and constant high humidity keep temperatures relatively moderate.

Singapore is strategically placed close to the narrowest point in the Strait of Malacca which joins the Indian Ocean and the South China Sea. This location and its large natural harbour have meant that it has long served as a meeting-point for Indian and Chinese cultures and as a centre for exchanging the products of Europe, India, and China. For more than 150 years, Singapore's wealth and economic base have relied on this entrepôt role and it remains the main port for Malaysia's rubber exports. It also

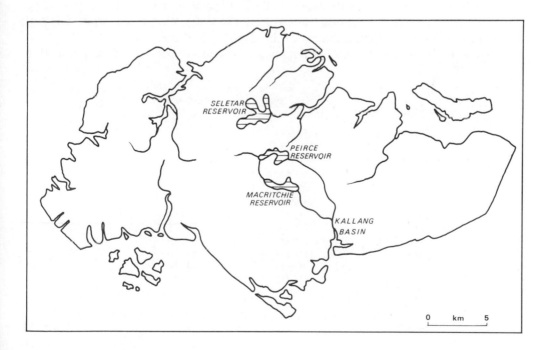

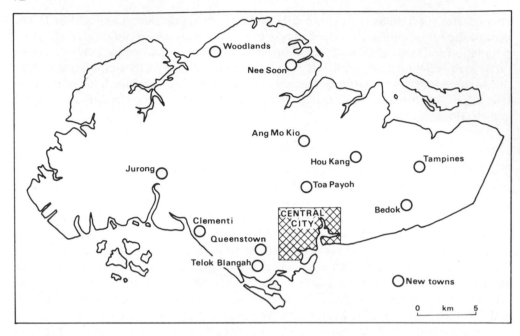

serves as one of the region's main oil refiners, importing crude and exporting petroleum products to nations such as Thailand, Japan and Hong Kong. The present government, in power since 1959, has encouraged the growth of manufacturing industries and more recently tourism with very considerable multinational investment allowed in.

Both the industrial sector and the economy as a whole have grown very rapidly since 1960. Between 1960 and 1978, per capita GNP grew on average by 7.4 per cent a year, a growth rate that is second only to Japan in Asia. With a per capita GNP of $3290 in 1978, it is among the richest of the Third World nations.

Despite the city's dominance of the main island, some 20 per cent of the population

New towns	Projected population	Distance from city centre (kilometres)
Queenstown*	150 000	5–8
Toa Payoh*	190 000	6–8
Telok Blangah*	70 000	5–7
Woodlands	290 000	22–25
Bedok†	225 000	10–14
Ang Mo Kio†	245 000	10–14
Clementi†	120 000	11–13
Nee Soon	200 000	19–21
Hou Kang	120 000	9–13
Jurong	160 000	14–19
Tampines	230 000	14–18

* Complete as of 31.3.79.
† Nearing completion as of 31.3.79.
Source: Housing and Development Board, Annual Report 1978/9.

lived outside the main city in the mid-1970s in new towns and rural communities. Agriculture and fishing make important contributions to national food needs although they only accounted for 2 per cent of GNP and employed 2 per cent of the labour force in 1978. Food remains one of Singapore's major imports.

Singapore's growing prosperity over the last 20 years has brought substantial benefits to most of its population. Economic growth has been accompanied by improvements in the quality of health services, public transportation, housing and education, and in nutritional levels. Life expectancy had risen to 70 in 1978. A foreign correspondant summed up Singapore as a modern, bustling phenomenon which at the moment at least is a remarkable success story. But this was qualified with the observation that 'personal freedom is strictly limited' and that 'when citizens are relocated, they are simply forced to move'.[22] However, the one party that has dominated the government since 1959 has been elected into office four times and in 1976 won all the parliamentary seats. No doubt the people accept limits on their freedom because of the prosperity and improved living standards that the present government's 20-year term of office has brought.

National Settlement Policies

India

Neither before nor after Vancouver has India announced a comprehensive settlements policy as envisaged by the Habitat recommendations. But recent Five-Year Plans have shown more concern with a better spatial distribution of development and suggest at least the basis for an emerging settlement policy.

Between 1956 and 1966, the Five-Year Plans concentrated on building up heavy industries. Then a shortfall in food production led to more emphasis on agriculture with the widespread introduction of high-yielding seed varieties and the infrastructure and services they needed. The fifth Five-Year Plan (1972–7) emphasized the need for a more equitable distribution of the benefits of development, a central concern of the Habitat *recommendations*. More emphasis was placed on meeting basic needs, on land reform and on promoting employment and higher incomes in rural areas. However, the sudden oil price rise in 1973 (and thus a soaring import bill), inflation and the after-effects of the Indo–Pakistan war culminated in the declaration of an internal emergency in 1975.

The emergency has been much criticized for its negative impacts. The abuses of power through imprisonment of political opponents without trial and through the sterilization programme are well known. So too is the generally negative effect of the city beautification programme which demolished inner city slums and transported the slum dwellers to makeshift colonies outside city limits. But two positive aspects were evident at the time. First, several items of the Prime Minister's 20-Point Plan included progressive measures such as socialization of urban land, abolition of bonded labour, minimum wages for agricultural labour and improved housing conditions in rural areas. Second, a national urbanization policy resolution was drafted as part of the Habitat preparations. In 1975, the Indian Government organized a seminar on urbanization policy to discuss the documents and resolutions prepared by the Town and Country Planning Organization (the federal government's advisory body on physical planning). The main objectives of the draft resolution for a national urbanization policy were the channelling of urban growth away from metropolitan areas to medium and small towns and new growth centres, the provision of a minimum level of services in rural and urban areas with rural–urban disparities reduced and a clear spatial pattern for economic development. Nevertheless, the bias was towards urban areas and many participants at the seminar pleaded for a more comprehensive settlements policy rather than simply an urbanization policy.

The seminar's draft resolution influenced India's National Report for Habitat. This Report recommended an integrated approach to development and settlement planning with the problems of rural and urban settlements to be dealt with at the same time. It accepted that present trends show the urbanization process to be irreversible. And it recognized that this is essentially a condition for and a consequence of economic development and industrialization. It listed a number of desirable objectives that integrated planning should seek to deal with such as minimizing rural–urban differentials, minimizing migration to major urban centres by developing service and growth centres and providing incentives to help the development of less-privileged sections of society and underdeveloped areas. It also identified the main areas of action at national, state (or regional) and local level. Thus, it outlined a framework for a settlements policy even if it did not actually define the policy itself.

In 1977, the Janata Party came to power, promising radical changes. Among other things, it promised a deletion of property ownership as a fundamental right, a new strategy for full employment, a stress on Gandhian values of austerity, the narrowing of rural–urban disparities with far more stress on rural and agricultural development, realistic public housing programmes and a social insurance scheme. It demanded that all metropolitan areas should have a regional plan and that every city of over half a million should have a masterplan with provision for a green belt around the city. Likewise, cities of over 100 000 should draw up masterplans with provision for slum improvement and housing for the poor. Licences for new industrial units close to cities whose 1971 population had exceeded half a million were to be very restricted. These policy statements were reflected in the sixth Five-Year Plan (1978–82) which aimed to remove endemic unemployment and underemployment, provide basic needs for all and ensure that the poor saw an appreciable rise in their living standards within ten years. Industrial investment was to concentrate more on village and small-scale industries, and funding for the Minimum Needs Programme was increased substantially.

Many of these changes have far-reaching implications for a future national settlements policy but no such policy appeared. And despite all its good intentions, the Janata Party embarked on an unknown and untried route of development for which neither the Party itself nor the bureaucracy that implemented it showed much inclination to go beyond deskwork. While wishing to promote the growth and development of rural settlements, there was no idea of the settlement structure the new policies were seeking to promote. It is by no means clear that the strength and will of the political leaders and the motivation and organizational power of local government was sufficient to implement such a rural-biased settlement policy. However, the question is somewhat academic since early in 1980 the Janata Party lost the election to Mrs Gandhi and the Congress Party. Thus, India's national policies related to settlements can be summed up as concerned but completely inadequate. Indian officials are well informed on all the issues. But no government has come close to putting these into the 'explicit, comprehensive and flexible national policy on human settlements' that Vancouver recommended as a central part of any overall national development policy.

Indonesia

Although Indonesia lacks an explicit and comprehensive national settlement policy, both spatial and economic planning have become more important under President Suharto. A National Planning Board (BAPPENAS) was set up to prepare draft

Five-Year Plans which, after approval by Parliament, provided the nation with its national development strategy.

In the early 1970s, settlement policies became more evident in national development plans. The aims of the second Five-Year Plan (1974–9) included reduced migration to large cities through the creation of new growth centres and rural development, a better distribution of development activities throughout the national territory and continued support for families to move from overcrowded rural areas to new settlements in underpopulated regions. Development action is at the provincial level—there are 26 provinces—with the provincial governor declared to be the Sole Power (Penguasa Tunggal). He is advised by Regional Development Planning Boards (BAPPEDA—essentially provincial versions of BAPPENAS) who prepare annual and five-year provincial development plans. To encourage coordination and cooperation between provinces, the second Five-Year Plan divided Indonesia into four economic development regions, each with two or three subregions which in turn encompass two or more provinces. 87 small and medium-sized cities were identified as potential growth centres by the Plan.

There is an important distinction here between decentralization and deconcentration. In Indonesia, central government favours deconcentration to promote development action at provincial level and its coordination through these new spatial subdivisions. But this does not involve decentralization of political power and influence. Deconcentration 'requires the building up of subnational capacities for planning, programming and budgeting systems in order to serve the national systems more efficiently and equitably'.[23]

Increasing attention has been paid to detailed urban and regional planning.[24] Neither BAPPENAS nor its provincial counterparts prepare detailed urban and regional plans. Their task is ensuring the various sectoral plans become a coherent and coordinated development plan. In 1965, the Directorate of City and Regional Planning replaced the Division of Spatial Planning. Its initial efforts in preparing plans for Bali and for Jakarta Metropolitan Area plus its surroundings prompted provincial governments to ask for similar plans for their regions. The failure or only partial success of provincial governments in implementing such plans led to the Ministry of Public Works and Electric Power (within which the Directorate of City and Regional Planning is located) helping to build up planning units at provincial level. These can work with the governor in formulating city and regional plans.

The Directorate of City and Regional Planning has been developing regional planning methodologies and techniques appropriate to Indonesian conditions. Several studies of the Jakarta region have been undertaken, often with different ideas as to how the central city's growth should be planned. A plan by the Provincial Development and Planning Board in 1973 recommended a concentric circle of growth poles beyond a green belt, 20 to 50 kilometres from the centre, while other plans have tended to favour growth axes radiating from Jakarta. An experimental study made by the Directorate with help from the Dutch government looked at Jakarta and three neighbouring districts[25] in 'Deconcentration Model Jabotabek' and recommended that Jakarta's growth should be steered to growth axes and thus divert much of the projected population growth away from the central city area.[26]

Indonesia's 'transmigration' programme to resettle people from overcrowded rural areas to sparsely populated islands began in 1905. After independence in 1949, it received high priority. The government sponsors migration from Java to areas like South Sumatra and South Sulawesi. Once new settlements are established with government help, the area is expected to attract spontaneous migration. Under this programme 1.25 million people were expected to settle in 500 villages during the 1974–9 Plan while the target for the 1979–84 Plan is for half a million families in 250 settlements in Sumatra, Sulawesi, Kalimantan and Irian Jaya.

Two other government programmes can be seen as part of settlements policy. One is a resettlement programme which aims to improve living standards among shifting cultivators in dry-farming areas. The other is to provide basic infrastructure and services to the hundreds of thousands of fishermen who live along Java's north coast and to bring them into larger settlements with a fishing harbour, cold storage and processing facilities.

Nepal

The new government in 1951 brought with it a commitment to planned development, no doubt influenced by India's example. Successive plans have outlined Nepal's development strategy and allocated development funds among the various sectors. The first three plans running from 1956 to 1969–70 did not bring the hoped-for economic growth with rapid expansion of industry and exports. Final achievements for each plan lagged far behind planned targets. But this is hardly surprising given the fact that the new regime inherited a nation with no dependable information on national resources, a fragmented and isolated economy, very inadequate infrastructure and no planning experience at all. Moreover, it possessed neither the administrative structure nor the expertise to effectively implement wide-ranging development programmes. And since much of the development budget was provided by foreign aid, the aid-donors' priorities no doubt influenced what are today regarded as misallocations—the development of a few, high-standard highways rather than a wider spread of investment to include upgrading local roads, muletracks and footpaths or the overconcentration on developing modern infrastructure and industry while doing little for the agricultural sector which provides the livelihood for nine out of ten Nepalis. The neglect of agricultural development in the Hills is one reason for the increasing inability of this region to grow sufficient crops to feed its population.

However, in the 1970s, a commitment to a wider spatial spread of development replaced the previous overconcentration of development investment in the Terai and the Kathmandu Valley. The accession of a new king marked a new attempt to spread the benefits of development more widely. The country has been divided into four regions—each with its own centre for implementing development plans—Dhankuta in the eastern development region; Kathmandu in the central development region; Pokhara in the western development region and Surket in the far-west development region. Planning remained centralized through the National Planning Commission, although it has set up branches in all four development regions. Within each of these, one or two major north–south growth axes linking each region's major settlements were identified.[27] The aim is to stimulate their development—and the links between them— in the hope that this will in turn stimulate a wider distribution of social and economic development.

The 1970s has also seen some strengthening of local government. In 1960, political parties were banned and the parliamentary democracy replaced by a four-tier system of local bodies (*panchayats*)— with 3915 village and 16 town, 75 district, 14 zonal and one national *panchayat*. All executive powers were vested in the King who rules with the help of a Council of Ministers. Although the *panchayats'* powers remain limited, the role of district and village *panchayats* in planning and implementing local development programmes has been increased. Village *panchayats* plan and implement village development programmes and can ask for funding and help from district level government offices, if approved by district *panchayats* who are responsible for coordinating village level activities and for preparing district level development plans. Districts are the focal point both for development programmes and for government administration. Many national departments have representatives at this level.

Two other developments in rural areas are worth noting. The first is a series of small area development programmes and small area package programmes which usually aim to complement some major development project with a wider development programme to improve, for instance, the area's social services, local industries, local soil management and farming practices and transport facilities. These are in an early stage of development and it is not yet clear who will implement them. The aim is to expand such programmes—there were 20 planned for the 1975–80 Plan—until, by the late 1980s, both the growth axes and these programmes will be subsumed into comprehensive, integrated regional development programmes.

The second important development has been the rapid migration of people to the Terai in the south. In 1963, the government set up the Punarvas Company to manage the resettlement of Hill people in the Terai in new planned communities with some 2 hectares per family, and with schools, clinics, potable water and other basic services. The company was also meant to guarantee the protection of forests, watersheds and lands unsuited to cultivation. However, the programme could not cope with more than a small proportion of the migrants. Thus, 'illegal' settlements sprung up in illegally cleared forest areas. Forceful attempts to evict them have placed such settlements under considerable difficulties. However, such settlers are now seeking sufficient political support to make the authorities legalize their settlements and give them services and infrastructure similar to those in official settlements. Reports suggest that many illegal settlements are in fact better than the 'planned' settlements which were based on the Israeli Moshav model which has little relation to Nepali culture and lifestyle.

Increasing attentic,' has been given to town planning. Up to the 1960s, there was no control of urban growth at all. Then town *panchayats* were given the power to control the design of urban houses—although this was primarily aimed at controlling the intrusion of modern buildings into traditional town landscapes of tile roofs with brick and wooden walls. In 1963, the Town Development Committee Act authorized the formatior ˀf committees to control urban development. The publishing of a development plan for Kathmandu Valley (although still not formally approved) increased the awareness of the need for planned urban development. Then in 1973, a Town Plan Implementation Act was passed to implement approved plans for the four regional centres. A Kathmandu Valley Town Development Board and implementation committees in each of the other regional centres were set up. Development plans for these four and for Lalitpur and Bhaktapur have been prepared—although these tend to be no more than land-use plans based on traditional masterplan approaches. Apart from the Town Development Committee Act, there is no policy document for the control of land and land use in urban areas and many officials think it necessary to extend the scope of such legislation to make it more comprehensive.

Philippines

The Philippines government has shown considerable enthusiasm for Habitat's settlement planning *recommendations*. In 1973, when preparations for the Habitat Conference were in their infancy, President Marcos created a Task Force on Human Settlements which brought seventeen government agencies together with the Development Academy of the Philippines to formulate a national settlements development 'framework', a development plan for metropolitan Manila and a national housing programme. This Task Force produced 'Human Settlements: The Vision of a New Society' that became the basis for national settlement planning.

Although the Task Force listed many policy goals, its aims were essentially to give spatial and settlement planning a more important role in national development planning and to use spatial planning to control the growth and development of metropolitan Manila while encouraging development in each of the other eleven planning regions. Resource surveys in each region would identify areas with potential for developing agriculture, livestock production, forestry, fishing and mineral extraction. And a total of 346 settlements were identified as potential growth centres whose development should attract urban migrants and urban developments away from Manila and disperse development throughout the country. These growth centres were to serve as focal points for intraregional and interregional linkages as transport and communication infrastructure was upgraded.

Development of 30 centres was given priority for the first five to ten years—two metropolitan centres (Cebu and Davao), eight regional centres, fifteen subregional centres (including four in the Manila Bay Metropolitan Region) and five growth centres also in the Manila Bay Metropolitan Region. A ban has been placed on most new industrial establishments within a 50 kilometre radius of Manila City centre with industrial development encouraged in these growth centres and transport links to the central city area improved.[28]

In 1976, the Task Force was replaced by a Human Settlements Commission which is, at present, seeking to implement the earlier Task Force's recommendations and broad settlement development strategy. Under its National Settlement Planning programme, resource inventory surveys have been completed for each of the twelve regions and comprehensive integrated regional development plans are being prepared. In addition, a longer term plan for 1975–2000 outlines the spatial aspects of the country's long-term development plan to complement the National Economic and Development Authority's 25-Year Plan. An Environmental Management Programme is working out an environmental impact assessment system to ensure that development plans do not neglect vitally important environmental aspects. In 1978, the Ministry of Human Settlements was created to coordinate all aspects of settlements policy with the Human Settlements Commission becoming its regulatory body.

Manila receives special attention through a programme to develop plans for the whole metropolitan area. A land-use map defining specific land uses is being prepared to guide the location of new activities, and the programme aims to delineate the functions of the various bodies operating in the metropolitan Manila area.

One gets the impression that present plans concentrate more on resource development, environmental protection and housing than on the delivery of basic services and infrastructure to the poor majority. The stress is also on urban development—and especially on 'saving' metropolitan Manila. However, the importance of relating national development plans to comprehensive spatial plans is clearly embedded in government policy and the new Human Settlements Ministry is a powerful body in the Philippines development administration.

Singapore

Economic prosperity and political stability have provided firm foundations for Singapore's settlement planning and development. In 1960 there was acute overcrowding in the central city. Its population was growing far faster than its housing stock. And around one-third of the population lived in slums or squatter settlements. There was also serious unemployment and underemployment. At first, the government gave priority to improving housing conditions; more recently, it has turned to urban renewal and to the construction of satellite towns around the central city.

Although there is no 'development plan', certain principles of settlement and physical planning are apparent in current government policies. The Ministry of National Development is responsible for planning and implementing development programmes; its activities encompassing public housing, urban renewal, public works, city and state planning and parks. It is the sole government institution responsible for formulating and implementing settlement plans at all levels. Two statutory bodies— the Housing and Development Board (the public housing agency) and the Urban Redevelopment Authority—implement its programme.

A masterplan guides all developments in the city-state. First approved by the government in 1958, this is reviewed every five years. A long-range physical plan for a population of 4 million was undertaken with help from the United Nations and long-range land-use, transportation and urban renewal plans were considered. This has allowed a wide range of proposals for Singapore's future development to be considered. Development proposals from both public and private sectors are submitted to the Planning Authority for consideration under the masterplan's guidelines.

One central thrust of Singapore's settlement policy has been to reduce overcrowding and replace slums in the city centre. Initially, public housing estates were built in clusters within 8 to 10 kilometres of the city centre. These rehoused many of the people displaced by slum clearance schemes and thus lowered densities in the congested city centre. By 1975, over 200 hectares had been cleared and redeveloped through urban development programmes with some 12 000 flats and 2000 shops built in their place.[29]

Eight new towns have been built (or are in the process of being built) to relieve congestion by providing houses and some jobs outside the central city. They vary in size from Queenstown with 150 000 people and Telok Blangah with 70 000, both complete and within 8 kilometres of the city centre, to Woodlands to the north, some 22 kilometres from the city centre which will eventually house 290 000 people. Public housing construction was concentrated at Ang Mo Kio, Bedok and Clementi for the

1976–80 Programme while the 1981–5 Programme will be largely concentrated in two additional new towns, Tampine and Hou Kang, and on greatly expanding Jurong's population.

The new towns have attracted some light industry and commercial development since they have a readily available workforce close by and can provide comparatively cheap and well-serviced industrial and commercial sites. The Housing and Development Board that is in charge of public housing also builds industrial premises in the new towns. Although no figures were available for the spatial distribution of jobs, it seems that most of the jobs for primary income earners remain in the main city centre. Thus, the new towns tend to serve simply as large suburban housing estates with most of the local jobs taken up by secondary income earners.

The public authorities have been trying to improve the urban environment through its Parks and Recreation Division. The main island has 35 parks, 20 of them within the city. The government runs a non-profit Plant Sales Centre and allows the cost of maintaining a private garden to be claimed as a deduction from income tax. This new stress on improving the urban environment relates to the government's strong promotion of Singapore as a tourist area. It recently became one of the few Asian nations to attract more than a million tourists a year.

Land

India

The amount of cultivated land per person in India is decreasing as 45 per cent of the national territory was cultivated in 1971 and there is little room to expand this percentage. In 1978, there was one quarter of a hectare for each person while in Kerala state, there was little more than one tenth. The main land issues tend to be rural since most of the population live and work in rural areas despite the comparatively low amount of cultivated land per person. Four principles for land reform have been laid down by the central government's Planning Commission: the elimination of intermediaries and idle landlords; a ceiling on holdings; specific permanent rights for cultivators (including the tenants' right to purchase their holding at a fair price); and the fixing of rents. But it is the state government's responsibility to devise and implement policies regarding control and use of land. This has resulted in each state adopting different land reforms with little coordination between them. Thus, tenure patterns, holdings and public control over land use differs from state to state.

Most operational land holdings are owner-occupied and operated. Figures for 1971 show that more than half of all holdings were under one hectare and represented only 9 per cent of the land. Large holdings of more than 10 hectares accounted for less than 4 per cent of holdings but represented more than 30 per cent of the land. Medium sized holdings of between 4 and 10 hectares represented 11 per cent of holdings and 30 per cent of land.[30] Some of the larger land holdings may have been broken up after the Central Land Reforms Committee lowered recommended ceilings in 1972. But of the four principles for land reform already outlined, land ceilings are the least implemented. Kerala and West Bengal have been at the forefront of implementing such ceilings but most other states lag far behind them. The Janata Party believed that the small, independent peasant farmer assisted by service coops should be the backbone of the rural economy. It stated that it would encourage the implementation of land reforms and impose a floor of 1 hectare on land holdings to prevent excessive fragmentation. But no concrete steps to implement these had emerged by 1979. And as in previous governments, there was little attempt to accept that land redistribution cannot solve the problems of the landless and the poorest farmers. There is not enough land to go round. But there was no move to give the landless labourers a minimum wage and more security in their work.

In addition, population pressures have caused serious environmental damage. Deforestation for fuel-wood and for extra cultivable land has caused an appalling reduction of forest land. As a result, flooding and soil erosion has increased and rainfall patterns have been disrupted. Desertification is spreading over widening areas of Haryana, Rajasthan and Uttar Pradesh. There is little effective control of this process and no simple or clear-cut solution when vital ecological needs to protect the productivity of the region clash with the immediate needs of the local population.

Until 1976, there had been no attempt to limit urban land holdings in a way comparable to rural land reforms. Urban capitalists had been given unlimited freedom to speculate in land. In response to this, the Land Ceiling and Regulation Act in 1976 aimed 'to take measures for exercising social control over the scarce resources of urban land with a view to ensuring its equitable distribution among the various sectors of society and also avoiding speculative transactions relating to land in urban agglomerations'.[31] Ceilings were set on urban land holdings, the larger the city the smaller the ceiling. State governments were empowered to acquire vacant land by paying 25/3 times the net average annual income during five consecutive years as compensation (with a maximum ceiling set for such compensation payments). Land used to build low-income housing was exempt. But this legislation has not been implemented in most states and urban areas. Even where it has, there are cases of owners forcibly removing squatters from their undeveloped urban land and building 'low-income' housing sold at prices low-income groups could not afford.

Quite apart from attempts to limit urban land holdings, urban planning and land-use control have met with little success. Most urban areas have larger percentages of land left undeveloped and their growth tends to be haphazard and unplanned. Although many masterplans have been prepared, most have been rigid and unrealistic. Few have been implemented. In addition, urban planning still tends to have aesthetic and traffic priorities. Orderliness of land use and wide roads are considered almost the prime aims of urban planning. The planners do not go beyond rigid layout designs and land-use plans so the concept of planning and stimulating urban development is totally lacking. There is no clear policy either from national or state government level.

Indonesia

Colonial occupation had a major impact on landholding patterns although Indonesia suffered less cultural disruption than the Philippines. After independence, there were two very different land tenure systems in force. Most of the nation's land were held under traditional 'Adat Land Law' which was largely unwritten. Land held under it was not usually registered with the public authorities. This traditional form of law stressed the communal aspect of land ownership in the spirit of *gotong-royong* (mutual cooperation). The rest, held under the former Dutch system, was registered with the authorities and stressed individual rights in land ownership.

In 1960, the government passed a Basic Agrarian Law which sought to adapt traditional concepts of land rights to modern needs and provide the basis for a unitary land law. The Law stated that 'all rights on land have a social function', in other words, that rights imply individual landowners have obligations to the community as in Adat law. The state has the right to determine and regulate land use and ownership. Individuals can have the right of ownership, building, exploitation and use but these rights are derived from the state. In addition, title-holders can grant secondary titles to others on the basis of a mutual agreement and thus lease the land, allow sharecroppers to farm it or use it as collateral for a loan. Extraction or exploitation of mineral resources requires a special government permit.

Thus, this land law promotes the right of the state (acting for the community) and diminishes individual rights as in traditional Adat law. The dual system of Adat and western land law legally ceased to exist but in practice, the dualism remains between registered and unregistered land. And for planners, the new law has its weaknesses. Although the state has the right to expropriate land in the public interest, there is no clear definition of 'public interest' and no guidelines for assessing compensation. Thus, urban development projects are delayed by the deficiencies in administrative procedure laid down by the Basic Agrarian Law. A City Planning Act 1971, applicable to all cities, makes provisions for the implementation of urban land-use plans and includes better procedure and clearer definitions for land acquisition.

Inevitably, in a nation as diverse as Indonesia with widely differing geographical regions, levels of development and cultures, land-use policies for the different regions will have to differ widely. The government is reluctant to let too much authority pass out of central hands. Furthermore, there is intense competition for development funds. A clear land-use policy has yet to emerge from such confusion. In addition, the government has not succeeded in controlling environmental degradation, particularly deforestation, as a result of population pressures on Java and other areas of very high population concentration. The government has sweeping powers to set out a rational land-use policy but political, economic and cultural factors seem to prevent it from making good use of this power.

Nepal

In an earlier section, we noted the serious ecological damage that has come from deforestation in this nation dominated by rugged and mountainous terrain. Forests cover some 30 per cent of the land but continuing population pressures are forcing people to clear and exploit land ill-suited to sustainable crop production. And the population's almost total dependence on firewood for fuel means that forest cover is probably diminishing quite rapidly. Although some programmes in the past sought to address this problem, they achieved very little. However, studies by the Planning Commission and various research bodies led to a recommendation by the National Development Council that this area be given more attention. A national land use plan is now under consideration.

In 1952, the state recognized that

> Unless the land tenure system is improved, the economic condition of the peasantry and agricultural production will not improve. Land ownership is passing from the hands of peasants to those of money lenders and other rich people. But the actual cultivators do not have security of tenure. This has reduced agricultural production and increased the number of landless peasants.[32]

A number of commissions and acts have tried ever since to improve the system without much success. The most important attempt was through the Land Act of 1964 which set ceilings for individual family holdings, abolished *jamindars*,[33] improved tenant security and sought to replace the village moneylender with government supervised credit schemes financed by compulsory savings. A special Ministry of Land

Reforms was set up with offices at district level to implement the Act. However, the district offices lacked records of who owned or had what rights to what land. They also lacked experienced and fully trained staff.

Some officials claim that implementation of the 1964 Land Act has been successful. By 1973, around three-quarters of the land in excess of the land ceilings was officially no longer in the previous owners' possession, but in effect most of them still controlled this excess land. A sample survey for 1973 of some 3000 households in twelve districts found that 63.1 per cent possessed less than 1 hectare and 10.6 per cent of total area while 2.1 per cent possessed more than 15 hectares and owned around 28 per cent of total area.[34] The study also showed one area in the Terai where about 60 per cent of the area was owned by landowners each with more than 30 hectares. The forced savings and credit scheme was dropped in 1968; the savings end was successful but its distribution as credit to replace village moneylenders was not. The land reform had some positive effects. The trend towards increasing concentration of land into a few hands was halted and tenants' rights were strengthened. But as in so many national land reform programmes, they did not achieve the fundamental changes in agrarian structure that was their aim.

We noted under Nepal's national settlement policy (page 78) the slow evolution of interest in town planning and within this of land-use control. Each Development Committee formed under the guidelines of the 1963 Town Development Committee Act can guide urban development and form a Board to implement its policies. This Board has powers to acquire land (paying its owner compensation). In addition, the Committee's approval is required for the sale, mortgage or subdivision of land or for changes in land use. Central government also has the power to acquire land for public purpose based on the 1961 Land Acquisition Act. But despite these powers, land-use control remains inadequate and generally ineffective.

There has been no effective recapture of unearned increments in land values. There is an annual land tax which makes a major contribution to central government revenues, but most of the yield is from rural lands. Municipalities are empowered to levy a house tax but a report in 1973 found that they did not seem to be making use of this taxing power. There is also a small duty levied on the transfer of property, and an urban property tax. But this same report stated that the revenue from both is not very significant.[35] Nepal's *National Report* to Habitat mentioned a new urban house and land tax, enforced in 1974–5, to try and discourage oversized urban plots which push house prices beyond the reach of low-income households and create urban sprawl.[36] We have no details as to the effectiveness of this new tax.

The Philippines

Landownership patterns suffer from the legacy of a Spanish colonial system to which were added some of the worst features of American capitalism. The Americans legalized the essentially feudal landholding pattern they found, leaving vast landholdings in both rural and urban areas in the hands of comparatively few families and institutions.

> Land based wealth became the chief source of economic power which, in turn, became the source of political power . . . For obvious reasons, political

power has held private property rights so sacrosanct that *jus abutendi* has come to mean in this country the right of the owner to exercise absolute and unlimited power over the thing owned, even to the extent of destroying it by any means, however inconvenient and prejudicial to the public interest or to the rights of others it may be.[37]

However, in recent years, the government has made some attempt to increase public control of land use in urban areas and to promote agrarian reform. A new Constitution in 1973 stated that public land cannot be sold and set ceilings on the amount an individual or corporation could lease. In addition, it allowed for the expropriation of private land. A subsequent land policy announced by the President stated that changes in use on private land were to be subject to government permission and expropriation of private land for public purpose (including housing) was allowed. However, the agrarian reform programme has not brought any pressure to bear on large landowners and landlords and has not benefited the tenant farmer in any major way. Between 1978 and 1982, there are plans to resettle nearly 33 000 families on public land.

In urban areas, the Human Settlements Commission is drafting a national land resource management code and a model zoning ordinance. It is also implementing the presidential decree for public control of land use within 50 kilometres of Manila City. Land-use planning in Manila dates back to 1940 when a zoning ordinance divided Manila into zones with specific land uses for each zone. Any urban development needed the permission of the Chief Engineer's Office. Other cities and municipalities followed Manila's example. Regulations governing the subdivision of land in urban areas and a National Building Code were prepared. However, political forces seem to have been more active than technical ones in determining urban land uses and most of the official standards were too influenced by western precedents and thus had little relevance to the culture and to the job that needed doing.

Within the new emphasis on settlements policy and planning described already, development plans for 175 urban centres were prepared by October 1977 with the Human Settlements Commission and the National Coordination Council for Town Planning, Housing and Zoning helping and coordinating local government land-use planning efforts. In addition, the government is paying more attention to the provision of urban land for low-income housing projects. The 1978–82 Plan talks of assembling land through negotiated purchase and expropriation of idle and underutilized private land and examining the use of public land to see if it is suitable for housing. It also talks of 'checking land speculation through taxation and other regulatory measures' with 'incremental tax on lands whose values increase mainly due to public infrastructure and change in land uses in the surrounding areas' being considered.[38]

In September 1979, President Marcos announced that some 600 square kilometres encompassing about 8 million people (that is the major built-up area of metropolitan Manila) had been declared an urban land reform zone. This meant that no land could be sold or building constructed without permission from the Human Settlements Commission. Large landowners were asked to sell land to people who had occupied it for at least ten years and some $20 million dollars were set aside for land expropriation, this land apparently to be allocated to landless and homeless people.[39] But in the past, the government has shown little ability to control speculation in land.

Urban land prices have soared and well-placed urban land has been left idle. A land-use study of metropolitan Manila in 1973 found that 64 per cent of the land within its boundaries was undeveloped open land.[40] One wonders if these new initiatives will achieve anything substantial, given the strength of powerful private interests in an uncontrolled urban land market. Although no assessment is possible since the initiatives are too recent, the reaction of an opposition leader, former Senator Jovito Salonga, was that the urban land reform in Manila would probably be as ineffective as the agrarian reform has proved to be so far.[41]

Singapore

Built-up areas cover a quarter of the main island while the city centre itself with four-fifths of the population covers 14 per cent. A quarter of the land area is devoted to agriculture; more than half to rubber and coconuts with most of the rest for vegetables, fruit and livestock for local consumption. The government (and public bodies such as the Housing and Development Board and the City Corporation) own approximately half of Singapore's land, including a quarter of the central city area. There are several major land reclamation projects to provide land for urban development. For instance, projects along the East Coast foreshore and at the Kallang Basin have reclaimed some 620 hectares while longer-range plans aim to reclaim more than 1000 hectares from the sea by 1985.

The public authorities have extensive powers for the purchase of needed land and the control of land use. Singapore's masterplan defines the use to which land can be put and all development proposals must receive planning permission (which remains valid for 2 years). The masterplan is reviewed at least once every 5 years. Proposals necessitating a change in the masterplan may be approved although development charges can be levied if, for instance, the change permits development in excess of the density prescribed in the masterplan.

Extensive public land ownership has allowed many major developments—new towns, public housing estates, urban expansion—to take place on public land. It has also allowed the development of parks throughout the island both within the city and in the hilly and coastal areas. But in addition, the public authorities have considerable powers for the compulsory purchase of land for a wide range of purposes including 'by any person, corporation or statutory board, for any work or any undertaking which, in the opinion of the Minister, is of public benefit or of public utility or in the public interest; or for any residential, commercial or industrial purposes' (Section 5 of the Land Acquisition Act).[42] The Housing and Development Board is the public body responsible for acquiring land and developing it (including the construction of public housing). However, private landowners may appeal against the level of compensation offered by the public authorities and so the Housing and Development Board often prefers to negotiate with private landowners rather than become involved in lengthy legal proceedings.

Various other measures complement the government's powers to acquire land and control its use. Property tax is payable on all lands and buildings based on the gross amount for which the property could be let with the rate of property tax varying with location. And the ownership of residential property is restricted to citizens and certain approved persons since a rush by non-citizens to buy residential property in the early 1970s pushed up property prices.

Shelter, Infrastructure and Services

India

As an official reference annual published in 1976 noted, 'there is an acute shortage of housing in urban and rural areas and much of the available accommodation is qualitatively of substandard variety'.[43] It went on to quote a National Building Organization study which suggested that by 1973 the urban housing shortage was of the order of 3.8 million units. We noted in the background section to India the cramped and unsanitary conditions under which most of India's rural and urban households live.

Since independence, the Indian government has steadily increased its involvement in housing. Although there is no long-term policy, successive Five-Year Plans have outlined housing programmes. Public urban housing programmes are essentially the responsibility of state governments although the federal government funds and designs most of the major programmes. These fall into two categories: subsidized and non-subsidized.

The Low-income Group Housing Scheme is the best established non-subsidized scheme, dating back to 1954. Individuals (or private cooperatives) receive loans for housing construction which cover up to 80 per cent of the cost (including land), if private incomes are below a certain ceiling. By the end of April 1975, 243 047 units had been completed under this scheme. There is also a Middle-income Group Housing Scheme, and schemes for dock and mining labourers in the non-subsidized category.

Under subsidized schemes, the Integrated Subsidized Housing Scheme had constructed 182 223 units by the end of April 1975. Originally intended only for lower-paid industrial workers, it was expanded to include economically weaker sections of the community with its standards changed to make them comparable to slum clearance and improvement schemes, the other major subsidized housing activity. With funding from central government, houses are constructed by both private and public bodies and rented out at well below market rates to eligible households.

India's programmes to improve living conditions in slums date from 1956 when the Slum Clearance and Improvement Scheme began. This gave financial assistance to states in acquiring slum areas and rehousing families living there; in improving environmental conditions in existing slums; and in constructing night shelters to accommodate pavement dwellers. This scheme had two guiding principles; there should be minimal dislocation of slum dwellers, and emphasis should be placed on providing essential services and minimum hygiene standards rather than construction of new units. In 1969, responsibility for this scheme passed to state governments with central government providing block grants or loans. Another initiative, the Central Scheme for Environmental Improvement in Slum Areas was launched in 1972. By 1974, it had reached 20 cities with the state governments receiving central government finance to help provide drinking water, sewerage, latrines, street lighting, etc. It was then transferred to state governments' control as part of the Minimum Needs Programme.

State governments can also receive funds from central government for acquiring and developing urban land for allocation to prospective builders. And open developed plots may be part of Integrated Subsidized Housing Schemes in major cities. The Housing and Urban Development Corporation, formed in 1970, is central government's major funder of 'social housing' that is built through the state housing boards, city improvement trusts, municipal corporations and so on.

By the end of April 1975, some 638 500 units had been constructed under the Low-income Housing, Middle-income Housing, Integrated Subsidized Housing and other 'social housing' schemes (excluding slum clearance and improvement) for an urban population that numbered some 120 million. In its first 5 years of operation, the Housing and Urban Development Corporation had sanctioned the construction of 151 409 units and the development of 23 819 residential plots. At this time, the number of urban households was growing at around 600 000 a year. So even with the new Corporation's increasing activity, it was not reaching more than a tiny proportion of those in need of housing. Central government has not provided enough funds for this sector. And there has been a tendency to look at housing problems as ones that can be solved by technology with new low-cost housing techniques. The problem is rooted in the poverty of most urban dwellers who do not have the resources to pay for even the lowest-cost house. Many of the low-cost houses were designed with no consideration for the lifestyle of the people involved. Little attention was given to the techniques by which layout can reduce costs. For instance, one sees large percentages of total area in low-cost housing schemes given to *roads* when those for whom the houses were designed could not afford *cars*. And their location was often on the urban periphery when the low-income households' primary need was cheap and easy access to sources of income. The government did not recognize the potential of the informal sector (including self-help efforts) to provide more realistic solutions for low-income families nor did it utilize the potential of an expanded construction programme to generate much-needed jobs.

The Janata Party proposed to encourage private construction except for luxury houses which were to be restricted. The target for 1978–83 was for over 2 million units by state governments and their agencies, 85 per cent of which were to be for the economically weaker sections. The urban housing objectives of the Sixth Plan (1978–83) include more stress on self-help housing and the strengthening of the Housing and Urban Development Corporation. However, the Janata Party's support for the private sector meant little or no attempt to control land prices and the removal of rent controls. An uncontrolled private land and housing market will not help low-income households. Indeed, it is more likely to drive up land prices and push legal, reasonable-quality housing still further from their grasp.

For urban infrastructure and services, there is no clear policy. Their provision is the state's responsibility and most states lack the funds. While national and regional transportation networks are well developed, in large urban areas and in rural areas they are very inadequate. For drinking water and waste disposal, present policies in most states tend to serve the upper classes, and the poor communities are worst served. There is no city in India with an adequate water supply or satisfactory environmental sanitation. Although funding for such basic infrastructure has increased in the 1970s, there is still a lack of clear policy that fixes priorities and chooses areas where urgent action is most needed. In addition, there is the need to evolve a pricing system which would ensure that the poor do not subsidize the rich and that the rich are taxed for overconsumption.

For urban services such as education and health care, once again their location, design and administration tends to favour middle and upper-income groups. Many of the better schools, colleges and medical facilities are too expensive for the poor. And although primary education and basic medical services are free, they are usually ill-designed to serve the needs and aspirations of the poor who often make little use of them.

Although much neglected in the past, rural housing, services and infrastructure are receiving more government support. From the early 1960s, a village housing and planning scheme provided loans to selected villages in groups to prepare layout plans and build houses. Another scheme helped state governments acquire land and give house sites to agricultural workers. Under the 20 point programme in the early 1970s, special attention was to be given to providing house sites for the underprivileged rural families. Up to 1975, 5.76 million free sites were allotted.

Kerala launched a large rural housing programme in the early 1970s and this has encouraged a number of other states to consider similar schemes. The programme involved mobilizing local *panchayat* committees who, assisted by volunteers and students from engineering colleges, built more than 50 000 houses for the landless. Several criticisms have been levelled at the scheme—on the design, location and allocation of houses and on the fact that the 100 000 target was not met. But the programme does show the type and scale of development action that can be achieved using local skills and materials (and in this case few government funds and no special implementing agency) if the political commitment is there. Indeed, it can be favourably compared to meticulous government planning and implementation in programmes of similar scale.

The Janata Party's manifesto revealed its commitment to rural development. It states that the Party 'will not only check growing disparities between town and country but pledges itself to initiate a comprehensive new village movement and promote rural growth centres'. The importance of political mobilization is stressed with mutual self-help providing skills and labour for improving rural housing. The Basic Minimum Needs Programme—initiated in the Fifth Plan (1972–7) includes education, health, nutrition, drinking water, provision of house sites, rural roads and rural electrification. This programme continued with substantially increased funding and more vigour under the Janata government. Goals and priorities have been set—for instance the provision of pure drinking water supplies to every village within 5 years. The rural health programme is to concentrate on preventive medicine and build up a cadre of medical, paramedical and community health workers to provide health care services to all rural areas.

Although the increased support for the Basic Minimum Needs Programme does aim to improve coordination of both service and infrastructure provision in rural communities, each component of the programme is treated separately, mostly at village level. A more effective development strategy would be the identification of needy households and the attempt to meet all their basic needs within a package with such a programme implemented within an overall settlements policy. Moreover, the Basic Needs Programme must not be considered as simply the provision of technology or improved houses. It must be part of a programme in which the appropriate government agencies work with the local community to ensure the continuous improvement of shelter, infrastructure and service standards. Otherwise, the new programme will have little significance and may indeed have a negative impact in the long run by making people more dependent on the fluctuating support of officialdom and bureaucracy.

Building Industry

Two-thirds of the population build their own houses. The informal sector is responsible for almost all housing in rural areas and small towns and for a large portion of that built in large urban areas. This sector makes use of traditional materials, mud bricks being the most widely used.

The formal building sector tends to follow western methods and models, despite the high price and continual scarcity of the modern building materials such techniques require. Attempts to build low-cost housing for lower-income groups using modern materials and prefabrication have met with little success. Since labour costs are relatively low, building materials can account for as much as 60 to 65 per cent of non-land construction costs.

The Central Building Research Institute pointed to one of the roots of housing shortages in urban areas and poor housing standards in rural areas: 'While the techniques used in urban areas mostly utilize costly and scarce building materials, without any attempt to utilize locally available material resources, the rural houses are constructed with local materials without any attempt to improve their quality or to make them more durable. Thus the former is wasteful and the other is substandard'.[44] Both government and private building contractors have ignored the fact that it is possible to combine advanced architectural and design techniques using indigenous building materials at relatively low cost. There have been a few encouraging experiments. The Janata housing scheme in Karnataka and the one *lakh* (100 000) housing scheme in Kerala used local techniques and materials. Mini cement plants have been developed at a cost and capacity to suit the needs of a small group of villages. Various groups are looking into the use of agricultural wastes in improved building materials. But inadequate attention has been given to developing and improving indigenous building material industries which better serve the needs and resources of low-income rural and urban dwellers. Government efforts have even inhibited the development of such industries. A national building code was prepared by the Indian Standards Institution several years ago with the aim of introducing standardization and mass production in the building industry. The code essentially promoted western-type buildings and inhibited the use of traditional materials and techniques.

Indonesia

Despite a predominantly rural population, the nation's major cities are hard-pressed to meet growing housing and service needs. Jakarta's population was little more than half a million in 1940; by 1971 it was more than 4.5 million, and projections made in the mid-1970s suggested it would have exceeded 7 million by 1980. A large percentage of Jakarta's households live in what are classified as temporary or semi-permanent houses. In an article in 1980, an official from the National Urban Development Corporation stated that 55 per cent of urban houses only have one room and that 48 per cent contained two or three families.[45] In 1972, BAPPENAS estimated that 300 000 units a year were needed in urban areas alone. Another estimate suggested that 1.2 million new units were needed in Jakarta between 1972 and 1983.[46] And yet until the mid-1970s, housing construction was almost entirely restricted to the private sector. The formal building industry built comparatively few apartments for middle-income groups. And most new households found shelter either in overcrowded existing structures or in squatter settlements. Surabaja and Bandung both had populations exceeding a million in 1970 and continue to grow rapidly. Such rapid growth has meant ever-increasing overcrowding, reliance on the informal sector for most housing construction and public authorities unable to keep up with increasing needs for basic services and infrastructure. By the late 1970s, only 10 per cent of the national population had access to safe water,[47] while only a small proportion of urban households were connected to sewage systems.

However, the last ten years has seen some concerted public action to improve living conditions in the major cities. Jakarta's municipal government has run a Kampung Improvement Programme since 1969 to improve community facilities and to provide basic infrastructure and services such as roads and footpaths, improved water supplies and washing facilities, toilets and garbage disposal to the poorest quarters. In addition, community health centres and schools have been built as part of the Presidential Instruction Programme (INPRES). The aim of such improvement programmes—since extended to other major cities—is to work with the local community in achieving considerable improvements but at a per capita cost that makes the scheme replicable and ensures that it can reach a large proportion of the low-income urban dwellers who live in *kampungs*. By the end of 1979, some 3.5 million people in Jakarta had benefited and during the 1979–84 Plan, minimum basic services should reach all low income residential areas. Costs per capita are around $40 to $65. There is little attempt at cost recovery but costs per capita are comparable to service provision in higher income neighbourhoods.

Around the beginning of the 1974–9 Plan, three new institutions were set up to increase central government's involvement in housing. A National Housing Policy Board was to formulate national policies while a National Urban Development Corporation (PERUMNAS) was to be in charge of implementing low cost and serviced-site housing programmes. And a Housing Mortgage Bank was set up to provide low-income households with long-term credit.

While Kampung Improvement Programmes are the responsibility of municipal governments, the new serviced site and low-cost housing programmes were to be the joint responsibility of local and central government with PERUMNAS as the main implementing agency. With serviced site projects, the aim is to provide lots in planned communities with all the basic services and infrastructure at a price low-income groups can afford. The programme began in Jakarta with the World Bank's support and there were plans to extend it to other large cities during the 1974–9 Plan. Similarly, the low-cost housing programme began with several pilot projects and is expanding during this Plan to cities such as Surabaja, Bandung, Semarang, Medan, Pandang and Jogjakarta. For the 1974–9 period, 90 000 low-cost housing units were planned, 54 000 built by the private sector, 16 000 built by non-profit organizations and 20 000 built by PERUMNAS. More than 200 000 serviced sites were planned for the same period with PERUMNAS undertaking 53 000 and non-profit organizations undertaking the rest. However, there have been problems in getting such programmes off the ground and the emphasis seems to be swinging away from serviced sites to public house construction with the new houses being too expensive for low-income groups. In addition, it seems that the civil service and military personnel will have priority allocation of such housing. Initial reports suggest PERUMNAS will not meet its target. By January 1978, an official from PERUMNAS stated that 'over 17 600 units' had been completed while the target for the 1974–9 Plan was for 73 000.[48] But even if PERUMNAS, the non-profit organizations and the private sector meet their target of 300 000 serviced-site and low cost housing units during this plan, this represents less than a fifth of the growth in urban housing needs in this same period.

During the 1979–84 Plan, the target is for 150 000 low-cost houses to be built by PERUMNAS and through the Housing Mortgage Bank.[49] This represents 30 000 units a year when the urban population is growing by around a million people a year.

In rural areas, the government's housing programme has concentrated on the provision of extension services and demonstration projects to stimulate and assist local communities in improving their housing, water supply and sanitation. About 1000 demonstration projects were planned for the 1974–9 Plan while the 1979–84 Plan aims to expand this programme to cover 6000 villages. Kendel, a remote village in Central Java, is held up as a model for what can be achieved through such efforts. The village was almost completely rebuilt using locally made trass-lime blocks with government and householders sharing the cost. In addition, the government paid for the construction of public baths, toilets, water supply and environmental improvements. The Building Information Centre from Jogjakarta provided technical advice and taught the villagers the basic principles of healthy housing. The provincial government in Central Java has since extended similar village modernization programmes to other villages.

The government is also seeking to improve education, health care and water supply in both rural and urban areas. During the 1979–84 Plan, it aims to increase the number of people with access to safe water from 10 to 30 per cent of the national population. 150 small cities are to be provided with a safe water supply. A major latrine construction programme is planned. In rural areas, basic health care services are to be spread more widely. Each subdistrict is meant to have a community health centre which in turn is to be supported by clinics and mother and child welfare centres. Cases beyond the competence of these centres can be referred to district or provincial level hospitals.

The Presidential Instruction Programme (INPRES) complements both the rural health and the village modernization programmes. Through this, every village (and urban settlement) gets a sum of money to undertake a project chosen by the local community (although the approval of the Provincial Governor is also needed). Initially, the money was usually spent on improving local roads, bridges and other infrastructure but more recently, the stress has been more on improved water supply and on the provision of latrines, community health centres and schools. Unfortu-

94

nately, no data is available on the results of this programme which seems particularly interesting in its funding of local projects chosen by the locality itself.

Building Industry

Most housing is built with traditional materials using traditional technology. In rural areas, villagers generally have little trouble building a house from local materials since the nation has abundant sources of construction materials—timber, limestone, natural pozzolana and clay for bricks. Although rural housing does not usually conform to minimum standards set by the Directorate of Buildings Research, everyone has a shelter.

In urban areas, most housing is self-built or constructed by small firms, jobbing builders and labour gangs using traditional materials and techniques. However, the supply of building materials is usually well below demand with the result that the price rises. The distribution and marketing of building materials is inefficient and also adds to its inflated price. And little effort has been made to develop more durable building materials based on indigenous resources. As an IDRC Report noted,

> as the bulk of building materials used in low-cost housing consists of traditional materials, ways and means should be found to solve the problem of improving its condition. Indonesia is not lacking in any of the major raw materials for the manufacture of building materials. As a matter of fact, large quantities of such raw materials are exported for processing and consumption in other parts of the world. Most tragically, the processed goods are being imported again into Indonesia.[50]

The Indonesian government is attempting to address the mounting housing deficits. Building information centres have been established at various places throughout Jakarta and in seven other provincial capitals. The National Urban Development Corporation is apparently going to build public housing units using its own prefabricated building factor. The government might do better to see how it can support the work of the traditional building sector and help it improve its productivity and the standard of unit it builds.

Nepal

We have noted already the concentration of the early plans on road construction and the development of other infrastructure. But in the 1970s, a shift of emphasis is evident. Physical planning, housing, health, sanitation, education and water supply all received special attention in the Fifth Plan (1975–80).

In urban areas, no major housing shortages were reported in the early 1970s, due, no doubt, to relatively slow urban growth. However, much of the housing is old and in need of repair. And the 1971 census showed that most urban houses did not have piped water and were not connected to a sewer—although households in Kathmandu itself were relatively well served. Government support for housing began with a modest programme of housing loans for government employees. During the Fifth Plan, the government asked UNDP's help in drafting the statute for a Housing

Corporation, a semi-public agency which will be responsible for land acquisition, serviced site development, sale of land and housing construction.[51] Prior to this, the only evidence of official housing programmes had been initiated by Town Development Boards in, for instance, the Kathmandu Valley, Pokhara, Dhankuta and Surket. These include two serviced site schemes in Kathmandu, self-help schemes for special communities in urban and surrounding rural areas in the Surket Valley and assistance to private development schemes such as those where the owners pool their land, install roads and other public amenities with local government help and reallocate private plots back to the original owners.

The provision of drinking water to both rural and urban communities has received higher priority in the 1970s. Three different bodies deal with water supply at different levels of community size. The Water Supply and Sewerage Board was formed in 1973 to implement IDA-financed projects in communities in the Kathmandu Valley and in Pokhara. The first stage built water supply systems in Kathmandu, Lalitpur and Bhaktapur (in the Kathmandu Valley) and in Pokhara while the second stage, starting in 1977, included the extension of sewage networks in Kathmandu and Lalitpur and a water supply system for Biratnagar. This Board will eventually become a statewide corporation. Then the Water Supply and Sewerage Department has responsibility for the design and construction of water systems in all other urban, regional and district headquarters as well as in rural communities exceeding 3000 people. A high percentage of the urban population is served by standpipes but less than 2 per cent of the population of settlements with under 10 000 inhabitants were served in 1971. The Department is also responsible for the design and construction of sewage systems— but no work had been done on this by 1978.

The Local Development Department is responsible for helping communities of less than 3000 people provide for their water supply and sanitation needs. Drinking water facilities have been provided in about 70 communities so far, mainly in the hill areas where water scarcities are more severe. But a recent survey found the quality of the water they supplied to be poor and maintenance of the taps and standpipes inadequate.

The 1970s has also seen increasing emphasis placed on health and education. A New Education Plan began in 1971 to spread primary education far more widely and to increase the supply of skilled personnel in all the major sectors needing development. There is also a long-term goal to ensure every community has a Junior Auxiliary Health Worker to provide primary health care. These are to be supported by health posts covering a larger area; 810 such posts were planned for the Fifth Plan. Then district headquarters were to have a hospital and rural health office (in 1975, more than half did) with regional centres having a general hospital. Thus, despite lack of trained personnel, high infant mortality rates, and low life expectancy, in the last decade, the Nepali government has given a quite new emphasis to meeting its population's basic needs. And initial reports suggest that the sixth Five-Year Plan, launched in 1979, carries this emphasis still further.

Building Industry

Nepal's formal housing construction sector remains underdeveloped with a lack of skilled personnel, of financial support and of demand for its products inhibiting its development. Most of the formal building industry is concentrated in the Kathmandu Valley. But many development projects use skilled labour and building firms from India. The formal sector also suffers from a lack of unskilled labour, especially for small-scale housing programmes as the building season and the harvesting season coincide. Farm labour usually provides unskilled building labour in the slack season.

Virtually all houses in Nepal are built in the informal sector using traditional materials such as mud-brick. Houses are usually self-built, often with help from other villagers. B. S. Bhooshan noted that this informal production process was often 'more purposeful than government initiated and completely programmed schemes'.[52] Although local development departments provide some help to informal sector construction, this institutional support could certainly be expanded very considerably. However, central government does recognize that a better supply of building materials based on local resources could aid this process. It noted that 'in order to build houses . . . in modern line, about 70 to 80 per cent of the total housing expenditure will have to be spent on construction materials alone',[53] most of them, no doubt, imported. A Construction Material Research Unit was going to be set up during the Fifth Plan.

The Philippines

In 1975, an article in the National Economic and Development Authority's *Journal* summed up past public action when it stated that government housing projects had 'not been very effective instruments of the national policy . . . to solve the country's housing problem'. Other critics were somewhat more severe of, for instance, slum clearance programmes with bulldozing and forced resettlement. In an earlier section, we noted housing shortages and the lack of basic infrastructure and services. A recent estimate suggests that 4 million urban dwellers are living in slums and squatter settlements with very limited access to water, often no sanitary facilities at all and very often considerable danger from floods during the rainy season.[54]

In 1977, the housing backlog in urban areas was put at 981 000 units, 227 000 households without houses, 656 000 with houses in marginal areas and 98 000 with houses in unsafe areas.[55]

In 1973, a national housing conference stressed the need for a new approach to housing with programmes integrated into wider development plans at national, regional and local levels. And the conference recognized that the root of the housing problems was poverty with its elimination representing the only satisfactory solution. In addition, it pointed to a primary reason for the failure of national housing and resettlement efforts being 'the existence of too many agencies with overlapping functions and plans implementing the programmes'.[56]

In 1975, all existing housing agencies were integrated into a single National Housing Authority. This was given the task of developing an integrated housing programme guided by the Human Settlements Commission which was planning and implementing the nationwide settlements plan. This new Authority would plan and implement programmes for metropolitan Manila and give support and guidance to local governments elsewhere who designed and implemented their own housing projects.

In a pre-Vancouver conference on human settlements, a series of recommendations were made that were then incorporated into the Five-Year Development Plan

(1978–82). These included increased government finance for a housing programme, the development of more realistic housing standards, an integrated approach to housing and encouragement for the use of indigenous building materials. Further-more, the conference suggested that the government assume responsibility for low-income housing while government and the private sector could work together in providing housing for lower-middle income groups. The private sector could cater for higher-income groups. The National Economic and Development Authority's long-term and Five-Year Plan envisaged a level of housing investment of at least 5 per cent of GNP up to 2000 with each housing development having basic infrastructure, health, education and community facilities, and access to income-generating activities.

The objective of the national housing plan outlined in the 1978–82 Plan is to 'establish, maintain and ensure adequate housing for families belonging to the low and middle-income levels' during a ten-year planning period while in the first five years 'prevent the housing backlog from increasing in urban areas' and 'discourage the growth of marginal settlements'.[57] The National Housing Authority was to be in charge of a programme to build over 200 000 units between 1978 and 1987 (72 137 in the first five years) mostly for low-income households. In addition, government finance would support the construction of over 100 000 additional units in the decade, 76 373 within the first five years. Slum and squatter upgrading programmes were to reach nearly half a million households in the decade, 144 245 in the first five years. And serviced-site programmes were to produce 88 392 units in the decade, 37 403 in the first five years. Along with various other housing programmes, including a major programme for military housing, the intention is to reach 547 000 households in the first five years and 1.1 million in the decade.

Since 1975, attempts to upgrade slums and implement serviced site schemes have widened in scope and apparently in success. Some early serviced site schemes in the 1960s in Manila met with little success but provided valuable lessons for the authorities. In 1974, the Tondo Foreshore Development Authority was set up to provide an integrated programme for slum upgrading with serviced sites for those displaced by the upgrading in what was one of Manila's poorest areas. In 1977, a Presidential Letter of Instruction created a nationwide Slum Improvement and Resettlement Programme which required local governments to define 'slums' in their areas and set up slum improvement and resettlement programmes. This was to include public acquisition of land, its development and then its leasing to local residents (with options for purchase). The experience in Manila programmes has shown the importance of minimum dislocation for slum families with the need to relocate families that are moved as close as possible to their original site.

These major new initiatives to improve urban housing conditions represent a considerable change both in government support and in the type of support that is being given. But it is too early to assess whether these new initiatives will achieve their stated goals of enormously increasing housing production and reaching lower-income families with their programmes. Before the National Housing Authority was formed, the People's Homesite and Housing Corporation was meant to build public housing units for those who could not afford decent houses on the open market. In 1972, the price of their houses plus the lot were far beyond the paying capacity of 84 per cent of Filipino families.[58] The National Housing Corporation, set up in 1968 to implement the government's mass-housing programme, and now under the direction of the

National Housing Authority, is to play a major role in constructing public housing units. Preliminary estimates suggest these will be too expensive for most urban families. And the targets seem overambitious when one considers that government housing construction for the low-income population totalled only 13 500 units for the 22 years up to 1972.[59]

The 1978–82 Plan also seeks to improve rural housing conditions, infrastructure and service provision. For rural housing, some 41 000 units are planned for families in rural farm resettlement programmes while demonstration projects to improve sanitation and promote housing improvement through self-help aim to reach 48 713 households.[60] Both the Five-Year Plan and the longer-term plans give priority to the provision of safe drinking water, sewerage, flood control and transportation. Long-term targets include safe drinking water for more than 90 per cent of the population and far more extensive sewerage and flood control systems by 2000. Long-term transportation plans aim to improve interregional links, rural roads, public transport in the three metropolitan centres and improve ports and airports for international links. For basic services, education programmes are to be strengthened and an expanded health programme will give more emphasis to preventive measures. Policy guidelines stress the need to reach the poorest, to mobilize human resources at local levels, to increase productivity, and to minimize dole-outs and palliatives.

Building Industry

In rural areas and small towns, virtually all houses are built using local resources and utilizing traditional techniques. Most areas have plentiful traditional building materials for this purpose. The large, organized building enterprises are heavily concentrated in the major cities and here the trend has been towards utilizing imported technology, cement and steel. The government has supported the spread of prefabricated techniques in the hope that these will speed up housing construction and lower unit costs. The National Housing Corporation, set up in 1968 to support a massive expansion of government housing construction, has built a factory in Tala, Caloocan City which can produce at least 12 000 prefabricated housing units a year.[61]

However, the shortage of modern building materials and the heavy import costs they entail do mean that researchers are now considering other approaches.

Singapore

Housing and service standards have improved very considerably in the 22 years since Singapore achieved internal self-government. In 1960, there was acute overcrowding. Estimates suggest that a quarter of a million people lived in central city slums while another third of a million lived in squatter communities.[62] Many of the squatter settlements were on land subject to frequent floods. The Housing and Development Board (HDB) was set up to replace the Singapore Improvement Trust and constructed some 230 000 housing units between 1960 and 1975 compared to its predecessor's total of some 21 000 between 1947 and 1960. Another 127 300 are expected to be completed by the end of 1980 and a further 85 000–100 000 are planned for 1981–5. By the end of 1980, more than two-thirds of Singapore's population was housed in HDB-built units and this proportion will rise to three-quarters by 1985.[63]

Since the early 1960s, the number of dwelling units completed by the formal construction sector has exceeded six (and in some years ten). This is probably faster than in any other Third World nation.

Most public housing units are standardized one, two and three-room flats in high-rise blocks with eight to ten storeys. At first, the HDB concentrated on basic one-room units within 8 kilometres of the city centre to rent to low-income families. As the most immediate housing deficit was reduced, standards were raised, higher-income families were allowed to apply for public housing and a home ownership scheme encouraged tenants to purchase their flats. In the 1970s, standards were raised again with many of the residential units built in new towns around the city centre. Four and five-room flats were introduced to provide for large and middle-income families. Home ownership of HDB flats became more popular and by the end of 1980, more than half the households living in HDB flats owned them. New housing estates have been planned on the neighbourhood principle—and such neighbourhoods in the new towns are well provided for in basic services, infrastructure and social amenities. A new company, the Housing and Urban Development Company,[64] was set up to build middle-income housing.

The HDB also played an important role in urban redevelopment. Singapore was one of the first Asian cities to launch a citywide slum clearance and comprehensive renewal programme—demolishing old and dilapidated structures in the central area and reallocating land uses guided by the masterplan. Some cleared sites were sold to private developers for new offices, hotels, flats or other developments while others were developed as markets, parks and recreational areas. In certain areas, especially the more congested central city areas, landlords may submit redevelopment plans for their property and if the plan is accepted, they may clear existing tenants from the buildings and give compensation based on government guidelines. In 1973, the division of the HDB responsible for urban renewal was set up as a separate statutory board and named the Urban Redevelopment Authority.

Services and infrastructure provision have also improved considerably since 1959. Nearly three-quarters of the population are served by waterborne sanitation while even rural areas are served by appropriate sanitation facilities. Primary education is free and universal. The effectiveness of health services is best shown by the life expectancy and infant mortality rates which compare favourably with First World nations.

The HDB's building programme is wholly financed by government loans. The annual rate of interest for the construction of rental units is $7\frac{3}{4}$ per cent for 60 years; for units to be sold it is 6 per cent for ten years. Flats are sold well below actual cost, with government funds meeting the HDB's annual deficit. For 1976–7, the housing subsidy was an estimated $59 million.[65] A considerable portion of Singapore's development funds come from its Central Provident Fund, a compulsory savings scheme. All employers and employees earning more than a stated minimum contribute, their contribution varying with their wage level. All employees earn interest on their account with their money becoming available for withdrawal when they are 55 or if they wish to purchase a flat in a public housing unit.[66]

Despite the public authorities' achievements over the last two decades, the powers they have been granted to effect such a radical change in Singapore's living environment have meant little real community participation. One commentator stated that 'slum clearance and urban redevelopment have adversely affected thousands of poor families and hundreds of marginally economic family businesses and backyard industries. Perhaps urban disturbances or riots have not occurred in Singapore only because the present economic prosperity has enough crumbs even for the urban poor.'[67] Many of the thousands of households affected by slum clearance and redevelopment schemes could not afford to stay in public housing despite concessional rates on what was already a subsidized rent. In addition, many of the earliest flats built by the HDB have sunk into almost slum-like conditions. A major initiative is now underway to upgrade or demolish one-room flats built in the early 1960s. Nearly 11 000 units will be demolished between 1981 and 1985.[68]

Building Industry

Most housing construction is undertaken by the private sector. But a large proportion of this is done under contract to the HDB whose units account for more than four-fifths of all new houses built. The Board is by far the largest developer in Singapore; according to a Report in 1975, its construction programme represents approximately a third to a half of total investment in construction.[69] The HDB's 1978–9 *Annual Report* mentioned that the feasibility of developing a prefabricated housing system for Singapore was being considered.

Although private contractors bid for the HDB's contracts, the Board helps to guarantee a steady supply of building materials through stockpiles and through setting up its own building materials industries. HBD plants supply granite aggregates, sand, bricks and wall tiles. In addition, the HDB places bulk orders for building materials well in advance of need and has been active in encouraging the use of new building technologies to increase labour productivity in the building industry.

Notes

The information in this section is based on the assessments of our colleagues at the Institute of Development Studies, University of Mysore which have been published in five volumes. Misra, R. P. General Editor (1979). *Habitat Asia: Issues and Responses* (New Delhi: Concept). Volume I, *India*: Misra, R. P. and Bhooshan, B. S.; Volume II, *Indonesia and the Philippines*: Suri, Donna, Misra, R. P., Achyutha, R. N. and Bhooshan, B. S.; Volume III, *Japan and Singapore*: Varma, Rameswari and Sastry N. N.
Bhooshan, B. S. (1979). *The Development Experience of Nepal* (New Delhi: Concept).
Misra, R. P. and Bhooshan, B. S. (1980). *Human Settlements in Asia; Public Policies and Programmes* (India: Heritage). For statistics for which no source is quoted, the reader should refer to these volumes and to the list of general sources in the Introduction.
1. Food-grain production has grown, on average, slightly faster than population ever since India achieved independence, although there have been notable setbacks in years with poor monsoon rains, for instance 1965–7 and 1972–3—Mellor, J. W. (1976). 'The Agriculture of India', *Sci. Amer.*, September 1976. In 1979 provisional figures suggested that India had a record food-grain harvest of 130 million tonnes.
2. The 1971 census data quoted in Bhooshan, B. S. and Misra, R. P. (1979). *Habitat Asia, Issues and Responses, Volume I, India*, Tables 2.2 and 2.3.
3. There are some exceptions to this rule. In 1971, there were 287 settlements classified as towns with less than 5000 inhabitants. But they accounted for less than 1 per cent of the urban population.

4. *Manorama Year Book* (1978). The Punjab had the highest per capita income while Haryana and parts of Andhra Pradesh had per capita incomes comparable to the more industrialized states because of prosperous agricultural and agroindustrial bases.
5. Tata Services Ltd (1978). *Statistical Outline of India 1978* quoted in Table 1.11 of Bhooshan, B. S. and Misra, R. P. (1979). *Habitat Asia, Issues and Responses, Volume 1, India*.
6. National Building Organization (1975) quoted in Bhooshan, B. S. and Misra, R. P. (1979). *Habitat Asia, Issues and Responses, Volume 1, India*, page 58.
7. Town and Country Planning Organization (1975). *Towards a Human Settlement Policy in India—2001*, Ministry of Works and Housing, pages 9 and 10.
8. Jakarta (1977) estimate from *Encyclopaedia Britannica Book of the Year 1978*. Bandung and Surabaja (1971) from *The Economist*, 'The World in Figures' (1976). Projections to 1990 from *Statistical Annex—Global Review of Human Settlements*, United Nations, Table 6.
9. Arndt, H. W. (1975). 'Development and Equality: The Indonesian Case', *World Development*, **3**, nos. 2 and 3 (February–March), page 79.
10. Small stretches and pockets of plain between the Siwalik Hills (also known as the Churia Range) to the north of the Terai and south of the Mahabharat Range (that marks the beginning of the Hills Region) are known as the Inner Terai.
11. The Hills and Mountains regions in this statistic include all of Nepal except for the Terai, the Inner Terai and the Kathmandu Valley.
12. Kathmandu (1976), Lalitpur (1976) and Bhaktapur (1976) from The Economist (1978) *The World in Figures*.
13. Zaman, Z. A. (1973). 'Evaluation of land reforms in Nepal', HMG, Kathmandu, quoted in Table 7.1 of Bhooshan, B. S. (1979), *The Development Experience of Nepal*.
14. Apacible, M. S. and Yaxley, M. (1979). *Manila through the Eyes of the Manilenos and the Consultant*, PTRC Summer Annual Meeting, 1979.
15. It seems the definitions as to what constitutes 'Metropolitan Manila' have changed recently. 'Manila Bay Region in the Philippines, Interim Report number 4' in Table 9, page 20 of *Housing in the Philippines*, NEDA Journal of Development Volumes I and II refers to the Manila Bay Region with an area of 18 000 square kilometres and a population of 8.56 million in 1970. The Task Force on Human Settlements' publication *The Vision of a New Society* (March 1975) talks of the 'Manila Bay Metropolitan Region' with a population of 9.6 million in 1970 and covering 29 997 square kilometres and the 'Manila Bay Metropolitan Area' within this region with a population of 5 million in 1970 covering 2238 square kilometres. Apacible, M. S. and Yaxley, M. (1979) state that, according to predictions, metropolitan Manila's population will increase from 6.6 million in 1977 to 7.7 million in 1980 to 10.5 million in 1990 in *Manila through the Eyes of the Manilenos and the Consultant*, PTRC Summer Annual Meeting, 1979. These figures are presumably for the 'Manila Bay Metropolitan Area'. A PADCO Report in 1978 (*Philippines Shelter Sector Assessment Volume 1*) noted on page 139 that there are at least eight definitions for 'metropolitan Manila' in use.
16. Projections based on Table 8, Ramos M. J. (1974–5). 'The Philippines: The Country and its People' in *NEDA Journal of Development*, **I and II,** page 19.
17. The 1963 figure is from Dwyer, D. J. (1975). *People and Housing in Third World Cities* (London: Longman), page 79. The 1975 figure is from Abesamis, F. D. (1974–5) 'Squatter-Slum Clearance and Resettlement Programmes in the Philippines', *NEDA Journal of Development*, **I and II,** page 301, and states that in 1975 there were 200 000 squatter families in metropolitan Manila. Assuming a family size of six (the assumption made by Abesamis on page 303), this means a squatter population of 1.2 million.
18. United Nations (1979). *Demographic Yearbook 1978*. Statistics are estimates for city populations, not for urban agglomerations.
19. Calculations based on 'Percentage Distribution of Families and Total Family Income by Income Class, Urban and Rural, 1961 and 1971', in Misra, R. P. and Bhooshan, B. S. (1979), *Human Settlements in Asia*, using data from *NEDA Statistical Year Book 1975*.
20. *The Economist* (**13 October, 1979**), page 58.
21. Ramos, J. M. (1974–5). 'Rural housing in the Philippines', *NEDA Journal of Development*, **I and II.** Tables 5 and 6, pages 418 and 419.
22. *Christian Science Monitor* (21 May, 1978), printed in The Hindu.

23. Fisher, B. H., 'Growth centre planning in transition: requiem for formalism, resurrection of informed commonsense', unpublished paper quoted in Misra, R. P. and Bhooshan, B. S. *Human Settlements in Asia*, page 89.

24. 'Regional' here refers to provincial and subprovincial level planning, not regional at the level of the vast Economic Development Regions.

25. The *kabupatens* of Bogor, Tangerang and Besaki, a *kabupaten* being a predominantly rural subprovincial spatial unit.

26. Michael, Richard (1978). 'A comparative analysis of plans and problems—Bangkok, Jakarta and Singapore', *Ekistics* **January.**

27. In the Far Western Region, Dhengari–Jogbura–Dandeldhura and Nepalganj–Surket–Dailekh–Jumla; for the Western Region, Palpa–Syangja–Pokhara–Jomson; for the Central Region, Birganj–Hitauta–Kathmandu–Dhunche–Barbise; and for the Eastern Region, Biratnagar–Dharan–Dhankuta–Hedangma.

28. Task Force on Human Settlements (1975). *Human Settlements; the Vision of a New Society*, G1/HC/PHI/501.

29. Sastry, N. N., and Varma, R. (1979). *Habitat Asia: Issues and Responses, Volume III, Singapore and Japan*, page 143.

30. *All India Report on Agricultural Census* (1975), quoted in Bhooshan, B. S., and Misra, R. P. (1979) *Habitat Asia: Issues and Responses Volume I, India*, Table 6.5, page 185.

31. Urban Land (Ceiling and Regulation) Act (1976). 'Statement of Objectives'.

32. *Nepal Gazette* (1952), **1,** no. 22.

33. *Jamindars* are intermediaries who were given the right to collect revenues from tenants on what was *raikar* or crown land. The crown reasserted its own right to collect land revenues direct.

34. Zaman, Z. A. (1973). *Evaluation of Land Reforms in Nepal* (Kathmandu: His Majesty's Government).

35. United Nations (1973). *Urban Land Policies and Land Use Control Measures Volume II: Asia and the Far East*, ST/ECA/167/Add.1.

36. His Majesty's Government (1975). *Nepal: National Report to Habitat*, page 26.

37. Casanova, R. A. (1974–5). 'Evolving a Philippine Land Policy for Low-Cost Housing', *NEDA Journal of Development*, **Volumes I and II,** page 361.

38. Philippines, Republic of (1978). *Five Year Philippine Development Plan*, NEDA, pages 219–20.

39. *International Herald Tribune* (12 September 1979).

40. PADCO (1978). *Philippines Shelter Sector Assessment, Volume I: Country Report*, page 85.

41. *International Herald Tribune* (12 September 1979).

42. United Nations (1973). *Urban Land Policies and Land Use Control Measures, Volume II; Asia and the Far East*, ST/ECA/167/Add 1, page 79.

43. India, Government of (1976). *India—a Reference Annual*, Ministry of Information and Broadcasting, page 347.

44. Quoted in Agarwal, Anil (1980), *Mud, Mud; the Use of Indigenous Building Materials in the Third World*, Earthscan Briefing Document.

45. Moochtar, Radinal (1980). 'Urban Housing in Indonesia', *Habitat International*, **4,** no. 3, page 325.

46. Yeh, Stephen, H. K., and Laquian, A. A. (1979). *Housing Asia's Millions* (Canada: International Development Research Centre), page 48.

47. Indonesia, Republic of (1979). *The Third Five Year Development Plan 1979–84 (Summary)*, Department of Information.

48. Moochtar, Radinal (1980). 'Urban Housing in Indonesia', *Habitat International*, **4,** no. 3, page 331.

49. Indonesia, Republic of (1979). *The Third Five Year Development Plan 1979–84 (Summary)*, page 48.

50. Abbas, Z. A. from *Housing and the Construction Industry*, quoted in Suri, Donna, Misra, R. P., Achyutha, R. N. and Bhooshan, B. S. *Habitat Asia; Issues and Responses Volume II*, page 79.

51. United Nations Development Programme (1975). *Country Programme for Nepal*, DP/GC/NEP/R.2.

52. Bhooshan, B. S. (1979). *The Development Experience of Nepal*, page 104.
53. Nepal, His Majesty's Government (1974). *Policy Guidelines for the Fifth Plan 1975–80*, National Planning Commission, page 110.
54. Turner, Alan (1979). 'Low income housing in the Philippines; the regional cities programme', paper presented at the PTRC Summer Annual Meeting, Warwick University (July 1979).
55. Philippines, Republic of (1977). *Five Year Philippine Development Plan*, NEDA, page 217.
56. **Accent** (1976), **IV,** no. 2.
57. Philippines, Republic of (1977). *Five Year Philippine Development Plan*, NEDA, pages 217-218.
58. Casanova, Ramon, N. (1974–5). 'Evolving a Philippine Land Policy for Low Cost Housing', *NEDA Journal of Development*, **I and II,** page 359.
59. PADCO (1978). *Philippines Shelter Sector Assessment, Volume I: Country Report*, page 75.
60. Philippines, Republic of (1977). *Five Year Philippine Development Plan*, NEDA, pages 225–6.
61 Tobias, Gaudencio, V. (1974–5). 'Prefabrication of Housing Components in the National Housing Corporation', *NEDA Journal of Development*, **I and II,** page 188.
62. Yeh, Stephen, H. K. (ed) (1975). *Public Housing in Singapore; a Multi-Disciplinary Study* (Singapore: University Press), page 5.
63. Housing and Development Board (1978–9). *Annual Report*.
64. This is jointly owned by the Housing and Development Board and the Urban Redevelopment Authority.
65. Varma, R. and Sastry, N. N. (1979). *Habitat Asia: Issues and Responses, Volume III; Japan and Singapore*, page 158.
66. According to the Singapore Survey by *The Economist* (December 1979), in late 1979 employers' contribution was 20.5 per cent of the wage bill while that of employees was 16.5 per cent. Interest rates on employers' and employees' accounts was 6.5 per cent a year.
67. Lim, William (1975). *Equity and Urban Environment in the Third World* (Singapore: DP Consultant Service), page 51.
68. Housing and Development Board (1978–9). *Annual Report*, page 24.
69. Yeh, Stephen, H. K. (ed) (1975). *Public Housing in Singapore; a Multi-Disciplinary Study*.

SECTION III: LATIN AMERICA

Bolivia, Brazil, Colombia and Mexico

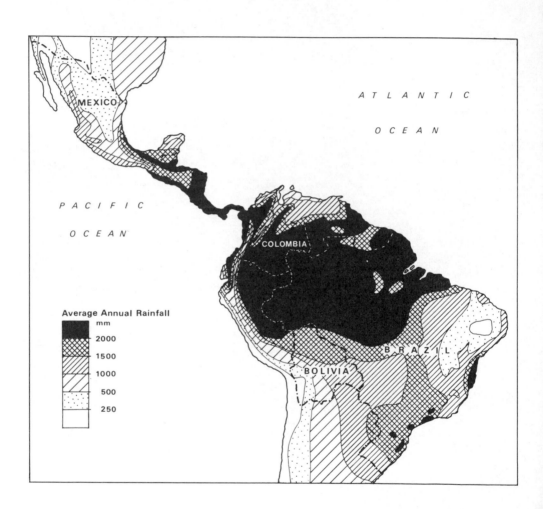

Average Annual Rainfall
mm

2000
1500
1000
500
250

Background

This landlocked republic in central South America is sparsely populated. In 1976 it had 4.7 million inhabitants[1] on a land area covering more than a million square kilometres. Projections suggest that the population will be around 9 million by 2000.

Three distinct geographical regions run from north to south. The Altiplano (high plateau) lies between two great parallel ranges of the Andes—the Cordillera Real and Cordillera Central to its east and the Cordillera Occidental to its west. With an average altitude of some 4000 metres, this contains more than half the national population on little more than a quarter of the national territory, despite being cool, relatively dry and windswept with generally poor soil. To the east, the low-lying Plains account for three-fifths of the national territory but contained only 14 per cent of the population in 1973. This vast region encompasses rainforests to the north, a humid subtropical central zone, and to the south the semi-arid Chaco. In between these two regions run the High Valleys, a complex region of deep valleys between high mountains. This region contains some 30 per cent of the national population on 13.2 per cent of the land.[2]

Bolivia was once part of the ancient Inca empire and later formed part of the Spanish viceroyalty of Peru. Silver mined on the Altiplano, especially at the great silver mine of Potosi, was a major source of Spain's colonial revenue. By the middle of the seventeenth century, Potosi was the largest city in the Americas while the town of Oruro was also a major colonial silver-mining centre. With independence in 1825, exports and economic activity remained centred around silver and later tin mining on the Altiplano. Economic and political power remained with the landowners and those who controlled the mines, banks and large urban businesses. Crises in commodity markets after 1927 and import difficulties after the Second World War forced the country to begin some industrial development. But such development for the domestic market was limited since most mine-workers and peasants were too poor even to enter it.

In 1952, after a long period of political instability, a revolution brought the Movimiento Nacional Revolucionario (a populist, urban middle-class party) to power under Victor Paz Estensoro who was elected President for a five-year term. The government nationalized the mines and in 1953 introduced a major land reform. Expropriated land was distributed to peasant families. Although this benefited the poor peasantry, it failed to bring about substantial improvements in agricultural production. Siles's presidency (1956–9) and Paz Estensoro's second term (1959–64) saw the advanced social programme instituted soon after the revolution cut back and the opening up of the plains with United States oil companies allowed in once again.

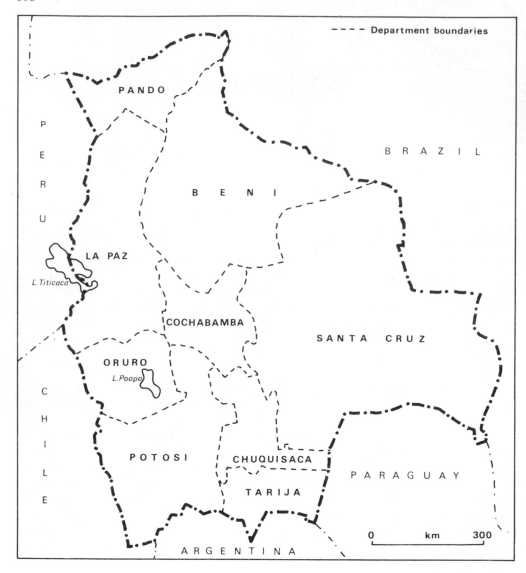

In 1964, the army took over power and, with changes in the leadership, has been there ever since apart from a civilian government for a few months in 1979.

Bolivia's development has been based on the dynamics of its extractive industries whose products accounted for over 95 per cent of merchandise exports in 1975. Tin remained the major export with tin mining concentrated in the Altiplano. However, rapid development of oil and natural gas resources based in south-east Bolivia meant these accounted for one-third of merchandise exports in 1975. This development 'towards the outside' has given rise to an enclave economy which makes little contribution to the development of a diversified economic base. Per capita GNP at $510 in 1978 was low for a Latin American nation. Manufacturing industries have been slow to develop; in 1978 they produced only 13 per cent of GDP. These along with most of the mines and service activities are concentrated along the highway axis defined by La Paz in the Altiplano, Cochabamba in the High Valleys and Santa Cruz in the Plains—and in the mining centre, Oruro, some 90 kilometres south of the axis. La Paz is the administrative capital and had 654 713 inhabitants in 1976. Cochabamba is surrounded by some of Bolivia's most productive farmlands and had 204 414 people in this same year. Santa Cruz is a major centre for locally grown tropical and subtropical crops and related industries. Road connections to Cochabamba and rail connections to the Atlantic coast through Brazil have greatly boosted its growth. In

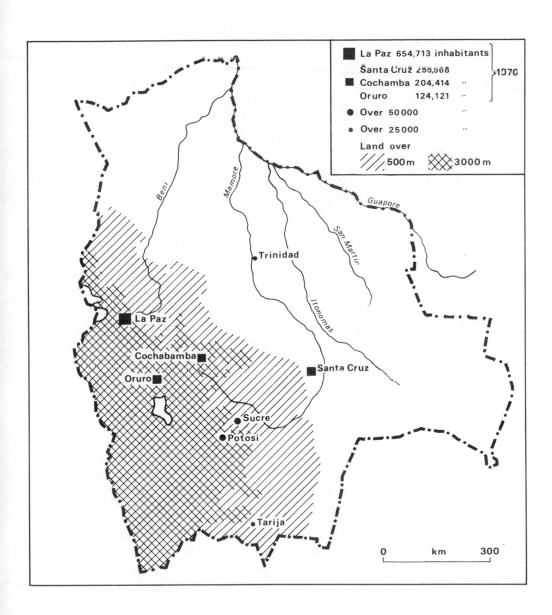

1976, it had 255 568 inhabitants, its rapid growth making it overtake Cochabamba as the nation's second largest city.[3]

These three cities accounted for some two-thirds of the population in settlements with over 20 000 inhabitants. And the three departments they were in (of the same name as the cities) produced two-thirds of GDP in 1974 and contained most of the manufacturing industries.[4]

By 1976, centres with more than 20 000 inhabitants had 32.2 per cent of the national population while those with between 20 000 and 2000 had 10.4 per cent.[5] If the urban population is defined as those living in centres of 2000 or more inhabitants, the urban population's annual average growth rate was 3.9 per cent between 1950 and 1976.[6] For the national territory as a whole, Bolivia does not have a network of urban settlements—from small market towns to regional and national centres—which bring each region and subregion into the national economy and thus allow a uniform spread of goods and services. The urban centres 'do not fulfil the functions of environment dynamizers'.[7] They also lack a firm and diversified economic base and are poorly served with basic infrastructure and services. Urban settlements of below 20 000 inhabitants are particularly ill-served; only a tiny minority of their households are connected to sewage systems or have a household connection for water.[8]

Despite the fact that more than two-thirds of the population still lived in rural areas in 1976, and that half of the workforce were still in the agricultural sector in 1978, agriculture has played a secondary role in Bolivia's economic development. Agricultural production grew by an annual average of little more than 2 per cent between 1962 and 1972, although it did show some signs of more rapid growth in the mid-1970s.[9] The rural population remains very poor. According to a United Nations Report published in 1977, more than three-quarters of the households living in settlements of less than 2000 inhabitants earn less than $50 a year. The agricultural sector's major roles have been providing a labour reserve for the mines and food for the urban and mining centres. Neither increasing oil production nor growing industrial activity is likely to have much effect on the poor rural majority. Bolivia's average life expectancy—52 in 1978—remains the lowest in South America. In many regions and subregions, mountainous terrain has hindered the linking of small, isolated rural communities to either major economic centres or neighbouring regions. The result is that agricultural production in most rural settlements is largely for consumption in the local market. In addition, the isolation and low purchasing power of many rural communities means that handicraft production still prevails there.

Brazil

The Federal Republic of Brazil occupies nearly half the South American continent, covering more than 8 million square kilometres. It is the world's fifth largest nation. Between 1960 and 1978, annual population growth averaged 2.8 per cent a year and its population was approaching 120 million by mid-1978. Projections suggest its population will reach more than 200 million by 2000.

The Equator crosses northern Brazil while the Tropic of Capricorn cuts across its southern territory. Despite its tropical and subtropical location, much of the country receives moderate rainfall and experiences no great extremes in temperature. However, areas such as the Upper Amazon Basin has very heavy rainfall, while the

COLOMBIA

RORAIMA   AMAPA

0   km   1000

A M A Z O N A S

P A R Á

MARANHAO   CEARA RIO GRANDE
DO NORTE

PARAIBA

P I A U I   PERNAMBUCO

ALAGOAS

ACRE   RONDONIA   SERGIPE

B A H I A

MATO GROSSO

GOIAS

B O L I V I A

M I N A S

G E R A I S   ESPIRITO
SANTO

GUANABARA

SAO PAULO   RIO DE JANEIRO

PARAGUAY

P A R A N A

A T L A N T I C

SANTA CATARINA   O C E A N

RIO GRANDE
DO SUL

- - - State boundaries

URUGUAY

northeast suffers recurring droughts with some areas in this region having an annual average rainfall of below 250 mm.

Brazil can be divided into four macro-regions: the South and Southeast with much of the population, virtually all the modern industry and most of the more productive agriculture; the sparsely populated North and Northwest which is dominated by the vast Amazon region; the Northeast, the early colonial period's economic centre but now an area of frequent drought, poverty and exhausted land; and the sparsely populated Centre–West which is dominated by the vast Central Plateau. Most of the national population—and most of the largest cities—are in or near the Atlantic coast. The South and Southeast contained three-fifths of the national population in 1970 on 18 per cent of the land area while the Northeast contained nearly a third also on 18 per cent of the land. The Centre–West and the North contained less than 10 per cent of the population on nearly two-thirds of the national territory.[10]

In the sixteenth century, the Portuguese established the world's first large-scale sugar plantations in the Northeast with imported African labour. But the discovery of gold and later diamonds in the Southeast shifted the nation's economic centre and stimulated the development of Rio de Janeiro through which the minerals were shipped to Europe. Brazil's present settlement pattern reflects such shifts in the economic centre's location, brought about by the expansion of different primary commodities for export. As gold deposits were exhausted, the growth of coffee exports made São Paulo state (and city) the main focus for economic growth. The coffee boom helped develop the urban economy with the expansion of railroads increasing the commercial importance of certain urban areas, especially Santos and São Paulo. By 1930, with the global depression, Brazil had a fairly large internal market which allowed import substitution to provide the base for industrial development up to the mid-1960s. Since then, with a military regime in power, industrial development has concentrated more on production for export with widespread use of foreign capital and technology. Industrial output grew very rapidly between the late 1960s and mid-1970s. Its annual average growth rate exceeded 10 per cent between 1970 and 1978 with GDP growing at almost the same rate. Per capita GNP rose to $1570 in 1978. Despite rapid industrial growth, primary products still dominate Brazilian exports with sugar, coffee, iron ore, soybeans and animal fodder accounting for half of all merchandise exports in 1975. However, agriculture's contribution to GDP had fallen to 11 per cent in 1978 while that of industry had grown to 37 per cent.

While national population more than doubled between 1940 and 1970, urban population (defined as the population in urban and suburban zones of administrative centres of *municipios* and districts) more than quadrupled. In this period, the number of cities with over 20 000 people grew from 53 to 351.[11] By 1980, 65 per cent of the national population lived in urban areas. This rapid urbanization process resulted in the Brazilian urban system becoming extended over virtually all the inhabited territory. By 1970, 70 cities had more than 100 000 inhabitants while eight had more than half a million. Vilmar Faria has suggested a number of reasons why the urban system is moving away from the primacy pattern which characterizes many Latin American nations.[12] Firstly, urban settlements had developed in the various regions which were once the nation's most dynamic centre. More recently, rapid industrial expansion has created new jobs in industrial centres. It has also indirectly promoted the economy of new centres which, with growing market integration, distribute goods and services among the more dispersed population. Changes in agriculture with its modernization, growing integration into the national market and the extension of the agricultural frontier have demanded new urban functions and centres. So too have the exploitation of new natural resources and the expansion of government activities. All these developments have helped increase the nation's urban base.

The South and Southeast remain the nation's economic core. In 1970, they accounted for more than two-thirds of the agricultural GDP, more than 90 per cent of the industrial GDP and more than four-fifths of the services GDP.[13] São Paulo, with more than 12 million people in its metropolitan area in 1980, encompasses most of Brazil's high productivity manufacturing enterprises and generates more than a third of the entire nation's GDP. Rio de Janeiro is the region's other major metropolitan area with more than 8 million inhabitants in 1975 and it remains the nation's largest port.[14] As we noted, the region produces much of the nation's agricultural GDP, most of this being grown within the São Paulo–Parana–Minas Gerais triangle. 73 per cent of the Southeast's population lived in urban areas in 1970.

The Northeast had major cities such as Recife, Salvador and Fortaleza, but only 42 per cent of the population lived in urban areas in 1970. In this same year, it contributed one-fifth of the national agricultural GDP, 5.6 per cent of the industrial GDP and 12.1 per cent of the services GDP. Not surprisingly, its per capita GDP was less than half that of the South and less than a third that of the Southeast. There has been steady net outmigration from the Northeast since 1940 with the Centre–West showing the most rapid inmigration for this period, no doubt due to the expansion of the agricultural frontier west of São Paulo (in the south of Mato Grosso and Goias) and the movement of the capital to a new city, Brasilia, located in this region. In all regions there has been continuous rural-to-urban migration, whether interregional or intraregional.

Despite the emergence and increasing consolidation of a national urban system, there are major regional differences in average wage, level of industrial development and provision of social infrastructure. São Paulo and Rio de Janeiro can be seen as the centre of the most urbanized and advanced region with subcentres at Porto Alegre, Belo Horizone and Curitiba. These subcentres and other cities with between half a million and 2 million inhabitants such as Brasilia and the Northeast's major cities have low industrial productivity and low average wages compared to both larger and smaller centres in and around Rio de Janeiro and São Paulo. Their social and economic infrastructure is also comparatively poor. Then the Northern region has a relatively well-distributed urban infrastructure but no solid economic base and a low level of services in medium and small centres. Finally, in the national periphery (which includes Amazonia and parts of the Centre–West), only now are the first signs of an urban network appearing.

By the early 1970s, it was evident that the poor majority had benefited little from the economic policies that had turned Brazil into a major industrial power. The uneven distribution of modern industry, agriculture and basic services over the national territory can be compared to the increasingly inequitable distribution of income. In 1972, the poorest 20 per cent of households received just 2 per cent of total household income while the richest 20 per cent received two-thirds.[15] Vast squatter communities surround most major cities. In São Paulo Municipality, the proportion of the population served by the water supply system actually fell between 1950 and 1973 from 61 per cent to 56 per cent. In the Greater São Paulo region, the proportion of the population served by the sewage system fell from 35 to 30 per cent between 1971 and 1975.[16] Infant mortality rates in major cities were growing rather than falling. Meanwhile, the Northeast had twice the South's infant mortality rate and twelve years less life expectancy.[17] Since 1974, as we shall see in later sections, there have been some attempts to improve the distribution of benefits from development.

Colombia

Covering more than a million square kilometres on the northwest corner of South America, Colombia had a population of 25.6 million in 1978. Its rapid natural growth rate during the 1950s and 1960s seems to be slowing and projections for 2000 suggest a population of some 37 million. It is a country with very uneven terrain and a wide range of regional climates. The Andes reach their northern end in Colombia, entering the country through Ecuador to the south and then splitting with the Cordillera Occidental running parallel to the Pacific Coast and the Cordillera Orientale reaching up to Colombia's northeast with a branch going into Venezuela.

Despite its tropical location, the Andean region's elevation gives it a temperate climate. This region has long been the nation's main political, economic and population centre. Today, it contains more than three-quarters of Colombia's population. The Caribbean lowlands are the only other area with major population centres. This region has a tropical climate with abundant rainfall and contains nearly a fifth of the national population. The other three regions—the Pacific lowlands, the Llanos to the east and the Amazonian rainforests to the southeast—contain less than 5 per cent of the national population. The Llanos and the Amazon rainforest region make up some two-thirds of the national territory and contain less than 2 per cent of the national population.

From the sixteenth century, through 300 years of Spanish rule, and for at least a century after independence in 1819, Colombia's economy was based on primary exports—gold, coal, blue dye, quinine, and finally coffee. After independence, coffee became the backbone of the economy. Its production in relatively small owner-occupied plots in the central Andean region supported small, dispersed towns which remained relatively isolated from each other. Indeed, until a few decades ago, each

region was virtually self-sufficient. The few interregional transport routes were built to service the movement of export crops rather than integrate the various population centres and their economies into a national system. By the 1920s, Colombia's coffee exports accounted for 10 per cent of the world market and the annual crop represented around 18 per cent of GDP. As in many Latin American nations, the

Great Depression in the 1930s caused an economic crisis as the price of primary products fell, but in the longer term it stimulated import substitution in industry. Then conditions after the Second World War favoured a more rapid development and diversification of industry. The industrial sector's growth rate averaged more than 5 per cent a year between 1960 and 1978. Meanwhile, per capita income grew to $850 by the end of this period.

The Andean region remains the nation's industrial and agricultural centre. Its climate is well suited to coffee production and just this one crop accounted for more than half of all export earnings in 1976. Textile yarns and fabrics are the major manufactured export with Medellin being the centre of this industry. The Andean region includes Colombia's three largest cities: Bogota, the national capital in the cold central plateau; Medellin in the temperate western highlands; and Cali in the southwest. By 1977, estimates put the population of Bogota at 3.5 million, of Medellin at 1.75 million and of Cali at 1.19 million.[18] Together with Barranquilla in the Caribbean lowlands (with some 868 000 inhabitants on this same date), these urban areas had monopolized much of the modern industrial development. By 1974, they employed nearly three-quarters of the nation's factory workers, and in the last four decades, they have absorbed four out of every five new industrial jobs. Bogota alone accounted for two-fifths of these new industrial jobs and has been the major centre for the tertiary sector's growth.[19]

The manufacturing industry's share in GDP had grown to 20 per cent in 1978. Mineral exploitation remains an important economic sector. Up to 1974, Colombia was self-sufficient in petroleum. The Cordillera Occidental's Pacific slope contains valuable gold and platinum deposits; the Cordillera Central has gold, silver and industrial mineral resources and the Cordillera Orientale has various industrial minerals and some of the world's finest emeralds.

Colombia's urban population has grown rapidly in the last three decades, especially during the 1950s and early 1960s. By 1980, 70 per cent of the population lived in urban settlements compared to 38.9 per cent in 1951.[20] But this relatively high percentage of population in urban areas is partly explained by the criteria used to define an 'urban' settlement. All settlements with a nucleus of 1500 or more inhabitants are urban.

In contrast to the considerable concentration of modern industrial and tertiary sector growth in the four major cities (especially Bogota), there is a fairly balanced distribution of urban centres in Colombia close to rank size pattern. In 1979, there were 69 towns with over 30 000 inhabitants and 46 with over 50 000.[21] Arenas Bonilla noted the 'high positive correlation between the urbanization level (associated with the highest increase in productivity and larger social division of labour) and the magnitude of migratory streams'.[22] In the intercensus period 1951–73, Bogota's population quadrupled while Medellin's tripled, Barranquilla's and Cali's increased 2.8 times and cities with 100 000 to half a million inhabitants doubled.

The traditional agricultural sector was unable to meet the demands of a rapidly growing urban sector and was replaced by more modern, capital-intensive agriculture in the main valleys where modern technology could be used. The traditional rural dichotomy between *latifundia* and *minifundia* was replaced by that between commercial and traditional agriculture. This led to growing unemployment for the agricultural labour force and rapid migration to urban areas. The peasants dispossessed by the

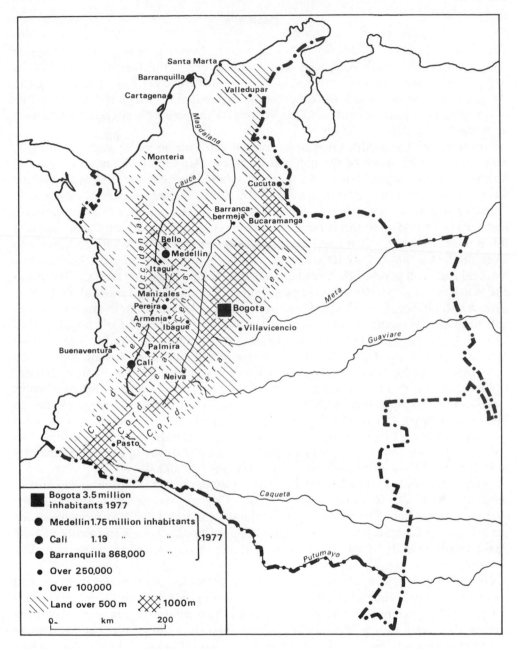

new modern farms were one major cause of *La Violencia*—the virtual war in the Colombian countryside in the late 1940s and most of the 1950s. A large proportion of the rural population still live on small subsistence holdings while the modern farms play a major role in Colombia's economy. Agriculture produced 31 per cent of GDP in 1978 while cash crops accounted for around three-quarters of the merchandise exports in 1977.

Mexico

The Federal Republic of Mexico is a vast nation, covering nearly 2 million square kilometres on the North American continent just below the United States. With a population of more than 65 million in 1978, it is the second most populous Latin American nation. Over the past few decades, its population growth rate has been one of the most rapid in the world[23] and projections for the year 2000 suggest a population of at least 125 million.

Positioned on the earth's great desert region and with no major rivers crossing it, water is scarce for much of the national territory. Two major mountain ranges run north–south close to the coasts—the Sierra Madre Occidental near the Pacific and the Sierra Madre Orientale, a continuation of the Rocky Mountain system, close to the Gulf of Mexico. Between them is the plateau that covers the interior from Mexico's northern border down to the Isthmus of Tehuantepec in the southern states. Much of this is over 1500 metres above sea level. Regional climates are very varied. Areas with more moderate climates are determined more by altitude than latitude. The California Peninsula and parts of the north and northwest have very low rainfall. The north and northeast regions which encompass Baja California Norte, Baja California Sur, Sonora, Chihuahua, Coahuila, Nuevo Leon, Sinaloa, Durango and Nayarit represent half the national territory but contained less than a fifth of Mexico's population in 1970[24]. Average rainfall tends to increase, moving southwards. And it is in a broad central band running from coast to coast that population densities are highest. In 1970, more than three-fifths of the population lived in such a band made up of Jalisco, Colima, Michoacan and Guanajuato (centre–west region); Zacatecas, Aguascalientes and San Luis Potosi (centre–north); Mexico state and the Federal District (Valley of Mexico); Morelos, Queretaro, Hidalgo, Tlaxcala and Puebla (centre); and the Gulf state of Veracruz. This band represents only a quarter of the national territory.[24] In the mid-Seventies, more than half of Mexico's cropland was in the predominantly rainfed central highlands which are within this central band.[25]

The Central Valley with Mexico City in its centre has been the nation's main area of settlement since Pre-Columbian days. Mexico City was the site of the great Aztec capital, Tenochtitlan. The native population in the Central Valley provided labour for the mines and *haciendas* and Mexico City became capital of the Viceroyalty of New Spain which extended from the Panama Isthmus deep into what are now central northern areas of the United States.

The development of settlements extended north as new silver mines were opened up (Mexico remains one of the world's major silver producers) and new agricultural lands exploited where water resources allowed. The central region and the mining areas to the north to which it was linked remained the main political and economic centre after independence in 1821. Late in the nineteenth century, Mexico's economy responded to the world market's increasing demand for raw materials and achieved high economic growth rates based on agricultural exports. Foreign capital helped to finance economic development while new railway networks brought many more areas into the national economy. Both boosted and modified the pattern of urban development. Strategically placed urban centres grew rapidly while Mexico City, the main destination of capital flows, began the 'demographic impulse that would turn it into a decisively pre-eminent city'.[26] Increasing capitalist penetration into the more

119

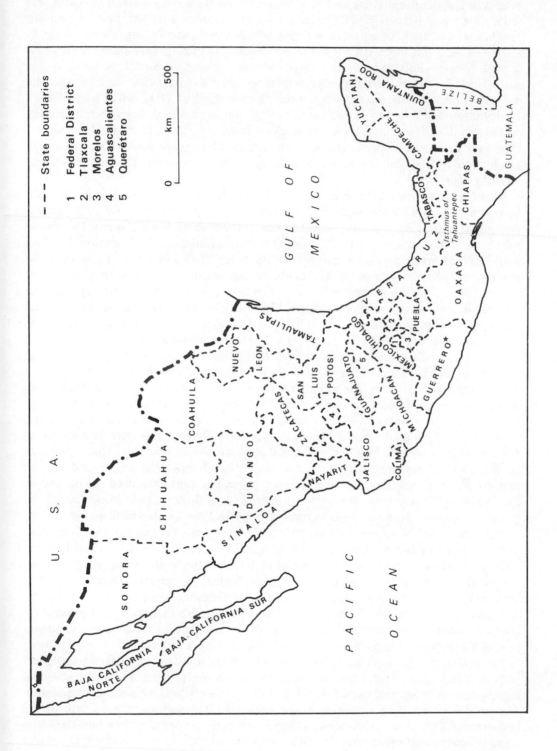

productive agricultural areas and land hunger both from dispossessed peasants and from rapid population growth inflamed social tensions and led first to peasant revolution and then to agrarian reforms which were patchily implemented up to 1940.[27] Then, for three decades, the so called 'stabilizing development strategy' turned Mexico into one of the Third World's major industrial powers. It has maintained impressive economic growth rates over the past two decades and the secondary sector now accounts for more than a third of GDP while agriculture's contribution had fallen to 11 per cent in 1978. But agricultural crops such as coffee, cotton, fruit and vegetables are still major exports. So too are mineral resources, especially crude oil. Oil reserves in south-eastern Mexico are massive and crude oil production nearly doubled between 1970 and 1976, becoming the nation's single largest export.

By 1978, per capita GNP had reached $1290. Rapid economic growth has been accompanied by relatively rapid and sustained urban growth rates. By 1978, metropolitan Mexico City was the world's most populous city with some 14 million inhabitants. Guadalajara had 2.34 million and Monterrey 1.92 million in their metropolitan areas on this same date.[28] Between 1940 and 1970, the number of settlements with more than 20 000 inhabitants grew from 37 (when they contained 18.4 per cent of total population) to 131 (when they contained 43.2 per cent) while the number of settlements with more than 100 000 inhabitants grew from six to 35 in this same period.[29] In 1980, 67 per cent of the population were living in urban settlements (which are officially defined as those with 2500 or more inhabitants).

However, neither urban nor industrial development was evenly distributed. The 'stabilizing development strategy' had meant subordinating the agrarian sector to 'urban-industrial interests, the monopolization of the economy, its denationalization and greater inequalities in personal as well as regional income distribution; the latter reflected by the extreme economic concentration in a few cities and in a reduced number of commercial areas'.[30] The statistics for 1970 bear this out. The Valley of Mexico with just over a fifth of the national population and little more than 1 per cent of the national territory accounted for two-fifths of industrial sector and half of tertiary sector production. Not surprisingly, it was the most urbanized region and its per capita GDP was twice the national average and three to five times that of the poorest regions—the three other central regions and the south–southeast.

The North and Northeast regions and the Gulf region (Tamaulipas and Veracruz) contain much of the modern commercial agriculture and grew more than half the nation's marketed agricultural produce in 1970. After the Valley of Mexico, they are among the most urbanized regions and had the highest per capita GDPs in 1970. The economies of the North and the Northeast have benefited from commercial, tourist and service links with the United States. Both have more than half their population living in urban areas. Monterrey is the north's financial and industrial capital and was one of the nation's fastest growing cities between 1940 and 1970.

In the centre, centre–west, centre–north and south–southeast regions (which do not include the Valley of Mexico), urbanization levels are much lower and traditional agriculture far more widespread. In 1970, they had nearly half the national population but produced less than a quarter of the national GDP and less than a fifth of the industrial GDP. The centre–west, a region of early settlement, has had declining mining activity and rapid rural to urban migration with the growth of commerical and

121

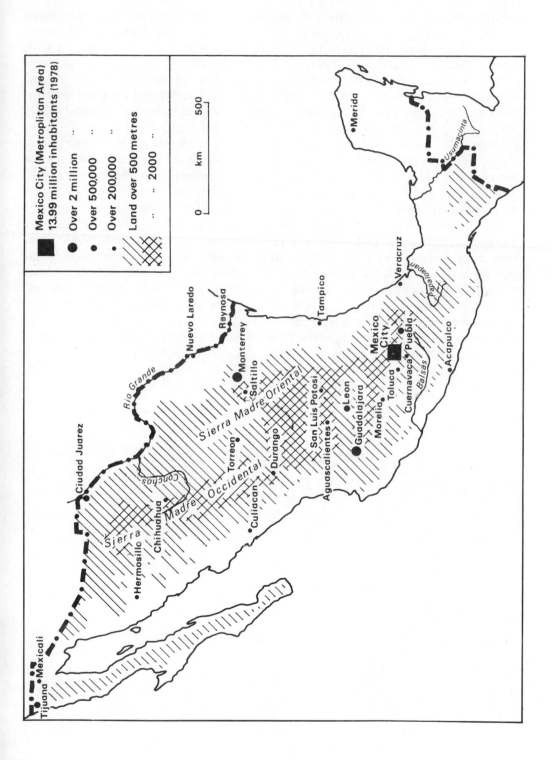

service centres and of Guadalajara. In the south–southeast and the other two central regions, urbanization has been slower. And in all four regions, many urban centres remain isolated from the main urban network and from industrial development while most of the rural population ekes out a precarious existence on what are generally subsistence holdings on poor land. Although in per capita GDP terms, the gap between these four regions and the Valley of Mexico diminished between 1940 and 1970, this is no doubt due to outmigration pushing the poor regions' per capita GDP up and inmigration pulling the Valley of Mexico's per capita GDP down.

Since 1970, there have been attempts to spread the benefits of economic growth more widely. Figures for 1977 reveal that the poorest 40 per cent of households received 10.3 per cent of total household income while the richest 20 per cent received 54.4 per cent and the richest 10 per cent received 36.7 per cent.[31] The 1977 figures suggest that the poorest 40 per cent have not increased their share of national wealth since the 1960s, although the lower-middle and middle-income groups seem to have increased their share quite considerably with the higher-income group's share decreasing. Mexico's vast oil reserves and the wealth this will inevitably bring could provide the financial underpinning for the much-needed extension of basic services and infrastructure to regions and rural communities largely bypassed by the nation's economic development. It could also help create jobs. At present, unemployment and underemployment are very high. They would be a lot higher were it not for the temporary and permanent migration of millions of Mexicans across the border to the United States, most of them entering the United States illegally.

National Settlement Policies

Bolivia

In the background to Bolivia (page 108), we noted that the present sociopolitical model is essentially the consolidation of that part of the middle-class which is associated with mining and closely linked to international capital. Direct foreign investment, intensified since 1972, has mainly been in mining, agro-industry, oil, foreign trade and services and has gone to the Departments of La Paz and Santa Cruz and to mining areas in Oruro and Cochabamba. This has intensified the 'march to the Orient' with the city of Santa Cruz as its centre. The spatial concentration of both private and public investment has delayed important development programmes in the Altiplano and High Valleys. For example, many small- and medium-sized urban areas in the Departments of Oruro, Cochambamba and Potosi have had no public works investment for over a decade.

Santa Cruz's expansion as a 'growth pole' should not be seen simply as an attempt to deconcentrate productive activities but as part of a process which is itself defining a new centre with relative autonomy both politically and administratively. Interregional conflicts might account for the lack of any clear national spatial plan. Proposed policies—where they exist—are 'mere aggregates . . . of separately designed regional strategies'.[32] Many regions have been completely forgotten by central government. And there is a lack of coordination between the committees or development corporations of each department or region, many of whom still come under separate ministries.

The Bolivian National Plan for Economic and Social Development (1976–80) notes the country's disjointed spatial structure and recognizes the obstacles this presents to the generation of the well-integrated national market that solid and sustained economic development needs. The Plan's 'spatial strategy' aims at the 'efficient integration of the national territory'.[33] Its objectives include: the central axis's consolidation and development, bringing new departments into its sphere of influence; the creation of new poles in the southeast (around Mutun's steel industry), in the northeast (around modern agricultural units) and in the southeast (around oil and natural gas deposits); and development of the area to be obtained on the Pacific.[34] National policies aim to create better urban conditions (especially for lower income groups) and to bring the vast peasant agricultural sector into the modern economy. Priority is given to investment in 'integrated projects and plans for rural development' designed to promote agricultural production, irrigation, improved agricultural technology and marketing structure, and the supply of basic social and economic infrastructure. But these objectives have not materialized in concrete action, for no national legislation has turned these into more precise and detailed policy guidelines.

The National Plan also gives high priority to the colonization of new lands which have potential for agricultural production to draw people from overpopulated rural areas on the Altiplano and in some of the High Valleys. But despite considerable potential in many areas, especially in the plains now that the more serious diseases have been virtually eradicated, there has been no well-planned and executed colonization policy. Up to 1965, various bodies (including the Ministry of Agriculture, the Mining Corporation of Bolivia, the United Nations Andean Mission, religious missions and other bodies) all had uncoordinated colonization programmes. In 1965, the autonomous Institute of Colonization and Development (later renamed the National Institute of Colonization) was created. Although reorganized several times, this has implemented a number of projects both with government funds and external aid. Many of the projects currently underway have the general objective of creating agricultural and cattle-raising bases in areas that link the Altiplano to the Plains and support and stimulate settlement development along newly developed roads and railways.

The result of programmes, at least up to 1972, has been limited and, in some cases, negative. Little support was given to most of the migrating peasants and the receiving areas were often ill-prepared for their new population. In some cases, for instance settlements in tropical areas, conditions were so bad that the migrants did not stay. In addition, an even larger process of spontaneous colonization is taking place without the government's direct cooperation.

One interesting result of Bolivia's agrarian reform[35] has been the spontaneous formation of peasant villages, mostly in the Altiplano. With their own holdings, peasants could engage in commercial agriculture and these new settlements sprung up as market and service centres for the peasant farmers. But for a great number of peasants, economic conditions have not improved as the land reform was not followed up with the needed technological and institutional inputs to raise their productivity. In fact, lack of opportunity in Bolivia and the exclusion of the poor majority from much of the development process has led to massive emigration. Estimates suggest that there are some 600 000 Bolivians temporarily or permanently in Argentina alone.

Brazil

Brazil still lacks an explicit settlements policy that implies a comprehensive view on the organization and distribution of human activity over its national territory. But since the 1950s, successive governments have tried to address the problem of economically depressed regions. More recently, they have been moving towards a national urban policy and showing more consideration for spatial aspects in national development plans.

In the late 1950s, an autonomous regional development agency, the Superintendency for the Development of the Northeast (SUDENE) was set up to promote development in the depressed Northeast with the aim, initially, of introducing basic reforms such as restructuring landholding patterns. But these structural reforms were never fully implemented, although SUDENE did develop infrastructure and encourage industrial development. After 1964, SUDENE was incorporated into the Ministry of the Interior along with other newly created agencies for regional development so the Northeast lost the political priority it had enjoyed. SUDENE had its powers cut and though there was a marked increase in modern industry and some improvement in infrastructure, the basic problems of high unemployment and poverty remained.

In 1970, a serious drought in the Northeast prompted a new policy. The poverty and unemployment there was to be eased by opening up new lands and exploiting natural resources in the Amazon Basin and directing outmigration from the Northeast to this frontier region. In addition, a new programme for land redistribution and for the Promotion of the Agricultural Industry in the North and Northeast (PROTERRA) was started in 1971. But neither met with much success. The Amazon colonization met with countless obstacles, perhaps the most important being that most of Amazonia's soil will not support sustained agricultural production. And PROTERRA concentrated on the promotion of agroindustrial firms which made the aim of seeking a better distribution of benefits from development fade away.

These attempts to develop the poorer or less developed regions were enlarged in the Second National Development Plan 1975–9. This emphasized the spatial aspects of the nation's development process more than previous plans. It also included the explicit objective of 'a better political and economic balance between the various regions. . . . The aim is to compensate for the diseconomies and disutilities generated by the acceleration of the industrialization and/or urbanization process.[36] So the Plan was concerned with a spatial reorganization which would contribute to the process of a more equitable social development. Regional inequalities were to be minimized by regional industrial complexes. The Plan talked of a 'national integration strategy', taking into account relationships between population, territorial space and the role of Brazil as an exporter of agricultural produce and thus to consider regions such as Amazonia and the Northeast in this light. Special 'integrated' programmes for Amazonia, the Northeast and Brasilia were part of the Plan. But the Plan did not specify what economic policy tools its objectives would demand if they were to be achieved. For instance, for the proposed industrial deconcentration, no details were given as to which industries would be steered to relatively backward regions, from where they would move, how they were to be chosen and what institutional mechanisms would be needed to make this work. Nor has it been made clear how such a policy could be made compatible with regional, state or municipal government plans and with basic social objectives such as assisting the lowest income groups. Thus, despite clear goals, there is little evidence of the explicit social and economic policies that might achieve them. This lack of institutional mechanisms to turn policy into practice is also evident in specific sectoral policies. Among the most important with regard to settlement policies is the National Urban Policy.

Brazilian urban policy began in 1964 as little more than an urban housing policy with the creation of the National Housing Bank (BNH) and the Federal Service for Housing and Urban Planning (SERFHAU). Although other aspects such as city and metropolitan area planning, water supply and sewerage were gradually added to the support for expanding housing construction, these remained fragmented, with no clear connection to national development policy. SERFHAU was no more than an appendix to housing policy until 1967 when it came to coordinate urban planning policy in municipalities of over 50 000 people with the creation of a National Planning System for Integrated Local Development and a fund for financing local development plans. But although many urban masterplans were prepared, most achieved little or nothing because of (among other reasons) the separation of preliminary planning studies (done by the private sector) from the authorities who actually had to implement them (and who generally lacked the power to do so), the lack of coordination with state and federal institutions and the sectoral nature of the plans which only covered physical aspects. In 1970, when SERFHAU's activities were coming to an end, there was an attempt to implement a Programme for Concerted Action in 457 municipalities which had been chosen for their major role in the development of their region. But again, coordination was lacking and the physical aspects received priority. In 1973, eight metropolitan regions were established—Belem in the North, Fortaleza, Recife and Salvador in the Northeast, São Paulo, and Belo Horizonte in the Southeast and Curitiba and Porto Alegre in the South (Rio de Janeiro was already a metropolitan region). This was designed to put the administration of the regions under the state.

The 1974 elections produced important changes in national urban policies. The Second National Development Plan advocated a more comprehensive and integrated national urban policy which would no longer be simply metropolitan and sectoral. Its two basic objectives were the definition of guidelines with operational mechanisms to ensure that the urban structure complemented development strategy, and then the translation of these guidelines into specific regional development strategies. Among many goals, the intention was to establish the nine metropolitan regions that had already been created and establish urban nuclei within each of these regions, to identify the functions that national and regional metropolises should perform, to define secondary poles of national or regional scope, to prevent the excessive growth of São Paulo and Rio, to promote urbanization in recently settled areas in the North and Centre–West regions, and to promote urban development in the Northeast. The National Commission on Metropolitan Regions and Urban Policy (CNPU) was set up to propose guidelines for national urban development policy (including the norms and tools needed to implement it) and to help coordinate the efforts of the metropolitan region governments, the superintendencies of regional development, the various sectoral agencies and other government agencies working in this field. The National Fund for Urban Development System was set up to regulate and direct federal funds for urban development according to criteria proposed by CNPU.

In 1976, CNPU produced a surprisingly radical Draft Law on Urban Development. Among its basic objectives are improved integration of federal, state, metropolitan and municipal institutions in urban development projects and improved basic services and social facilities in all urban areas. But its main innovation is a revision of land ownership rights in urban areas, giving far more power to the state to buy land and control development.[37] By stating that urban property owners had social obligations, it aimed to give the state pre-emption rights for the purchase of real estate in special interest areas and the right to demand that an owner of real estate should develop it and thus not be allowed to leave it vacant.

So, since 1974, there are signs of a more comprehensive approach to urban problems with an attempt at better coordination between different levels of government and the various agencies involved. But according to Andrade,[38] the Ministries of Planning and the Interior were in dispute right from the start as to who should be responsible for metropolitan policy. He suggested that the functions assigned to CNPU would have required ministerial level powers to be effective with the institutional position to deal with the many agencies involved in urban development. Instead, it was put in the Ministry of Planning.

To sum up, there is still no clear definition of priorities and of mechanisms to put priorities into action and thus face up to the nation's urban problems. The objectives of urban policy remain too broad and imprecise, and, as always, the nation's political and economic strategies have a profound influence on the kind of urban policy that can be implemented. As Hamilton Tolosa points out,

> if the national objective is to accelerate the GNP growth rate, it would be highly effective, from the economic point of view, to concentrate all the activity in São Paulo. But if the issue is to implement a development model that is effective from the point of view of achieving a certain degree of equity among cities and regions, then things are different and the spatial configuration must be different.[39]

The first model would inevitably result in rising unemployment and underemployment in most other urban areas, while the second could engage in a programme to steer new investment to other urban areas and reduce unemployment there but at some cost to the national growth rate. Clearly the choice between the two is political. And national trends in urbanization can be seen to reflect the general socioeconomic process. The problems they generate cannot be solved by partial or sectoral action. They demand a more comprehensive, precise and distributive social policy. But even so, the draft law proposed by CNPU, if implemented, would represent real progress, despite its limited subject area.

Colombia

Between 1957 and 1975, Colombia was ruled by the 'National Front', a coalition of the two largest parties (the Liberals and the Conservatives) who took turns for the Presidency. Various settlement policies and programmes were tried during these years. But they changed every few years. Successive presidencies saw first rural and then urban questions become the main emphasis of development plans. And in urban and regional planning, although substantial policies were suggested, they did not become law.

The 1960s saw the beginning of urban and regional policy after the National Council for Economic Policy and Planning was set up as the top planning body to advise the President. The Ten-Year Plan 1960–70 sought to promote heavy and intermediate industrial development and to accelerate the transformation of generally low productivity *latifundia* into modern commercial farms. The first half of this decade (under Valencia, a Conservative President) saw a concentration on rural policies in the belief that these could slow rural outmigration and lessen social tensions. But the 1961 Law on Agrarian Reform and the Colombian Institute for Agrarian Reform set up to implement it achieved little. It did not eliminate sharecropping. Very few tenancies were converted to freehold. And it did not succeed in stimulating increased productivity in large portions of land farmed extensively. Its only major achievement was the expansion of cultivated area, granting family units title on public land.[40]

In 1966, under a new Liberal President, Carlos Lleras Restrepo, more attention was given to urban and industrial policies while continuing the attempts to implement agrarian reforms and promote the development of commercial agriculture. A supplementary Law of Agrarian Reform in 1968 gave tenants and sharecroppers of less than 15 hectares the right to purchase the land they farmed, but peasants' expectations were destroyed through very slow implementation and costly repayment terms to the former owners. In addition, the development of commercial agriculture continued to expel peasants.

This administration saw the development of a regionalization model as the basis for a better distribution of population and productive activities over the national territory. The model defined eight planning regions and five urban classifications. Bogota, the national metropolis, was to have its growth checked. Support metropolises in Medellin, Cali and Barranquilla were to balance Bogota by developing manufacturing and modern tertiary activities. Regional centres and minor intermediate cities (with between 30 000 and 200 000 inhabitants) would become commercial and service centres. If located in rich agricultural areas, attempts would be made to integrate agricultural and industrial production. And finally small centres would be developed as service centres for their area and, where appropriate, as craft and tourist centres.

Then the eight planning regions were to have regional development committees to advise national government and mobilize national agencies into implementing regional development plans. New metropolitan governments were proposed for large cities who would levy 'added value tax' and would be responsible for preparing and executing the urban region's development plan. The proposal for metropolitan and regional bodies finally became law in 1973 although four autonomous regional corporations were set up between 1966 and 1971.[41]

But the change in government in 1971 coincided with the discarding of the Regionalization Model, except for considerably reduced support for infrastructure development in the intermediate cities. The model's policy of seeking balanced regional development was seen to require excessive public participation for a government now under a Conservative President. The new development plan—the Four Strategies—emphasized increasing exports, increasing agricultural productivity, redistributing income (mainly through a progressive tax system and public expenditure on services) and the promotion of building activities in urban areas to generate employment. The Integrated Programme for the Urban Development of the Oriental Zone of Bogota was launched with much publicity, supposedly a 'gigantic program of public interest which would benefit the whole of the low income population living in that sector of the city'.[42] In fact, nearly two-thirds of the budget went on constructing the Avenida de los Cerros, a great avenue whose main purpose was to decongest Bogota's central district, and complementary works.

After 1975, under a new government administration, no important changes were made in regional and urban policies. Instead, there was a relative weakening of state action, no doubt partly due to the ending of the formal agreement between Conservative and Liberal parties for the National Front government and due to lack of agreement among the many factions in Congress. The new national plan 'To Bridge The Gap' sought to close the gaps between rural and urban incomes, between poor and rich income groups and between differential access to education and other public services. In urban areas, the intention was to make the internal development of cities more rational. The idea of 'cities within the city', formulated by the previous administration for Bogota, was taken up, the intention being 'to decentralize in several nuclei the various metropolitan activities, avoiding overcrowding in a single urban centre and reducing transport expenses as much as possible'.[43] New nuclei within the major metropolitan regions would serve as centres of jobs and services for their local population. To implement this, metropolitan areas would come under public institutions which would take over some of the functions of the various municipalities. In addition, associations of municipalities could undertake projects of interest to all of them. Autonomous urban development enterprises were to be set up, bringing local administrators and national government together. And subsidies and technical assistance were to be extended to small- and medium-scale industries to help them develop and thus create jobs—and to develop such industries and public services in small- and medium-size towns. The Higher Council of Housing and Urban Development was created in 1976 to act as advisor to the Ministry of Economic Development and implement the Law on Urban Reform if (or when) it became law.

In rural areas, a Programme of Integrated Rural Development sought to aid peasant farmers who continue to produce a substantial proportion of Colombia's domestic food. This Programme aimed to provide credit, technical assistance and new marketing associations and, at the same time, improve basic services and infrastructure. Attempts are to be made to speed up agrarian reform, especially the granting of land to peasants.

Although it is perhaps too early to judge these new initiatives since 1975, here, as in previous policies, it is not clear what institutional mechanisms will be used to meet stated objectives. In this respect, Colombian experience has not been very encouraging. Attempts to pass a Law on Urban Reform began in 1960 (Law 81 imposed progressive taxes on vacant land) and successive draft laws have not been passed. In 1978, Congress passed the 'Organic Urban Development' (Law 61) but this was partially annulled by the Courts.[44] This frustrated the original intentions of the 1975 proposals to Congress. Thus, urban policy to date has been only isolated programmes, many of which result from agreements with international funding agencies and so have to be adapted to meet their requirements. In rural areas, laws have underpinned policy but implementation has been slow and often ineffective with partial interruptions and successive restructuring of the institutions hindering any long-term programme.

Mexico

So far, no settlement policy explicitly covers the most important aspects of the nation's settlement process in an integrated and coordinated way. But in recent years, important steps have been taken towards formulating a national settlements policy and to reorganizing the government to undertake such a policy. It remains to be seen whether this progress will result in real policy actions—and the extent to which these actions will achieve stated objectives.

National planning efforts date back to the 1930s but these were sectoral with no spatial strategy in the allocation of public funds. In the two plans covering 1962 to 1970,[45] there were attempts to make the spatial spread of public expenditure more rational but to little effect. However, successive governments implemented policies which had direct or indirect effects on settlements. Redistribution of land under the land reform programme (described in the later section on Mexican land policies, page

137) since 1915 appears to have been a major factor in encouraging the dispersal of rural communities. Communal land holdings that had been taken over by *haciendas* were now returned to villages, but the villages themselves were difficult to reach with infrastructure and services. Public investment in irrigation infrastructure in the north probably played a major role in encouraging rapid development there while exacerbating regional inequalities. Within the agricultural modernization process, which enormously increased national production, the only policies for regional development were through Commissions for coastal basins on the Gulf and Pacific, based on the Tennessee Valley Authority model. They fulfilled to varying degrees objectives such as electricity production, flood control, irrigation and land reclamation. But the expected boost to urbanization and industrialization and thus decentralization of some industrial development from the Central Valley did not materialize. These commissions worked separately in what has been described as 'disarticulated regional planning'[46] and lacked the power and status to effectively promote regional development. Other plans sought to develop certain areas and had some local impact. But their contribution to regional inequalities was insignificant. Meanwhile, federal policies did little to encourage industrial investment in the more backward regions. Infrastructure and service expenditure remained concentrated in Mexico City. Tax incentives were meant to encourage private investments in certain industries outside the Federal District (Mexico City's central area). But the advantages of investment there often outweighed the lack of incentives. Besides, the incentives applied virtually everywhere else so they encouraged private investment in the more advanced regions and cities. And the incentives also applied to Mexico State into which the Mexico City conurbation had grown. So many firms benefited from the incentives while being in or close to the capital's metropolitan area.[47] Similarly, a Guarantee and Promotion Fund for the Small and Middle Size Firms sought to help enterprises setting up outside the Federal District and Monterrey. But a large number of its loans went to firms in the capital's metropolitan zone just outside the Federal District. In the 1950s and 1960s, various industrial parks were set up, many of them by private enterprise. But once again, most of the industrial area these provided was in the Federal District. Thus, up to 1970, we see some sectoral attempts to promote regional development and industrial decentralization but with very little success and without a national settlement policy within which each of these should operate.

The 1970s have seen a new commitment to the problem of large regional inequalities aimed, no doubt, at reducing the social and political tensions such inequalities generate. Under Echeverria's presidency, Committees for the Promotion of Socioeconomic Development sought to promote development in depressed states such as Oaxaca and Chiapas on the southern border with Guatemala. Incentives for industrial decentralization were stepped up. One example of this is the enlargement of the Guarantee and Promotion Fund for Small and Middle Size Firms whose contribution to a new venture now depended upon the area's degree of industrial concentration. A Comprehensive Rural Development Programme sought to promote development in 40 micro-regions through providing agricultural credit and improved infrastructure and social services. A new Committee for Reordering Land Tenure was set up in 1973 whose objectives included securing space for urban growth, drawing up masterplans for some cities (mainly ports) and attempting to create an institution in charge of planning at metropolitan level in the Central Valley.

In 1975, Committees for the Promotion of Socioeconomic Development had been set up to cover the whole of the nation (except the Federal District) with the General Division of Regional Development set up in 1974 to support and coordinate their work. In 1975, a National Commission for Regional Development was set up to head the whole regional development system. Then in 1976, the General Law on Human Settlements was passed which made the new National Commission responsible for coordinating regional and urban development with sectoral plans and administrative policy. These changes in 1976 relate closely both to the organization and to the spirit of the Habitat Conference. Although the Conference itself was not directly responsible for these changes—the Mexican Government was moving towards an integrated approach to spatial planning anyway—the Conference almost certainly hastened the approval of the legislation.

Thus, the legal framework for a national settlement policy was set up with constitutional reforms and a national law. In amendments and additions to the Constitution, the state was instructed 'to make an equitable distribution of public resources, to take care of their preservation, to achieve balanced development throughout the country and the improvement of living conditions for rural and urban populations'. The public authorities were empowered to adopt guidelines needed to plan settlements, execute public works and plan and regulate 'the creation, preservation, improvement and growth of population centres'.[48] Congress could issue laws requiring the federal government to work with state and municipal governments and all three were empowered to issue land-use regulations, implement plans, carry out public works and services and regulate the land market. Both federal and state governments could issue human settlement laws. The national settlement system was to be ordered and regulated through a new national plan for urban development and through state, metropolitan and municipal plans.

By the end of 1976, with Jose Lopez Portillo's administration in power, the Ministry of Public Works had become the Ministry of Human Settlements and Public Works (SAHOP). This was to formulate and direct national settlement policy and housing and urbanization programmes. It was also to promote community development and direct public works programmes. It contained three subministries—Public Works, Real Estate and Urban Works, and Human Settlements. The Human Settlements subministry was made responsible for implementing the new Human Settlements Law and for formulating and implementing the National Plan for Urban Development. The new inter-ministry National Commission for Urban Development brought together representatives of the various institutions in government concerned with urban development. Chaired by the Minister for Human Settlements and Public Works, this worked with SAHOP in implementing the National Plan for Urban Development. Through this Commission, the aim is to coordinate the work of all the various sectoral institutions and thus make sectoral plans and settlement plans compatible.

In 1978, as field-research for this study was being completed, the government was finishing a proposed Urban Development Plan which would promote 'communication and development axes' to help bring backward areas and regions firmly into the development process. The national urban system would have thirteen urban zones with their areas of regional influence. Within these, there would be hierarchies of central city, support city, intermediate city and rururban centre. The Plan would aim to develop 'support' and 'intermediate' cities, to redirect internal migration there and to improve service and infrastructure standards in rural areas through the rururban centres. Programmes for Concerted Action would make it possible to integrate the actions and investments of federal, state and municipal governments in each of the urban systems with the National Commission for Urban Development as the main coordinating agency.

It is too soon to make an evaluation of how effective these new moves will be. Clearly, implicit in these policies is an understanding of the spatial element in settlement problems. But one problem posed by the model of a national urban system with its orderly hierarchy of settlements in each region is the extent to which such a model actually reflects the functioning of the whole Mexican socioeconomic system in spatial terms. The actual relationships existing in the economic system can determine locational patterns for activities and for income that differ from those expected—or even planned for. In addition, the Mexican government has not made explicit the tools that will be needed to implement policies and plans. SAHOP itself lacks the resources and direct control to implement them itself. Indeed, the allocation of public resources and major decisions for economic policy will strongly influence the extent to which the plans can be implemented. Powerful government ministries and agencies with large budgets and richer states and municipalities can execute their own plans which may contradict the national or regional development plan. Indeed, any local government whether at state or municipal level is responsive to powerful demands from within its own area and these may run counter to wider spatial plans. Thus, SAHOP will have to convince other powerful agencies that its spatial plans provide the best framework for guiding all major development expenditure.

Land

Bolivia

In 1950, Bolivia had one of Latin America's most inequitable landownership patterns with 8 per cent of the landowners occupying 95 per cent of the privately held farmland. Most of the large landowners in the Altiplano lived in the major cities or abroad. In 1953, the revolutionary government passed an Agrarian Reform intended to 'raise the country's present productive levels, to transform the feudal system of land tenure and use, establishing a fair redistribution among those who work it, and to incorporate the indigenous population into national life . . .'.[49] *Latifundia*[50] were subject to total expropriation without compensation unless the owner returned to work the estate and invest in it. *Colonos*[51] who had worked the large estates were given immediate ownership of their existing plots with the aim of distributing standard holdings in the future. But most peasants simply subdivided the land themselves with the land reform agency arriving later and simply legalizing the new landholding pattern. Every Altiplano peasant was given the right to land in the Plains and many thousands took up the offer.

Thus, the colonization programme was an important part of the agrarian reform. And within this policy, the Decree-Law foresaw the need to locate new towns and hamlets within the colonized area. Municipalities were given the responsibility of determining their location either 'by themselves or at the request of at least fifty families'.[52] The National Colonization Institute allocates land to the migrants. To give an example of this allocation, in the programme for San Julian Chane Piray, a distinction is made between three categories of grantees: peasants who get 30–50 hectares; professionals who get 125 hectares; and entrepreneurs who get up to 500 hectares. The land is granted provisionally for two years and then ownership reverts to the holder. The holder may sell the plot (with the public authorities' authorization) but cannot subdivide it. The programme is intended to favour landless peasants and *minifundia* owners and the Institute tried to promote cooperative land utilization but on private land.

The agrarian reform had profound effects on Bolivia's social and economic structure and, to some extent, on redistributing population over the national territory. By 1975, more than 16 000 large estates had been expropriated and 18 million hectares distributed among some 480 000 families. But the next stage, the support of rural people so they can develop their land, has hardly begun. And many *latifundia* managed to evade expropriation by various means.

For provincial capitals (which means, essentially the largest urban areas), a decree known as 'Law on the Reform of the Ownership of Urban Land' issued in 1954 set a ceiling of 10 000 square metres on urban property. The land expropriated from the large urban landowners was to be sold by the State to those who had no land on condition that they built dwellings on it within three years. This should also have reduced the large number of vacant urban plots held for speculative gain. But this law was only implemented in La Paz and Cochabamba, and even there implementation was very inadequate. In addition, so as to define the space on which the agrarian reform was applicable, tight limits were established around each urban area. This meant that land speculation could continue outside these limits on land that urban growth would soon need.

However, both urban and agrarian reforms imply a new concept of property rights. Article 22 of the Constitution states that 'private property is guaranteed provided that its use is not harmful to public interest. Expropriation is made on account of public interest or when the property does not fulfil a social function, determined by law and with fair compensation.' This suggests that the government could pass legislation giving the public authorities far more extensive urban land use controls. Urban masterplans have been prepared by municipalities which proposed restrictions on the use of urban plots according to zones. But the masterplans have not been implemented and no new legislation giving municipalities power to determine land use has emerged.

The 1976–80 Plan for Economic and Social Development contains no explicit land policy on which the settlement process it proposes for the 'efficient integration of the national territory' is to be based. The Plan does include the proposal 'to control the use and appropriation of urban land' but gives no details as to how this is to be done.

Brazil

There is no explicit land policy. The National Constitution does establish the principle of property's 'social function', making it explicit in the case of land. For rural land, it establishes procedures for its expropriation and for determining compensation. No explicit reference is made to urban land which means it remains subject to the old Civil Code with its clear liberal orientation and hence lack of support for public rights over land use and ownership.

In rural areas, according to Russell King, over three-quarters of the agricultural population is landless and less than 5 per cent of landowners share 81 per cent of the farmland between them.[53] The traditional, low-productivity *latifundia* did not meet the requirements of those in power and this led to the 1961 Law on Agrarian Reform. But this reform did little to redistribute land, and today much of the best agricultural land remains firmly in the hands of a small élite. We noted under Brazil's Settlement Policy that initially, the Amazonia development policy included land distribution to migrants, mainly from the Northeast. But this has been replaced by the sale of large tracts of public land, the tracts being too large and expensive for small- and medium-size enterprises to afford. Generous tax incentives have encouraged large firms, many of them multinational, to invest in vast logging and cattle-raising estates.

Until the last few years urban land policies hardly existed. Municipalities set up city planning norms to regulate land-use and these acted as guidelines for urban growth. A betterment tax on landowners who benefited from public works improvements was not enforced. Real estate rates were kept low. As one commentator pointed out, 'the Political Power's policies tend to be more favourable to real estate speculation than to true community interests'.[54] The result of no effective land-use controls is perhaps most visible in São Paulo city where large amounts of land remain undeveloped since they are profitable, speculative investments. According to one estimate in 1977, São Paulo's urbanized area on that date could accommodate a two-thirds increase in population.[55]

As we noted earlier (page 126), increasing urban problems finally gave rise to the National Commission on Metropolitan Regions and Urban Policy (CNPU) in 1974. To date, the only initiative to become law is one that improves some aspects of the 1937 law on land subdivision, increasing a land subdivider's obligations and giving the public authorities more power to repress clandestine subdivisions. It also proposes to transfer the power to legislate on urban land-use from municipalities to states and metropolitan authorities.

CNPU's Draft Law on Urban Development sought to adapt the private sector's right to build in urban areas to the National Constitution's principle of property's social function. In effect, it proposed that ownership rights be separated from development rights. This is seen most clearly in two measures. The first is the demand that private builders would have to pay for any 'created area' their development involved—that is, usable floorspace exceeding the plot-size. Thus, the landowner has the right to build on his plot to a floor area equivalent to the size of the plot. If he wishes to build to a higher density, he must obtain a special permit from the Prefecture. If granted, this permit has to be paid for, the cost being related to the amount of 'created area' the intended building contains and the prevailing real estate rate. The amount paid up to twice the plot value would go to the municipality while the rest would go to the State Fund for Urban Development. This law would allow more public control of private developments and mobilize funds to pay for increasing infrastructure capacity to meet the demands of high-density developments. It would also deter the replacing of sound buildings with others of higher density simply because the latter become more profitable as land values rise.

The second measure introduces the idea of 'compulsory development'. In areas of social interest, the government could tell a private landowner that his plot was of social interest and force him to develop or improve it. If the owner refuses, the government can purchase it. This would allow municipal governments to force development on vacant lands held for speculative gain.

Both these measures affect large interest groups and face opposition from the powerful urban real estate sector. And by 1979, the fate of this draft law was still not clear.

Colombia

The National Constitution states that 'property is a social function that implies obligation' and that 'private interest must give way to public or social interest' when a conflict arises between the two in a law issued in the public or social interest. This provides the legal basis for both rural and urban land reforms. In rural areas, despite comprehensive legislation, agrarian reforms have not been implemented—as we noted in discussing Colombia's settlement policies in which such reforms figured prominently.

A small élite of rural landowners continues to hold much of the best farmland. In 1970, there were more than 650 000 farms of under 5 hectares which represented less than 5 per cent of the farmland. In contrast, less than 9000 farms of over 500 hectares accounted for more than 40 per cent of all farmland while some 50 000 farms of over 100 hectares accounted for two-thirds of all farmland. The 1960s had not seen land distribution become more equitable although there was a noticeable decline in the number of small farms, no doubt due to urban migration and to peasant farmers becoming agricultural labourers.[56]

The 1961 Law (promising enforcement of a 1936 law) intended to give sharecroppers and tenants more security (or indeed tenure of the land they worked) and expropriate inadequately used land, distributing it to landless peasants. However, expropriation of 'inadequately used' land usually meant only the worst land from the large estates could be expropriated and the state had to pay commercial prices for it. In fact, most of the land distribution took place with public land. A supplementary Agrarian Reform Law in 1968 did little to speed up land distribution, although this was its intention. The failure of these reforms meant continuing invasions of large estates which intensified in the 1970s. Indeed, large rural landowners demanded government guarantees to preserve their property, and in 1973 a law made it more difficult for the state to purchase private land and thus be able to legalize invasions by expropriating the invaded land.

In urban areas, the Constitution's acceptance of property ownership's social function has not led to comprehensive land-use controls. A tax on unearned increment—a direct tax on private land that had benefited from public investment—was approved as law in 1921 to recoup some of the public cost of irrigation and flood control. This was later extended to cover all 'works of public service' and then in 1966 to 'works of public interest'. Legislation on urban subdivision demanded that all land be supplied with infrastructure before being sold. This made urban plots too expensive for low-income groups so speculators illegally subdivided their land and sold it to the low-income sector. A 1978 study by the Institute for Territorial Credit (essentially the national urban housing agency) found that 9 per cent of Colombia's urban population live on these 'pirate' developments.[57] An unofficial estimate suggested that 45 per cent of Bogota's population lived in these or other clandestine developments by the late 1970s. A law in 1968 to suppress these proved politically impossible to implement since it sought to stop the lower-income groups' only housing solution. In 1973, regulatory decrees established more realistic infrastructure standards to tackle this problem. Apart from these, various attempts have been made at urban reforms. One in 1969 sought to make urban property fulfil its social function but it was never passed.

Around 1973, the 'cities within the city' concept for major urban areas was put forward—and then taken up under Lopez Michelson's rule 1975–8. An official document stated quite bluntly that

> the belief in private initiative, so necessary in other areas of the economy, has led in urban issues to the supply of a hardly satisfactory, and in many cases, chaotic, product. Vast extensions of utility networks and buildings are under-used or deteriorating while the urbanization process, guided by the incentive of private profit, proceeds with no control to the confines of the country's most productive agricultural land.[58]

But the public authorities found it difficult to purchase land on the market to implement the new strategy. A capital gains tax on profits made on land sales led to forged selling prices in private transactions, minimizing the 'capital gained' and thus the tax due. If the government was to be the purchaser, no such forging could take place. So the authorities in the shape of new urban development enterprises found there were no sellers when they wanted to buy land needed for public developments. However, an assessment of the tax on unearned increment—or valorization tax—made by the World Bank suggested that it had worked successfully in Colombia's major cities in helping fund needed public works. Although 'it has not significantly altered income disparities and has probably increased the private return on to land development in the cities affected, it seems also to have been instrumental in enlarging the choice and accessibility of lower income groups to jobs and to residential building sites'.[59]

A small and usually underused programme undertaken by the Institute for Territorial Credit is also worth noting. This extends loans and technical assistance to municipalities, individuals or community groups for studies or surveys which help transfer urban plot titles to squatters. This programme will be expanded as part of the programme to improve living conditions for lower income groups in Colombia's smaller cities—which is described later. Some 30 000 households should get titles through this programme during phase 1 of this programme between 1977 and 1981.

Mexico

Mexico was the first nation in Latin America to institutionalize a policy of land redistribution after a revolution. And since 1915, with around 80 million hectares distributed among 2 222 662 *ejidatarios* and the return of 14.4 million hectares of communal land to 272 687 *comuñeros*, it has been one of the Third World's largest land redistributions.[60] Even if Mexico's present pattern of landownership does show a relatively small group of farmers monopolizing much of the best farmland in private hands, the reform reversed a centuries-old process in which 'the *hacienda* gradually gained ascendency and slowly but steadily devoured the village lands and even the villagers themselves'.[61] The Law in 1915 restored the *ejido*, a communal landholding, so that the usually landless peasant got a share in land that had been taken illegally from the village and also land expropriated from adjacent properties. Since that date, successive governments can be characterized by the way they implemented the agrarian reforms. For instance, under Lazaro Cardenas between 1934 and 1940, 18 million hectares were distributed to a million beneficiaries and more than 10 000 *ejido* communities set up. By contrast, the next two administrations saw a rapid drop in the land distribution programme and the rise of private commercial farmers, as Mexican agricultural production grew very rapidly. In fact, new *latifundia* have been formed based on large, productive and prosperous commercial plantations. Echeverria's administration gave priority to agricultural development and *ejido* organization. Between December 1970 and September 1973, more than 7 million hectares of land were distributed among some 100 000 *ejidatorios*. A Federal Law of Agrarian Reform in 1972–3 included a provision granting the *ejido* legal status that allowed it to sign contracts and thus function more effectively as a producing unit.

The *ejido* status also needed clarification in urban areas. Settlements had grown and encroached on *ejido* land. According to the Law, such land could neither be sold nor subdivided. If *ejido* land is to be developed, the public authorities had to buy the land from the *ejidatarios* and compensate them with other plots or with housing and such *ejido* expropriation had to be approved by national government. Perhaps not surprisingly, *ejido* land had been illegally subdivided with both original *ejidatarios* and new settlers living on it. In 1973, a Commission for the Regularization of Land Tenure was set up to clarify the status of settlements on *ejido* land. Regularization meant expropriation and payment of compensation to *ejidatarios* (both in plots and cash) with the rest of the revenue going to FONAFE, a decentralized agency in charge of managing and reinvesting funds the *ejido* communities receive in rural areas, once 10 per cent has been deducted to cover the Commission's administrative expenses.

In 1976, the Constitution was amended to give the nation 'the right to impose on private property the modes determined by public interest'. Furthermore, it stated that

> the needed guidelines will be adopted for the planning of human settlements and the establishment of adequate provisions, uses and reserves for land, water and woods, for the execution of public works and for planning and regulating the creation, preservation, improvement and growth of population centres; for the subdivision of *latifundia* so as to arrange, within the Regulatory Law, the organization and collective utilization of the *ejidos* and communities; for the development of the small agricultural properties under cultivation for the creation of new centres of agricultural population . . ..

This provides the basis for continuing efforts at agrarian reform and at urban land legislation.

The Law of Human Settlements establishes that the public authorities (whether at federal, state or municipal level) should 'dictate the pertaining regulations so that the land, depending on its fitness, water and woods should be used according to the function they have been assigned in the respective plans' and 'regulate the land market and also the real estate market destined for popular housing, which will be done through laws or relevant administrative provisions'. This Law also creates the basis for specific urban development plans to set up reserve areas to accommodate settlements' future growth.

In 1977, discussions began on the draft Urban Development Plan which sought 'to establish the rational and socially productive use of land within the frame of reference of the General Law of Human Settlements' and 'to promote the public property of urban land, so as to improve the capacity of human settlements for assimilating population changes and movements'. Thus, with the Constitutional changes, the new General Law on Human Settlements and the draft National Urban Development Plan, we see considerable consensus on the need for greater public control of the urban land market and land-use for the benefit of society. Even if the draft urban plan does not become law, new national policies increasing public control of urban land-use are likely to come into force.

This new approach is also evident in 'Elements of a National Housing Policy' prepared by the recently created Secretariat for Human Settlements and Public Works. Its proposals include the creation of mechanisms that would guarantee land serving its social functions—especially *ejido*, communal or public land destined for urban uses—and encouraging the optimal use of urban land, discouraging private landowners from leaving their land vacant in urban areas for speculative gains. In addition, two new State Laws show the direction urban land policies seem to be taking. The Law of Urban Development in the State of Mexico establishes the public authorities' right to set up land-use plans. They have the power to prevent artificial land price rises, to block building and development which do not follow the approved plans, to have priority in purchasing real estate destined for uses, reserves and provisions and to authorize the use of state land for social housing and complementary services.

Jalisco State's Law of Human Settlements[62] is more limited in scope. But it does represent a significant step towards increased public control of the urban land market. The public authorities can dictate and adopt policies needed to regulate land speculation 'when this is contrary to social interest through regulating its market price as well as that of real estate for popular housing'. The Law also establishes a tax on 'the increment of value and the specific improvement of the property that are the immediate and direct consequence of the execution of works foreseen by this law'.

Shelter, Infrastructure and Services

Bolivia

There are no detailed studies of Bolivian housing that give, for instance, data on their physical state or on overcrowding. However, a United Nations Team's Report,[63] written after visiting Bolivia, suggested that 19 200 urban houses and 20 700 rural houses were needed annually to meet demographic growth and replace substandard units (urban areas being taken to include all settlements with over 2000 inhabitants). The Report also estimated that 59 per cent of urban households were not connected to public water systems and more than three-quarters were not connected to sewage systems. For settlements of between 2000 and 20 000, the deficit exceeded 90 per cent for both of these. More than 90 per cent of rural households lacked access to public standpoints for water; 98 per cent of rural households were too poor to be able to afford the cheapest 'low cost' unit built by the formal sector. And in urban areas, of the 19 200 needed annually, more than 7000 are for the lowest income groups who cannot afford the cheapest 'low-cost' formal sector-built unit.

A National Housing Institute, set up in the mid-1950s, built only 836 units in eight years. In 1959, it had been given administrative, legal and economic autonomy with funds from a 2 per cent payroll tax from employers. Its role was restricted by the fact that trade unions held part of the funds and that the law required it to absorb 50 per cent of each unit's cost. In 1964 it was replaced by the National Housing Council also funded by the 2 per cent payroll tax and by a 0.7 per cent sales tax on industrial products. With international loans from the Inter-American Development Bank, it completed 7249 units in nine years, that is just over 800 a year between 1964 and 1973. However, since 1970, political pressures caused the public housing programme to be divided with separate housing councils for each trade union sector and this made it far more difficult to achieve a coordinated national housing policy.

Between 1973 and 1974, several changes aimed at a more coherent policy. The Ministry of Housing and Urban Planning was made responsible for formulating and controlling national housing policy. In 1974, the Housing and Construction Bank was set up to try and overcome the compartmentalization brought about by separate housing councils. This bank was to promote and finance the construction, repair and expansion of houses, the construction of basic infrastructure and the modernization of the building industry. The National Housing Council was allowed to extend its efforts to help those who made no direct contribution to its funds (for example, those not formally employed and thus not subject to the payroll tax) and to implement programmes for those living in peripheral marginal settlements. The aim was to more effectively reach lower income groups. In the private sector, the housing finance system is made up by the Central Savings Bank, the National Mortgage Bank, the

Mutual Saving and Housing Loan Associations and the commercial banks. Naturally, these served the income groups that could afford to pay market rates for housing loans. In the mid-70s, Mutual Saving and Loan Associations were attracting savings by offering depositors 10 per cent annual interest. They were granting housing loans at 12 per cent annual interest (plus a charge for insurance). The Central Savings Bank guarantees these Associations' loans and oversees their operations. By the end of 1976, they had more than 40 000 depositors but had granted only 4032 loans. The National Mortgage Bank and the commercial banks also give housing loans.

Between 1970 and 1975, the housing councils loaned and invested some $19 million in the construction of 6459 units. But—as in previous programmes between 1964 and 1969—this only met the needs of comparatively well-off households. When added to the private sector's contribution, the formal sector met only a few per cent of the 39 900 units needed annually. Housing programmes did not reach the lowest income groups in peripheral squatter settlements. They did not tackle the problems of deteriorating slums in the older cities. And they did not seek to improve housing standards and provide potable water and sanitary removal of human and household wastes although this would do much to alleviate the continuous ill-health suffered by the rural population. The 1976–80 Plan for Social and Economic Development does state that the 'actions concerning housing during the five-year period are . . . oriented to improving living conditions by providing or improving the related services (such as water, sewerage, electricity and others) and to reducing the housing deficit by giving special attention to the needs of the lowest income sectors of the population'.[64] This will not be achieved unless government programmes focus on the low income group's real needs and accept their very limited financial resources.

Building Industry

The informal sector produces virtually all rural housing and most urban housing. The formal construction industry is far less developed than in the three other Latin American nations studied here. The country produces cement, bricks, adobe blocks and wood components but must import material such as steel, aluminium, asbestos and pipes. The need to import many building materials pushes up their costs and very often delays construction operations. But for much of the imported material, lower cost substitutes based on local resources could be developed.

Brazil

In the early 1960s, when the sheer scale of Brazil's housing problem began to be recognized, various estimates sought to quantify the existing deficit and future needs both through replacement of deficient stock and provision for new households. Estimates suggested that between 8 and 11 million units would have to be built between 1960 and 1975 to give every family a house of its own with at least 6 million built for families with less than three basic salaries.[65]

The government's response in 1964 was to set up a National Housing Bank (BNH) to implement an ambitious housing programme by providing loans to lower income groups to purchase houses, and through such a policy to stimulate employment in the construction industry and build substitutes for the *favelas* (squatter settlements). The

Bank became the guarantor and ultimate deposit for funds coming from voluntary savings schemes within the Brazilian Savings and Loan system. These included Savings and Loans Associations and Real Estate Credit Societies. In addition, it initially received Federal Government funding. It then lent to state and municipal housing corporations and private housing cooperatives. Moreover, it provided loans to the building material industry and to contractors for purchase of materials. Lower income groups got preferential interest rates and, initially, a ceiling was set on the cost of a house BNH loans would support. Gama de Andrade points to three innovative features in such a policy.[66] Firstly, the central institution was a bank rather than a popular fund or a social security agency. As such, it must work within the market and not make a loss. Secondly, all loans and depositis were corrected to compensate for inflation which successfully attracted private savings and guaranteed a continuous provision of funds. And thirdly, the intention was to combine public financial support with the private sector who would in most cases build the houses.

Between 1964 and 1971, various changes were made both in the funding and in the institutional arrangements. In 1967, the BNH's funding base was widened very considerably by a new Employment Guarantee Fund[67] through which an employer had to deposit 8 per cent of each employee's salary with the BNH. By 1969, the BNH had become Brazil's second largest bank and the largest institution in the world specifically concerned with housing problems. In 1969, its assets exceeded a billion dollars, and by September 1978, $12 billion. This allowed the BNH to widen the scope of its activities. It began a programme for the Financing of Construction Materials to overcome a bottleneck in their supply and organized the first sanitation programme (FINASA) which in 1970 became PLANASA, the National Sanitation Plan.

Then in 1971, it became a second-line bank to escape continued criticism from house purchasers with BNH mortgages who found it increasingly difficult to maintain loan repayments. Responsibility for collecting repayments and for assessing prospective clients' creditworthiness passed to local financial agents such as municipal and state authorities and private housing cooperatives.

By this point, BNH was clearly failing in its original objective of providing housing for low-income groups. From the very beginning, there were basic contradictions, firstly between attracting private savings and entrepreneurial initiative and building houses for people with very low purchasing power, and secondly between loans and deposits corrected for inflation (essentially benefiting depositers but making it very hard for people with loans) and an economic policy which effectively reduced the basic salary's purchasing power. BNH was meant to serve the 'popular' market for families with incomes between one and three basic salaries, the 'economic' market for families with between three and six basic salaries and the 'middle' market for families with more than six basic salaries. But by the end of 1974, the proportion of loans granted to the 'popular' and 'economic' sector was 18.6 and 20.3 per cent respectively; a total of 38.9 per cent compared to 69.5 per cent in December 1967. The cost-ceiling on units BNH would support was revoked soon after the programme began. And transferring responsibility for repayment collection to intermediaries meant that an even higher proportion of funding was channelled to housing construction for higher-income groups who represented far lower risks for loan repayment. The programme completely bypassed up to half the urban population who earned less than one basic salary and did not have steady jobs. As such, they did not qualify for BNH loans. For instance, in Greater Rio de Janeiro, 37 per cent of the population had monthly incomes lower than one basic salary. In 1973, a considerable portion of BNH-financed mortgage-holders were behind with their payments—or had informally sold their new dwelling. Many of those defaulting on their payments were families forcibly moved to these new estates as their homes in the *favelas* were destroyed. In Rio, many estates reported three-quarters or more of their families behind with their payments.

In 1973–4, attempts were made to reform the housing programme so that it addressed its original social objectives. In 1973, a National Low Cost Housing Plan (PLANHAP) sought to build some 2 million units in ten years for families with an income of one to three basic salaries. In 1974, the basic salary was revalued and new tax allowances were given to house purchasers. Repayment periods on BNH-backed loans were extended to 25 years and interest rates for the popular sector were reduced to 1 per cent a year. PLANHAP was extended to cover families with incomes lower than one basic salary and the BNH provided backing for all state and municipal government investment in this programme. And a new programme, PROFILURB, was introduced to fund serviced urban plot provision both in existing *favelas* and in new sites. By December 1976, the BNH had financed 1 470 061 units but by the middle of 1977, loans to low-income sectors only amounted to 423 616.[68] By 1976, the total number of credits granted through PROFILURB was 9 326. Thus, BNH had stimulated increased urban housing construction and had helped expand employment in the construction sector. But total production had fallen a long way short of the needs outlined in the early 1960s. The programme cannot be judged only by the shortfall in absolute numbers. Ricardo Cortijo commented that 'eleven years after the creation of the housing financing system, workers still have no house and those who believed in the BNH's promises cannot pay their instalments because salaries have not risen in the same proportion as these have'.[69] The innovative housing programme that did away with direct subsidies and adopted a new, technocratic programme in conjunction with private entrepreneurs did not fulfil its social objectives. Indeed, the BNH obtained its funds from compulsory savings from all registered workers and, in effect, used it to support housing for middle and high-income groups, thus increasing social inequalities. Credit favoured the construction industry and, above all, the financial sector. Since it was not accompanied by a public land policy, land speculators and private real estate agents also benefited very considerably. However, public policy has changed recently and the BNH claims that the number of 'problem-making cases' has decreased drastically. But it is still too early for any accurate assessment to be made of the new initiatives.

With regard to sanitation policy, when PLANASA's activities began in 1970–1, out of 60 million urban inhabitants, only 26 million had running water and only 13 million were connected to sewers. By the end of 1976, these services had been extended to 43 and 21 million inhabitants respectively, although the total number of urban inhabitants had grown to more than 70 million. The plan hoped to extend running water to four-fifths and sewage to half the urban population by 1980.[70] However, since the BNH took over this sphere, municipalities have stopped granting subsidies and costs to consumers have increased as rates were adjusted for inflation. Thus, the organizations providing the services had their investment capacity protected while users had to meet ever-increasing bills.

Building Industry

An analysis of Brazil's building industry[71] pointed to the presence of two coexisting levels of technology—industrial and traditional craft—in housing construction. The tendency in urban areas is for the general adoption of industrialized production techniques both in building materials and in construction. This trend has not proved advantageous. The price of housing produced with industrial techniques has been equal or higher than that for housing produced by traditional techniques. The use of capital-intensive techniques has limited employment creation and has increased the pressure on capital resources and on the balance of payments from increased imports of equipment and certain building materials and through payments for royalties from technology transfer. In many cases, imported industrialized housing systems have produced units ill-suited to the local climate and rainfall. In addition, the existence of monopolies and oligopolies in the building industry means that a few large enterprises are in a position to obtain the major building and building material contracts.

We noted earlier that public action through the National Housing Bank to improve housing in urban areas favoured the construction industry and the financial sector. There is still very little government promotion of alternative forms of housing production based on the needs and possibilities of the informal sector, who continue to supply most of the housing built in urban areas and virtually all that built in rural areas.

Colombia

According to official statistics, the quantitative urban housing deficit grew from 87 000 units in 1951 to more than three-quarters of a million in 1974.[72] An unofficial estimate for 1973 yielded comparable figures—a half a million deficit of adequate urban housing or a three-quarter million deficit if lack of basic public services is included in the definition of an adequate house.[73] This deficit is heavily concentrated among the lower-income groups in the five major metropolitan areas which had been the most most rapidly growing urban areas between 1951 and 1973. Close to 70 per cent of Bogota's housing is categorized as substandard and the total deficit for 1977 was an estimated 247 000 units with a yearly growth rate of some 15 000. Housing construction by the formal sector was only some 5000 a year on that same date.[74] By the mid-1970s, a quarter of the urban population was estimated to have no access to public water supplies while more than a half were not connected to sewage systems. In rural areas, more than half the population lack access to protected water supplies.

In 1956, the Institute for Territorial Credit became exclusively concerned with urban housing. In the early 1960s, with funding from the Central Mortgage Bank, the national budget and the Alliance for Progress, its activities expanded considerably. Under the presidency of Restrepo (1966–70) attempts were made to increase funding for housing construction through a new National Savings Fund and an expanding funding base for the Central Mortgage Bank and the Institute for Territorial Credit. In addition, attempts were made to reduce the blocks that a virtually unrestrained urban land market brought to housing and urban development. But the Draft Urban Reform Law was never passed. According to the World Housing Survey 1974, the number of dwellings completed per 1000 inhabitants when measured by the number of permits granted fluctuated between 1.2 and 1.4 for each year between 1966 and 1972 inclusive. Simply to meet annual growth in urban demand would have required five per thousand or more.

Under Pastrana's Presidency (1970–4), another attempt was made to stimulate savings and channel these into housing construction. Savings and loans in private savings and loan associations were adjusted to reflect changes in the cost-of-living index. These then funded private housing corporations who constructed houses for higher-income groups, mostly in the major cities. The Central Mortgage Bank is the whole housing finance system's central agency, selling inflation-proof bonds to saving and loan associations. It also administers the Urban Development Financial Fund which lends money to municipalities through the Institute for Territorial Credit (ICT) and the urban development enterprises. Despite its name (a remnant of its original task of loaning money to improve housing conditions for agricultural workers) the ICT is solely concerned with public urban housing development.

The ICT designs and funds various kinds of public housing project and has become increasingly involved in both serviced-site and house-upgrading schemes. Between 1966 and 1971, it supported an average of some 12 700 units a year. Since then its programme has expanded somewhat with serviced-site and house-improvement programmes beginning in 1972. Between 1972 and 1975, 20 000 or more households were reached by ICT programmes each year with more than 5000 serviced sites being completed by the end of this four-year period. For 1975–6, 25 000 units were constructed through ICT programmes with an additional 42 000 receiving improved public services. But only 10 000 were serviced plots or 'minimum units'. Over 9000 were 'basic' units which served lower-middle-income groups, not the low-income groups who suffer most from inadequate housing and account for most of the housing deficit. In 1976, urban housing needs grew by around 115 000 units, one-third of these being for low income groups.[75] Thus, despite considerable expansion in public housing policies, with more programmes to benefit lower income groups, they were still falling a long way short of growing needs and not even beginning to tackle the accumulated deficit.

After 1976, a new programme was launched to try and raise the living standards of the poorest half of the urban population and to encourage urban migration away from the four principal cities to other urban areas. The 'Programme for the Integration of Services and Community Participation' became a central element of the 1975–8 National Plan for Social and Economic Development. In its first phase, up to 1981, it sought to improve living conditions for some 550 000 people in 23 cities which did not include Bogota, Medellin, Cali and Barranquilla. A new agency, the Popular Integration Secretariat, was set up in 1975 to implement this programme, working with ICT on housing and urban land aspects and with the relevant government agency on health, education, infrastructure and employment creation aspects.

The Colombian government has also shown a commitment to reaching more people with basic services, sanitation and clean water. Universal primary education was the target for 1979. And more support has been given to a primary health care system reaching both rural and urban populations, through a National Health Plan begun in 1975. The Colombian Institute for Family Welfare is extending 'Integrated Child and Family Welfare Centres' to more communities. And the National Municipal Development Agency, charged with the installation and operation of water supply and sewage systems in urban areas, has been extending its activities.

So there is more government action in seeking to improve housing and living conditions for a wider section of the population. More effort is being directed to smaller cities after, for instance, the ICT's activities in the 1960s and early 1970s had been heavily concentrated in the four largest cities.

Building Industry

Virtually all rural housing and a large proportion of urban housing is built by informal sector construction activities. At the top of the formal sector are a few large firms who have in recent years become more involved in real estate promotion with land rents yielding benefits as high as those from building. Most of the buildings firms however are small with low labour productivity and produce units that are beyond the price range of large portions of the urban population. Thus the main housing construction activities in urban areas are in 'pirate' quarters and invasion areas. Indeed, the informal sector's demand for building material is of major importance in the building materials industry.

Mexico

In 1970, an estimate based on census data suggested that there was an absolute housing deficit of 843 000 units with 2.5 million existing units in poor condition and 1.7 million overcrowded. More than a third lacked potable water and more than half were not connected to a sewage system. The absolute housing deficit—which had risen to an estimated 1.5 million units by 1978—was concentrated in urban areas while overcrowding and poor state of repair was as common in rural as in urban areas.[77]

Between 1960 and 1970, the public sector supported the construction of 175 000 units while the private sector built 503 000.[78] Estimates as to the annual average needed between 1970 and 1980 vary from some three-quarters of a million to a million or more. Thus, the number of new units needed annually during the 1970s was higher than the formal sector's total construction efforts for the previous decade.

Housing conditions in Mexico are bad by international standards, especially when compared to nations with comparable per capita incomes. The overcrowding index is one of the highest in the world with an average of 2.6 persons per room in 1970. On that same date, 40 per cent of housing units only had one room and in 1976, an average of 5.6 persons lived in each one-room dwelling.[79] In Mexico City's metropolitan area, half the population live in irregular peripheral settlements with few basic services while 10 to 15 per cent live in overcrowded tenements in the central area.[80] After two decades of intense industrial development, only 2 per cent of the national population lived in houses promoted by the state in 1964.

The first attempt at a national housing policy began in 1963 when a new housing finance system was set up. This sought to attract private funds to finance mortgage credit and thus expand the housing market. FOVI (the Fund for Operation and Banking Discount to Housing) channelled funds from the Federal Government and international loans to credit institutions and private banks to finance housing. FOGA (the Fund for Housing Guarantees and Credit Supports) guaranteed housing loans made by credit institutions, especially those made to low-income groups, and subsidized mortgage loans to borrowers who could not meet the minimum criteria for a standard mortgage. Private banks were allowed to devote 30 per cent of their deposit liabilities to financing housing of 'social interest' and interest rates for mortgages were reduced from 14–15 per cent to 8–9 per cent. An evaluation of these programmes shows that a savings and loans sector did not develop. 85 000 units were built between 1964 and 1970, most of them in Mexico City's metropolitan area.

Attempts at a new approach to the housing problem was one of the elements of the new government's social policy in 1970. Three new funds were set up to expand the financing of housing, based on the Brazilian model. The Institute of the National Housing Fund for Workers (INFONAVIT) created in 1972 drew its funds from a contribution by all employers equal to 5 per cent of their payroll with additional funds from the federal government. Government employees and the armed forces had their own agencies, FOVISTE and FOVIMI respectively. These loaned funds to those wishing to buy or enlarge their houses and thus helped expand the housing market and give it more continuity. According to one study, three-quarters of the INFONAVIT credits went to families with incomes lower than two basic salaries, thus to an income group that does not usually represent effective demand on the housing market. Other institutions such as INDECO (The National Institute for the Development of Rural Communities and Popular Housing) and the National Bank of Public Works and Services also helped to finance housing loans.

These new agencies all helped to ensure the expansion and continuity of funding for housing and brought about a marked increase in the production of government-sponsored units. They also helped create (directly or indirectly) thousands of new jobs by such an expansion. Between 1970 and 1974, 1.2 million units were built, over 200 000 supported by the state.[81] But in fact government efforts favoured the construction industry and owners of real estate. Much of the government-promoted housing was only accessible to middle or lower-middle-income groups who had the purchasing power to represent effective demand on the housing market and a lower risk of loan default.

The vast majority of the population have to solve their own housing problems. In urban areas, this often means on illegally occupied land. The state has not paid sufficient attention to ensuring serviced land is available to accommodate urban expansion. The complications of converting *ejido* and communal land to private urban plots and very rapid urban expansion have both led to illegal occupation of land. In some cases, as in the old reservoir of the Lago de Texcoco, the land is unfit for settlement.

If we compare Mexican housing production for the 1950s, the 1960s and the first four years of the 1970s, we see increasing state and diminishing private sector participation. In fact, the state sector seems to have increased its role only at the expense of the private sector since the informal sector's role has remained at some two-thirds of all housing construction for the whole period. Of estimated housing needs between 1978 and 1982, nearly three-quarters was for families earning less than one basic salary.[82] It is this, the lowest-income group, that has to go on devising its own solution for shelter with little or no help from the public authorities.

Building Industry

For housing construction, it is possible to identify three different scales of operation with different levels of technology. There are a few major enterprises with large fixed capital investments and technical capacities and many small units operating with limited capital and a wide use of labour. Then there is informal sector operations using traditional craft technology and which accounted for close to two-thirds of all housing production between 1950 and 1974,[83] including virtually all rural housing construction.

The growth in labour productivity for the construction industry was the lowest of any economic sector in the 1960s,[84] and its products are not generally within the price range of large portions of the urban population. Present government housing policy shows that the public authorities are aware of the need to improve labour productivity and to support informal construction efforts. There is increased understanding that housing is a process, with individual units improved and extended over time. It is suggested that alternatives to support for the conventional building construction firms should be increased, including the provision of serviced plots and 'foot of house' units (concrete bases with sanitary units) and support for house improvements. The Ministry of Human Settlements and Public Works is conducting a study into the implications of supporting the various types and forms of housing on costs and the use of labour.

Since no policy on construction technology and support for the informal sector has emerged, no final judgement can be made. But such factors as the economic power of the conventional construction industry and the structure of urban land ownership may well hinder the implementation of a programme designed to support progressive housing construction.

Notes

The information in this section is based on *Assessment of the Vancouver Recommendations for National Action* written by our colleagues Oscar Yujnovsky, Ruben Gazzoli and Beatriz Cuenya at the Centro de Estudios Urbanos y Regionales in Buenos Aires, Argentina. A revised version of this was published under the title *Politicas de asentamientos humanos* by Ediciones SIAP in Argentina in 1979. For statistics for which no source is quoted, the reader should refer to the list of general sources in the Introduction and to this volume.

1. Different sources given different figures for Bolivia's national population. This is taken from the 1976 census. However, the World Bank's *World Development Indicators 1980* gives Bolivia's mid-1978 national population as 5.3 million which implies that its population in 1976 was around 5 million.

2. Hardoy, Jorge E. (editor) (1976). *Reforma Agraria y Reforma Urbana en America Latina*, Centro de Estudios Urbanos y Regionales, ITDT, Anexo Estadistico Bolivia, Table number 4.

3. La Paz (1976), Cochabamba (1976) and Santa Cruz (1976) from 1976 Census data supplied by the Bolivian Embassy, London, in 1980.

4. Hardoy, Jorge E, (editor) (1976). *Reforma Agraria y Reforma Urbana en America Latina*, Table 15.

5. There is some uncertainty as to what constitutes an 'urban' settlement for Bolivia. The United Nations Report listed in (6) below talked of an urban population of 1 984 499 in 1976 which encompassed the inhabitants of all centres of 2000 or more inhabitants. This meant 42.6 per cent of the population lived in 'urban' settlements on that date. However, the United Nations in its *Global Review of Human Settlements—Statistical Annex* published in 1976 listed the urban criterion for Bolivia as those living in the cities of La Paz, Oruro, Potosi, Cochabamba, Sucre, Tarija, Santa Cruz, Trinidad and Cobija and in Table 1 gives the percentage of the population living in urban settlements as 37.2 per cent in 1975. *World Development Indicators 1980* (World Bank) gives a figure of 33 per cent for 1980, its data

coming from 'unpublished estimates and projections by the United Nations Population Division, supplemented by data from the World Bank and from various issues of the United Nations *Demographic Yearbook*', although the criteria for defining an 'urban' settlement are not listed.

6. United Nations Habitat and Human Settlement Foundation (1977). *Policies on Human Settlements in Bolivia*, Summary of the Report prepared by a Mission that visited Bolivia in 1976, page 6.

7. Federico, Alberto M. (1978). 'Notas sobre la cuestion regional en Bolivia', paper presented to the seminar on 'La Cuestion Regional en America Latina' in Mexico (April 1978), page 19.

8. United Nations Habitat and Human Settlements Foundation (1977). *Policies on Human Settlements in Bolivia*, page 33.

9. Average growth for agriculture was put at 2.1 per cent for 1962–72 in Hardoy, Jorge E, Editor (1976). *Reforma Agraria y Reforma Urbana en America Latina*, Table 14, while the average for 1970–8 was given as 3.6 per cent a year in *World Development Indicators 1980*.

10. IBGE (1974). *Anuario Estadistico do Brazil.*

11. Bremaeker, Francois E. I. de (1976). 'Tres decadas de urbanizacao no Brasil; 1940–70', Revista de Administracao Municipal No. 134 (January–February 1976), IBAM, Rio de Janeiro.

12. Faria, Vilmar (1976). 'O sistema urbano brasileiro: un resumo das caracteristicas e tendencias recentes', *Estudos CEBRAP* (October–December 1976), São Paulo: Ediciones CEBRAP, pages 91 to 115.

13. These and later statistics on the spatial distribution of economic activities in Brazil from Redwood, John (1975). 'La distribucion espacial del desarrollo economico reciente en Brasil', *Eure*, **IV** (December 1975), no. 12, Universidad Catolica de Chile, Instituto de Planificacion de Desarrollo Urbano y Regional, CIDU–IPU, pages 9 to 51.

14. São Paulo's population— a projection— and Rio's an estimate from United Nations (1976). *Global Review of Human Settlements—Statistical Annex*, Table 6.

15. World Bank (1980). *World Development Indicators.*

16. Batley, Richard (1977). 'Expulsion and exclusion in São Paulo: an overview', paper presented at Conference on Access to Housing, Institute of Development Studies, Sussex (March), page 2.

17. *The Economist* (1976), special supplement on Brazil.

18. Banco de la Republica (1979). *Colombia's Socio-Economic Indicators 1970–78*, Economic Research Department, Table 3 page 13.

19. Arenas Bonilla, Roberto (1977). 'El desarrollo economico y la politica urbana: la experiencia colombiana' in *Revista Interamericana de Planificacion*, **XI,** no. 41 (March), Mexico: SIAP.

20. DANE (1973). 'Censos de Poblacion', quoted in Arenas Bonilla (see note 19), page 104.

21. Mora-Rubio, Rafael (1980). 'Colombian experiment', *Mazingira Magazine*, number 12, 'Habitat for the Poor', page 18.

22. Arenas Bonilla, Roberto (1977). 'El desarrollo economico y la politica urbana: la experiencia colombiana'.

23. In 1979, the United States Census Bureau claimed that Mexico's birth rate had fallen dramatically with population growth rates falling from more than 3 per cent a year in 1975 to around 2.5 per cent in 1979.

24. Unikel, Luis (1976). 'El desarrollo urbano en Mexico: diagnostico e implicancias futuras', El Colegio de Mexico.

25. Wellhausen, Edwin, J. (1976). 'The agriculture of Mexico', *Sci. Amer.* (September), **235,** no. 3, page 130.

26. Unikel, Luis (1976). 'El desarrollo urbano en Mexico: diagnostico e implicancias futuras'.

27. Details of the agrarian reform are discussed under the section on Land in Mexico, page 137.

28. United Nations (1979). *Demographic Yearbook 1978.*

29. These and later statistics on regional urbanization and distribution of population are drawn from Unikel, Luis (1976). 'El desarrollo urbano en Mexico: diagnostico e implicancias futuras'.

30. Lavell, A., Pirez P. and Unikel, L. (1978). 'El estado y la cuestion regional en Mexico', paper presented at a seminar on 'La cuestion regional en America Latina', El Colegio de Mexico.

150

31. World Bank (1980). *World Development Indicators*, Table 24.

32. Federico, Alberto M. (1978). 'Notas sobre la cuestion regional en Bolivia', paper presented at the seminar on 'La cuestion regional en America Latina', El Colegio de Mexico (24–29 April).

33. Bolivia, Republic of (1975). 'Plan de desarrollo economico y social 1976–80' (summary), Ministerio de Planeamiento y Coordinacion, La Paz, Bolivia, pages 29 and 30.

34. Bolivia's government is seeking access to the Pacific coast after losing territory on the coast to Chile in the late nineteenth century.

35. For details of the agrarian reform, see later section on Land in Bolivia (page 133).

36. Lu, Martin (1976). 'II PND. Pode O empresario integrar-se?', *Journal Visao* (**19 April**).

37. Described in more detail under the section on Land (page 134).

38. Gama de Andrade, Luis Aureliano (1976). 'Politica Urbana no Brasil: O paradigma a organizacao e a politica', *Estudos CEBRAP,* **18** (October–November), page 144.

39. Tolosa, Hamilton (1976). 'Debates sobre Desenvolvimento Urbano', in Kacowitz, Mateus (editor), *Desenvolvimento e politica urbana*, Rio de Janeiro: Instituto Brasileiro de Administracao Municipal.

40. Colombia's agrarian reforms are discussed more fully in a later section on its land policies (page 135).

41. These were for the Choco, Quindio and Ubara regions and for a group of three cities—Manizales, Salamina and Aranzazu.

42. Pradilla Cobos, Emilio (1974). 'La Politica urbana del Estado colombiano', *Ideologia y Sociedad,* **9** (January–March), page 51.

43. Departamento Nacional de Planeacion (1975). *Parra Cerrar la Brecha, Plan de Desarrollo Social, Economico y Regional 1975–8,* Colombia, page 97.

44. Information given to us by architect Rafael Machado.

45. *Plan de Accion Inmediata 1962–74* and *Programa de Desarrollo Economico y Social 1966–70.*

46. Carrillo Arronte, Ricardo (1974). 'Las experiencias en la Planificacion Economica de Mexico', *Economia Politica,* **XI,** no. 4 and **XII,** no. 1, 1974–75.

47. The Federal District is Mexico City's central area while the Metropolitan Area encompasses the whole urban agglomeration. In 1970, the Federal District included around 80 per cent of the whole agglomeration's population.

48. Article 27 of the Constitution reported in Centro de Documentacion, Informacion y Estudios del Desarrollo Regional y Urbano (1976), *Asentamientos Humanos*, no. 1 (**November**).

49. Decree-Law 03464.

50. Term dating from Roman times—large estates given out by colonizers after confiscation from conquered communities. The term is widely used in Latin America to describe any large estate.

51. *Colonos* are peasants working the land of others and paying for it with cash and/or a percentage of their crop.

52. Decree–Law 03464, article 109.

53. King, Russell (1977). *Land Reform: A World Survey,* Bell's Advanced Economic Geographies, page 8.

54. Marchezan, Nelson (1977). *Jornal do Brasil* (**7 November**), 1° Cuaderno.

55. Bolaffi, Gabriel (1977). Quoted in a lecture given at the Institute of Development Studies, Sussex (17 March).

56. Araya, Juan Enrique *et al.* (1975). *La politica agraria en Colombia 1950–75*, Fundacion para la Educacion Superior y el Desarrollo.

57. Mora-Rubio, Rafael (1980). 'Colombian experiment', *Mazingira,* **12,** page 18.

58. Sierra, Pedro Javier Soto (1977). 'Transformacion en el sector urbano', VI Congreso Interamerican de Vivienda, Interhabitat 77, Medellin.

59. Doebele, W. and Grimes, O. (1976). 'Valorization charges as a method of financing urban public works: the example of Bogota, Colombia', World Bank working paper, number 254.

60. Cardenas, Cuauhtemoc (1979). 'Los procesos de reforma agraria: el caso Mexicano', *Revista del Mexico Agrario* (**April–June**), XII-2, 101.

61. Whetten, N. (1948). *Rural Mexico*, Chicago University Press, quoted in King, Russell (1977) *Land Reform: A World Survey*.

62. Jalisco State is one of the more urban Mexican states; Guadalajara is its major urban centre and has many towns and cities around it.

63. Ministerio de Urbanismo y Vivienda–Fundacion de las Naciones Unidas para el Habitat y los Asentamientos Humanos (1977). *Informes sobre politica de los asentamientos humanos en Bolivia*, La Paz.

64. United Nations (1977). *Policies on Human Settlements* in Bolivia, United Nations Habitat and Human Settlements Foundation, Summary of the Report prepared by the mission (September), page 2.

65. The basic salary is a sum periodically adjusted by the national government that is meant to represent what an average worker's family could live on. In fact, the cost of living has risen far more rapidly than the 'basic salary' and an average family required two or more basic salaries to meet basic expenses, excluding rent or mortgage payments by 1978.

66. Gama de Andrade, Luis Aureliano (1976). 'Politica urbana no Brasil; o paradigma, a organizacao e a politica', *Estudos CEBRAP*, **18** (October–November–December), pages 117 to 148.

67. Essentially a compulsory savings programme, each registered worker having 8 per cent of his or her salary deposited with the BNH where it is corrected for inflation and collects interest—and can be withdrawn on retirement, illness, unemployment and other specified circumstances.

68. *BNH en Resumo*, number 5, Rio de Janeiro (1977) and Lopes, Helio (1977), 'O BNH e a habitacao popular', BNH.

69. Cortijo, Ricardo (1975). 'Os 11 anose de fracasos de BNH', *Opinão* (**1 August**), page 8.

70. Schulman, Mauricio (1977). 'A politica brasileira de poupanca', *BNH en Resumo*, **6** (March–April).

71. Seelenberger, Sergio H. (1976). *Politicas habitacionais e desenvolvimento*, Instituto Brasileiro de Administracão Municipal, Desenvolvimento e Politica Urbana, Rio de Janeiro: IBAM.

72. DANE (1973). *Boletin Mensual de Estadistica* nos. 262–3 (June), Bogota, page 88.

73. Molina, Humberto, Mondragon, Luz Angela, Reig, Martin and Toro (1977). *El problema de la vivienda en Colombia* research study SIAP–CIID, Bogota.

74. Negret, R. and Azuero, O. (1977). 'Un caso especifico de solucion en Bogota, Colombia', paper presented at the seminar on marginal human settlements, Jalapa, Mexico (September), pages 6 and 7.

75. Low income groups being those with monthly incomes below C$1500 in that year. In 1974, 84.2 per cent of the national urban housing deficit was found by ICT to be among families with monthly incomes below C$1280.

76. Izquierdo, Victor Ramirez (1978). *La vivienda en la politica de empleo*, CIDIU I–3, page 53, Mexico.

77. Covavinbias, Francisco (1978). *La vivienda en el plan nacional de desarrollo urbano*, CIDIU I–2, (July–August), page 49.

78. Garza, Gustavo and Schteingart, Martha (1976). 'La produccion de vivienda en Mexico', *Planificacion*, n. 18, Table 1, page 55.

79. Covavinibias, Francisco (1978). *La vivienda en el plan nacional de desarrollo urbano*, CIDIU I–2, page 50.

80. COPEVI (1977). *Investigacion sobre vivienda. La produccion de vivienda en la Zona Metropolitana de la Ciudad de Mexico, Volume II*, Mexico.

81. Garza, Gustavo and Schteingart, Martha (1976). 'La produccion de vivienda en Mexico', *Planificacion*, no. 18.

82. Covavinbias, Francisco (1978). *La vivienda en el plan nacional de desarrollo urbano*', CIDIU I–2, page 51.

83. Garza, Gustavo and Schteingart, Martha (1976). 'La produccion de vivienda en Mexico', *Planificacion*, no. 18.

84. Romero, Gustavo (1976). 'El papel de la industria de la construccion en la determinacion de la produccion de vivienda', Sociedad Mexicana de Planificacion, *Planificacion*, no. 19 (August).

SECTION IV: SUB-SAHARAN AFRICA

Kenya, Nigeria and Tanzania

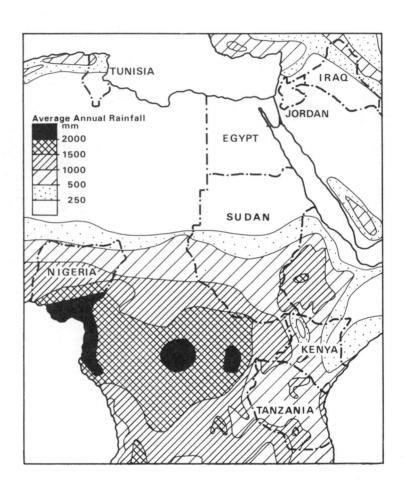

Background

Kenya

Sitting astride the equator on the East African coast, Kenya (like its somewhat larger southern neighbour, Tanzania) had a poor, predominantly rural population. It had 15 million inhabitants in 1978 and with one of the world's most rapid population growth rates 1960–80, the population is likely to double between 1980 and 2000.

Kenya's seven provinces, covering over 583 000 square kilometres, show considerable contrasts in geography, climate and population density. The fertile and intensively cultivated area around the Lake Victoria Basin is in Nyanza and Western Provinces. Although these are Kenya's two smallest provinces covering less than 5 per cent of the national territory, they contain nearly a third of the national population with population densities exceeding 300 persons per square kilometre in higher and better watered areas. The second major population concentration (which contains more than a third of the national population) is in southern central Kenya, including Nairobi and Central Province and is just east of the Rift Valley that runs from Lake Rudolf in the north right through to Tanzania. The Coastal Province has around 9 per cent of Kenya's population and includes Mombasa, Kenya's major port and second largest city which also serves as a major port for landlocked nations such as Uganda and Burundi. The vast Eastern and North-eastern Provinces that make up half the national territory contain only a fifth of the population. Much of this area and the northern half of the Rift Valley Province is arid or semi-arid.

Kenya has a seasonal climate with its rainy season from late March to May. The coast is hot and humid while temperatures are more moderate inland in the southern half due to increasing elevation. Much of the two western provinces and the southern central area is over 1500 metres above sea level. And the major population centres which are in these areas are those with the most favourable rainfall.

Under British rule, Kenya was brought increasingly into the world market with cash crops developed for export and railways extended to serve the major growing areas. Nairobi rose to prominence as East Africa's major commercial and industrial centre. After Independence in 1963, the Kenyan economy developed with rapid and sustained growth in industrial production. Most industry (and indeed agriculture) remains in private hands. Construction and food processing industries grew rapidly in the late 1960s and early 1970s. So too did oil-refining based in Mombasa with crude oil the nation's major import and petroleum products one of its major exports. Tourism has also grown rapidly to more than 400 000 visitors a year to become black Africa's largest tourist industry.

Nairobi with a population of some 959 000 in 1978[1] remains the hub of Kenya's expanding modern sector. In 1977 it contained more than half the nation's wage-

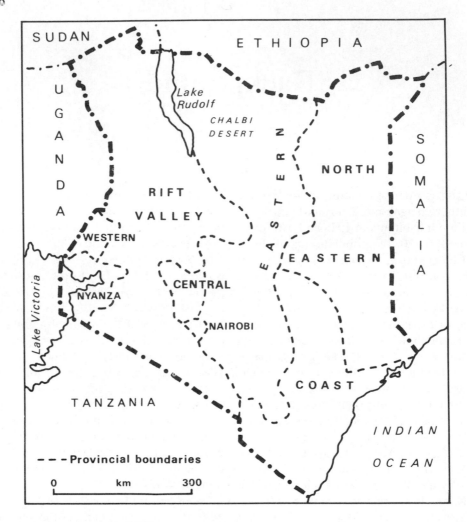

earners and close to half its urban population. Mombasa is Kenya's only other large city, with 401 000 inhabitants in 1978 and around a fifth of the nation's wage-earners. No other urban areas approach these in size and in concentration of industrial and service sector wage employment, although Kisumu with 115 000 inhabitants in 1978 had doubled its population in the previous decade. Meanwhile, Thika, 40 kilometres north east of Nairobi, Nakuru and Eldoret had between 40 000 and 80 000.

Settlements are classified as 'urban' when they have over 2000 residents. In 1978, there were 68 of them, containing 14.3 per cent of the national population. Nine of the largest settlements after Nairobi and Mombasa have been designated municipalities and were 'growth centres' for the 1974–8 Plan. In recent years, urban growth rates have been very rapid, averaging 7.7 per cent a year between 1969 and 1978 and projected to keep on rising by more than 7 per cent between 1978 and 1983. The number of settlements classified as 'urban' is projected to rise to 108 by 1983.

Most of the major towns are in the highlands where Europeans settled and were originally founded as centres of administration and transportation. The only pre-

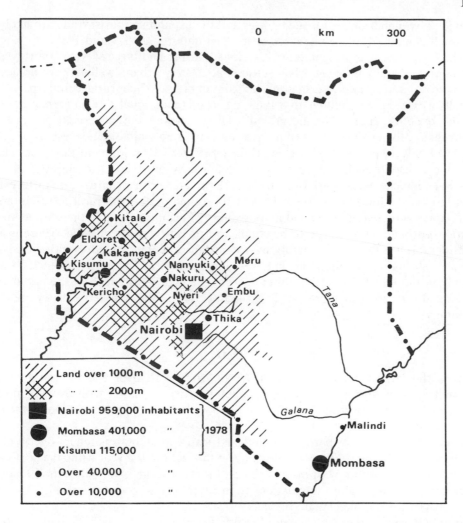

0   km   300

Kitale
Eldoret
Kakamega
Kisumu
Nanyuki   Meru
Nakuru
Kericho   Nyeri   Embu
Thika
Nairobi
Tana
Galana
Malindi
Mombasa

Land over 1000 m
   "   "   2000 m
Nairobi 959,000 inhabitants
Mombasa 401,000   "   } 1978
Kisumu 115,000   "
Over 40,000   "
Over 10,000   "

European urban settlements were Arab trading ports and towns established near or on the coast.

However, the vast majority of Kenya's population—86 per cent in 1980—live in rural areas.[2] The transfer of foreign settlers' land to Kenyans has proceeded peacefully since independence. In some areas, large former European estates have been replaced by smallholdings, although nationally only a small proportion of the rural population has benefited from land redistribution.

A small minority of farmers prosper while the majority still largely depend on subsistence-level farming. In the north and northeast, where the land and climate will not support agriculture, nomadic pastoralists such as the Masai live. Agriculture remains the backbone of the economy and provides the livelihood for some three-quarters of the population. Tea, coffee, fruit and vegetables are major exports with agricultural produce accounting for more than two-thirds of total merchandise exports in 1976. With increasing prices paid for coffee on the world market in this same year, coffee alone accounted for 37 per cent of export earnings. But the boost provided by higher prices for such goods and the expanding tourist trade are likely to be small compared to the increased cost of oil imports in 1979 and 1980.

The government is struggling with serious housing and basic services shortages in the nation's rapidly growing urban settlements. Many urban dwellers have no access to basic sanitation and live in squatter communities. Their rural counterparts are usually worse served. Figures from 1969 suggested that a small élite had received most of the benefits from economic growth. These showed the richest 20 per cent of Kenyans receiving 68 per cent of all income generated while the poorest 40 per cent received only 10 per cent. However, Kenya's 1979–83 Development Plan does claim that these disparities had been reduced significantly by 1976.[3] The majority of very low wage income earners are working for the private sector in agriculture or forestry. The last census found that 70 per cent of those migrating from rural to urban areas were apparently landless and had no possibility of acquiring land in their home areas. Rural-to-urban migrants tend to be young and relatively well-educated. There is also considerable rural-to-rural migration—for instance people forced to move by land-lessness, drought or famine. One in ten rural residents had access to a protected water supply in the mid-1970s. Adult illiteracy remains high. And much of the population outside the richer and more fertile farmlands have little contact with the modern economy.

Nigeria

This is the largest coastal nation in West Africa with over 900 thousand square kilometres. It is also by far the most populous African nation with over 80 million people in 1978.[4] Projections suggest that the population will be 153 million by the end of the century.

Located on the lower part of the great African continental plateau, Nigeria has a tropical climate. The southeast is hot and wet throughout the year while the north and southwest has less rain with distinct dry and rainy seasons. Annual rainfall tends to decrease and temperature fluctuations to increase as one goes further inland. In the far north, a dry steppe climate prevails.

Within Nigeria, there are some 250 ethnic groups, each with its own customs, traditions and language. This great diversity is no doubt linked to the nation's strategic location on transcontinental migration routes. There are three major areas of population concentration: to the southwest, dominated by the Yoruba culture; to the southeast, dominated by the Ibo and Ibibio; and the northern central and western areas, dominated by the Hausa and the Fulani people. In the cocoa-growing region to the southwest, the southeastern region west of the Cross River and parts of the north, population densities exceed 195 persons per square kilometre. Indeed, in parts of this southeastern region, population densities can reach 300 or more persons per square kilometre. These northern and southern population centres are separated by a large · middle belt which is sparsely populated. The northeast is also sparsely populated.

Present Nigeria dates from 1914 when the two British Protectorates of Southern and Northern Nigeria were joined. At that time, the south was a major producer of cash crops while the populous north remained cut off from the export-oriented colonial economy. The gradual extension of railways linked the main northern towns of Kaduna and Kano to Lagos (the capital) in the southwest and to Port Harcourt in

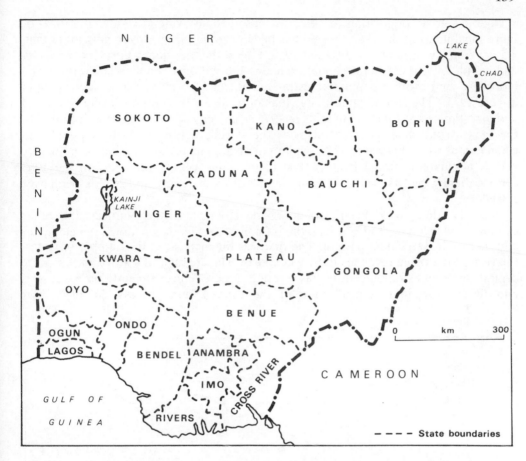

the southeast. In fact, Nigeria's major urban areas such as Ibadan, Lagos, Kano and Onitsha were important traditional urban centres which then developed as centres of commercial activities and for colonial administration. Others, such as Port Harcourt (a major port and railway terminus), Enugu (a coal mining centre) and Kaduna (an administrative and military centre) were developed to serve the colonial economy and administration. In 1960, Nigeria gained independence.

In the mid-70s, three-quarters of Nigeria's population lived in rural areas.[5] Around one-third of the national territory is cultivated, generally in small, scattered land-holdings around small villages. Most rural areas are self-sufficient in food production, although some densely populated rural areas cannot grow enough for themselves, and national production cannot meet the rapidly growing demands of major urban centres. In 1977, 13 per cent of Nigeria's merchandise imports were food. In addition, Nigeria's major cash crops of palm nuts, cocoa and groundnuts have suffered from wildly fluctuating world prices and generally poor returns for the farmers growing them. In 1960, these and the oil derived from the nuts accounted for more than 60 per cent of all export earnings; in 1976, they accounted for less than 5 per cent. During the late 1970s, the government was seeking to reduce food imports through 'Operation Feed the Nation' and through extending the land area under cultivation.

Nigeria's urban population (defined as those people living in centres of 20 000 or more inhabitants in the 1963 census) has been growing rapidly, averaging more than 4.5 per cent a year between 1960 and 1980. Lagos, the traditional Yoruba coastal city and, until 1975, the federal capital, remains the nation's commercial, service and industrial centre with a population estimated at some 3.5 million in its metropolitan area in 1975.[6] The second largest city, Ibadan, is also a traditional Yoruba town and had an estimated 847 000 inhabitants in 1975. Kano city, whose origins as a capital of the Hausa state date back 900 years is the north's major city with a population estimated at some 399 000 in 1975, while Port Harcourt is the southeast's major city with a population estimated at 242 000 in the same year.[7] According to the 1963 census, there were 183 towns with more than 20 000 inhabitants and 24 cities with over 100 000.[8]

Recently, there have been two major developments, one political, the other economic, which have had considerable influence on Nigeria's national development and thus on its settlement pattern. The first was the increase in the number of states, the second the rising revenues from oil exports. The creation of states and thus state capitals as administration centres has resulted in new centres for state bureaucracies and thus a certain decentralization of the urbanization process. In 1956, four

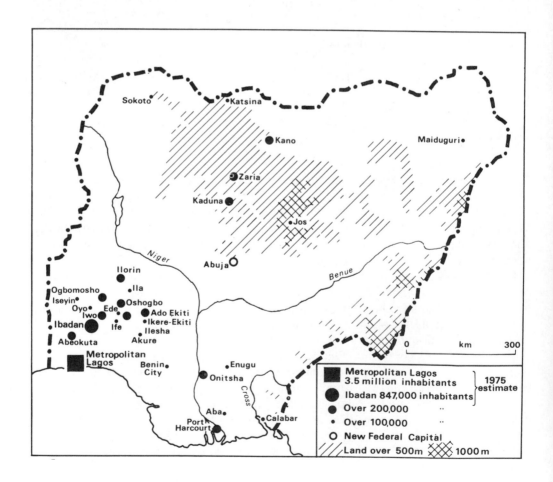

administrative centres covered the whole nation—Lagos (federal), Ibadan (west), Enugu (east) and Kaduna (north). During this period, Lagos dominated commercial activities, drained the rest of the nation of manpower and remained the main port of entry for consumer goods and the main port of exit for cash crops. The other regional administrative centres tended to dominate their region's development and became centres for rapid industrial development. In response to strong political differences between the north, east and west (and the ethnic groups there) which eventually resulted in civil war, the number of states was increased to five, then to twelve and finally, in 1976, to nineteen. The federal capital was moved to Abuja, located in the centre of Nigeria almost equidistant from the original three states. Although Lagos metropolitan area remains the dominant industrial and commercial centre, there are also major manufacturing centres at Kano (Kano State), Jos (Plateau State) Kaduna and Zaria (both Kaduna State) in the north; at Abeokuta (Ogun State) and Ibadan (Oyo State) in the west; at Port Harcourt (Rivers State), Aba (Imo State) and Onitsha (Anambra State) in the southeast; and at Sapele, Warri and Benin City (Bendel State) in the south mid-west. Outside of Lagos, these account for around half the nation's manufacturing activities.[9] Each of these urban centres had more than 60 000 inhabitants in 1971 while all but Sapele, Warri and Jos had more than 120 000.

Since the oil price rise in 1973, Nigeria has enjoyed an economic boom. Oil exports account for more than 90 per cent of total export earnings and have come to provide between three-fifths and four-fifths of the federal government's revenues. These provided capital for investment in industry. The Second Plan (1970–4) saw emphasis placed on expanding light industry while the Third Plan has concentrated more on the development of heavy industry—iron and steel, cement, petrochemicals[10]—and the assembly of automobiles and trucks from imported parts.

But sustained economic and industrial growth (with per capita income rising by an average of 3.6 per cent a year between 1960 and 1978) has not been translated into effective programmes meeting basic needs for the poor majority. There is little data on income distribution but there are wide gaps between earnings in urban and rural centres, between foreign and local personnel and between management and workers. Real income disparities are obscured by the free medical care, subsidized housing and even on occasion, free agricultural produce given to government and quasi-government employees. Clerks will usually earn more than skilled workers. The privileges—and the government reservations with high quality houses in garden city-like surroundings for senior staff—are hangovers from colonial times but still remain strong. There have been some attempts to reduce disparities. Minimum wage levels were raised by 30 to 100 per cent in 1975 and the federal government has recently cut down on car loans and allowances to its employees. Rent control was introduced. There are major differences in average per capita income among cities. Not surprisingly, the highest are found in Port Harcourt (where petroleum industry earnings tend to inflate the average) and in Lagos.

Meanwhile, public authorities have fallen further and further behind with basic infrastructure and services. Nigeria's *National Report* to the Habitat Conference[11] reported that in Kano, Kaduna, Benin and Ibadan, between half and three-quarters of the houses had no piped water while comparatively few were connected to a sewage system. In Lagos, the telephone and electricity systems are constantly breaking down, there are perpetual traffic jams, and the sewage and water supply systems are grossly inadequate. In rural areas, minimal support for rural and agricultural development has simply swelled the flow of rural migrants to urban areas and increased the pressure on their inadequate service base. Many rural areas remain virtually excluded from all social and economic investment with little or no services and infrastructure provided. This helps explain Nigeria's massive food import bill. It also helps explain why average life expectancy in 1978 was only 48.

Tanzania

Bounded by a series of lakes to the west and the Indian Ocean to the east, the United Republic of Tanzania[12] had a population of 17.5 million in 1978 spread over a national territory of 945 000 square kilometres. Projections suggest that by 2000 the population will exceed 30 million.

Population distribution over this vast nation reflects the distribution of rainfall, fertile soil and more moderate climate. Three major areas of high population concentration are around Lake Victoria to the northwest, along the northern border from Arusha to the coast and to the southwest around Mbeya. Here the equatorial climate is moderated by altitude (virtually all inland Tanzania is over 1000 metres above sea level) and by generally adequate rainfall. Population densities on Lake Victoria's southern shores and on the lower slopes of Mount Kilimanjaro to the north range from 100 persons per square kilometre to 200 or more. The coast, hotter and more humid than inland, also has areas of high population densities. And the islands of Zanzibar and Pemba off the northeast coast are densely populated. By contrast, much of the immense plateau that dominates west and central Tanzania has very low population densities due to tsetse fly and lack of water. The Masai Steppe in central-northern Tanzania is also sparsely populated due to lack of water.

In the first half of the twentieth century, Tanganyika was first under German colonial rule and then under British rule after the First World War. It had the poorest natural resource base among the British East African territories and was the least developed under colonial rule. Nairobi (in Kenya) remained the major commercial and industrial colonial centre. However, due perhaps to the unity in its nationalist movement, it became the first to gain independence in 1961, despite being one of the poorest and least developed nations in the world. In 1964, the Sultan of Zanzibar was overthrown, the long Arab dominance of the island ended and the United Republic of Tanzania including Tanganyika, Zanzibar and Pemba was formed.

Tanzania's economic base remains predominantly agricultural. More than four-fifths of the population live in rural areas and agricultural production accounted for 51 per cent of GDP in 1978. Cash crops are Tanzania's major export earners; cotton, coffee, cloves, sisal and tobacco being the major exports in 1976. The main cash crop-producing areas are around Lake Victoria, Mount Kilimanjaro and the Southern Highlands. Cash crops provided some base for industrial development. Food processing industries have developed rapidly since independence and the textile industry is also being developed. Petroleum is a major import with some of the products from its oil-refining process being exported.

Dar es Salaam with some 600 000 people in 1976 is by far the largest urban area. It contained more than two-fifths of all urban formal wage sector employment in 1974,

including half of all urban manufacturing employment. It was the national capital until Dodoma was chosen as the site on which a new capital would be developed. Ministries and other central government offices are slowly being transferred from Dar es Salaam to Dodoma. Dar es Salaam has been growing very rapidly. In 1967, it had only 273 000 inhabitants. By 1981, the population will have exceeded 900 000.[13] Eighteen towns besides Dar es Salaam had more than 20 000 inhabitants in 1976, many originally established as colonial centres of administration with their growth and development being boosted by the coming of the railway.[14] Moshi and Arusha, close to Mount Kilimanjaro, Tanga, on the coast to the north, Mwanza by Lake Victoria and Morogoro, 150 kilometres inland from Dar es Salaam, are the major manufacturing towns. These, along with Dodoma, Mbeya, Iringa and Tabora had between 50 000 and 100 000 people in 1976.[15] All but Iringa and Mbeya are on railways originally built in colonial times. And these two towns are on a new highway linking Dar es Salaam and Zambia while Mbeya is also on the Tazara railway.

Urban areas are growing very rapidly. In 1976, an estimated 12.8 per cent of the population lived in settlements with more than 5000 inhabitants with the annual average growth rate for such settlements averaging a fantastic 11.6 per cent a year between 1967 and 1976. For settlements with 20 000 or more inhabitants, annual average growth rates between 1970 and 1980 were put at 8.3 per cent with 12 per cent

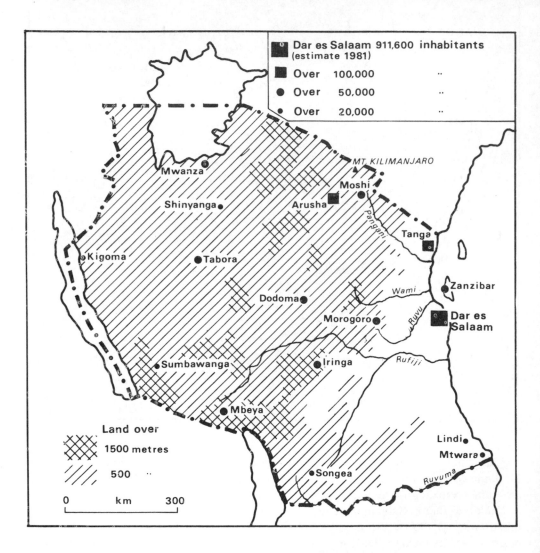

of the national population living in such settlements in 1980.[16] Such growth and the rapid rural-to-urban migration that is its principal cause brought with it considerable problems in terms of shelter, infrastructure and service provision. There was a rapid growth in slums and squatter settlements. Urban areas' economic bases did not grow fast enough to provide sufficient job opportunities for such growth. And the Tanzanian mainland had no strong urban tradition, and hence no established policies and institutions with which to deal with this growth.

Altogether, there are 369 settlements with more than 2500 people and roughly 8000 villages, most of which have between 1000 and 2500 people. Much of the formerly scattered rural population was brought into these villages as part of the villagization programme that began in 1967 and accelerated between 1974 and 1976.

Despite its continuing poverty, small industrial base and lack of resources, Tanzania's development programme has been comparatively successful in reaching a substantial proportion of the population. Considerable progress has been made in spreading adult literacy, primary education and basic health care. Per capita GDP has grown by an average 2.7 per cent a year between 1960 and 1978, although the industrial sector has not managed to sustain the rapid growth rate it achieved in the 1960s. The country remains vulnerable to periodic droughts. One in 1974–5 coincided with oil price rises and low world prices for Tanzania's major agricultural exports and caused an economic crisis. More recently, Tanzania's war against Amin's regime in Uganda and its support for the new government have been a serious drain on the nation's resources. National development policy has been guided since independence by the writings and work of their President, Julius Nyerere.

National Settlement Policies

Kenya

As yet, there is no fully comprehensive settlements policy which covers the whole of Kenya. But since independence in 1963, development plans and programmes have increasingly recognized the importance of linking spatial policy to socioeconomic policy and of the need to build up a planning framework which covers the whole nation but which can include local input and guide local and provincial development planning. In the 1970s, more emphasis has been given to extending basic services to rural areas and to encouraging the growth and development of 'intermediate' urban areas. Both the 1974–8 and the 1979–83 Development Plans include broad policy aims and guidelines for the growth and development of settlements and a commitment to a more equitable spread of basic infrastructure and social services across the nation. But these spatial objectives should be seen as subordinate to socioeconomic goals such as increasing GDP, decreasing income disparities and greatly expanding the wage sector to provide employment for the rapidly growing national labour force and even more rapidly growing urban populations.

The whole of Kenya is covered by physical development plans for the seven provinces and these were incorporated into the 1974–8 Plan. Nine intermediate towns were designated as growth centres to which industry was to be steered and infrastructure and services improved. These were Kisumu, Kakamega, Kitale and Eldoret in the southwest and Thika, Nyeri, Nakuru, Embu and Meru in southern central Kenya, between 40 and 260 kilometres north of Nairobi. In the 1979–83 Plan, greater emphasis will be given to those in southwestern Kenya with Bungoma, Kericho and Kisii added as new growth centres there. Kisumu will get special priority. Machakos some 40 kilometres southeast of Nairobi, is to be added to Thika as a growth centre close to Nairobi to which industrial investment will be steered. Similarly, Malindi, 120 kilometres up the coast from Mombasa, is to be developed to slow the latter's growth. Finally, four new growth centres, Garissa, Isiolo, Kapenguria and Narok are to be developed as 'gateway towns' linking arid and semi-arid areas to more developed regions and their markets. The nine older and nine new growth centres will get priority in funding for social and economic infrastructure and for rural development. Government investment allowances will encourage investment here too, these allowances being based on the number of jobs the new investment creates. Such allowances are not available to new firms setting up in Mombasa and Nairobi. Kenya's *National Report* to Habitat stated that the government 'has pursued a vigorous policy of persuasion and provision of incentives to private developers to locate in smaller centres'[17] but it is not clear how successful this policy has been to date. As we noted earlier, Nairobi and Mombasa between them accounted for nearly three-quarters of the nation's wage earners in 1977.

Both the 1974–8 and the 1979–83 Development Plans outline a National Service Centre Hierarchy through which the government aims to reach 90 per cent of the national population with improved infrastructure and social services. This hierarchy consists of 86 small urban centres (not including the eleven major urban centres), 420 market centres, 1015 local centres and 150 rural centres. Each category aims at a different mix of services and infrastructure to serve the surrounding areas. For instance, an urban centre will probably serve as a local government centre and have a hospital and possibly higher educational institutes to serve a catchment area of between 100 000 and 150 000 people. A market centre would provide a lower level of service for at least 15 000 people and might over time acquire a health centre, secondary school and a post office. The local centre serving at least 5000 people may have a primary school, dispensary and some shops. Through such a hierarchy, the government aims to bring most rural communities into the development process.

The Physical Planning Department of the Ministry of Lands and Settlement is responsible for physical planning and for ensuring settlement policies are reflected in national development plans. Regional plans have been prepared for all seven provinces and a representative from the Physical Planning Department sits on each of the Provincial Development Committees. There are plans to extend the Department's staff down to district level. This would match that of the Ministry of Finance and Planning which has permanent representatives on both provincial and district development committees. These committees are the major planning and implementing bodies for development policies. The Department of Physical Planning also works with the Ministry of Commerce and Industry guiding private and public industrial development to intermediate towns, and is responsible for preparing physical plans for all townships other than Mombasa and Nairobi (which have their own planning departments).

Thus, we see an increasing emphasis on spatial aspects in development policy. The principle of more input from local and regional levels at the planning stage is gaining acceptance. And a 'Strategy on Human Settlements in Kenya' prepared by the Ministry of Lands and Settlement was used in preparing the 1979–83 Development Plan. However, as yet the commitment given to settlements policy in terms of financial support and the trained staff needed for planning and management falls short of need at both national and local levels. Despite district level planning, there is still the tendency to concentrate important planning decisions at national or provincial level. Nairobi and Mombasa continue to get a large proportion of national development funds. And the intermediate towns also receive a disproportionate share, compared to rural areas where most Kenyans live and will continue to live for at least the next few decades. Coordination in planning and implementation is often lacking. An estimated 30 agencies are involved in some aspect of settlement planning in Kenya but their work is not coordinated within a comprehensive strategy. Local government's dependence on central government grants has increased recently as two local revenue sources, graduated personal tax and school fees, were abolished. Central government grants to compensate for these have proved inadequate and local government cannot hope to implement effective development programmes if it lacks the financial base to do so. But it is still very early to give an assessment of Kenya's recent initiatives in moving towards a national settlement policy. Perhaps the success of the 1979–83 Development Plan in meeting its spatial objectives will be the best judge of whether it is effective.

Nigeria

There has been no explicit national settlements policy to guide Nigeria's development over the last 20 years. However, Nigeria's development in colonial times and its political development since independence has produced a relatively decentralized pattern of industrial and urban development. At first, processing plants were built in each region to serve local cash crops: in the north for cotton lint for British textile mills; in the east for palm oil extraction (and later soap factories based on palm oil); in the mid-west for rubber processing and sawing timber; and in the west for hulling rice. Then after independence, regional governments invested their resources in the major regional towns, developing industrial infrastructure there. Private investment (including foreign investment) was attracted to major centres in each region and consumer industries such as beer, cigarettes, shoes and matches grew rapidly in the 1960s and early 1970s. The Third Plan (1975–80) saw a switch of emphasis to heavy industries and consumer durables such as automobile and truck assembly plants. The final location of federally funded industrial development projects is often more influenced by interstate political competition than by conventional, sectoral cost-benefit analyses.

Urban and metropolitan development over the next 50 years is likely to be concentrated around Lagos, the state capitals, Abuja (the new federal capital) and the manufacturing centres mentioned in the Background section. Apart from the Lagos region and associated port and coastal urban centres, major metropolitan concentrations are likely to develop around Port Harcourt and Warri with their strong and viable oil industry on the Niger Delta; around metropolitan Ibadan and other major urban areas close by; around Abuja; and around Kano, Kaduna and Zaria in the north. Intermediate cities may well develop in all the other state capitals but their growth and development will be strongly influenced by whether federal investments continue to aim at balancing the development of all nineteen states.

The Third Development Plan 1975–80 shows an important shift from financial and sectoral planning to regional development based on the states. Its objective is to achieve national economic growth and development along with balanced regional development, and 'to enhance the quality of life for all citizens as development progresses'. The regional distribution of federal investment funds for such sectors as water, housing, community development, sewerage and drainage, and town and country planning does show that backward states are not neglected. The Plan also outlines a strategy for managing urban development, including the establishment of local government machinery both in rural and urban areas. The strategy also emphasizes that state governments should play a more direct role in the new local government system.

A new Ministry of Housing, Urban Development and Environment was set up to initiate and coordinate urban policy (although this was dissolved in 1977 when state governments took over housing programmes). Rural policy sought to boost agricultural productivity and provide basic infrastructure and services. Environmental planning was introduced, with slums, inadequate water supply, lack of sewage and poor waste disposal seen as the most serious problems. Industrial pollution was viewed as a secondary problem, although a National Coordinating Committee on the Environment was established with similar committees at state level to work out environmental policies. Efforts were made to improve interregional transportation and communication facilities with some success. Massive federal funding was given to housing (which had only received serious attention for the first time in 1973). Regional development projects, such as the river basin at Lake Chad in the extreme northeast and Kainji lake in the northwest were started.

However, the Third Plan contains major weaknesses. A detailed study of allocations to town and country planning in two states—Lagos and Kano—has shown an emphasis on urban development in major administrative centres to the virtual exclusion of rural development. Nationally, there are some signs of agricultural production reversing its long stagnation but the policy of encouraging agribusiness is likely to make the small farmer worse off and, no doubt, to hasten the migration of rural poor to urban areas and exacerbate urban problems there. Massive public investment in housing and urban development has driven up the price of all construction materials and helped create endemic inflation. This inflation—especially the increasing cost of food and transport—has hit the poor hardest. And development projects do not seem to benefit the poor living there. Indeed, they often aggravate the poor's living conditions. For much of the development investment reflects the bias of policy-makers and professional consultants which often seem to run counter to what is actually needed. For instance, there has been an overconcentration on improving roads within urban areas but little or no attempt to improve mass transit. In the road-building process, much-needed housing was often demolished. In public housing projects, imported industrial techniques have built houses that are too expensive, even with subsidies, to benefit the lower-income groups. And they in no way relate to the national background rich in both indigenous traditions and urban history.

The Third Plan has provided funds for masterplans for all urban centres. To date, the lack of planning has meant haphazard urban growth and sprawl with very inadequate basic services and communal facilities. Metropolitan Lagos itself has numerous organizations responsible for planning and building but there is very little coordination between them. With the help of UNDP and federal funding, Lagos State has prepared a masterplan for metropolitan Lagos. But here, as in other states, the conflict between city and state authorities inhibits the development of an effective metropolitan-wide planning authority. In Lagos itself, there is the additional problem of conflicts between state and federal levels of government. Local governments—including town and city authorities—lack trained personnel, political initiative and a firm and clearly defined tax base. Different levels of conflict between federal and state governments and between local and state governments over land-use and areas of authority underscore the impotence and ineffectiveness of local councils. Their role is often little more than the provider of a city hall and the maintainer of basic urban services. Perhaps the return to civilian rule will be marked by government response to citizens' demands and needs at all levels of government, a response that was noticeably lacking under military rule.

Tanzania

It is difficult to separate national settlement policy from socioeconomic policy for both work together with the long-term aim of improving the welfare of the entire population and achieving a more balanced distribution of population and development throughout the nation. For rural areas, settlement policy is explicit, based on the policy paper *Socialism and Rural Development* by Julius Nyerere, published in 1967. No single document outlines a national urban development policy but successive five-year plans and ministerial statements have shown some consistency in promoting an urban development strategy.

Villagization is the key to Tanzania's national settlement policy. It aims at the structural transformation of rural society, bringing a generally scattered rural population into villages where basic services can be provided and new economic activities stimulated. Initially, the programme stressed the formation of *ujamaa* villages where agriculture, marketing and other economic activities were to be done collectively. More recently, less emphasis has been placed on collective farming. Estimates vary for the proportion of rural people now living in villages. But certainly the majority of rural people now live in or close to villages. Since independence, rural development has been a central part of Tanzania's national development plans. The hope is that these new villages will provide the means for reaching the rural majority with improved infrastructure and services and increased incomes through more developed and diversified agricultural production and new economic activities. The long-term goal is to slow rural-to-urban migration and promote equitable development throughout the nation.

For urban areas, the primary goals have been to slow Dar es Salaam's growth, to encourage development in nine regional centres to counterbalance its growth and to encourage the development of other small urban centres to serve their rural surrounds. The nine growth centres—Morogoro, Dodoma and Tabora on the railway line running west from Dar es Salaam; Arusha, Moshi and Mwanza in the north; Mbeya to the southwest; and the coastal towns of Tanga to the north and Mtwara to the south—were identified in the second Five-Year Plan (1969–74). Masterplans have been prepared for seven with interim land use plans for the other two. Fiscal incentives sought to attract private and public enterprises there while industrial infrastructure in each was improved. The Small Industries Development Organization, a government organization attached to the Ministry of Industry, has been developing industrial estates in 20 regional centres which include these nine growth centres. In 1978, seven had been completed and several more were underway. This organization also ran training programmes and helped entrepreneurs and local cooperatives set up new enterprises in small- and medium-sized settlements. As we noted earlier, Tanzania's central government is moving from Dar es Salaam to Dodoma. The third Five-Year Plan (1976–81) and long-term industrial policy seek to establish a heavy industry base to support the development of basic consumer goods industries and to promote and develop small and medium-scale industries at regional and district level. The southwest around Mbeya is likely to develop as a major heavy industry centre as local coal and iron ore deposits are worked and a steel industry developed there.

Tanzania has developed an extensive planning system to link local, regional and national planning. Tanzania is divided into 21 regions, each of which are divided into districts. Regional and district authorities are responsible for the detailed planning of towns and villages (guided by national policy) and for implementing them. These authorities come under the Prime Minister's Office which turns all the regional plans into a single plan. This is passed to the Ministry of Finance and Planning[18] which puts in regional budgetary estimates and these, along with other ministerial plans, are submitted to parliament for approval. Parliament then allocates money to both regions and ministries. Two-fifths of the budget and the civil service have been decentralized to the regional level. This has improved both planning and implementation of regional programmes very considerably, including better coordination of economic and physical planning since both come under the Regional Commissioner's Office.[19] The major towns are regional capitals while Dar es Salaam is itself a region and Dodoma has its own Capital Development Authority.

An assessment of Tanzania's settlement policies is difficult in that much of it is aiming at long-term goals. Clearly, a considerable amount reflects the Habitat *Recommendations*, even if many of its policies actually predate the Conference itself. The concentration on developing rural settlements is unusual. Most other Third World governments have given far less attention to the rural sector, despite what are often predominantly rural populations. Basic services have been extended to a large proportion of the villages with efforts continuing to reach those not yet adequately served. However, there is no evidence to suggest that rural-to-urban migration has been slowed. And rural policy must concentrate on consolidating past achievements. In many new villages, especially the larger ones, there is an urgent need for land-use planning to guide their growth and development. Some may need substantial modification since in the rapid villagization programme, their growth and development did not match local water or soil resources. There is also a need to encourage surplus population in densely populated rural areas to move and help develop new areas. Incentives are being given to people in areas such as Kilimanjaro or Bukoba and Ukerewe on Lake Victoria to move to such areas as Tabora, Mpanda and Chunya to the west.

In urban areas, most of the regional centres are growing rapidly. The 1976–81 Plan estimates that Dodoma, Tanga and Arusha will have populations exceeding 100 000 by 1981 (although this may overstate Dodoma's growth rate as economic difficulties have slowed the movement of government offices there). But there are no signs of Dar es Salaam's growth slowing down. Nor is it clear to what extent government run industries are supporting the policy seeking to develop industrial bases in the regional capitals. Dodoma's future as an industrial centre is somewhat uncertain given the lack of local water resources and natural resources. There is a need for a more explicit national settlement policy that more clearly addresses the problems and tradeoffs involved in seeking to decentralize urban and industrial development. But with its concentration on developing rural settlements and on stimulating urban development away from the primate city, the foundation for a national settlement policy is there.

Land

Kenya

Land is held under both traditional tribal concepts and western concepts of private and state ownership. In 1971, more than two-thirds of Kenya's national territory was held in trust, administered by country councils on behalf of tribal peoples. Former crown land has become state land, administered by the Commissioner of Lands. Individuals can lease land from the Commissioner or from country councils. The Commissioner of Lands grants long leases—usually 99 years for urban and 999 years for agricultural land. Private freehold land represented only a tiny proportion of all land in 1971 but this included much of the richest farmland and the best placed urban land. In many urban areas, much of the land is state-owned. For example, large portions of Nairobi are held either by the Commissioner of Lands or by public bodies. But, as in rural areas, private ownership patterns established in colonial times have been transferred to Kenyans. Much of the best-located and thus most valuable land is in private hands and there is considerable land speculation in major urban centres.

In urban areas, national policy tends to give maximum scope to private developers as long as their developments are within prescribed guidelines such as zoning regulations and building codes. Despite the fact that large portions of Nairobi are publicly owned, much of the development takes place on private land. However, public authorities can acquire private land by compulsory purchase in the public interest. This is increasingly used to buy up land on urban peripheries that the expanding urban area will need. The City of Nairobi has recently acquired land to expand the airport and to provide sites for low-cost housing projects. Mombasa's city council has also been active in compulsory purchase operations to provide land for low-cost housing schemes and for public developments such as oil refineries and the airport. Efforts by urban authorities to acquire land well in advance of development and to release inexpensive land to individuals for residential and industrial development has not succeeded in halting widespread land speculation. This has led to high compensation costs for government compulsory land purchases. There have also been cases of public land acquisition programmes hampered by opposition from the landowners and from political leaders.

Control of urban land-use is exercised by local and central government through zoning (regulating densities, plot sizes, types of development etc), by clauses in leases and by building codes. Urban development plans prepared by the Physical Planning Department (except for Mombasa and Nairobi with their own planning departments) include zoning and estimates of future land requirements to guide public land acquisition policies. Three property taxes exist: a site value tax based on the value of the unimproved site; a capital gains tax which applies to all assets; and an estate or death duty tax. However, these taxes have not controlled speculation. To avoid estate tax, land has been subdivided while clandestine land transactions have avoided capital gains tax.

In rural areas, in contrast to Tanzania, the emphasis has been on changing traditional communal tenure patterns into private freehold with the aim of increasing rural incomes through support for individual farms producing cash crops. Rural land policy has had two major components. One has been the settlement of independent African farmers on land formerly farmed by Europeans. The other has been the granting of formal titles to individuals or groups for land previously held under customary tenure. In the very fertile White Highlands, from where African farming was excluded under colonial rule, some 4000 European farmers have been replaced by 200 000 Africans.[20] Although only a small percentage of rural people benefited from this programme, it was implemented in a relatively short time after independence with little disruption to agricultural production. The rural land programme also includes the surveying and mapping of virgin lands with a view to establishing new settlements and extending the area under cultivation and irrigation, and afforestation schemes. Land control boards at district level control all transfers and transactions in non-urban land. They can veto the sale on such grounds as the sale price being too high or the purchaser being foreign.

Thus, public control of landownership and use has been operating with some success for several decades. The public authorities have met with little success in controlling speculation on land in or close to urban areas. Zoning and other land-use regulations are often not enforced. And capital gains tax that should help recapture some of the unearned increment in land values has been reduced recently and is commonly evaded. Rural policies have bypassed most of the poorer families. It would be in the nation's interest to address these deficiencies and to make both rural and urban land policies more effective.

Nigeria

Traditionally, land was owned by the community and held in trust by community leaders and heads of families. Individuals acquired the right to use it and kept that right as long as they met their obligations to family and to society. Anyone might apply to the community head for the right to use a piece of land.

As a result of British colonial rule, land became subject to acquisition in the public interest with compensation paid to the former occupants. Thus, for the first time, land acquired a commercial value. And colonial governors and succeeding governments had the power to acquire land, something that traditional community leaders had not possessed. By the middle 1970s, traditional land law and use rights remained strong except in southern urban areas where land ownership had become mostly private. Such urban land obviously had a very high commercial value and was a good speculative investment in the rapidly growing urban areas. High land values pushed up the price of housing. Speculators bought land on the periphery of cities such as Lagos and Ibadan, subdivided it and then sold the plots for housing. This not only pre-empted infrastructure and service provision; it also created a haphazard and sprawled pattern of city growth. Meanwhile, since basic infrastructure and services were very lacking in many parts of the major urban centres, those few areas which were well served and had easy access to areas of middle-class employment had very high rents.

Government's power to acquire land has had considerable influence on present urban forms. It has helped segregate senior staff in government and in private enterprises in the government reservations originally set up for colonial staff. These usually enjoy a comparatively high standard of services and infrastructure. The power to acquire land has also been used to move those people that stood in the way of new developments. The Gwaris were moved once so that Kaduna could be built and they are now being moved again to make way for the new federal capital, Abuja. Similarly, many people have been moved to make way for the Kainji lake behind the new dam. But despite this power, public authorities in the south have found many urban projects prohibitively expensive because of land costs. A number of important projects in the Second Plan (1970–4) could not take place because of the high compensation demanded by private landowners.

By 1975, it had become clear that government had to find a way of reducing soaring land costs in southern urban areas. Land costs—and the difficulty in acquiring clear title to the land—was also a major block to private development. It was decided that land banks would be set up and compensation procedures streamlined. In 1976, a land panel was set up along with the rent and anti-inflation panels. Then in 1978, the government issued the Land Use Decree, which stated that all land was to be held in 'trust and administered for the use and common benefit of all' under the state governor's authority. Thus it abolished private landownership although private ownership of urban developments (and the right to sell such developments) remained. The Decree established land-use committees in rural and urban areas for the purpose of land allocation. And it stipulated that each individual should have the right to no more than half a hectare of undeveloped urban land in each state. In rural areas, the ceilings were 500 hectares for agriculture, 5000 for grazing and 400 for mining building materials. Building codes and permits and housing regulations were to remain as the major instruments for regulating land-use.

As yet the institutional machinery to effectively enforce this Decree has not emerged. The ceilings on urban plots are comparatively large—and do not limit private holdings of developed urban land. The Decree contained no financial measures such as property taxes although these are much needed. One immediate effect in metropolitan Lagos was to slow down private housing construction (which provides the bulk of all new housing) as the private investors feared their investment in housing would not be safe and because banks refused to accept undeveloped urban land as collateral for their loans. However, in the long run, the government should be able to acquire land more easily and without paying inflated prices. Furthermore, the Decree should reduce speculation and, if implemented effectively, reduce unplanned urban sprawl on the urban peripheries. In rural areas, the ceilings along with recent policy statements and incentives for agribusiness suggest that mechanized farming will increasingly displace traditional rural farmers.

Tanzania

All land in Tanzania is public property. In 1963, freeholds were converted into government leaseholds,[21] and in 1968 all land was nationalized.[22] The state grants right of occupancy to individuals, institutions and enterprises, usually for 33, 66 or 99 years, with conditions attached as to the use to which the land can be put. The Ministry of Lands, Housing and Urban Development oversees land policies although regional land development offices have been given powers to grant rights of occupancy. Thus, individuals have the right to use land for specific periods with this right protected by law. But the state can revoke right of occupancy in the public interest (with compensation paid). For instance, the Capital Development Authority of Dodoma has the power to acquire property on land it needs for the new capital's development. Right of occupancy can also be revoked if the conditions under which it is held are broken.

In rural areas, people may still hold their land under customary land tenure although feudal forms of tenure have been abolished. Plantations are held under rights of occupancies but are gradually being replaced by state farms. Individuals may sell their agricultural produce and can sell the right to farm the land they have been granted—but not the land itself. The state enforces soil erosion control and other conservation measures such as forbidding cultivation on steep slopes and settlement in areas subject to flooding.

In urban areas, land-use changes are controlled by regional urban planning offices. Masterplans guide the growth of the major urban centres. However, squatter communities have appeared around industrial sites and on the edge of towns. Unplanned and often located on unsurveyed land, these settlements are usually inadequately served by basic infrastructure and services. During the 1970s, squatter upgrading programmes (including secure tenure for the squatters) and serviced site schemes have been the main component of Tanzania's urban housing programmes. Public land ownership and control of land-use made these possible without the problems and high costs many public authorities face when trying to provide land for housing low-income groups. A Land Rent and Service Charge equal to 10 per cent of the unimproved land's economic value, is levied annually with the land values being determined (and periodically reassessed) by government valuers. This ensures that unearned increments in land values that accrue to individuals' sites through public developments are recaptured.

Shelter, Infrastructure and Services

Kenya

As the Habitat Conference met, Kenya was in the middle of its 1974–8 Development plan. This aimed at a four-fold increase in urban housing construction over the previous plan period, 1970–4, when approximately 25 000 urban housing units were completed, some 20 000 of which were funded by the government.[23] In the new Plan, the government was to provide 60 000 serviced sites or core houses while the National Housing Corporation was to build some 40 000 two-room units, four-fifths of them for lower income groups. Rural housing was to be left primarily to self-help efforts and the private sector.

There have been new and important initiatives in Kenya's major urban centres in the last decade that sought to increase the rate of housing construction. In Nairobi, the efforts of both public and private sectors have been falling far behind the demands of a city population expanding by some 7 per cent a year.[24] In the early 1970s, the private sector was completing over 1000 units per annum, although this dropped to little more than 500 in 1976 and 1977.[25] The public sector had managed between 600 and 1500 units or serviced sites up to 1977. Combining public and private formal sector efforts, the total never exceeds 3000 units although Nairobi's population was growing by some 60 000 annually and at least 10 000 units were needed annually just to meet this growth. A Housing Development Department has been set up to implement serviced-site and squatter upgrading projects. The Dandora Community Development project[26] implemented between 1975 and 1978 showed that many poor urban households can build their own housing to acceptable standards, pay back loans and meet mortgage payments. This has now been extended to a city-wide programme that aims to provide 17 700 serviced sites and aid the upgrading of some 2050 squatter houses by 1983.

Mombasa and Kisumu have also established Housing Development Departments. In Mombasa, a city growing by some 5 per cent a year, the Housing Development Department aimed to implement serviced-site and squatter upgrading schemes for 3400 households between 1974 and 1978. The National Housing Corporation planned to construct 11 700 units in this same plan period.

However, it seems that achievements fell far short of targets. The 1979–83 Development Plan stated that 'over the last plan period, only 8 per cent of the low cost units planned were in fact completed and these cost on average five times the expected cost. Excessively high and unrealistic standards for building design, occupancy and municipal services were clearly a major contributing factor'.[27] It also seems that the serviced-site programme was falling far behind targets. Between 1975 and 1977, only 1031 had been completed in Nairobi with 815 completed elsewhere.[28] Total urban housing needs were estimated to grow by 160 000 units between 1974 and 1978 and a report in 1975 stated that '50 per cent of these needs will be met satisfied through government funded programmes'.[29] The final achievement was probably no more than 5 per cent.

Thus, despite new government initiatives such as serviced-site and squatter upgrading programmes in Nairobi and Mombasa, housing conditions are continuing to deteriorate. The majority of uncontrolled settlements in Nairobi still lack adequate safe water supplies and basic sanitation. Water shortages are troubling many rapidly growing urban centres. The public authorities have made little attempt to address such basic matters as a revision of building codes, public health regulations and town planning guidelines, many of which still resemble those in force in Europe several decades ago, and are totally inappropriate both to most urban household's resources and to local culture and building material availability. The activities of informal sector operations which remain the main housing provider have often been frustrated by demolition of small-scale businesses and houses on health grounds. Various attempts have been made to review and revise these but with little success to date.

The 1979–83 Development Plan has less ambitious housing targets than its predecessor. During the plan period, the public sector target is for 47 332 low-cost housing units and 28 022 plots, this representing some 24 per cent of the housing units with the remainder provided by 'private agencies and voluntary organizations'. And '90 per cent of all urban development funds allocated for housing through the National Housing Corporation will be used to finance site and service schemes and other forms of low-income housing'. The Development Plan states that all municipalities 'will review their housing standards in order to make them appropriate for the settings to which they will be applied and to reduce them to the minimum consistent with the provision of low-cost housing needs at reasonable cost'.[30]

However, it is by no means certain that public housing units can be constructed at a cost the lower-income households can afford, even if municipalities do enormously reduce public housing standards. And even if targets are met, publicly sponsored projects will meet only a small fraction of urban housing needs.

In rural areas, government programmes in the 1974–8 and 1979–83 Plans concentrate on improving infrastructure and extending basic services to a wider proportion of the population. We noted the National Service Centre Hierarchy under the National Settlement Policy section on Kenya (page 16). Considerable progress has been made in spreading primary education. In 1978, more than 85 per cent of children between 6 and 12 years old were enrolled in primary school. This should increase to over 95 per cent by 1983. A Literacy Survey 1976–7 found reading ability in rural areas limited to 65 per cent of men and 31 per cent of women over 15. A mass literacy campaign is now planned. Medical services and the primary health care network will be expanded; and adequate water supply should be available to the entire population soon after 2000.[31] Mention should also be made of the *harambee* (pull together) movement. *Harambee* projects are self-help projects (which may have the support of government or private organizations) where the local community build or finance such projects as a school, nursery, village polytechnic or even institute of technology.

Building Industry

In Kenyan virtually all rural housing and most urban housing is constructed by informal sector operations. In housing construction, three scales of operation can be identified. Major contracts still tend to be undertaken by a few established Asian or European building contractors. Some of these large firms use industrialized methods of construction. Then there are smaller building contractors who tend to use concrete blocks and other manufactured building materials to build houses based on western designs. These two scales of operation which could be classified as formal sector construction are heavily dependent on imported materials, especially cement and steel, and the rising cost of imported materials has been an important factor in the escalating cost of construction in the 1970s. The cost of building materials essentially doubled between 1972 and 1977. Rising costs led to a slow down in housing construction, especially in the private sector. It has also meant that the price of legal, officially approved houses has been pushed further away from what the majority can afford. The third scale of operation is informal sector operations where construction is usually largely self-help with traditional materials such as mud and wattle.

Official government policy does back increased self-sufficiency in building materials. The National Construction Corporation was set up in 1968 to help Kenyan building firms develop. Under it, the National Construction Company aims to provide management assistance to Kenyan subcontractors and to help develop local building material production. The company has helped small-scale local contractors get contracts and has provided some financial and technical assistance. In addition, the Housing Research and Development Unit at Nairobi University and the Industrial and Commercial Development Corporation have been promoting the development and use of local building materials. The Kenya Bureau of Standards is looking into the revision of standards so they can better meet local requirements and local industry's capabilities. But, as a Kenyan architect points out, 'in his wish to become modernized and noting the contempt with which his tradition's were regarded by the colonial powers, Kenya's African architect or administrator has accepted unreservedly whatever has come from the West and has, up to now, joined his western colleagues in disregarding the local traditional building materials and methods'.[32] Publicly supported housing projects tend to scorn the use of traditional materials and techniques. And official government regulations in municipal areas usually forbid their use.

In fact, there is a wide range of local materials in Kenya well suited to low-cost housing which can be developed into permanent or semi-permanent materials and meet minimum safety and health standards. The Housing Research and Development Unit has shown that soil cement blocks can be produced comparatively cheaply. But, as the Kenyan *Report* points out, 'it is unlikely that officials will allow an easement of the byelaws permitting wide usage of stabilized mud bricks'.[33] Oil companies are reported to be interested in the possibility of using an asphalt emulsion to produce 'asfadobe' blocks. UNICEF's Village Technology Unit is promoting the use of soil-cement blocks through courses for teachers working in rural polytechnics. But the development of local building materials needs more government support both in research and in encouraging their use.

Nigeria

By the mid-1970s, the quantitative urban housing deficit was put at between 840 000 and 1 025 000 units with projections suggesting that 1.6 million or more units would be needed by 1985 to solve the accommodation problem.[34] The last two decades have seen housing deficits growing in every major city. One estimate put the increase in urban housing at less than 2 per cent a year in most cities while urban population growth has been close to 5 per cent a year.[35] A survey from 1970–1 found that nearly three-quarters of Lagos households lived in one room with the average number of persons per room for the whole city being close to four. Meanwhile, Port Harcourt, Warri, Kaduna and Kano had between half and three-quarters of their households living in one room and between one-quarter and three-quarters of their houses lacking piped water.[36] In rapidly growing urban centres such as Lagos, the expansion of water supply lags far behind demand. Many city dwellers have to rely on wells sunk in their backyard while comparatively few urban households are connected to a sewage system. In addition, electricity shortages are very serious with frequent blackouts.

Until the 1970s, there was no government policy at all that sought to help lower-income groups find housing. National policy was essentially the provision of high-quality houses and infrastructure in low-density gardencity type residential areas for the more senior public officials. Such a policy dates from the colonial period when the government reservations were created for colonial staff. But the provision of high-quality houses in exclusive enclaves with subsidized rents for such groups as the armed forces, police, senior civil service and senior staff in public utilities continued after independence. The colonial government also instituted an African Staff Housing Scheme to give loans to Africans to build their own houses. In 1956, the Nigerian Building Society was established to grant loans to senior staff with sufficient credit in their pension entitlements to build their own housing. In the same year, regional governments also began staff housing schemes. Housing corporations or development authorities were set up for the northern, eastern and western regions while one for Lagos had existed since 1929. These built houses or provided sites and services for creditworthy citizens, with considerable subsidy in each unit.[37] Meanwhile, most urban housing was being built by the private sector and then let at very high rent. Thus, two rental markets ran side by side, the private one with very high rents and the public one where upper-income groups paid heavily subsidized rents. Government employees who have been able to build a house with a long-term government low-interest loan usually remain in their government-subsidized house and rent out the house they have built. And private individuals fortunate enough to get a site in a government-serviced neighbourhood through one of the housing authorities often cannot get a loan to construct the house. They therefore turn the site over to a contractor who builds the house, and gets the right to rent this out for five or more years. By the mid-1970s, the public sector was accounting for 20 per cent of housing construction in urban areas—essentially for the upper-income groups and those with influence—and the private sector accounted for the rest. Meanwhile, the poor urban majority received no help either from public or private commercial sources. They lacked the collateral for a loan from the private sector. Either they rented accommodation which cost a high percentage of their total income or they built their own houses in a piecemeal fashion on the urban periphery with few or no basic services and infrastructure, using the informal sector for the skilled work. Inappropriate government slum clearance schemes also exacerbated housing shortages. Over the last 40 years, slum clearance schemes in Lagos have displaced between 250 000 and 300 000 people, and redevelopment rarely provides improved housing for those displaced. Indeed, much of the land (and a lot of public investment) has gone into new roads, bridges and flyovers in the vain hope of improving traffic circulation. Part of the reason for this was the belief that Lagos could be rapidly shaped to become a 'modern' city. But those displaced tended to go to other potential slums. And given very inadequate public transport services, new vehicles rapidly filled any new roads.

In 1971, the federal government changed the Nigerian Building Society into a Federal Mortgage Bank giving housing loans at 3 per cent annual interest for owner-occupier housing and 6 per cent for commercial housing. In addition, in 1973, the federal government announced that it was to build 54 000 units for low and middle-income groups and established a Federal Housing Authority to do so. The first phase was to build 9000 units within 15 months in Kaduna and Lagos for participants of the Second World Black and African Arts Festival. Then in 1975, under the Third Plan, the public housing target was raised to 200 000 for completion by 1980, the houses to be distributed among the (then) 12 state capitals. In 1975 and 1976, rent control regulations were introduced. In 1977, responsibility for most of the National Housing Programme shifted to the 19 state governments;[38] 8000 units were to be built in each state with federal funds financing 4000 of these and infrastructure works for all units. In addition, the Federal Housing Authority would build 50 000 units in Lagos metropolitan area.[39] Private companies with more than 500 employees were required to build houses for their middle-echelon workers. And at state level the decision was made to stop providing highly subsidized urban plots by Lagos's housing corporation.[40]

These policy changes show a new awareness on the part of the federal government that mounting urban housing shortages have to be tackled. The massive public housing programme involves the expenditure of some 2.256 billion *naira* (some $3.5 billion at 1977 exchange rates), 2 billion from federal funds and the rest from state governments.[41] It represents the first major attempt to reach the public (rather than senior government employees) with a major housing programme. But even if the ambitious housing targets are met, they will only make a small impression on growing needs. The five-year target is little more than the annual growth in urban housing needs. And initial reports suggest that the targets are not being met and that the units are beyond the range of low-income families. Despite large government subsidies for the Festival Village housing project, units were still too expensive for low-income groups.[42] A study in Owerri, capital of Imo state, found that the 3000 units planned under the 1975–80 programme represented only a small portion of housing needs and most of these units were to go to higher income groups.[43] The Federal Mortgage Bank's capital base has not been able to cope with the demand for its loans. In June 1979, total applications amounted to 500 million *naira* while its share capital recently raised in the Third Plan was only 150 million *naira*. The policy demanding that large companies provide houses for some of their staff may increase housing construction but will tend to create company-owned housing neighbourhoods similar to the government enclaves.

It is perhaps too early to say whether all the new initiatives described here and under Land (page 174) will improve housing conditions. But the housing policy has not addressed some of the root causes of the present shortages—the high cost of building materials, rates of urban growth boosted by rural policies (or lack of them) and unrealistic housing and planning standards. Most building materials are imported and thus expensive and hard to get. Even locally produced timber and cement are expensive owing to low output, high demand and no price controls. And, no doubt, the announcement of a massive public housing programme served to inflate building material prices still further. Housing standards tend to be too high, given the population's limited financial resources and the high cost of other inputs into housing. Private housing (for which local government approval is mandatory) must conform to the 1937 *Building Codes and Planning Regulations* (last amended in 1947) in most areas. These can demand a minimum number of rooms, the use of expensive imported material or minimum size for rooms which push house prices beyond the means of most urban families. And the various housing corporations and town planning departments tend to emphasize low-density residential developments, especially when the public authorities build the houses themselves. Such a policy can only increase unit costs, infrastructure costs and urban sprawl. Finally, the dilapidated state of so much of the urban housing stock must relate to the dominance of rented accommodation. Now government resources—and those of major companies—are to be invested in housing that these bodies will have to manage and maintain. The enormous investment this represents would have been better spent providing funds for individuals and cooperatives to construct houses for owner-occupiers and to help people improve and extend their houses.

We have noted already the lack of basic services and infrastructure in urban areas. Despite government bias in favour of urban areas, demand continually outstrips supply. In Lagos, sewage continues to be dumped in its lagoon. And only a minority of urban households are connected to sewage systems. In most rural communities, the schools, roads and clinics were provided either by the community's own efforts and resources or by missionaries. The cost of such communal efforts were met by a development levy on those living in the community and on the sons of the community living and working in the urban areas. Between 1960 and 1966, rural community development was encouraged by the civilian regime who provided some financial support. More recently, the government is trying to spread basic facilities for health and education throughout the nation.

Building Industry

Virtually all rural housing and four-fifths of urban housing is built in the private sector. In rural areas, as in most other Third World nations, houses are built using traditional, locally produced materials by the people themselves.

In urban areas, the 20 per cent of houses built by the public sector include those constructed by universities, public corporations such as the National Electric Power Authority and the civil service for their senior staff.[44] The public sector utilizes the larger building concerns, including foreign concerns and some of these are partly state-owned. Of the rest, much of the housing is built by individuals in a piecemeal fashion, gradually purchasing materials as they can afford them. For instance, when an individual has accumulated enough cement, he may hire a local builder to lay the foundation and build the walls. At a later stage, he may employ local artisans to install the plumbing and the wiring.

Up to 80 per cent of the materials in the formal construction sector are imported. In 1978, a report stated that 70 per cent of Nigeria's cement consumption was imported.[45] Heavy demand for modern building materials from government development projects has tended to push up their prices, leading to rapidly increasing construction costs. This is one major reason why the unit costs of public housing projects are so high. And as David Aradeon points out, 'the increasing dependence on systems building and instant package houses with their imported technology and dependence on machinery contributes to rendering the available unskilled manpower redundant'.[46] At least up to the late 1970s, the official view seemed to be that government-backed public housing projects in sufficient quantities would solve the housing problem. Furthermore, official views seemed to be that 'only houses build of sandcrete blocks rendered with sand–cement mixtures and painted both internally and externally, covered with asbestos roofing sheets on an asbestos ceiling, can be regarded as a properly built house'.[47] The result is houses that are usually too expensive for most households (even with a subsidy) and often ill-suited to local climatic conditions.

A more appropriate response to mounting housing problems would be a government policy to stimulate people to build and improve their houses and to ensure that the building materials are available, at a reasonable price, to allow them to do so. This implies a considerable expansion in the use of local resources for building materials, including research into how local resources can be used to produce cheap but durable building materials. Some initial steps have been taken in this direction. The Third Plan (1975–80) backed the manufacture of clay bricks, and efforts are being made to expand timber production and to reforest logged areas.

Tanzania

The government regards the provision of adequate shelter, infrastructure and services to all its people as central both to settlement development and national development. Various new institutions have been set up since independence to tackle urban housing deficits and improving housing conditions in rural areas. A National Housing Corporation was set up to provide housing for low-income families and undertake urban renewal projects. All buildings worth more than 100 000 shillings were nationalized with the Registrar of Buildings set up to manage these and construct houses for higher-income groups. The Tanzania Housing Bank was set up to provide loans for individuals, cooperatives and public corporations. All these work under the Ministry of Lands, Housing and Urban Development which guides their work and formulates national housing policy.

In 1962, the National Housing Corporation was set up to tackle growing urban housing deficits and to improve housing standards throughout the nation. During the first Five-Year Plan 1964–9, its efforts fell far short of expectations. Most of its work was concentrated in Dar es Salaam where around 4700 units were built. But most of these were built as part of slum clearance programmes so the net addition was estimated to be less than 600 a year which did little to alleviate housing problems. Slum clearance schemes were also extended to towns such as Dodoma, Mtwara and Morogoro. Its total programme had aimed at more than 25 000 houses and only 6327 were built.

During the second Five-Year Plan, 1969–74, slum clearance schemes were abandoned and the annual need for urban housing was put at 25 000 houses and 2500 serviced plots a year. The Plan recognized that the housing problem 'cannot be solved in a period of five years'.[48] In these five years, the combined output of the National Housing Corporation and other public bodies was little more than 2000 units a year. Once again, the Corporation's performance was far below expectations, with less than half its target met.[49] And despite its aim of building units for low-income families, the cost of constructing 'minimum standard' housing with prices inflated by expensive imported building materials proved far too costly for low-income groups. The monthly economic rent for a new NHC two-bedroom house was roughly the same as the annual minimum wage. Anything approaching an economic rent would be beyond the means of most urban households. And by now, between 40 and 70 per cent of the population of most urban centres were living in slums or squatter settlements.

The emphasis in urban housing policies then switched to squatter upgrading and to the provision of serviced plots to accommodate new urban dwellers in planned communities. Squatters were given secure tenure and provided with basic infrastructure and services such as piped water, primary schools, community centres, electricity, clinics, and storm drains. Under the first project begun in 1974, 8932 serviced sites were provided in Dar es Salaam, Mwanza and Mbeya. With 8800 existing houses affected by improvements, some 160 000 people benefited. In a second phase begun in 1978, 315 000 low-income urban dwellers should benefit in Dar es Salaam, Morogoro, Tanga, Iringa and Tabora. This aims to reach two-fifths of all existing houses in these settlements and satisfy three-quarters of the need for new plots in these five towns. By the end of the project in 1981, 475 000 people should have benefited. Standards have been kept low compared to western practice. In the second phase, only surveyed plots in residential layouts were provided. But this has kept per capita costs low enough both for relatively low-income households and for the public authorities whose limited resources can reach more low-income households as a result.

The Tanzania Housing Bank[50] was set up in 1972 to promote development and finance projects that were 'economically viable, socially desirable and technically feasible in urban and rural areas of Tanzania'.[51] It gives loans to both rural and urban people, including loans for the purchase of building materials and it has helped to popularize the use of locally produced building materials—for instance, burnt bricks instead of concrete blocks. It loans money to the National Housing Corporation, private individuals, housing cooperatives and various institutions. By 1974, it was providing loans for some 2000 dwellings per year with lower-income groups receiving preferential interest rates. It has increased its role in rural areas. It administers a 'Workers' and Farmers' Fund' which was created by a levy of 2 per cent of the wage bill paid by employers with ten or more employees which concentrates on giving low-cost loans in rural areas with priority given to *ujamaa* villages or housing cooperatives. By 1981, this fund aims to have helped construct 32 200 permanent village houses with a yearly capacity raised to 11 000 by then.[52] The Bank now has offices in each of the 20 regions.

In the late 1970s, the total output of the formal housing sector, which includes the National Housing Corporation, the Registrar of Buildings, the Tanzania Housing Bank, other parastatals building houses for their employees and the small private sector, were constructing some 3000 units a year in urban areas compared to actual urban needs of some 34 000 a year. Thus, self-help builders and the informal sector were accounting for nine out of ten urban houses constructed. The construction of residential units by public bodies has shifted away from Dar es Salaam to other towns with Dodoma receiving special attention.

In rural areas, the commitment to improved infrastructure and services dates back to independence. More recently, a rural housing policy has sought to improve rural housing conditions. We have noted already how the Tanzanian Housing Bank has extended its lending activities to rural areas. One important reason for the restructuring of the administration with more power and resources steered to each region was the disproportionate share that urban areas (especially Dar es Salaam) had received in development funds during the second Five-Year Plan. The Ministry of Lands, Housing and Urban Development and the Prime Minister's Office have launched a campaign to improve rural housing conditions, and this aspect of national policy has been strongly stressed in the third Five-Year Plan. Mobile construction units in each district will offer technical assistance and help organize self-help housing schemes in the villages. By 1980, these rural construction units should exist in most districts.

Tanzania's achievements in providing basic services and infrastructure in rural areas are very considerable. Universal primary education was achieved in 1977. Primary health care facilities are now far more widely available in rural and urban communities. Three-quarters of the national health budget goes to rural health care, very different from the usual pattern of national health budgets dominated by supporting a few major hospitals in larger urban centres. The final goal is a dispensary in every village and a hospital in every district. Targets for 1980 include a dispensary for every 6000 to 8000 people, and a rural health centre for every 50 000 people. Provision of piped water within less then half a kilometre of all consumers is the target for 1991 with intermediate solutions being devised before then. Again the stress is on incremental improvement that match local resources and needs. Major adult literacy programmes have raised adult literacy to one of the highest levels in Africa and a vigorous health education programme has spread knowledge about basic health care. A major programme has improved and upgraded roads linking regions, districts and major agricultural areas. In addition, rural feeder roads have been constructed, usually by the community itself with some government help. Electricity supplies are being extended to more towns and large villages and used chiefly for small industries and community facilities. During the 1977–8 financial year, an additional fifteen small towns were provided with electricity for the first time.

So, after a policy of public housing construction in the 1960s, Tanzania has adopted a more realistic approach to shelter, infrastructure and services. In doing so, it has improved the lives of far more people, although some critics doubt if such ambitious programmes can be maintained, given limited resources and scarce skilled manpower. No clearly defined policy regarding the legalizing of squatter communities has been made but present policy is to legalize squatters' tenure and help them improve their living conditions. Such legalization should be accompanied by appropriate taxes to broaden the settlement's financial base so the provision of services and infrastructure can be maintained and indeed improved. But one notes that many households with housing improvement loans from the Tanzania Housing Bank have been unable to meet loan repayments[53] so care must be taken not to overcommit low-income families and demand too much of them in loan repayments.

Building industry

The formal sector's dependence on imported building materials and construction technology has severely hampered its construction activities. A major factor in the failure of the National Housing Corporation to meet its targets for public housing units (both in number and in unit cost) was the escalating price of building materials. Their high price also hampered informal sector activity in its efforts to build or upgrade houses.

Government policy is to reduce the construction sector's dependence on imported materials, components and technology. The 1976–81 Plan aims to quintuple national cement production in the five-year period[54] and expand the production of many other building materials. Some based on widely available local resources have also been developed. Factories making burnt clay bricks have been set up around the country and their bricks are being used in the construction of houses in both rural and urban areas. The Small Industries Development Organization is helping to set up building material production in regional and district towns. And the Building Research Unit continues to research into the use of indigenous resources for the production of cheap but durable building materials.

Notes

The information on Kenya, Nigeria and Tanzania is based on *Post Habitat Evaluation in Sub-Saharan Africa: Volume 1, Nigeria*, by David Aradeon; *Volume II, Kenya*, by N. Gebremedhin, T. Chana and D. Lamba; and *Volume III, Tanzania*, by G. Mayao and S. M. Kulaba, which were prepared under David Aradeon's direction. For statistics for which no source is quoted, the reader should refer to this work and to the list of general sources in the Introduction.

1. The Kenyan urban statistics presented here are drawn from the Republic of Kenya's *Development Plan 1979–83 Part 1*, Tables 2.3 and 2.4.

2. This figure from the *World Development Indicators 1980* differs somewhat from the figure given in Kenya's *Development Plan 1979–83* which states that 85.1 per cent of the population lived in rural areas in 1978 and this would fall to 82.8 per cent in 1983 (Table 2.4).

3. Morrisson, C. (1972). 'Income distribution in Kenya', paper prepared for the Development Research Centre, World Bank. Kenya, Republic of (1979). *Development Plan 1979–83 Part 1*, page 5.

4. As this went to press, no reliable, up-to-date demographic statistics were available for Nigeria. As Aradeon noted in the report on Nigeria, 'the 1973 census (cancelled in 1975) has been generally regarded as unreliable. Hence demographic studies have been based largely on projections of the 1963 census which reflected the 1952 census. The 1952 census itself has been contested by the South on the grounds that it had been designed to give political control to the North.' Both political power and the allocation of federal revenues to the states relate to state populations so figures have been exaggerated. Thus, all demographic statistics for Nigeria remain estimates. And very often different sources give very different estimates for the same thing.

5. Different sources give very different figures. This is taken from Nigeria's *National Report* to the Habitat Conference (interim version), A/CONF.70/NR/54, 1975, which states that over 25 per cent of the population live in settlements of 20 000 or more inhabitants. *World Development Indicators 1980* puts the figure for 1980 at only 20 per cent. We should also note that the Nigerian urban criterion—that is the population living in settlements with 20 000 or more inhabitants in 1963—makes Nigeria's urban population appear very small since the urban criteria for most other nations ensures they include the population of far smaller settlements.

6. United Nations Development Program/Lagos State Masterplan project.

7. United Nations (1978). '*Demographic Yearbook 1977*' page 256.

186

8. Figures for Kano, Port Harcourt and number of towns and cities from Nigeria's *National Report* to the Habitat Conference (Interim Version), page 3.

9. Aboyade, O. (1968), 'Industrial location and development policy: the Nigerian case', *Nigerian Journal of Economic and Social Studies*, **10**, no. 3.

10. Despite its oil production, Nigeria has to import fuel since Nigerian refineries cannot meet rapidly growing domestic demand.

11. Interim Version.

12. Includes the islands of Zanzibar and Pemba.

13. The third Five-Year Plan for Economic and Social Development, 1976–81, gave Dar es Salaam's projected population for 1981 as 911 600.

14. Mayao, G. and Kulaba, S. M. (1978). *Post-Habitat Evaluation Report on Human Settlements in Tanzania* (Kenya: Mazingira Institute), Table 1.3.

15. Although 1976 estimates put Dodoma's population at some 50 000, Hayuma, A. M. in his paper 'A review and assessment of the contribution of international and bilateral aid to urban development policies in Tanzania', *Ekistics* (**November 1979**), stated that the 1978 census figure for Dodoma was only 45 600.

16. The figures for settlements with more than 5000 inhabitants are from Kubala, S. M. (1977), *National Settlement Analysis and Policy Formulation in Tanzania—Country Report*, (New York: Ad-Hoc Expert Group, United Nations Centre for Housing, Building and Planning), while those for settlements with more than 20 000 are from *World Development Indicators 1980*.

17. Kenya, Republic of (1975). *National Summary Report for Habitat: The UN Conference on Human Settlements*.

18. Early in 1980 it was reported in the *Tanzania Daily News* that this Ministry was to be split with a New Ministry of Planning and Economic Development being formed. As we went to press, no information was available as to how this new institutional arrangement would affect regional planning procedures.

19. Also known as the Regional Party Secretary's Office.

20. King, Russell (1977). *Land Reform; A World Survey*, Bell's Advanced Economic Geographies, page 342.

21. Freeholds Title (Conversion) and Government Leases Act.

22. Customary Lease Hold Enfranchisement Act.

23. Kenya, Republic of (1975). *National Summary Report for Habitat*, page 33.

24. Kenya, Republic of (1979). *Development Plan 1979–83, Part I,* page 48, Table 2.4.

25. Kenya, Republic of (1979). *Statistical Abstract 1978*, Central Bureau of Statistics, page 161, Table 142.

26. In 1975, the Dandora Community Development Project began as a result of earlier recommendations by the Nairobi Urban Study Group with support from the World Bank. The Dandora Community Development Department was then merged with the newly formed Housing Development Department to implement the wider programme, also with the support of the World Bank.

27. Kenya, Republic of (1979). *Development Plan 1979–83, Part I*, page 50.

28. Kenya, Republic of (1979). *Statistical Abstract 1978*, Central Bureau of Statistics, page 163, Table 145(b).

29. Kenya, Republic of (1975). *National Summary Report for Habitat*.

30. Quotes in first half of paragraph from page 107; quote in final sentence from page 50.

31. Statistics on education, literacy and water from Kenya, Republic of (1978). *Development Plan 1979–83, Part I.*

32. Mann, Erica (1978). 'The development of human settlements and architecture in Kenya', Department of Physical Planning, Ministry of Lands and Settlement, Kenya, presented at the 13th International IUA Congress, Mexico City (October 1978).

33. Gebremedhin N., Chana T. and Lamba, D. (1979). *Post-Habitat Evaluation Report on Human Settlements in Kenya* (Nairobi: Mazingira Institute).

34. Romconsult. 'Study concerning a Ten-Year Federal Housing Programme in the 1976–80 Period', prepared for the federal government.

35. Okpala, Donatus C. I. (1978), 'Housing standards: a constraint on urban housing production in Nigeria', *Ekistics* (**June 1978**).

36. Survey by the Federal Office of Statistics made during 1970–71 and quoted in the *Third National Development Plan,* **Volume I,** page 307.

37. The subsidy was hidden since the prepared site and the services were paid for by public funds and not charged to the owner or lessee.

38. The newly created Ministry of Housing, Urban Development and Environment was dissolved in 1977 with the Housing and Urban Development Department going to the Ministry of Works, and Environment going to the Industry Ministry.

39. Osobukola, F. O. (1977). 'Socioeconomic Problems of Low-Cost Housing Scheme in Nigeria', Fourth Conference on Housing in Africa, US AID.

40. Originally called the Lagos Executive Development Board, now called the Lagos State Development and Property Corporation.

41. Nigeria, Federal Republic of, *Third National Development Plan 1975–80 (Revised).*

42. Aradeon, David (1978). 'Regional assessment of human settlements policies in Nigeria', *Habitat International,* **Volume 3,** no. 3/4.

43. Udeogu, J. A. (1978). 'Nigeria's housing policy and its application at local level', *BEI-Bulletin,* **8,** (Netherlands: Bouwcentrum).

44. The relatively small contribution of the public sector to urban housing provision has been true since 1960. It is unclear to what extent the 1975–80 Plan's public housing programme will change this but it is worth recalling that initial reports suggested the targets were not being met.

45. *Business Times,* Nigeria, 18 August 1978.

46. Aradeon, David (1979). *Post Habitat Evaluation Regional Reports on Human Settlements* **Volume I:** *Nigeria,* page 34.

47. Agarwal, Anil (1980). Quote by Kunle Ade Wahab of the University of Ife in *Mud, Mud; The Use of Indigenous Building Materials in the Third World,* Earthscan Briefing Document.

48. Tanzania, Republic of (1969) *Second Five-Year Plan for Economic and Social Development* (Dar es Salaam: Government Printers).

49. Tanzania, Republic of (1976). *The Third Five-Year Plan for Economic and Social Development 1976–81,* **Volume I,** page 75.

50. This took over the assets and liabilities of the Permanent Housing Finance Company of Tanzania which had financed the construction of houses for upper-income groups on a commercial basis. It had originally been set up as the First Permanent Building Society under British Colonial rule.

51. Tanzania Housing Bank (1975). *Reports and Accounts, 1974.*

52. Tanzania, Republic of (1976). *The Third Five-Year Plan for Economic and Social Development, 1976–81,* page 77.

53. *Urban Edge* (1979), **Volume 3,** no. 7.

54. Tanzania, United Republic of (1976). *Third Five-Year Plan for Economic and Social Development,* **Volume 1,** page 70.

SECTION V

Comparative Analysis

Background

Despite enormous diversity among the seventeen nations in such factors as size, population, climate, degree of urban and industrial development, economic growth rates, resource endowments, life expectancy and per capita wealth, there are four important areas where governments are faced with similar or at least comparable circumstances. The first is a settlement pattern still showing the profound influence of colonial rule. The second is the way world economic forces have influenced and moulded the settlement pattern since independence. The third is in current settlement trends—the move to an increasingly urban and non-agricultural society. And the fourth is in current settlement problems, many of which arise from or are linked to this move. Before assessing the seventeen nations' housing, land and settlement policies, we will examine the background to these policies under these four subject-headings: colonial influences, world economic forces, settlement trends and current settlement problems.

Colonial Influences

A nation's settlement pattern—the spatial distribution and relative size of the various metropolitan regions, cities, towns and villages—inevitably reflects its political, social and economic development over time. Clearly, it has been influenced by physical factors with permanent settlements drawn to areas with fertile land, plentiful water resources, temperate and healthy climate, mineral resources and access to building materials. As interregional trade develops, settlements are also drawn to convenient points along transport routes—for instance to natural harbours or to places on the transition between two ecological areas to facilitate trade between them. The history of different settlements' growth, stagnation or decline naturally coincides with the area's economic and political history. Indeed, a study of changing settlement patterns and hierarchies through time within any nation or region provides important and interesting insights into the development both of the economy and of the society.

In looking at the seventeen nations, each with their own unique society, culture and history, one is struck by the fact that all but Nepal have the legacy of an urban system largely implanted and developed under colonial rule.[1] This is as true for East Africa as it is for Latin America, even if the colonial process was three centuries or more apart. In all four of the Third World regions, present economic structure remains profoundly influenced by colonial developments. For Latin America, colonization brought this region into inter-continental trade; for Africa, Asia and the Middle East, where such trade links were centuries old, colonial powers came to expand and then dominate these links. Although such matters of economic history may seem of little immediate relevance when looking at government housing, land and settlement policies (after all Spain and Portugal began colonizing Latin America nearly five centuries ago), settlement patterns established during colonial times have played a major role in defining primate cities and those which have become major regional, industrial or administrative centres. They brought about significant (and often radical) changes in rural–urban linkages and in the distribution of population from precolonial settlement patterns and trends. And they played a major role in defining which regions have been linked to the monetary economy (producing for domestic consumption or for export), and which remain largely outside the monetary economy with a large proportion of their population largely deriving their living from growing subsistence crops or cattle raising.

Settlement patterns, especially the growth and distribution of major cities, reflect economies that grew and developed as exporters of minerals or cash crops. Port cities, developed in colonial times, are very often the largest or second largest cities today: Manila, Jakarta, Rio de Janeiro, Dar es Salaam, Lagos, Mombasa, Alexandria, Port Sudan, Tunis and the city of Singapore. Calcutta, Bombay and Madras, India's first, second and fourth largest urban areas, were the major colonial ports.

In Latin America, the Spanish and Portuguese conquerors founded trading posts on the coast and settlements inland to secure control of territory and facilitate resource exploitation. Where the colonizers came up against advanced urban cultures, they also formed settlements to utilize the indigenous peoples' labour. Thus we see early Spanish towns developing in the interior close to population centres of the Aztecs in Mexico, the Incas in Peru and in the highlands of Bolivia and the Chibchas in Colombia. Most of Latin America's principal cities and ports were founded between 1530 and 1600, including La Paz, Cochabamba, Santa Cruz and Potosi in Bolivia; Bogota, Cali and Cartagena in Colombia; São Paulo, Rio de Janeiro, Recife, Salvador and Santos in Brazil; and Mexico City, Puebla, Guadalajara, Monterrey and Veracruz in Mexico. Although urban populations as percentages of national populations remained low, the population of ports and administration centres generally grew steadily under colonial rule while those of mining centres varied as the profitability of mining operations rose or fell. Thus, the major settlements grew and developed only because they benefited (directly or indirectly) from trade links with the colonial powers and as administrative/political/military centres.

Among the five Asian nations, Singapore owes it foundation in 1819 and its subsequent development as a port and entrepôt centre to colonial rule. In India, the British East India Company founded trading posts in Calcutta, Bombay and Madras in the seventeenth century. Their regional (and national) primacy was reinforced by their role as major colonial ports and centres on the railway system. Under British rule, many millions of formerly self-sufficient peasants were brought into the export market and thus into reliance on fluctuating world market prices for their livelihood. Industrial development was either suppressed or strictly controlled. In both Indonesia and the Philippines, the economies were developed by Western powers to serve their primary produce needs. Both Jakarta and Manila were developed as early colonial ports and trading posts. India and the Philippines still rely on the export of cash crops developed under colonial rule for a considerable portion of their export earnings. So too would Indonesia if it did not have oil as its major export. And in all three nations, a large proportion of the national population depend on earnings from cash crop production for their livelihood.

In Sub-Saharan Africa, there are important parallels with regard to how and why major settlements developed, even though colonization of the interior took place much later and the mode of colonization and treatment of the native population was very different. Initial European trading posts were established as early as the mid-fifteenth century. But until the nineteenth century, they nearly always remained only on the coast to facilitate either the export of slaves or of ivory and precious metals. Lagos in Nigeria, for example, emerged as a major settlement through its role as a slave trade centre. Then, when the European powers partitioned Africa, economic development took place in those regions that became involved in the export of primary produce back to Europe. Mombasa in Kenya, Dar es Salaam in Tanzania and Lagos and Port Harcourt in Nigeria developed as colonial ports. In Nigeria, the railways were developed in the last few years of the nineteenth century and the early twentieth century to bring cash crops and minerals to Lagos and Port Harcourt for export. In Kenya, the line from Mombasa to Kisumu on Lake Victoria built between 1898 and 1902 and later extended into Uganda sought to consolidate British power in Uganda. But then settlement was encouraged close to the railway to help pay for its operation. Nairobi was no more than a convenient waterhole for the new railway. Once the railway was built, however, it became an important settlement as its climate and surrounding land were found to suit agriculture and thus exploitation by European farmers. It also became a provincial capital in 1902 and then a capital for the whole East Africa Protectorate in 1905. Similarly, Dar es Salaam was no more than a small port until it became the capital of German East Africa in 1891 and then the starting point for a railway to exploit rich agricultural areas in the interior in 1907.

There are also important parallels in the five Arab nations included in this study. Although urban civilizations originate in the Middle East, most particularly in Egypt and Iraq, each of the five nations studied still shows the profound effect of colonialism both in economic structure and settlement pattern. The Ottoman Empire's indifference to commercial development allowed western powers to gain considerable rights, concessions and privileges for trading and the exploitation of resources. Much of the region's railway system was developed (and owned) by foreign interests. Although in Tunisia, Egypt and Iraq, major urban centres had existed for centuries (or even millenia) sustained by international trade, the colonial period reinforced the primacy of some centres. Cairo, located at the head of the Nile Delta at a convenient crossing-point, became the centre of the nation's railway system, well located close to fertile land and linking the major cotton-growing areas with the port of Alexandria. In the Sudan, both the capital (Khartoum–Khartoum North–Omdurman) and the major port (Port Sudan) were developed from very small settlements under colonial rule. In Jordan, Amman was little more than a watering place for nomads in the nineteenth century. It was only developed as a city after the British separated Transjordan from western Palestine after the First World War and made Amman the capital.

Thus, the colonial period played a major role in shaping most of the seventeen nations' national economies and the distribution of major settlements over space. But urban settlement patterns established during colonial rule have also exerted powerful influences on subsequent settlement development. Industrial developments were usually drawn to pre-eminent colonial centres since only these had the markets, infrastructure, financial institutions, transport links (both internally and internationally), labour force and government contacts the new industries needed. Obviously, there are exceptions, but major colonial centres usually monopolized much of the industrial and commercial development after independence. We noted earlier how Nairobi contained more than half of Kenya's wage-earners in 1977, how Dar es Salaam had half of Tanzania's urban manufacturing employment in 1974, how São Paulo's metropolitan area encompasses most of Brazil's high productivity manufacturing enterprises, how the Valley of Mexico in which Mexico City is located contained two-fifths of industrial sector and half tertiary sector output in 1970 and how Khartoum Province (in which the capital is located) contained two-thirds of all manufacturing output in 1970–1.[2] The metropolitan areas of Cairo, Amman, Lagos, Manila and Bogota have comparable concentrations of their nation's modern industry and service sector employment.

The concentration of much of the modern industrial and service sector in one or two cities within each nation was, no doubt, reinforced by governments' general concentration on economic growth since the 1950s. Indeed, economists from the industrialized nations advised them to do so, suggesting that the benefits of rapid economic growth would 'trickle down' to encourage development in the peripheral regions and that once a nation achieved economic maturity, differentials in regional per capita incomes that diverged with early developments would then converge.

A second colonial legacy which had profound implications on the way settlements developed was the introduction of new patterns of rural and urban landownership and of new concepts under which land was owned. In rural areas, the imbalance between small percentages of landowners who control much of the best land and the majority with little or no land in nations such as Brazil, Colombia, and the Philippines dates back to colonial times. Rural landownership patterns in nations such as Mexico, Bolivia, Egypt and Tunisia were also profoundly influenced by colonial rule, although efforts have been made in recent decades to lessen the inequalities. Clearly, the pattern of agricultural land ownership profoundly affects the type and volume of economic activities villages or market towns will support. It also has considerable bearing on population growth rates, on migration patterns and on the interest of governments in installing basic services.

The new concepts of private ownership rights over land that colonial rule introduced have generally proved more intractable blocks to housing and settlement policies than in the former colonial powers' own development. In the Philippines, the Americans legalized the essentially feudal landholding pattern, leaving vast landholdings in urban (and incidentally rural) areas in the hands of comparatively few families and institutions. In Indonesia, Kenya, Nigeria and Tunisia (among others), traditional ownership concepts were disrupted by the new stress on individual ownership rights. Ottoman Land Law, traditional law in many parts of SubSaharan Africa, and Indonesian traditional land law had stressed the importance of community rights over land. In Latin America, Portuguese and Spanish rulers alike stressed the rights of private landowners over those of the community.

A third colonial legacy which has continued to influence settlements' development is the mass of building and planning concepts and regulations which were developed in Europe and North America in response to what were (or are) seen as their major settlement problems. Building codes, infrastructure standards and planning legislation in Third World nations may even date from colonial times, especially in Africa or Asia. Or they may be based on European or North American models. This legacy is further reinforced by the fact that Third World professional staff's perception of settlement problems and their response are also powerfully influenced by the 'conventional wisdom' developed in the industrialized nations. Of course, many of their planners, administrators and engineers were trained in the West or in institutions whose curricula were based on those used in the West. And foreign consultants working in the Third World also bring with them a perception of problems and a range of skills and techniques developed in the West in response to settlement problems there. An obvious illustration, evident in many of the national settlements policies examined earlier, is a central concern in national and city plans for improving the road system. What the planners fail to tackle is the fact that the majority of the nation's population still live in poor, ill-serviced houses on inadequate incomes. Another illustration is in building codes and infrastructure standards which bear little relation to the basic needs and resources of the population and the resources available to governments. We will return to this point later. A third illustration is the continual development of masterplans for which little or no legislative base or administrative and financial capacity exists to implement them. An over-preoccupation with growth poles and new towns can be seen in the same light.

Thus, in this very brief summary, it becomes clear that the colonial period has had important and lasting influences on the growth, development and distribution of settlements. Although it would be naïve to blame all Third World settlement problems on colonial legacies, their importance should not be underestimated when examining the way national governments have sought to change their 'geography of development' and control urban land markets.

World Economic Forces

After a Third World nation finally achieves political independence, clearly the international market continues to exert a powerful influence on the national economy. And for all seventeen nations, world economic forces have tended to help maintain and often reinforce the settlement hierarchies first formed during the colonial period.

This is particularly evident in Latin America where Third World nations first achieved political independence. National economies' dependence on the export of primary commodities remained and was further reinforced as demand rose in Europe and then North America for industrial raw materials and for food. This demand, coupled with far cheaper transportation costs, first by sea and then overland because of the railway, allowed the export of a greater variety of cash crops and minerals which had formerly been too expensive to transport to the coast and then ship overseas. These developments also stimulated the import of manufactured goods from the West's rapidly growing industrial sector. The advances in transport technology reinforced the primacy of ports and main railway stations while regional economies often stagnated as their products were undercut by imports. For instance, in Mexico, cities such as Guadalajara and Monterrey were developing independently of Mexico City with Mexico City's growth being comparatively slow for much of the nineteenth century. But with its central place in the railway system and in the nation's finance system, Mexico City's primacy over other urban centres was reinforced as Mexico's economy responded to increased world demand for primary produce.

In addition, ports and strategically placed urban centres became the centres of increasing national and foreign investment in new transport and communications technology and in commercial activities related to the export of primary produce. Many new settlements were founded during this period but these tended to be new administration centres, service and transport centres for areas producing agricultural or mineral goods or tourist centres. Very few have grown into major cities to challenge the dominance of the older established centres. Belo Horizonte and towns along the Mexico–United States border are obvious exceptions.

The older established centres generally became natural centres for industrial development. They had the transportation and communications, infrastructure and banking facilities. If industrial produce was for export, then the factory had to be on major transport routes with good access to the port. If the produce was for internal consumption, the major cities had large, easily accessible consumer markets including a high proportion of the middle and higher-income groups. The Great Depression of the 1930s and the collapse of prices for primary produce exported to Europe spurred industrial development in many Latin American nations, especially those with some industrial infrastructure and an internal market such as Mexico, Brazil and Colombia. The growth of the major cities was swelled by rural migrants, forced off the land by the collapse in primary produce prices, as they had been in (for instance) Brazil, by waves of immigrants some three decades previously.

Among the nations in other continents, all of whom (bar Nepal) only achieved political independence in the last 50 years, there were comparable developments. Industrial and commercial investment was drawn to existing cities for the same reason as in Latin America. And efforts by national governments to change the 'colonial' economic structure and hence colonial settlement patterns have been inhibited by their lack of power in the world market and thus by other economic priorities. Each of these nations has to exist within this market. And attempts to increase their power and earning capacity within this market generally reinforces the concentration of investments and high productivity (and hence higher income) jobs in the richer and more developed regions and settlements.

A priority given by government to increasing the nation's industrial capacity—and on developing the infrastructure and services this needs—will tend to further reinforce the concentration of investment and new jobs in major urban centres. Such a priority involved the import of technology since no nation at Independence had the skilled manpower and the technological base needed to produce and develop their own. Indeed, few have the beginnings of such a base today. Machinery and transport equipment accounted for a third or more of all merchandise imports in 1977 for Kenya, Indonesia, Egypt, Tunisia, Colombia and Jordan while for Nigeria it was close to half and for Iraq it was more than half. Although statistics for 1977 for Tanzania, the Sudan and Nepal were not available, no doubt machinery and transport equipment figure large in their import costs.

In addition, among the seventeen nations, most are partially or totally dependent on the import of oil or oil-derived fuels. In 1977, fuel imports accounted for more than a tenth of total merchandise imports for Tunisia and Tanzania, more than a fifth for Kenya and the Philippines and more than a quarter for India and Singapore. With rapid oil price rises in 1979/80, import costs for oil are likely to have risen faster than export earnings. Estimates for 1980 suggest that roughly half of India's and Tanzania's total import bill is for oil. Only five nations—Iraq, Nigeria, Mexico, Egypt and Indonesia—aren't net importers of oil.

Meanwhile, increasing export earnings has to be a high priority to pay for needed imports. Most of the seventeen nations have serious balance of payments problems and rapidly growing debts. To give only one example, estimates for 1980 suggest that for Brazil, the cost of oil imports and servicing the foreign debt will exceed total export revenues. Yet most of the seventeen nations still rely on the export of primary produce to generate most of their export earnings. In 1977, primary products other than oil or oil-derived fuels accounted for half or more of total merchandise exports in the Philippines, Tunisia, Jordan and Brazil and three-quarters or more in Nepal, Tanzania, Kenya, the Sudan, Colombia and Bolivia. Certainly from the mid-50s to the early 70s, the price of primary commodities on the world market declined relative to the price of manufactured goods. And world prices for many primary commodities have been subject to wild fluctuations which removes the long term economic stability governments need to implement development plans.

Thus, government policies are with good reason oriented towards increasing and diversifying exports. Those with the technological base to do so have sought to increase the contribution of industrial goods to exports. For nations such as India, Egypt, the Philippines, Tunisia, Mexico, Brazil and Singapore, manufactured goods are major export earners, accounting for a quarter or more of total merchandise exports in 1977. But once again, industrial development for the export market will tend to go to the few regions and settlements with the infrastructure to support such development and with good transport links with the international market. So new export industries tend to develop in existing major cities, reinforcing their primacy.

For nations such as Nepal, the Sudan and Tanzania, building or developing industries for export could also mean less dependence on fluctuating world prices for primary produce. Yet this means entering a competitive world market and competing against other nations with advanced industrial infrastructures (and the many major institutions and services a major industrial sector needs) already in place and many decades of industrial development behind them. And it means doing so during a major global recession with increasing protectionism protecting most of the major markets for the kinds of industrial exports they might develop. Inevitably, they have to turn back to increased cash crop exports to earn the foreign exchange to pay for the oil, machinery and transport equipment their economy needs. But this usually means increasing production in the more developed and prosperous regions. These tend to have the fertile soil, water resources and developed infrastructure that is needed to do so. The return they give in terms of increased output per unit of capital invested is far quicker and generally higher than the return from investing in more peripheral regions. Alternatively, mineral production can be increased, again centred on deposits already developed. Unexploited or underexploited resources in the more peripheral regions may have great potential. But the lead time needed to develop them—and the capital too—deters the needed public investment in, for instance, roads and electricity provision when the government urgently needs to increase exports to pay for rapidly rising import costs. So the richer, more developed regions are usually the main beneficiaries of a drive to increase exports.

In addition, continuing dependence on cash crop exports not only helps maintain their lack of power in world markets and their lack of capital for development. It also helps maintain their dependence on food imports. A concentration on increasing cash crop production for export is usually at the expense of increased food production for the home market. In 1977, every one of the seventeen nations we have statistics for except Brazil and Kenya had food representing 10 or more per cent of total merchandise imports. Thus, Nigeria, Tanzania, India, Indonesia, the Philippines, Singapore, Colombia, Mexico, Iraq, Jordan and Tunisia each had food imports in this year representing a tenth or more of total merchandise imports. For Egypt, they represented 23 per cent.

Table 1 Structure of merchandise imports 1977 (percentage shares of merchandise imports)

Countries	Food	Fuels	Other primary commodities	Machinery and transport equipment	Other manufactures
Africa					
Kenya	6	22	4	34	34
Nigeria	13	2	2	47	36
Tanzania*	10	18	5	35	32
Asia					
India	16	26	15	19	24
Indonesia	16	12	5	37	30
Nepal	—	—	—	—	—
Philippines	10	24	7	26	33
Singapore	12	26	9	26	27
Latin America					
Bolivia	—	—	—	—	—
Brazil	7	34	7	26	26
Colombia	12	7	7	38	36
Mexico	13	3	8	45	31
Arab nations					
Egypt	23	2	10	35	30
Iraq	15	—	3	54	28
Jordan	18	9	3	35	35
Sudan	—	—	—	—	—
Tunisia	13	11	7	34	35

Source: World Development Report 1980, World Bank
— Not available
* The figures for Tanzania are for 1976.

Thus, a concentration on building up an industrial sector and on increasing exports—which may well be essential to economic survival—tends to reinforce the existing pattern of economic development over the nation. Here we come across a contradiction which surfaces in many development plans—that the need to concentrate on economic priorities conflicts with stated government goals of spreading economic development more widely and fostering urban and industrial development away from the major centres.

However, although there are very considerable constraints imposed on government action by world market forces and by economies still locked into dependence on primary produce exports, this does not mean that governments remain completely powerless to change their 'geography of development'. Although such constraints limit government action—and here one should note the special difficulties faced by landlocked nations such as Nepal and Bolivia whose lack of access to the sea increases the cost of importing and exporting goods—several among the seventeen nations have effected considerable changes in the spatial spread of development in the last twenty years. These efforts are examined (and assessed) under 'National Settlement Policies'.

Settlement Trends

Of the seventeen nations, all but Singapore experienced rapid growth rates in their urban population between 1960 and 1980. Singapore is the exception only because most of its population is already in the central city and because its size ensures there is very little rural population. All comparisons between the remaining sixteen nations' urban growth rates listed in Table 2 (and indeed between the percentages of their population in rural and urban areas) are open to misinterpretation because of the very different criteria used by each nation to define what constitutes an 'urban' settlement.[3] The reader should refer to the note on 'Statistics and Definitions' in the Background section which discusses why such international comparisons are only of limited validity. But since we have no other statistics to work with—and at least all national 'urban' definitions include all major settlements—the text will draw broad conclusions based on these. For the sixteen nations, annual average urban growth rates exceeded 3 per cent for this period. For Bolivia, Brazil, Mexico, Nigeria and Jordan they exceeded 4 per cent, while in Iraq it exceeded 5 per cent, and in Kenya, Tanzania and the Sudan they exceeded 6 per cent.

Since national population growth rates varied so much, it is worth looking at the differences between annual average urban growth rates and population growth rates. This difference was 1 or more per cent for all nations except Singapore and the Philippines. For Nigeria, Nepal and Iraq it exceeded 2 per cent, while for Kenya, the Sudan and Tanzania it exceeded 3 per cent. The reason the Philippines appears to have a relatively slow rate of urban growth seems to be due to the official criteria by which a settlement is defined as urban not being related to its population size.[4] Certainly for settlements with 10 000 or more people in 1960, annual growth rates between 1960 and 1970 exceeded population growth rates by more than 1 per cent.

Table 2 Urbanization

Countries	Urban population			
	As percentage of total population		Annual average growth (per cent)	
	1960	1980	1960–70	1970–80
Africa				
Kenya	7	14	6.6	6.8
Nigeria	13	20	4.7	4.9
Tanzania	5	12	6.3	8.3
Asia				
India	18	22	3.3	3.3
Indonesia	15	20	3.8	3.6
Nepal	3	5	4.3	4.7

Table 2 *cont.*

Countries	Urban population			
	As percentage of total population		Annual average growth (per cent)	
	1960	1980	1960–70	1970–80
Philippines	30	36	3.9	3.6
Singapore	100	100	2.4	1.5
Latin America				
Bolivia	24	33	4.1	4.3
Brazil	46	65	4.8	4.3
Colombia	48	70	5.2	3.9
Mexico	51	67	4.8	4.5
Arab nations				
Egypt	38	45	3.6	3.0
Iraq	43	72	6.2	5.4
Jordan	43	56	4.5	4.5
Sudan	10	25	6.9	6.8
Tunisia	36	52	3.8	3.8

Source: World Development Report 1980 (World Bank)
Note. Other sources suggest Iraq's percentage of population in urban areas is somewhat lower (see note 8, Section I, page 50) while Nigeria's is somewhat higher (see note 5, Section IV, page 185).

Of the seventeen nations, only Singapore, Iraq and the three richer Latin American nations (Mexico, Brazil and Colombia) had three-fifths or more of their population in urban areas in 1980. India, Kenya, Indonesia, the Sudan, Tanzania and Nigeria had a quarter or less of national population in urban areas on that same date while Nepal had less than a tenth. Clearly, the larger the percentage of population in rural areas, the larger the potential role of rural-to-urban migration as a cause of urban growth.

In all but India, Colombia and Brazil, the largest urban agglomeration contained around one-quarter or more of the entire nation's urban population in the late 1970s. In Nepal, it contained more than half, in Kenya, Egypt and Jordan, it contained around half while in Tunisia, Iraq, Bolivia, the Philippines, Tanzania and Mexico it contained around a third or more.[5] Both India and Brazil are somewhat in a class of their own, being by far the largest among the seventeen nations. Even so, Brazil had more than a quarter of its urban population in two metropolitan areas in the centre-south region, São Paulo and Rio de Janeiro. Colombia's urban pattern is unusual in that its mountainous terrain inhibited interregional transport links so its major cities developed and grew in the different regions where minerals or fertile land could be exploited. But even so, Bogota in 1977 had more than a fifth of the nation's total urban population.

Table 3 The three largest urban agglomerations in each nation

	1950	Most recent figure (mostly estimates)	Projection
Kenya			
Nairobi	135 000	959 000 (1978)	1.895m (1990)
Mombasa	159 000 (1960)	401 000 (1978)	504 000 (1983)
Kisumu	23 526* (1962)	115 000 (1978)	169 000 (1983)

Table 3 *cont.*

	1950	Most recent figure (mostly estimates)	Projection
Nigeria			
Lagos	267 407* (1952)	3.5m (1975)	5.443m (1990)
Ibadan	459 196* (1952)	847 000* (1975)	1.625m (1990)
Kano	127 205* (1952)	399 000* (1975)	—
Tanzania			
Dar es Salaam	148 000* (1960)	600 000* (1976)	911 600* (1981)
Arusha	—	89 000* (1976)	101 900* (1981)
Tanga	—	70 000* (1976)	120 600* (1981)
India			
Calcutta	5.15m	7.03m (1971)	13.7 m (1990)
Bombay	3.34m	5.97m (1971)	13.11m (1990)
Delhi	1.74m	3.65m (1971)	8.96m (1990)
Indonesia			
Jakarta	1.45m*	6.18m (1977)	11.45m (1990)
Surabaja	679 000*	2.27m (1980)	3.46m (1990)
Bandung	511,000*	1.84m (1980)	2.82m (1990)
Nepal			
Kathmandu	121 000	415 000 (1976)	
Biratnagar		45 100* (1971)	
Nepalganj		23 523* (1971)	
Philippines			
Manila	1.78m	7.7m (1980)	10.5m (1990)
Cebu	178 000*	418 517* (1975)	
Davao	124 000	515 520* (1975)	
Singapore			
Singapore	938 000 (1947)	2.33m (1978)	
Bolivia			
La Paz	300 000*	654 713* (1976)	1.13m (1990)
Santa Cruz		255 568* (1976)	
Cochabamba		204 414* (1976)	
Brazil			
São Paulo	2.45m	12.49m (1980)	18.66m (1990)
Rio de Janeiro	3.05m	8.33m (1975)	14.15m (1990)
Belo Horizonte	353 000	2.59m (1980)	4.05m (1990)
Colombia			
Bogota	607 000*	3.5m (1977)	6.84m (1990)
Medellin	341 000*	1.75m (1977)	2.72m (1990)
Cali	269 000*	1.19m (1977)	2.47m (1990)
Mexico			
Mexico City	3.19m	13.99m (1978)	21.63m (1990)
Guadalajara	378 000*	2.34m (1978)	4.17m (1990)
Monterrey	332 000*	1.92m (1978)	3.23m (1990)
Egypt			
Cairo	2.50m	8.5m (1979)	11.98m (1990)
Alexandria	1.04m*	2.32m* (1976)	4.11m (1990)
Mahallah al Kubrah	129 000*	292 853* (1976)	
Iraq			
Baghdad	540 000	2.92m* (1977)	7.45m (1990)

Table 3 *cont.*

	1950	Most recent figure (mostly estimates)	Projection
Mosul	140 000	350 000 (1974)	
Basrah	100 000	423 000 (1974)	
Jordan			
Amman	25 000* (1948)	775 800* (1978)	
Zerqa	106 080* (1961)	282 700* (1978)	
Irbid		146 070* (1978)	
The Sudan			
Khartoum	253 600 (1955/6)	1.05m (1978)	2.5m (1990)
Port Sudan	47 600* (1955/6)	250 000 (1978)	530 000 (1990)
Wad Medani	47 700* (1955/6)	112 000* (1973)	
Tunisia			
Tunis	615 000	925 000 (1975)	1.31m (1986)
Sfax		174 900* (1975)	247 300* (1986)
Sousse		80 500* (1975)	113 800* (1986)

m million
Figures with * are city populations, not urban agglomeration populations.
Virtually all the figures in this table are estimates or projections. The source of each statistic is listed in note (6) at the end of this section. Rather than rely on census information for the most recent figure—which can mean having to give figures for the early Sixties for some nations—we have used estimates drawn from a wide range of sources. In many instances, we found widely differing figures for the same city or urban agglomeration for the same year. When listing the sources for the statistics, mention is made of when the statistic's accuracy is open to question. Furthermore, when giving a city's population, many sources did not specify whether the figures was for the city or the urban agglomeration.

Furthermore, in each of the seventeen nations, between 1950 and the late 1970s (Table 3), the largest urban agglomeration more than doubled its population. Cairo more than tripled its population in this period while the population of Mexico City, Manila, Jakarta, Bogota and the Sudan's three town capital (Khartoum–Khartoum North–Omdurman) more than quadrupled. Meanwhile, São Paulo's and Baghdad's population grew more than five-fold, that of Nairobi, Lagos and Dar es Salaam by more than seven times and Amman more than 20-fold.

No simple generalizations can be made about growth rates for other urban centres, due mainly to a lack of data. In nations such as Kenya, Nigeria, Tanzania, Jordan, the Sudan, Egypt, Indonesia, Colombia, Iraq, Nepal and the Philippines, the largest urban agglomeration remains among the fastest-growing urban settlements. In India, Brazil and Mexico, this is no longer the case. In Brazil, cities such as Fortaleza and Porto Alegre were growing at roughly the same rate as São Paulo and a lot faster than Rio de Janeiro between 1950 and 1980 while Belo Horizonte, Brasilia and Curitiba were growing a lot faster than both. All these Brazilian cities had more than a million inhabitants by 1980. In Mexico, Guadalajara and Monterrey grew faster than Mexico City between 1950 and 1980. And in India, Calcutta was actually one of the slowest growing of the thirteen cities that had more than a million inhabitants in 1980 between 1950 and 1980. But the sheer size of population in Calcutta, São Paulo and Mexico City will ensure that their share of total urban population will only decline slowly, if this trend is sustained. Unfortunately, information on the population and the growth rates of other settlements is too scanty for any generalizations to be possible.

Table 4 Labour-force

| Countries | Percentage of Labour-Force in | | | | | |
| | Agriculture | | Industry | | Services | |
	1960	1978	1960	1978	1960	1978
Africa						
Kenya	86	79	5	8	9	13
Nigeria	71	56	10	17	19	27
Tanzania	89	83	4	6	7	11
Asia						
India	74	74	11	11	15	15
Indonesia	75	60	8	11	17	29
Nepal	95	93	2	2	3	5
Philippines	61	48	15	16	24	36
Singapore	8	2	23	38	69	60
Latin America						
Bolivia	61	51	18	24	21	25
Brazil	52	41	15	22	33	37
Colombia	52	30	19	23	29	47
Mexico	55	39	20	26	25	35
Arab nations						
Egypt	58	51	12	26	30	23
Iraq	53	42	18	25	29	33
Jordan	44	27	26	39	30	34
Sudan	86	79	6	9	8	12
Tunisia	56	45	18	24	26	31

Source: Table 19, *World Development Report 1980* (World Bank)

Not surprisingly, the percentage of the workforce in the industrial sector and this sector's contribution to GDP reflected the rapid growth in urban population. In virtually all seventeen nations, the proportion of GDP produced by agriculture fell between 1960 and 1978 while the contribution of industry rose (Table 8). Similarly, the percentage of the labour force in agriculture fell while that in the industrial sector grew. One notable exception was India. Here, the percentage of the labour-force in the agricultural and the industrial sector were the same in 1978 as they had been in 1960 even though the industrial sector's contribution to GDP grew from 20 to 26 per cent while that of agriculture declined from 50 to 40 per cent in that same period.

Current Settlement Problems

All seventeen governments are or have been confronted with comparable housing and settlement problems. On the one hand, most have large urban centres growing more rapidly than their housing, infrastructure and services base. It is not uncommon to find half or more of a major city's population inadequately served by potable water and sanitary waste disposal. Smaller cities' populations tend to be even worse served. Cities with a million or more people living in squatter settlements are becoming increasingly common. The formal construction sector provides housing units for only a small minority of the urban population. On the other hand, much of the rural population and those living in smaller settlements are often largely excluded from economic development and lack basic services. Very few governments have managed to extend services as basic as potable water to villages and small towns. Even fewer have successfully improved housing conditions in rural areas.

Among the seventeen nations studied, we found the majority of people badly housed and lacking direct access to the most basic services. It is worth recalling some of the statistics given earlier. In Egypt, the quantitative urban housing deficit was put at more than 1.5 million in 1975. On that date, urban housing needs were growing by some 150 000 a year while the combined efforts of both public and private enterprises in the formal sector was some 61 700 units. In East Jordan, official estimates suggest that housing needs are growing by more than 16 000 units a year between 1976 and 1985 (not including efforts to reduce the existing deficit) and yet the formal sector's target for 1976–80 was for 6200 units annually. In the Philippines, the housing backlog in urban areas was put at 981 000 units in 1977 while a recent estimate suggested that 4 million urban dwellers were living in slums and squatter settlements with very limited access to water, often no sanitary facilities at all and very often considerable danger from floods during the rainy season. In India, in 1973, the urban housing shortage was put at 3.8 million units. In Nigeria, the quantitative urban housing deficit was put at between 840 000 and 1 025 000 in the mid-1970s. In Kenya, urban housing needs grew by some 160 000 units between 1974 and 1978. The government aimed to meet half of these needs through publicly funded low-cost housing and serviced sites. It probably met no more than 5 per cent of these needs. In Bolivia, the formal sector (including publicly funded units) met only a few per cent of the annual growth in urban housing needs between 1970 and 1975. In Colombia, the quantitative urban housing deficit grew to three-quarters of a million units by 1974. In Bogota alone, in the mid-1970s, close to 70 per cent of the housing was categorized as substandard with the total quantitative deficit put at 247 000 units.

Although such figures are not directly comparable with each other since different criteria are used to estimate housing deficits, they do show how housing needs in major urban centres have far outstripped housing construction by the formal sector. Statistics on the state of rural housing are usually less precise or less up-to-date. Actual deficits are usually far less serious, since acquiring a site on which to build is less of a problem and materials are usually to hand. However, the condition of rural housing (particularly the health hazards presented by the use of traditional materials and the environment in which the rural population live) make it as pressing a problem as urban housing. This is especially so in nations with a large portion of their population in rural areas. Among the seventeen nations, Kenya, Tanzania, Nepal, Nigeria, Indonesia, India and the Sudan have three-quarters or more of their populations in rural areas in 1980. And yet, the tendency in each of these nations has been for government housing, infrastructure and services budgets to concentrate on serving urban populations, especially those in the largest settlements.

Most or all of the seventeen nations share other problems related to settlements. An obvious one is the list of environmental problems faced by large portions of their populations: lack of adequate sanitation, lack of efficient garbage collection, lack of primary health care and lack of control over dangerous discharges from industries and commercial enterprises. Another is the lack of basic services such as education or public transport. Such problems are not easily resolved since local governments so often lack the resource base and authority to do so. And the people most in need of improved services are usually those with the least ability to pay for them. In urban areas, it is certain sectors of the lower income groups who suffer most from poor public transport systems since the cheapest housing sites tend to be those with poorest access to employment opportunities and central city services. Thus, those least able to afford long bus rides are often those who have to make them.

There are, of course, many other shared problems which do not relate directly to housing conditions but have a major bearing on living standards. The most obvious example is the lack of income sources to match the needs and aspirations of the growing population. In all seventeen nations bar Singapore, the labour-force is likely to grow at an annual average of 1.8 per cent a year or more between 1980 and 2000. For Tanzania, the Philippines, Colombia, Nigeria, Bolivia, Tunisia and Brazil, the figure is 2.5 per cent or more while for Mexico, Iraq and Kenya it is 3 per cent or more. This gives one an idea of the speed with which economic development must create new jobs.

However, the number of jobs that guarantee individuals or households a steady income above any reasonable definition of minimum subsistence is already far short of needs. Even with generally rapid economic growth in the 1950s and 1960s, the growth in the labour-force usually far outstripped the creation of what are often referred to as 'formal sector' jobs. The result is an increasing proportion of the labour force working in the 'informal sector' which is characterized by fluctuating and generally below subsistence-level incomes. We do not have figures for the rate at which formal sector employment is expanding for each of the seventeen nations. But the *World Development Report 1979* stated that in the 1960s, the low-income nations (which include Nepal, Tanzania, Kenya, India the Sudan and Indonesia) absorbed less than 20 per cent of the growth in their labour-force each year.[7] For the middle-income nations (which includes all the other nations in this study) with their generally more rapid industrial growth, less than 35 per cent of the growth in their labour force was absorbed into the industrial sector.

The result is unemployment or underemployment for large numbers of people with all that this implies in terms of incomes below subsistence level. For rural areas, surplus labour is not automatically drawn off to new urban employment opportunities. And in the urban areas, unemployment and underemployment becomes endemic with large percentages of the labour-force having to rely on insecure sources of income and, often, very low hourly returns for their work. With regard to housing conditions, this lack of secure income-earning opportunities relative to growing needs in both rural and urban areas implies a large and possibly growing proportion of households lacking the income to pay for improved housing or for charges to pay for basic services. This, perhaps more than any other factor, constrains any government attempt to improve housing conditions. In addition, the lack of purchasing power among the majority of people limits the generation of new economic activities within settlements to meet local consumer needs.

However, basic settlement problems—deteriorating housing conditions and lack of basic services—have been compounded by the generally low priority these have received in the allocation of government resources. Indeed, in most of the seventeen nations, they still are. The major multilateral lending agencies have also given little support to housing and basic service projects. Up to 1978, fifteen major multilateral agencies had committed only 1.8 per cent of their loans and grants to housing, site and services, slum upgrading, urban development and urban transport in their entire history. Only 5.2 per cent had gone to water supply and waste disposal projects, and 0.5 per cent had gone to building material projects. And the trend is for much of this multilateral aid to be concentrated in projects in the larger urban agglomerations.

However, rapidly deteriorating settlement conditions and the failure of economic development (by itself) to begin to tackle such problems have been forcing a rethink. As the earlier sections have shown, all seventeen governments are giving more attention to settlement problems. A few have done so to considerable effect over a number of years. Some have done so over a similar period but to relatively little effect. And others are only just beginning to consider what policies are appropriate in dealing with mounting settlement problems. We will now assess the extent to which national settlement, land and shelter policies are contributing to 'the rapid and continuous improvement in the quality of life' and the 'satisfaction of basic needs'. For these are the cornerstones of all the Habitat *Recommendations*.

Table 5 Multilateral aid agency commitments to settlement projects (Selected years, US$ millions)

Agency	Period during which aid was given	Total agency commit-ments	Amount and percentage of total agency commitments to projects of 'direct impact' (see notes below)					
			Urbanization urban transport, urban housing		Water supply, waste disposal		Building materials	
			Amount	%	Amount	%	Amount	%
International Bank for Reconstruction and Development[a]	1947–78	58 419	864.1	1.4	2048.7	3.5	193.0	0.3
European Development Fund	1960–78	2 308	8.7	0.3	129.5	5.6	—	
United Nations Development Programme[b]	1959–77	2 513.5	7.8	0.3	39.2	1.5	0.8	—
Interamerican Development Bank	1961–78	13 988	533.0	3.8	1330.0	9.5	91.8	0.6
Caribbean Development Bank	1971–78	180.1	15.1	8.4	c39.0	21.7	—	
Central American Bank for Economic Integration	1961–77	899.0	103.3	11.5	109.6	12.2	—	
Andean Development Corporation	1971–78	352.6	—		—		11.0	3.1
Latin American Savings and Loan Bank	1975–78	66.0	66.0	100	—		—	
Asian Development Bank	1968–78	5404.0	37.7	0.7	512.5	9.5	—	
African Development Bank	1967–78 1974–78	753.2 576.2	— —		102.6 157.3	13.6 27.3	8.2 —	1.2
Arab Bank for Economic Development in Africa	1975–78	282.7	—		14.0	5.0	32.8	11.6
Islamic Development Bank	1976–78	452.5	5.13	1.1	8.6	1.9	47.7	10.5
Arab Fund for Economic and Social Development	1974–77	1074.5	—		113.9	10.6	57.0	5.3
OPEC Special Fund	1976–78	927.2	—		6.9	3.4	—	
Totals	Various	88 296.5	1640.8	1.8	4611.8	5.2	442.3	0.5

Source: Blitzer, Silvia and Hardoy, Jorge E. (1980). *Aid for Human Settlements in the Third World: A Summary of the Activities of Multilateral Agencies during 1977 and 1978*, International Institute for Environment and Development

Notes

Care should be taken in quoting or interpreting this data. Researchers wishing to use this should refer to the original paper from which it is drawn which explains how the projects which the multilateral aid agencies sponsor are broken down into those of 'direct', 'less direct' and 'indirect' impact on settlements.

[a] Includes International Bank for Reconstruction and Development, International Development Association and International Finance Corporation.

[b] As all of UNDP resources are in the form of technical assistance, the assistance has been broken down according to category, and not included as a lump sum.

[c] Construction of roads, electricity and water supply are included in this category, according to the Caribbean Development Bank's 1978 *Annual Report*.

National Settlement Policies

The Habitat *Recommendations*

The improvement of the quality of life of human beings is the first and most important objective of every human settlement policy. These policies must facilitate the rapid and continuous improvement in the quality of life of all people, beginning with the satisfaction of the basic needs of food, shelter, clean water, employment, health, education, training, and social security without any discrimination. . . . . In striving to achieve this objective, priority must be given to the needs of the most disadvantaged people.
Declaration of Principles, General Principles, paras 1–2

All countries should establish as a matter of urgency a national policy on human settlements, embodying the distribution of population and related economic and social activities, over the national territory.
Recommendation A1

Such a policy should . . . embody a firm political commitment and . . . be based on a critical assessment of the present situation of human settlements, the emerging trends, and the impact of past policies.
Text below Recommendation A1

A national policy for human settlements and the environment should be an integral part of any national economic and social development policy.
Recommendation A2

Human settlement policies should aim to improve the condition of human settlements particularly by promoting a more equitable distribution of the benefits of development among regions; and by making such benefits and public services equally accessible to all groups.
Recommendation A4

National human settlements strategies must be explicit, comprehensive and flexible.
Recommendation A5

There must be institutions at national, ministerial and other appropriate levels of government responsible for the formulation and implementation of settlement policies and strategies for national, regional and local development.

Recommendation F1

National Action

As the sections on each nation's national settlement policy show, the general trend among the seventeen nations is for governments to become more involved in guiding economic development and give more consideration to the spatial distribution of social and economic investments. There is a growing acknowledgement that market forces operating both within and from outside the nation cannot by themselves promote development in the poorer and more undeveloped regions and cannot solve many of the settlement problems confronting both national and local governments. The pattern of industrial and agricultural development which market forces and past government policies have produced are recognized as one of the root causes of rapid urban growth in larger urban centres and, very often, economic stagnation in less urbanized regions and rural areas.

In the 1950s and 1960s, virtually every national development budget or development plan concentrated on promoting economic growth. The emphasis was on expanding the 'productive sector'—which usually meant industry and the infrastructure such as roads and powerplants that supported its development. Most of the seventeen nations had annual growth rates in GDP and in industrial production averaging 5 or more percent between 1960 and 1970. The exceptions tended to be the poorer nations such as the Sudan and Nepal. In some, emphasis was also placed on expanding agricultural production although concentration was usually on cash crops for export. We noted earlier the dependence of many of the seventeen nations on food imports while cash crops remain their major export.

The emphasis on expanding the productive sectors usually meant that social investment received low priority. And spatially, certain agglomerations (plus their hinterlands) and agricultural areas benefited from an expanding economic base while the rest of the nation was largely excluded from the development process. The concentration of industrial and commercial investment in a few major cities often resulted in much of the nation's public investment also being concentrated there as city governments struggled to keep up with infrastructure and service demands both for the expanding industrial base and for rapidly growing populations. The concentration of both private and public investment in a few settlements and regions inevitably exacerbated regional inequalities in both income levels and development.

By 1974, when preparations for the Habitat Conference began, most of the seventeen nations had much of their modern industrial sector in a few (or even one or two) cities. Per capita incomes and levels of service provision varied very considerably among regions, and large portions of the population still lacked access to basic services.

However, by the late 1960s and early 1970s, national development plans were giving more attention to the provision of social services and were trying to make explicit their intention to spread social and economic development more widely. National Plans for Economic Development now became National Plans for Social and Economic Development. All seventeen nations now have national development plans, most taking the form of five-year plans. And by 1979, each of the national governments was claiming that one of their key goals was to steer the benefits of economic development more widely than the operation of market forces alone would produce. Most of the national plans—including those of Egypt, Tanzania, India, the Philippines, Kenya, Jordan, Colombia and Mexico—talk of slowing migration to the major urban centres and encouraging industrial and commercial development in smaller urban centres. Several national plans including those of Indonesia, Kenya, Tanzania, Egypt and the Philippines identify specific settlements which are to be developed to counteract the attractions of the major city or cities. In both Brazil and Mexico, more attention is being given to a national urban policy. We should also recall Egypt's ambitious long-term settlement strategy to steer population growth away from Cairo and other 'overcongested' areas to rapidly developing cities along the Suez Canal, to satellite cities around Cairo and to new developments in previously undeveloped areas. Some governments, those of Tunisia, Kenya, Tanzania and Mexico among them, are seeking to reach a large portion of their rural population with improved services and infrastructure for settlements spread over the national territory. This development of 'intermediate centres' to counter the attraction of major metropolises and the spread of basic services to the rural population is very much in line with the Habitat *Recommendations* (especially B5). But despite certain similarities in the trend by governments to give more attention to spatial aspects of development policies—and certain similarities in strategy—enormous differences exist both in their scope and in the scale of political support they enjoy.

These differences are perhaps best highlighted by contrasting the experiences of five very diverse nations: India and the Sudan which have yet to develop anything approaching the beginnings of a national settlements policy and Singapore, Mexico and Tanzania where policies are more developed. India's Five-Year Plans have provided the framework for its national development policies for more than 30 years. The early Plans in the 1950s contained statements about the need for balanced regional development even if they included no major initiatives to try and achieve this. The Fourth, Fifth and Sixth Plans (covering 1969–83) have sought to identify people and areas largely bypassed by development. There have been discussions about the need for a national urbanization policy. The Janata government, in power between 1977 and 1979, included major spatial goals in its development policies including more emphasis on rural development, on meeting basic needs and on steering new industrial and commercial developments to the smaller urban centres. But such major spatial goals had no national settlement policy within which to operate. As the Asian *Report* points out, 'there is no clear idea . . . of the type of settlement structure the new policies are going to promote'.[8] The nation lacks a long-term development (and thus a long term national settlement) policy which addresses the fundamental causes of poverty and underdevelopment. Policies tend to be statements of intent that remain unimplemented.

In the Sudan, the Six-Year Plan (1977–8–1982–3) states that it intends to help more backward areas develop. But despite this, and despite the fact that the government recognizes that settlement policy should be intimately linked to socioeconomic development policy, the plan remains essentially sectoral in nature with its major emphasis being on expanding 'the productive sector'–agriculture and industry. And since much of the public and private investment continues to be in the three-town capital and below it adjoining the Blue and White Nile, the more backward areas seem unlikely to receive much benefit from economic development.

In Singapore, the government has been committed to reaching the whole population with improved infrastructure and services. Together with successful economic development since 1960, most of the national population has benefited very considerably both in terms of income, and education, health and quality of life. Although there is no explicit national settlements policy, the government has in effect pursued a consistent long-term settlements policy through a masterplan and through government controls on type and location of development. But Singapore's size, population and economic base makes it a special case. Any comparison with nations such as the Sudan has limited validity: the one being a tiny nation with high population density and a booming economy; the other, huge, underpopulated and lacking economic development. The main island of Singapore covers only some 600 square kilometres. It is best seen as a metropolitan area where city government has successfully decentralized urban growth to new towns (which are essentially residential suburbs) and to new nuclei within the metropolitan region. In doing so, it has brought most of the area's population into the development process.

Tanzania is unique in several ways. It was one of the first Third World nations to come close to an explicit settlements policy and to use such a settlements policy as the spatial framework within which socioeconomic development policy occured. Furthermore, the settlements policy concentrated on rural areas. A villagization programme starting in the late 1960s and accelerating in the mid-1970s has brought most of a formerly scattered rural population in or close to villages. The aim was to stimulate new economic activities, to provide the rural population with basic services and to encourage communal enterprises. Since more than four-fifths of the population live in rural areas,[9] the long-term aim is to slow migration to the major urban centres and bring the whole nation into the development process. While there is no sign of urban migration being slowed—indeed, available figures suggest Tanzania has one of the world's most rapidly growing urban populations—and the programme's economic impact has been criticized, the villagization programme has allowed a very considerable proportion of the rural population to benefit from better health care, education and water supply and from more involvement in government development plans. For urban areas, although there is no explicit long-term policy, successive Five-Year Plans have been consistent in seeking to promote industrial and commercial development in regional capitals (especially in nine designated as 'growth centres'), on steering migrants away from Dar es Salaam and, more recently, on moving the government to a new capital in Dodoma. Again, the aim is a better spread of urban and industrial development throughout the national territory.

In Section III, we noted Mexico's increased commitment to a national settlements policy and to setting up the institutional structure such a policy demands. In 1975, committees to promote regional development were set up to cover the whole nation except the Federal District (the centre of Mexico City metropolitan area). In 1976, amendments to the Constitution and a General Law on Human Settlements set the legal framework for a national settlements policy. The Ministry of Public Works became the Ministry of Human Settlements and Public Works. Its Minister became chairman of the interministry National Commission for Urban Development set up in 1977, which aimed to coordinate the work of all the various sectoral government agencies and thus make their plans and national settlement plans compatible. The Commission was to work with the new Ministry in implementing the National Plan for Urban Development. The draft plan being discussed in 1978 would aim to encourage the growth and development of smaller cities and to improve infrastructure and service standards in rural areas.

Simply picking on these examples does not mean that other governments among the seventeen nations have also not begun to evolve settlement policies. The Philippines, like Mexico, has been developing a national settlement policy and setting up the institutional structure to implement it. Kenya's 1974–8 Plan included nine intermediate towns designated as growth centres to which industry was to be steered and where infrastructure and services were to be improved. The Plan also outlined a National Service Centre Hierarchy of small urban centres, market centres, local centres and rural centres through which the government intends to reach most of the rural population with improved services. The 1979–83 Plan's spatial aims remains consistent with those of its predecessor and some new growth centres are also to get special attention. The Indonesian 1974–9 Plan identified 87 small and medium-sized cities as potential growth centres within 26 provinces (from where most of the development action is implemented) and groups the provinces into four economic development regions to promote coordination and cooperation between provincial development plans. The Nepali government is seeking to spread urban and industrial development more widely. The nation has been divided into four development regions, each with its own development centre. And in each, growth axes linking major settlements on a north south axis are to be developed.

In fact, each country section on national settlement policies noted some government attempts to spread urban and industrial development more widely than has been the case in the past. But there are enormous contrasts as to the success of spatial strategies, to their realism, and to their long-term effects.

Assessment

A settlement policy of the kind envisaged by the Habitat *Recommendations* is essentially political for it arises from the need to address social and spatial inequalities created by economic development. The aim of such a policy is no less than the 'rapid and continuous improvement in the quality of life of all people, beginning with the satisfaction of the basic needs' that the Declaration of Principles explicitly states. It must also include special attention to the most disadvantaged. Most governments claim these are among their most important goals; but few have made a major attempt to put into place a policy that has some hope of achieving such goals.

Policies to achieve such goals demand certain preconditions which the *Recommendations* spell out. They must embody a firm political commitment, which implies long-term financial support too. They must have the institutional framework to implement such a policy. This implies some concept of the settlement pattern and population distribution pattern the policy seeks to promote. They must be based on a critical assessment of current trends, past policies and the present settlement pattern. And they must be explicit. Since these points—and a commitment to a more equitable spread of development and to meeting basic needs—are the essence of Habitat's *Settlement Policy and Planning Recommendations*, these will be the main focus of the assessment.

In fact, most of the seventeen nations fail on the majority of these counts. Only Tanzania and Singapore, each in their own very different ways, come close to meeting these preconditions. Tunisia has moved some way towards doing so in the last ten years. Mexico, Kenya and the Philippines have also moved some way, although the initiatives are too recent for any results to be in evidence.

Settlement Policies and the National Economy

As we have seen, several among the seventeen governments are giving settlement policies more political (and even financial) support. Institutional changes are being made. But emerging settlement policies are so often not based on a critical assessment of current trends and past policies. Governments are not recognizing the limits and constraints imposed on settlements policy by national and international forces over which they have little or no control.

Each nation's settlement pattern and its change over time inevitably reflects the pattern of economic activities and how this is changing. If a nation has rapidly expanding metropolitan centres and stagnant villages, this simply reflects economic trends. If a backward region is to be developed, the government has to reverse or modify social and economic trends which caused the region to be backward. If there is to be economic development, it has to increase the region's comparative advantage either within the national or the international market.

Governments use three direct methods of increasing investment in specific towns or regions. The first is direct investment in basic services—improving health and education services, providing protected water supplies and so on. The second is by public investment in new economic activities there—say a new publicly owned factory or state plantation. The third is by using public funds to encourage private investment there by, for instance, developing infrastructure or giving cheap credit. (There are also structural reforms such as changes in taxation or agrarian reforms which can have profound effects on the spatial distribution of private investment but these are discussed in the next subsection).

The first option, direct investment in improving basic services, is perhaps the most direct way of improving living conditions for lower-income groups without major structural reforms. And yet, few governments have maintained a sustained programme to reach most of their population with basic services. The various responses (and the beginnings of a change in government attitudes) will be examined in more detail later. But only a minority of governments have shown a serious commitment to providing rural populations with improved services, even when they represent half or more of total population.

The second option is only open to governments who are responsible for part (or most) of productive sector investment. But there are constraints here to the public sector's ability to more equitably spread industrial growth and development across the nation. A new enterprise, whether publicly or privately owned, will have to sell its products or services to create incomes (and thus contribute to the area's economy). Public sector industrial investment is often located with no careful assessments as to which location will best serve both economic efficiency and a more equitable spread of industrial development. The location of such investment may well be determined by political bargaining—a point to which we will return in the next subsection. The result is often government-owned enterprises working below capacity with few local linkages or producing relatively expensive goods since the location does not suit the operation.

But in addition, powerful sectoral ministries such as the Ministry of Industry must agree that the benefits of locating one of the new government funded plants in a backward area outweights the possible diseconomies. Officials from industry ministries or from national economic planning offices are under pressures to maximize their own sectoral achievements, regardless of wider social and spatial goals.

The third option open to governments is to use public funds to encourage private investment in specific towns or regions. This can take the form of improved infrastructure such as the provision of electric power or upgraded road networks. Or it can take the form of financial incentives such as cheap credit or special tax allowances. A combination of these have been widely used in both First and Third World nations. In most of the seventeen nations, the location of private investment was a (if not *the*) major factor in determining where development took place. Private investment will not go to a relatively backward or undeveloped region or settlement unless this appears the most profitable course. Government incentives to encourage investment in such regions can only achieve their objective if they make it worthwhile for private investors to do so.

But even if a government programme is successful in steering industrial and commercial development to a backward region, this by itself does not guarantee development that benefits a substantial proportion of the population. Third World governments do not have much control over the type of technology used although this has important implications on the type of development that takes place, the number of jobs created (directly or indirectly), the associated economic activities it will generate or support locally and so on. If the result of a regional development programme is simply a few capital intensive industries or mines, in the region itself, a small élite will benefit. The products are very often destined for markets outside the region or even the nation; so too are the operations' profits. Meanwhile, the majority of people in the region have seen little improvement in their life as a result, despite economic growth in the region's GDP (and even an increase in the proportion of national GDP the region produces).

Indeed, public investment in a relatively poor region may even help impoverish lower income groups still further. Improved transport infrastructure may allow enterprises from outside the region to take over markets formerly supplied by local enterprises who had remained competitive only because of poor (and thus expensive) interregional transport links. In addition, most of the population in a poor region lacks the resources to take advantage of government incentives to help increase production. Thus, the élite may strengthen their position by having access to cheap credit. Or they may be in the best position to take advantage of, for instance, public investment in water projects encouraging wider use of irrigation. Incentives offered to local farmers to help them increase production usually results in the displacement of rural labour (through increased mechanization) and tenants being dispossessed since it is now more profitable for the landlords to farm the land themselves. There are numerous examples in nations such as the Philippines or India or Indonesia where the more wealthy landowners have had the resources to make use of new technology and new seeds so they become the main beneficiaries of agricultural development programmes. And there have even been cases where agricultural development programmes have increased the price of basic crops for the local population since the development is geared to increasing exports, not increasing national consumption.

Thus, there are internal limitations as to what a government can achieve in changing the 'geography of development' spatially and who benefits within each area's society. There are also external limitations, as we discussed in the previous section from world economic forces. The drive to increase exports because of serious balance-of-payments problems may go against development aims. No government can fund a major social investment programme without a reasonably healthy economy. Tanzania's ambitious social and spatial development programmes will suffer if it is forced to adopt economic policies (such as increasing cash crop exports or cutting public expenditures on basic services) that go against the longer term social and spatial goals.

In most of the government policies studied, there seems to be an inadequate understanding firstly of what a settlement policy should be and secondly of what it can and cannot achieve. There is a lack of 'critical assessment of the present situation . . . the emerging trends and the impact of past policies' (*Recommendation A2*). There is, for instance, little attempt among most nations to carefully examine the spatial distribution of public investments the various sectoral development plans imply with careful projections as to the pattern of private investment this will promote. Many proposed policies or strategies do not take full account of the factors limiting the spread of economic and social development more widely or preventing the slowing of the growth of major urban areas. And there seems to be an inadequate understanding of the possible conflict between social and economic development. It is significant that according to *Recommendation A4*, settlement policies should aim to improve settlement conditions by 'promoting a more equitable distribution of the benefits of development among regions *and* by making such benefits and public services equally accessible to all groups'.

Perhaps the major failing in emerging settlement policies is the lack of sectoral coordination. A settlement policy is intended as the spatial framework within which all public investments are made. It seeks to guide private investment while recognizing the limitations on its abilities to do so. It is not only a question of steering new investment to a certain region or settlement but of devising complementary social and economic investment patterns at local or regional levels which fit within national policies.

Examples of the limited success of regional development programmes are common. In India, encouraging industrial development at Rourkela and Bhilai did little to stimulate development around them and raise living standards for their local population. In Mexico, the regional development commissions for coastal basins on the Gulf and the Pacific based on the Tennessee Valley Authority model did not produce the hoped-for boost to industrial and urban development and thus some decentralization of industrial investment away from the Central Valley. In Brazil, we have noted already the failure of regional programmes in the Northeast to address the basic needs of the region's population. The same is true for the Brazilian government's programme to develop the vast Amazon region. At one time, the construction of the Trans-Amazon Highway was to be accompanied by land distribution to settlers from the Northeast each side of the new road. But emphasis switched from providing low-income families with land to encouraging development by large companies by giving generous incentives to encourage investment there. Although some of these developments may have created many jobs, most of them have displaced indigenous Indians, settlers and squatters while having worrying long-term implications regarding the stability of the region's soil and micro-climate. Furthermore, the products from the large estates owned by companies there are primarily for export.

Certainly, some of the settlement policy goals formulated in the last few years seem unrealistic, even though it may be too early for evidence of whether or not they are working. For instance, an official publication on the Philippine's settlement policy states that part of a policy of industrial dispersal includes 'a ban on new industrial establishments within a 50 kilometre radius of the city of Manila'.[10] It seems unlikely that new industrial investments will be severely curtailed in what is the nation's economic core. Similarly, one wonders to what extent the Janata government in India succeeded in its policy to steer industrial investment away from major cities to village and small-scale industries.

Even in the richer, more urban and more developed nations such as Brazil and Colombia, emerging spatial goals do not seem to be backed with policies that might allow the goals to be met. In Brazil's 1975–9 National Development Plan, there is talk of a national integration strategy to achieve a more equitable spread of social and economic development, the aim being 'to compensate for the diseconomies and disutilities generated by the acceleration of the industrialization and/or urbanization process'.[11] Regional inequalities are to be minimized by regional industrial complexes, with special 'integrated' programmes for Amazonia, the Northeast and Brasilia. But the Plan does not specify the economic policy tools to achieve these goals and to steer industrial development to the more backward regions. Nor has it been made clear how the national policy is to be made compatible with regional, state and municipal level plans and with basic social problems. Colombia's new programme aiming to raise living standards for the poorest half of the urban population in smaller cities also aims to reduce migration to the four major urban centres. But if private industrial and commercial investment continues to concentrate in these four cities, it is unlikely to achieve this second aim, however successful it is at improving living conditions.

Tanzania's 1976–81 Plan claims that the policy of encouraging growth in nine growth centres, first formulated in the 1969–74 Plan, has failed because 'Dar es Salaam has remained a major gravitational centre for investments, population and other social utilities'.[12] It is unrealistic to assume that they could make such rapid changes in prevailing settlement trends. The results of Tanzania's settlement policy can only be judged in ten or more years. By then, it should be possible to see whether a concentration on rural development has slowed rural-to-urban migration, whether the development of alternative growth centres has reduced Dar es Salaam's primacy and whether urban and industrial development has been decentralized without too great a cost to economic efficiency.

With good reason, Egypt's long-term spatial plans seek to accommodate virtually all population growth over the next two decades in areas away from the Nile Delta and Valley. Rural population densities are among the highest in the world there, but there are limits on what can be achieved. As Tanzania has discovered—and many other nations before them—stating in government plans that a settlement's growth is to be slowed or controlled is no guarantee that it will happen. The Egyptian plans have designated certain settlements as 'overcongested' so they will have population decreases over the next two decades. Meanwhile 'saturated' areas are to have no more population growth while what are today virtually uninhabited 'virgin' areas are to accommodate 14 or more million people by 2000. It seems unlikely that the Egyptian government can effect such radical changes in the distribution of population and development. Despite the very real boost to the economy that oil production (and exports) are already bringing, one wonders where the government can raise the money needed to develop areas in the Western Desert so they support 10 million people by the end of the century. No doubt, there are new settlements which can be developed with new irrigated lands in the New Valley and new industries around Mirsa Matruh if the Qattara Depression can be developed to produce cheap electricity. But are these two regions likely to absorb the equivalent of one third of all Egypt's population growth between 1979 and 2000? One wonders if Cairo's growth can be suddenly halted and reversed. Previous plans to limit it met with little success. One also wonders if private investment will go to 'virgin areas' and at what cost to the government in having to develop infrastructure and offer incentives. Such an ambitious plan can only drain government resources much needed in improving basic services and infrastructure in the villages, towns and cities where the population is living now. Thus, part of the Egyptian long-term spatial strategy does not seem to take full account of what government intervention is able to achieve.

Clearly, settlement policies which make use of economic trends are likely to have far more success. In Nepal, when malaria was virtually eradicated from the Terai, an underpopulated region with fertile soil was opened up. Not surprisingly, there was rapid migration from the Hill and Mountain areas with generally less fertile soil and very often serious population pressures and soil erosion. Thus, the Nepali government's policy of encouraging migration to this region was likely to meet with success. In fact, the government company set up to manage the resettlement programme could not cope with the rush of migrants, and illegal settlements sprang up. Similarly, the Egyptian government is likely to have more success in the part of its spatial strategy which aims to encourage the growth and development of cities along the Suez Canal. This is an area whose economic base is growing and likely to continue doing so. It also has well-established (and relatively short) transport links with Cairo. In conclusion, then, although it is somewhat of a truism to state that changes in settlement pattern can only reflect changes in the pattern of economic activity, it seems that most emerging national settlement policies do not take full note of this.

Settlement Policies and the Socioeconomic Structure

Clearly, the different levels of income, access to basic services and quality of the living environment within any nation reflect the differences in the economic and political strength of the various social groups that make up the nation. The nation's socioeconomic structure largely determines who benefits (and who does not) from economic development. We noted in the previous subsection how richer income groups or larger enterprises are obviously in a better position to benifit from the development of infrastructure or special incentives offered by government to encourage investment in a backward area. And clearly, settlement policies (or the lack of them) are moulded or influenced by powerful groups so they serve the group's interest. The type and distribution of public investment in national development plans can point to the relative strength of certain pressure groups in influencing government policies since the policies so obviously serve their interests. The low priority given by a development plan to social investment shows the lack of political strength for the group demanding this. And the general concentration of social investment in urban areas shows the relative strength of the urban population in influencing resource allocations compared to their rural counterparts.

Throughout the Habitat *Recommendations*, meeting basic needs, special help for the most disadvantaged and bringing the whole population into the development process are continually stressed. But although national development plans increasingly claim that these are among their principal aims, few governments have shown a serious commitment to implementing the structural changes that are a precondition for progress towards them. Furthermore, the type and distribution of public investment in national development plans has not generally changed to reflect such aims.

Perhaps the most pertinent example of where structural change is a precondition for settlement policies of the kind Habitat recommended is in land legislation. The legislation governing who has what right over what land (and the extent to which the legislation is enforced) is a major influence on settlement development. It also powerfully influences the distribution of wealth and the spatial distribution of income (and hence settlement development). Although an analysis of government land policies belongs to a later page, lack of government action in this area illustrates the lack of serious commitment to achieving the *Recommendations*' central goals. The *Recommendations* note than land 'cannot be treated as an ordinary asset, controlled by individuals and subject to the pressures and inefficiencies of the market'. They also state that an unchecked land market 'may become a major obstacle in the planning and implementation of development schemes'. And yet few of the governments have made fundamental structural changes in the last five years; none have done so in rural areas. So although the concept of 'meeting basic needs' is becoming more popular in national development plans, there have been few efforts to actually change the prevailing landownership pattern that helps lock both rural and urban poor into continuing poverty.

Implicit in many government plans seems to be the belief that basic needs can be met and development spread to include the rural and urban poor with few (or indeed no) structural changes. As we noted in the previous section, the present workings of the economic system do not guarantee the distribution of wealth to peripheral regions and to lower income groups, even if the system's wealth is growing rapidly. But few among the seventeen governments seem prepared to make changes that would improve that distribution. There is a wide range of structural changes that could have a profound effect on the distribution of benefits. One obvious example is tax reform; another is in agricultural policies that do not exclude small farmers and enterprises from government-sponsored credit and incentive schemes. For instance, cheap loans are likely to benefit lower-income families if less rigid guarantees and less collateral is demanded as the condition for the loan. A third is the terms of trade between rural and urban areas which are affected by government controls on the price of crops. Tax structure and the whole system of government supports for agricultural and industrial production profoundly influences the distribution of income and all that this implies in terms of each settlement's or region's purchasing power and thus the type of additional economic activities it will support and the living standards of the population.

Although our survey of the seventeen nations did not examine in detail either agricultural policies or tax structure, we did find many of the national 'social and economic development plans' with powerful biases running counter to stated social and spatial aims. The most common, not surprisingly, was the the rhetoric of 'uplifting the poor' with policies that best served the elites. One major example we will examine in detail in a later section is the gap between stated aims in improving housing conditions and the realities of a housing programme that chiefly serves relatively prosperous urban households.

Another major example is evident in development plans which concentrate public investment in urban areas, especially the largest cities. In fact, the bias is more social than spatial in that it reflects the relative power of social groups based in urban centres rather than the urban centres themselves. At the same time, public investment in rural areas can also reflect the relative political power of social groups there since such investment (as we have seen) chiefly benefits the larger and more prosperous landowners.

Nigeria's Third Development Plan 1975–80 illustrates this bias. One of its stated objectives is 'to enhance the quality of life of all citizens as development progresses'. Yet public investment continues to be heavily concentrated in urban areas, despite the fact that more than four-fifths of the population still lived in rural areas at the beginning of the Plan. The Plan also gave unprecedented support to housing provision for low-income urban groups entailing public investments of more than $3 billion during the Plan period. Relatively little went to provide basic services in the smaller towns and rural areas while nothing was planned to improve rural housing conditions. As we noted in Section IV, a detailed study of allocations to town and country planning in Kano and Lagos states showed an emphasis on urban development in major administrative centres to the virtual exclusion of rural development. After years of neglect, the agricultural sector is receiving more support. But the major thrust of this support seems to be incentives to encourage agribusiness to develop large commercial farms. Such a policy is unlikely to promote improved living conditions for the vast majority of rural people and will probably hasten migration to the major urban areas where the new public housing programmes are making little impression on rapidly deteriorating housing conditions.

There are similar biases in the Sudan's development budget, despite the 1977–8 to 1982–3 Plan's stated intention to help more backward areas develop and check migration to urban areas. More than four-fifths of the nation's population lived in rural areas in 1975. Yet development expenditure in the Plan is concentrated in urban areas and in specific, large agricultural schemes in the areas to the south and east of Khartoum. The same is true in Kenya during the 1974–8 Development Plan. By the end of the Plan period, the eleven municipalities and Nairobi in particular had monopolized much of central government's grants to the 50 or so local government units. And as local governments lack their own funding base for development investment—as in many other nations—a lack of supra-local development funds limits basic service and infrastructure provision.

This kind of bias in sectoral allocation of public investment and in overall development policies in most of the seventeen nations further enhances the attraction of major cities (or indeed one or two cities) to private capital. Housing budgets tend to concentrate on urban housing and usually only on projects in major cities. Very few have any major component for improving rural housing conditions despite the fact that in 1980, ten of the seventeen nations had more than half their population in rural areas while six had more than three-quarters. Rural housing programmes in Tunisia and, more recently, Tanzania, are the only notable exceptions. Mexico, too, has had some modest programmes and projects with some emphasis on improving living conditions in rural settlements. Infrastructure and service expenditure also tends to concentrate on major urban areas and urban services may be heavily subsidized while rural services remain almost non-existent. A more subtle form of urban bias is the fact that commerce, industry, financial services and major building enterprises may have to be close to government offices to function properly. Only through such close proximity can they easily secure the trade licences, import licences, low-interest credit and government orders on which their profits depend. Clearly, vested interests based in urban areas are far more successful at influencing development expenditure to serve their needs than are rural groups.

Urban biases in development investment are also reflected in the grants and loans given to Third World nations by the major multilateral aid agencies. When the spatial distribution of loans and grants from eight major multilateral aid agencies in Latin America were analysed, the general trend was for projects to favour large urban agglomerations with very little support given to projects in smaller towns and rural areas.[13]

Rural policies, too, often work against such commonly stated national objectives as 'slowing rural-to-urban migration'. Both the Nigerian and the Sudanese plans show this. In each, agricultural development programmes tend to benefit large commercial farming operations. Although arguments such as the need to increase export earnings or to rapidly increase food production may be advanced to justify such programmes, if these remain the major thrust of agricultural policy in nations with surplus rural labour, increased urban migration is the likely result. Alternatively, agricultural policies based on a revision of land tenure and encouragement of crop production that increases poorer rural households' income may slow such rural outmigration.

But governments seem unprepared, unwilling or incapable of making the needed structural changes to put such a policy into practice. Land redistribution and then technical and financial support for the smallholder to increase his contribution to national production has proved an effective remedy for lessening rural poverty and for increasing social and economic development. But it is not a path followed by such nations as Brazil, the Philippines and Colombia, despite the reserves of unutilized or underutilized land each nation has. Mexico in the 1930s and Bolivia and Egypt in the 1950s began major land redistribution programmes. But later development policies have not consolidated this redistribution by supporting the smallholder in developing the land and increasing his income. And legislation on maximum landholdings has been moderated or evaded for much of the richest agricultural land in all three nations.

The powerful vested interests influencing the type and spatial spread of public investment do not only act from outside government. Powerful sectoral ministries such as a Ministry for Industry must agree that the benefits of locating one of the new government funded or backed plants in a backward area outweighs the possible diseconomies. Officials from industry ministries or from national economic planning offices are under pressure to maximize their own sectoral achievements, regardless of wider social and spatial aims. Similarly, powerful state or city governments with their own resource bases and political influence at national level must also agree to work within national guidelines if an effective national settlements policy is to be put into place. Teriba and Kayode noted that in Nigeria, the location of many federally funded industries had been 'determined by the sheer balance of political bargaining by the regional political pressure groups in the federal government rather than by any conscious policy of achieving a rationally distributed pattern of industries among the regions'.[14]

Thus, a national settlement policy has no hope of working unless it has the support of sectoral ministries and subnational levels of government. It also has no hope of achieving some of the major Habitat goals unless it has sufficient powers and resources to enable it to implement policies that inevitably conflict with powerful private interests. This is why the *Recommendations* suggest that institutions and national, ministerial and other appropriate levels of government will be needed to formulate and implement settlement policies (*F1*). Only in Mexico and the Philippines have ministerial-level bodies concerned with national settlement policy emerged. And even there it is not clear whether their efforts to spread the benefits of development more widely, socially and spatially, will not be shackled by powerful interest groups. Nor is it clear whether these can convince powerful public bodies to work within their framework.

Mention could be made of many other government policies which go against explicitly stated government goals. For instance, government intervention in keeping food prices down or in appropriating a larger share of the revenues from cash crop revenues inevitably restricts rural development. And it may be that policy-makers know full well that such goals as 'slowing rural-to-urban migration' and 'spreading development over the whole national territory', stated in national plans, have no chance of being fulfilled because needed structural changes and appropriate sectoral policies are not in place.

But when reading government plans, one gets the impression that government planners are quite surprised that such goals are not being achieved. It seems they still believe that poverty can be attacked and a far wider proportion of the population brought into the development process without any major changes in the socioeconomic structure. It also seems that they still believe the problem of regions largely bypassed by the nation's economic development will be solved by continued economic growth; the effects of the economic cores' growth eventually stimulating growth and development in the peripheral areas.

Although the national studies on which this is based did not make a special study of, for instance, how regional income disparities had changed over time (the data was simply not available for most nations), we found no evidence to support either of the above hypotheses regarding automatic redistributive mechanisms spreading the benefits of economic development both socially and spatially. Furthermore, even if such mechanisms do eventually come into play once a certain level of economic development and per capita wealth is achieved, many Third World nations may never achieve such levels. Thus, government planners relying on such mechanisms to increase the share of benefits reaching the poor majority in both rural and urban areas are likely to continue waiting in vain.

Settlement Policies and Political Models

A government's ability to implement an effective settlements policy must relate to the strength and nature of its power base, that is, to the strength and nature of the group or groups that keep it in power. Combating poverty in large portions of the national territory may depend on fundamental structural changes that the government cannot (or is not prepared to) make. While social investments such as improved health care, education or protected water supplies can improve living standards for the poor, they do not necessarily get to the root of the poverty—lack of land or lack of income. Structural changes such as land redistribution or legislation limiting landlords' tenancy terms may be a precondition to an effective basic needs policy in rural areas. It may also be a precondition for stimulating growth and development in villages or small towns. Only with broadly based agricultural development can the community's purchasing power increase sufficiently to support increasing commercial activity and possibly some light industrial development too.

No simple generalizations are possible about the type of government which can implement a settlements policy based on the *Recommendations*. Clearly, it must be committed to a high level of social investment and meeting basic needs. It will need a strong power base since some policies will inevitably conflict with the interests of powerful groups. And within the government, there will generally have to be a group that continually promotes the cause of the rural poor. In many of the seventeen nations, the rural population's illiteracy, lack of organization and isolation from politicians' eyes ensures that their needs are usually ignored, since they have relatively little power as a political force, despite their numbers.

There also has to be some consensus in government as to what the settlement policy is seeking to achieve and as to what form it should take. The policy has to have long-term goals and needs consistent policies to support these goals. Two nations with major differences in size, ideology, wealth and level of urban and industrial development—Singapore and Tanzania—have both had a long-term settlement policy stretching back a decade or more. But there are interesting points of comparison in their political models. Both have what are often judged to be authoritarian or even almost totalitarian regimes. Both have what are essentially one party states (although with periodic elections). But it seems that the majority of each nation's population endorses or at least accepts their government's actions over the last 20 years. Both governments have been in power since the early 1960s unchallenged by serious social dissent. Both have a strong commitment to improving living standards for the whole population and both, in very different ways, have met with some success in doing so. And both have had a certain consistency in their settlement strategies and in the way they have been implemented.

A strong and comparatively long-term power base seems a necessary (if not sufficient) precondition for a successful national settlements policy. In Brazil, rapid economic growth rates between the middle 1960s and middle 1970s with a strong military government not answerable to an electorate could have allowed for effective state action in implementing a national settlement policy. *Politicas de asentamientos humanos*[15] suggests that Brazil's social policies after the military took over in 1964 can be seen to reflect the degree of social control the government achieved. After coming to power, government housing policies sought to obtain the support of the urban lower-income groups. But once firmly entrenched, the new government's policies switched to supporting the private sector while doing little to tackle mounting income disparities and continued poverty for large portions of the national population. More recently, increased support for social programmes and low-income housing can be seen as ways of dispelling tensions created by overconcentration on economic growth.

A similar reason may be suggested for increased commitment to a settlements policy in the Philippines and for more concern with settlement problems in Indonesia. They, like Brazil, have a highly centralized administrative system and a national government in which a small group wield enormous power and in which military or ex-military personnel figure prominently. Economic power is also in the hands of a relatively small élite who have prospered (directly or indirectly) from rapid industrial and economic growth over the last two decades. All three have large portions of their population benefiting little (if at all) from such development. And in all three, the government has claimed to support the uplifting of the poor, but in the past has done far less than its rhetoric has suggested. The tendency has been to sidestep changing the socioeconomic structure. Past experience suggests that their new commitment will not actually help the poor much, although it is too soon to judge the results of new initiatives. Certainly, in the Philippines the government's commitment to a major human settlements policy has been constantly stated with a ministerial-level body—the Ministry of Human Settlements—recently set up to direct the new initiatives.

Countries with powerful polarized interests continually competing for office will usually have the greatest difficulty in formulating and implementing any long term development policy. If government ideology changes every few years, a consistent settlements policy is not likely to be implemented. In Colombia, between 1957 and 1975, a coalition 'National Front' ruled with two major parties, Conservatives and Liberals, taking turns for Presidency every four years. But spatial policies tended to change with each president. The Regionalization model with its eight planning regions and hierarchy of settlements to be developed to check Bogota's growth and bring the whole nation into the development process was dropped in 1971. The new Conservation government that came to power in 1970 under Misael Pastrana regarded the model as involving excessive government interference. The development plan that replaced it was more sectoral in nature.

One reason for India's lack of a long-term settlement policy seems to be the opposing factions who concentrate on short-term political issues. For instance, the polarized debate between rural and urban supporters obscures the real issues and prevents the implementation of a consistent development policy (and hence a consistent settlements policy). Another is its sheer size of population. Administrative and legislative power are centred at state and federal levels. With such centralization (many states have more than 40 million inhabitants while Uttar Pradesh has more than 100 million), national and state representatives remain distant from local problems while local governments lack the resources to tackle them.

Clearly in all nations, the spatial organization of government and the relative powers (and resources) available to different levels of government down the hierarchy from national to local has a major bearing on the distribution of public investment and thus development. Nigeria is a particularly interesting case. In response to strong political differences between the north, east and west—and then within these regions—the number of states was increased from three in 1956 to five, them twelve and finally, in 1976, to nineteen. Although Lagos remains the dominant commercial and industrial centre, major manufacturing centres have developed in many of the states. Since the 1950s, state governments have sought to develop their own industrial base. Federal investments could not afford to favour only a few select states with industrial investment. Despite the problems already discussed of federally funded industrial projects' locations being guided more by politics than by careful choice, this has ensured a comparatively decentralized pattern of urban and industrial development nationally, even if within each state, this development has tended to concentrate in the regional capital.

By its nature, a federal government will tend to address inequalities in development levels among its states in a way unitary governments do not feel obliged to do. Perhaps the Mexican government's concern with regional development programmes which dates back to the 1940s and the Comprehensive Rural Development Programme under President Echevarria (1970–6) owe their origin to demands by state-level groups for a more equitable spread of development. And the new institutional developments including a new sub-ministry to head national settlement policies (as Habitat recommended) suggests a new commitment to addressing the needs of the rural population and the less prosperous states. But it is too early to judge whether the new institutional arrangements will have the political and financial power to ensure that an effective settlements policy is formulated and implemented.

However, the generalization that a federal government will tend to address regional inequalities more than a unitary government does not hold true for Brazil. A large portion of the nation's most productive export agriculture and much of its industry are concentrated in the state of São Paulo. Within nations, whether federal or unitary governments prevail, the relative strength of regional political forces in the decision making process must be a major factor influencing the spatial distribution of government funds. This also relates to the relative role of regional, district and local authorities in formulating development plans and in implementing them. Few generalizations are possible about the seventeen nations, as each has its own unique political structure. But despite the prevailing tendency for major planning decisions to remain concentrated in the hands of central government, several nations have recently strengthened the role of subnational levels of government. In the Philippines, regional and local bodies have been given more planning powers. And the National Economic and Development Authority's long-term plans suggest that this will be further consolidated when the twelve planning regions have their own regional governments with their own legislature and executive councils. Tanzania has also given its 21 regions more power both in formulating and implementing development programmes. With two-fifths of the budget and the civil service decentralized to the regional level in 1971, the planning and implementation of regional programmes was reported to have improved very considerably.[16] In Kenya, regional (provincial) and district authorities are being given a greater role in planning as well as implementation. In the Sudan, a new physical planning law seeks to decentralize settlement planning and implementation to the regional level, to work along the same lines as local government structure, decentralized in the early 1970s. The Tunisian government has recently strengthened both the regulatory powers and the funding base of municipal governments and has decentralized the institution in charge of housing construction for lower income groups into four; one each to serve the north, Tunis, the centre and the south.

In some other nations, subnational levels of government play major roles in implementing development programmes but remain comparatively weak in actually formulating development plans. This is true for nations as diverse as Nepal, Indonesia and Egypt. In Indonesia, provincial administrations under the governor implement development programmes while the 26 provinces are also grouped into four economic development regions to promote interprovincial cooperation. But major planning decisions remain at central government level. In Nepal, district level offices play the leading role in implementing development programmes with the 75 districts grouped into four development regions. But again, all major planning decisions remain in the hands of central government. Egypt has the hierarchy of governate, town/district and village councils but these subnational levels are hardly involved in policy formulation at all. In some cases, the lack of plan formulation at subnational levels of government may relate to the lack of professional staff. In others, it relates more to central government's desire to retain control over all major decisions. This second reason seems to apply in several of the seventeen nations, including Indonesia, the Philippines and the Sudan. National borders tend to be somewhat arbitrary lines drawn during the colonial period which brought culturally and ethnically diverse peoples into the same nation or divided a strong single group. Central government's control of major decisions may relate to its attempt to unify the nation and suppress regional groups' powers.

Settlement Policies and Level of Development

As we noted in the Background (page 195), a nation's performance in the world market inevitably affects development possibilities and hence the possibility of effective settlement policies. For poorer nations, desperate to close widening balance-of-payments deficits or find investment capital for their plans, a concentration on developing those settlements and areas which give the quickest payoff in terms of industrial or agricultural development is an almost inevitable response. The result is often platitudes in national development plans about the need for regional balance or for improving living standards for everyone but with plans which have little or no hope of doing so. Alternatively, it may be ambitious settlement policies whose achievements depend on a level of economic success which the country is unable to attain. Tanzania planned to move its capital from Dar es Salaam to Dodoma as one of several policies designed to lessen Dar's primacy. However, Dodoma's growth and the movement of ministries and other government offices have had to be slowed due to national economic problems. Settlement policy, like the whole development effort, will inevitably be constrained by economic difficulties.

However, the poorer and relatively rural nations do have the advantage of being latecomers in that their urban pattern is still in the process of formation. Despite the formidable problems confronting nations such as the Sudan, Nepal, Tanzania, Kenya and Bolivia, the governments could have the ability to influence the pattern of industrial and economic development while essentially directing the pattern of social development in a way that other nations with longer urban traditions and a higher percentage of people in urban areas do not have. In 1978, none of these nations had a city with a million people, even if Dar es Salaam, Nairobi, and the Sudan's three-town capital were approaching this figure. A careful assessment of what each government can achieve, given its limited powers and lack of financial resources, could help to produce a national development pattern and settlement pattern less inequitable both spatially and socially than those of societies with longer histories of urban and economic development. Clearly, Tanzania is aiming at just this, and has already done much of the groundwork. Kenya has gone some way too, and so has Nepal. In the Sudan, there is evidence of government planners giving more consideration to spatial issues. But current development expenditure is concentrated in the few major towns and in major agricultural schemes in the central region around the three-town capital.

Thus, the governments of such nations have the possibility of steering social and economic development in a way that mitigates such development's tendency to concentrate in a few select areas or settlements without sacrificing economic efficiency. Clearly, some regions and settlements will inevitably continue to be relatively more prosperous than others. But as experiences have shown in Tanzania (and in such nations as China and South Korea not covered by this survey), basic services can be extended to reach a large proportion of the rural population without excessive government expenditure. And as we noted earlier, some economic development can often be stimulated in the poorer regions, if the government is able and willing to make the needed structural reforms. Such changes may be more easy to put into place in nations with a high proportion of their population still in rural areas and most of their labour force still in agriculture. In such nations, the urban-industrial élite are not sufficiently strong to block changes that moderate inherent urban biases in development plans. As Galbraith commented, 'with increasing well-being, all people become aware, sooner or later, that they have something to protect'. One of a national settlement policy's goals is to put into place the type and spread of public investment and guidance of private investment that precedes the emergence of an urban-industrial élite sufficiently strong to ensure that all government policies become biased in its favour.

Land

The Habitat *Recommendations*

Land, because of its unique nature and the crucial role it plays in human settlements, cannot be treated as an ordinary asset, controlled by individuals and subject to the pressures and inefficiencies of the market. Private landownership is also a principal instrument of accumulation and concentration of wealth and therefore contributes to social injustice; if unchecked, it may become a major obstacle in the planning and implementation of development schemes. Social justice, urban renewal and development, the provision of decent dwellings and healthy conditions for the people can only be achieved if land is used in the interests of society as a whole. *(Preamble)*

Land is a scarce resource whose management should be subject to public surveillance or control in the interest of the nation.

(Recommendation D1)

Changes in the use of land, especially from agricultural to urban, should be subject to public control and regulation.

(Recommendation D2)

The unearned increment resulting from the rise in land values resulting from change in use of land from public investment or decision or due to the general growth of the community must be subject to appropriate recapture by public bodies (the community) unless the situation calls for other additional measures such as new patterns of ownership, the general acquisition of land by public bodies.

(Recommendation D3)

Public ownership, transitional or permanent, should be used wherever appropriate, to secure and control areas of urban expansion and protection and to implement urban and rural land reform processes and supply serviced land at price levels which can secure socially acceptable patterns of development.

(Recommendation D4)

Past patterns of ownership rights should be transformed to match the changing needs of society and be collectively beneficial.

(Recommendation D5)

The supply of usable land should be mainted by all appropriate methods . . ..
(*Recommendation D6*)

Comprehensive information on land capability, characteristics tenure, use and legislation should be collected and constantly updated. . . ..
(*Recommendation D7*)

National Action

Among the seventeen nations, there is evidence of governments seeking to increase public control over land-use and, in certain cases, limit private ownership rights. Many of the initiatives to do so have come in the 1970s. And most governments would now admit that private land markets and land-use in urban areas have to be guided and controlled by public policy. We noted in Section III (page 136) the Colombian document which stated that 'the belief in private initiative, so necessary in other areas of the economy, has led in urban issues to the supply of a hardly satisfactory and in many cases chaotic product. Vast extensions of utility networks and buildings are under-used or deteriorating while the urbanization process, guided by the incentive of private profit, proceeds with no control to the confines of the country's most productive land.'[17] Officials in the other sixteen nations would no doubt agree with this diagnosis (even if some may have reservations about the judgement on private initiative's role in other sectors).

However, the scope of the seventeen governments' control over landownership and use varies enormously. So too does the effectiveness of this control in tackling settlement problems. At the risk of repeating what was stated in earlier sections, it is worth recalling briefly some of the urban land policies under four headings: patterns of ownership, (the definition of public and private rights); control of land-use changes; public ownership; and recapture of plus value. Government policies will then be assessed.

Patterns of Ownership (Recommendation D5)

The first step in any comprehensive urban land policy has to be the clear and unambiguous definition of public (or community) rights and private rights over landownership and use to ensure that society's needs are safeguarded. This is the essence of *Recommendation D5*. Considerable progress was made in the 1970s in establishing the principle of public (or community) rights that limit private land-owners' rights. But the legislation and the political will to follow this up have not been so forthcoming.

Public authorities in each of the seventeen nations have the right to expropriate land in the public interest. In the four Latin American nations, the national constitutions establish the principle that individual rights over private property are not absolute. A new Constitution in the Philippines, introduced in 1973, allowed for the expropriation of private land for public purpose. In Mexico, the Constitution was amended in 1976 to give the nation 'the right to impose on private property the modes determined by public interest'.

But in several of the seventeen nations, despite the constitutional basis for government land expropriation 'in the public interest', government action has been very limited. Little attempt has been made to formulate and implement effective legislation that, for instance, allows public authorities to acquire land for low-income housing or serviced-site projects. In Indonesia, the public authorities have faced considerable difficulties in acquiring land for such projects, the land acquisition being hindered by no clear definition of what constitutes 'public interest' and no clearly stated guidelines for assessing compensation. In Colombia, attempts to pass a law clarifying public rights to land expropriation and control date back more than a decade. As yet, no law has been passed. Bolivia's 1976–80 Plan included a proposal 'to control the use and appropriation of urban land' but gave no details of how this was to be done.

In four of the seventeen nations—Singapore, Tunisia, the Sudan and Tanzania—substantial progress has been made. In two others—Nigeria and Mexico—there have recently been major changes recently. And in Brazil, initial steps towards such a policy may have begun.

In Tanzania and the Sudan, virtually all land is publicly owned. This ensures public authorities have the powers to guarantee public rights in land-use. We also noted how in Tunisia, despite widespread private ownership of urban land, two public agencies have the power to expropriate land they need for housing developments. The Agencie Foncière d'Habitation buys undeveloped urban land (by expropriation if necessary), develops it and sells it at cost price to private developers. The Société Nationale de la Tunisie (SNIT), set up to undertake 'social interest' housing projects for lower-income groups, can also expropriate land needed for public housing schemes.

In Singapore, the government laid down clear and explicit expropriation procedures, including the definition of how much compensation should be paid. Public authorities, including the major public housing agency, the Housing and Development Board, have considerable powers for the compulsory purchase of land. Although assessments of government urban housing policies belong to later pages, it is worth noting that these four nations, the Sudan, Singapore, Tunisia and Tanzania, have among the largest urban housing or serviced-site programmes relative to the size of their urban populations.

During Nigeria's 1970–4 Plan, the public authorities found it difficult to acquire land for public projects. Despite expropriation powers, public land acquisition was hampered by the level of compensation demanded by private landowners. Various initiatives were taken in 1975 and 1976 including a decision to set up land banks and to streamline compensation procedures. But the most fundamental change was made in 1978 with the Land Use Decree. This stated that all land was to be held in trust and administered for the use and common benefit of all under the state governors' authority.

In Mexico, the new General Law on Human Settlements backed by the changes to the Constitution set the legal basis for more effective land-use control by public authorities. Land-use powers at federal, state and municipal levels were strengthened. The Law also allows for specific urban development plans to set up reserve areas for accommodating future growth. Although no Federal Law on urban development had emerged by 1978, two state laws show the direction urban land policies are taking. The State of Mexico's Urban Development Law established the public authorities' rights to set up and enforce land-use plans while the State of Jalisco's Human Settlements Law enables public authorities to regulate land speculation and establishes a tax on unearned increments in land value.

In Brazil, the National Commission on Metropolitan Regions and Urban Policy's Draft Law on Urban Development seeks to separate ownership rights from development rights. This separation is evident in two measures: the fact that private builders would have to gain approval for and pay for any 'created area' their development involves; and the fact that government would have the power to force private landowners in areas of 'social interest' to develop or improve their land.

Control of Land-use Changes (Recommendation D2)

In virtually all settlements in the Third World that have experienced rapid population increases, urban growth has been haphazard and unplanned. Even when masterplans have been prepared, they are not usually enforced. It is to this problem that this *Recommendation* is addressed. And it makes special note of the need for public control of unplanned urban encroachments onto agricultural land since many major settlements are sited next to fertile soil and their uncontrolled growth has been at the expense of this valuable resource.

Earlier sections have shown how certain nations have recently sought to improve public control of changes in land-use. In the Philippines, some 600 square kilometres of land encompassing much of metropolitan Manila's population was proclaimed an 'urban land reform zone' in September 1979. The President stated that no more land could be sold and no building constructed without permission from the regulatory commission of the Human Settlements Ministry. In addition, more effort is being made to control urban growth in other major urban centres.

In Tunisia, the regulatory powers of municipal masterplans were strengthened during the 1973–6 Plan. In Mexico, changes to the Constitution and the new Human Settlements Law should provide the legal basis for more effective land-use control by state and municipal authorities.

In Egypt, a Comprehensive Planning Law has been under discussion for several years. If implemented, this would demand both rural and urban masterplans covering all settled areas and give governates and local authorities more power to control illegal subdivisions and protect agricultural land. In Singapore, the masterplan defines the way in which all land can be used. Planning permission is needed for all development projects, and the public authorities' control of changes in land-use is effectively enforced through such a system. In the Sudan, the fact that land is publicly owned allows the public authorities sufficient scope to control changes in land-use and to protect valuable agricultural land.

Public Ownership (Recommendation D4)

This recommends the use of public ownership (transitional or permanent) where appropriate for three distinct tasks. The *Recommendation* is very specific about the first two: securing and controlling areas of urban expansion; and implementing urban (and rural) land reform. The third is less specific: the supply of serviced land 'at price levels which can secure socially acceptable patterns of development'. For our analysis, this is taken to mean the supply of serviced land at price levels which do not automatically exclude lower-income groups. Few students of urban problems would disagree that the exclusion of large portions of the population of most Third World cities from the urban land market (because they cannot afford to enter it) is the most 'socially unacceptable' aspect of land policies.

Many of the seventeen nations have examples of local or national governments increasingly using public ownership as an important part of urban land policies. As we noted earlier for Tanzania and the Sudan, virtually all land is publicly owned. However, it is worth noting that *Recommendation D4* includes the comment that 'public ownership of land cannot be an end in itself; it is justified in so far as it is exercised in favour of the common good rather than to protect the interests of the already privileged.' There have been instances in both industrialized western nations and in countries with centrally planned economies where replacing land-use allocation by market forces with allocation by public authorities, has not led either to more efficient or more egalitarian practices. However, in Tanzania, and increasingly in the Sudan, public ownership of urban land has led to a marked increase in the supply of urban land for housing at a price low-income groups can afford. The scale of both nations' housing-plot schemes would not have been possible without public landownership. The governments would not have had the resources to purchase needed land from private owners at market prices and then supply plots at a price lower-income groups could afford.

Singapore's case is somewhat similar for it too has made good use of public land reserves in settlement policies. In the early 1960s, when confronted with massive housing problems, Singapore's public authorities were fortunate in having a large portion of the national territory under public ownership, including land located in or close to the city centre. The scale of their public housing programme since then would not have been possible if the government had had to expropriate all the land needed both for public housing estates in or near the city centre and for the new towns built around the island.

In both Jordan and Iraq, state land has been used both for public housing and for selling to housing cooperatives. It has been sold at prices well below market rates in order to stimulate housing construction (and presumably keep unit costs down). In Egypt too, publicly developed land is sold at cost (rather than at market value) to encourage housing construction.

In Tunisia and Kenya, public authorities have been active in buying up land needed for expanding urban areas. City councils in Mombasa and Nairobi have been buying up land both for public developments and for low-cost housing projects (although high compensation costs have hindered this programme). Nigeria's public housing programme has also been hindered by such high compensation costs. In Tunisia, the Agencie Foncière d'Habitation was set up to acquire land in advance of need, install infrastructure and sell it to developers. Mexico's Human Settlements Law allows for specific urban development plans to set aside areas that will accommodate future urban growth—but the initiative is too recent for any results to be in evidence.

In Bolivia, India and Nigeria, initiatives have sought to place ceilings on urban land holdings. Bolivia's Law on the Reform of Ownership of Urban Land dates from 1954. In the other two nations, the initiatives have been more recent. India's Land Ceiling and Regulation Act in 1976 set ceilings on urban land holdings and state governments were empowered to acquire surplus land with a specified formula set to determine compensation. In Nigeria, the Land Use Decree set ceilings on undeveloped urban land-holdings of half a hectare in each state. In the Philippines, as part of the recently declared 'urban land reform zone' within metropolitan Manila, large landowners were asked to sell land to squatters who had illegally occupied it for more than ten years while a $20 million fund was set up for land expropriation, this land to be allocated to landless and homeless people.

Recapturing Plus Value (Recommendation D3)

This includes a list of the various ways public authorities can recapture the unearned increment in land values which result from changes in land-use, from public investment or from the community's own growth. They include taxes such as capital gains tax on land sales, annual taxes based on land values with special rates for lands left vacant and betterment charges. They can also take the form of development charges for allowing changes in use which increase the property's value. Compensation rates for land expropriated by public authorities may be fixed according to the land's value at a specified time rather than its commercial value once the possibility of the public development becomes known. Land which is leased from public authorities can be on terms that ensures the unearned increments in value return to the community. All these in theory tend to reduce land speculation.

Taxation is the method most commonly used among the seventeen nations. Property taxes are levied in many of them although, it seems, with no special attempts to recapture unearned increments by having land values regularly reassessed and special rates for land left vacant. Singapore is an exception with property taxes levied on all lands and buildings based on the gross amount for which the property could be let, the rate of taxation varying with location. In addition, all developments have to be approved by the public authorities and development charges can be levied before permission is granted. Planning permission remains valid for only two years to ensure that land is not left vacant. And in 1978, compensation payments for land expropriated for public purpose were fixed at the property's value in November 1973.[18] In Tanzania, a Land Rent and Service charge plays the same role as a property tax; 10 per cent of the economic value of unimproved urban land is levied annually with land values periodically reassessed. Kenya, too, has a site value tax based on the value of the unimproved site together with an estate (or death duty) tax applicable to land holdings and a capital gains tax (introduced in 1975).

In Colombia, land transactions are also subject to capital gains tax. In addition, Colombia has a betterment levy (or tax on unearned increment) which dates from 1921 when it was put in place to recoup some government expenditure on irrigation and flood control. In 1943 it was extended to cover 'works of public service' and in 1966 to cover 'works of public interest'. This has been used to recapture some of the costs of street construction and road improvement, of establishing parks and of redeveloping deteriorating communities in Colombia's larger cities. Although no federal law in Mexico deals with the recapture of unearned increment, the state of Jalisco's Human Settlements Law established a tax on unearned increment.

In Jordan and Iraq, the public authorities have the right to appropriate one-quarter of a property without compensation if the value of that property has appreciated in value as a direct result of public works. Iraq also has a tax on vacant land while Jordan's 1976–80 Plan includes proposals for such a tax, for a capital gains tax and for an increase in the proportion of land which can be appropriated free of charge to 35 per cent. Both Jordan and Egypt have a tax based on a percentage of the sale price of land. And in Egypt, an annual tax on vacant land has been proposed.

Many of the measures outlined under previous headings help public authorities recapture some of the unearned increments in land values. For example, Brazil's Draft Law on Urban Development could recoup unearned increment through the development charges for 'created area'. And any measure that dampens the speed with which land values rise helps reduce the scale of the 'unearned increment'.

Assessment

All growing urban areas have conflicts of interest between the various groups seeking land for specific uses—from the lowest-income groups seeking accommodation close to possible sources of income, to a multinational seeking a site for a new factory, to an individual seeking to invest in urban land (and leave it undeveloped) since this gives a non-depreciating investment which rapidly grows in market value (in real terms). The major conflict in most urban centres was found to be between the private landowners and the housing needs of a large portion of the population. Another major conflict is between the public authorities in their efforts to control and guide the settlement's growth and those who operated contrary to public regulations: by squatting; by selling illegally subdivided land; by setting up commercial or industrial operations contrary to an area's zoning regulations; by individuals or enterprises constructing buildings contrary to official standards. The purpose of an urban land policy is to define the balance between individual citizens' land-use rights, every citizen's own land-use needs (for instance housing) and community needs (for instance public works and community facilities). It is to this task that the Habitat *Recommendations* were addressed.

Rather than seek to analyse in detail what each specific measure by each national government has achieved—a task beyond the scope of this study—we shall concentrate on two aspects. Firstly, how successful have national urban land policies been in ensuring a sufficient supply of land for housing with a price range that ensures every urban citizens' individual land-use needs for housing are met. Secondly, have urban land policies succeeded in guiding and controlling urban development.

Land for Housing

In most of the major urban areas in the seventeen nations, there is an inadequate supply of serviced land for housing. The price of legal, serviced plots generally puts them—and even the lowest cost units built on them—beyond the range of the majority of households. The market, by itself, does not cater for this need, nor have the public authorities met with much success in influencing the market so that it does so. The only response open to those who cannot find accommodation in existing houses is to go outside the law—to squat on public or private land or to purchase or lease illegally subdivided land. Since such land is illegally occupied, only very rarely does it have basic services. Very often, it is ill-suited to permant habitation. Squatter settlements appear, sometimes almost overnight, on swamps, dangerous slopes, ravines and areas subject to flooding if these can give the occupants the access they need to possible sources of income. In Cairo, an estimated million people are squatting in the City of the Dead. In Bogota, more than a million people live on illegally subdivided land. In 1973, metropolitan Manila had well over a million squatters in settlements in or around the city. Up-to-date statistics on the extent of squatting in most major cities proved impossible to get. However, the *Global Review of Settlements* produced by the United Nations for the Habitat Conference showed that in the late 1960s and early 1970s, 30 per cent or more of the population of Nairobi, Mombasa, Ibadan, Rio de Janeiro, Port Sudan, Tunis, Dar es Salaam, Bogota, Buenaventura, Mexico City, Bombay, Calcutta, Delhi and Manila lived in 'slums and squatter settlements'. Official up-to-date statistics on the number of people living in overcrowded, unsanitary and ill-serviced units are rarely available. It is, for instance, usually impossible to obtain a breakdown as to the percentages of a city's population living in slums, on illegally occupied land or on illegally subdivided land. But in virtually every urban area where statistics were available, the slum and squatter populations were growing far faster than the total population. We have no reason to suspect this trend has changed much. Indeed, when current rates of formal sector housing construction are compared to urban population growth rates and when local researchers' estimates are considered, we would suggest that the few available official statistics considerably understate the magnitude of the problem.

Darin Drabkin points to the peculiar nature of the urban land market as being the major factor in this widening gap between the land needs of the low income urban majority and the reality of what they can obtain legally.[19] This peculiar nature is seen most clearly in the fact that urban land's value is largely created by society's development but appropriated by a small elite of private individuals. Urban land's value is largely created by the development of the whole settlement (including public investment in infrastructure, services, and social/cultural facilities) but private landowners usually receive most or all the benefits of its rising value. Indeed, the landowners frequently leave the land undeveloped since the land itself does not suffer from depreciation over time and rising demand further increases its value. Such speculative withholding of urban land from development further limits supply and thus further pushes up land prices.

In addition, since the value of urban land relates as much (or more) to its location as to the building on it, its supply does not automatically expand to moderate rapid price increases as a result of rapidly growing demand. The value of urban land relates to the access it gives the user (whether living or working there) to income earning opportunities, services and infrastructure, important contacts, pleasant environment and so on. Although public investment in services and infrastructure can increase the supply of well located and serviced urban land, the reality in most Third World cities is that demand for such land is growing far more rapidly than city governments can increase supply.

As both private and public investment continues to concentrate in the major cities, and as these cities' populations continue to grow rapidly, obviously the demand for well located and serviced land also grows rapidly. Its scarcity and non-depreciating character makes it an attractive investment without the need (and expense) of developing it. This is especially so in nations with high inflation and limited investment opportunities. And rapidly growing urban areas will demand more land for commercial and residential use so landowners may further limit the supply of land for development by not selling or developing their land in anticipation of changes in use which will enormously increase its value.

Thus, the amount of well located and serviced urban land can only be expanded slowly. In most cities among the seventeen nations, demand for such land is rising rapidly. In examining government responses in the previous sub-section, clearly most governments are trying to limit private gains from the urban land market and are increasingly entering the urban land market themselves to increase the supply of land for housing. In most cases, neither has been successfully used to ensure there is an adequate supply of serviced land for housing the growing urban population. Controls on land speculation are usually ineffective. Nor do the public authorities attempt or seriously commit themselves to recapture much of this unearned increment. The Arab *Report*[20] noted that in Egypt, Iraq and Jordan, this recapture has not been successful. In both Amman and Cairo, large amounts of well-located land remain undeveloped since they represent valuable speculative investments. New initiatives in Jordan and Egypt may help remedy this. In Kenyan urban areas, speculation has not been controlled by three property taxes—capital gains, estate (or death duty) and site value. Site value tax is very low, estate tax has been avoided by subdividing landholdings while clandestine land transactions have avoided capital gains. In Colombia, too, forged selling prices in private land sales have minimized the 'capital gained' and thus the tax due. In the Philippines, the government has shown little ability to control very rapid rises in urban land prices and well-located urban land is often left undeveloped. However, the tax in Colombia on unearned increment seemed 'to have been instrumental in enlarging the choice and accessibility of lower-income groups to jobs and residential building sites' and to 'have important financial benefits' for the municipality, according to a World Bank paper in March 1977.

Regarding the success of public authorities entering the urban land market themselves, there are a few more examples of success. Perhaps the most fundamental has been governments' slow and generally unwilling recognition that legalizing tenure for squatters or those living on illegally subdivided land is more effective than destroying their settlements—or trying to rehouse them elsewhere through public projects. This seems to be the principle behind Colombia's Programme for the Integration of Services and Community Participation which is seeking to improve living conditions for the poorest half of the urban population in 23 intermediate cities. Its aim is to minimize the number of households relocated and to give secure tenure to those living on illegally occupied or subdivided land. Another important trend has been that of governments recognizing that the major block to low-income households finding accommodation is not so much lack of houses but lack of serviced plots on which houses can be built. But both of these kinds of project are best assessed under 'shelter' and will be looked at in the next subsection.

Apart from some notable serviced-site and squatter legalization programmes, most public authorities have been reluctant to enter into urban land markets on a scale which has some hope of lowering the cost of housing projects or indeed moderating speculation. Tanzania and the Sudan are, once again, exceptions because virtually all land is publicly owned. Despite the fact that on a per capita basis, these two nations are among the poorest of the seventeen, the public authorities' control of urban land markets and their willingness to keep the price of leaseholds or 'rights of occupancy' down is at the basis of their large and relatively successful housing-plot programmes.

Singapore, too, presents rather a special case. We should recall that large amounts of the island belong to the public authorities, who also have strong and efficient expropriation procedures as well as an array of property taxes and development charges. Although land prices have risen rapidly over the last 20 years and although public authorities often prefer to negotiate with private owners rather than expropriate (thus avoiding expropriation procedure), the combination of public land reserves and public control have undoubtedly checked land speculation and thus the level of compensation private landowners have to be paid. Indeed, for a city with serious constraints on the land area over which the urban area can expand and with one of the fastest-growing economies in the world between 1960 and 1978, the government's achievement in controlling land prices and guaranteeing a supply of land for housing that ensured the houses were not too expensive for low-income groups is very considerable.

We noted that public authorities in Iraq, Jordan and Egypt have sold urban land at well below market prices to stimulate housing construction. But none of them complemented this with steady public investment in urban land in advance of need. And although this policy may have increased housing construction in the short term, the massive and still rapidly rising urban housing deficits in each nation suggest the policy has little long-term significance.

In nations such as Tunisia, Mexico, Kenya, Nigeria and the Philippines, the initiatives are too new for results to be much in evidence. The entry of public authorities into the land market in Tunisia and Kenya could help ease housing shortages if undertaken on a scale that gets close to need and in a way that does not make the land too expensive. The Tunisian programme may be beginning to achieve this already. But in the Philippines, the ineffectiveness of longstanding agrarian reforms does not augur well for the prospects of urban land reform being implemented. And in Kenya, the allocation of public land to serviced-site and low-income housing projects in Nairobi in the past at very low cost made little impression on deteriorating housing conditions.

Controlling Land-use

Not surprisingly, there is a clear link between national (or city) governments who have successfully increased the supply of urban land for housing and those that have had some success in guiding and controlling urban development. The fact that a public agency in Tunisia has become the major supplier of subdivided and serviced land for housing in major urban centres allows such developments to conform to city plans. Government policies supplying cheap land for housing in Tanzania and the Sudan has the same effect. This kind of policy lies at the heart of Singapore's housing strategy. No doubt, this is one of the aims of public authorities in Nairobi, Mombasa and Kisumu in Kenya who have been purchasing large quantities of land for housing. This suggests that either the use of public land reserves or advance acquisition of land by public authorities (or both) can play a major role in helping to guide and control urban development, especially in rapidly growing urban areas.

There have been few successful attempts among the seventeen nations to improve land use control through negative controls—the enforcement of zoning, subdivision and building regulations or masterplans containing a combination of these. The rapid and unplanned physical expansion of urban areas which characterized Third World cities in the 1950s and 1960s is even more generally true today. The picture is one of municipal governments lacking the political power, the legislative and financial base and the trained personnel needed to guide and control the growth and development of the area under their jurisdiction. The land use controls they have at their disposal are so often based on those developed in the West for controlling their own cities' growth. These ill-serve the community's needs and the planners' real responsibilities. There are also numerous problems of overlapping jurisdiction. The area over which the city authorities have jurisdiction often does not grow with the city itself. Unplanned urban growth very often occurs over valuable agricultural land outside city limits. No doubt public authorities in Egypt echo the cry of the Colombian quoted earlier bemoaning the fact that the urbanization process proceeds with no control to the confines of the nation's best agricultural land. Between 1950 and the late 1970s, Egypt lost more than 10 per cent of its most productive farmland to urban encroachment—much of it through illegal squatting or subdivision. And this is in a nation desperately short of fertile and well watered land.

One basic dilemma in seeking to improve public control of land-use (and indeed in wider questions related to limiting private rights over land-use and ownership) is in regard to the level at which land policies should be formulated and implemented. Legislation by governments far removed from municipal authorities often lacks an appreciation of what needs to be done and what local authorities can actually achieve. And yet if local governments' powers to formulate and implement land-use policies are increased, local vested interests may be the chief beneficiaries. This problem is especially acute in large and populous nations such as India. Here, central government can and does give directives on the use and control of land but only state government legislation can actually put the directives into practice. Only state governments have the power to devise policies regarding the control and use of land. But even though this formulation and implementation of land legislation is decentralized to state level authorities, these authorities are also distant from local government. Several Indian states have populations exceeding 40 or 50 million while Uttar Pradesh alone with 88.3 million in 1971 was more populous than all but Brazil and Indonesia among the other sixteen nations.

In fact, state level legislation in India on which urban land-use planning is based is both inadequate and outdated. Most of it is still based on the concept of rigid masterplans which ill suit the tasks urban authorities must tackle. This is, no doubt, one major reason why 'more than 500 masterplans prepared in the last twenty to twenty five years in the country lie mostly as documents on paper. Perhaps only about 20 per cent of these plans have been implemented in one form or another.'[20]

But if a large portion of the urban population can only afford accommodation by going outside the law, the public authorities can never hope to guide and control urban development. If a quarter or more of the urban households (including most of the lowest-income households) and much of the increase in population every year is housed 'illegally' at little cost to the public authorities, any enforcement of negative controls by themselves can only make housing problems worse. It seems that the only effective strategy to halt or control haphazard and unplanned sprawl and to control land-use changes involves substantial government intervention into the land market for housing. This may—and often does—go against the ideology of the government in power. It almost certainly goes against the wishes of powerful vested interests, who are so often well represented in local government. Zoning and subdivision regulations are frequently used to protect the élite's interests. But this does not invalidate the conclusion—that only where the legal land (and housing) market does not exclude a large portion of an urban area's population (because they cannot afford to enter the market) will government have some hope of guiding and controlling land-use.

In summary, we find only four nations—Singapore, Tanzania, the Sudan and Tunisia—where urban land policies are seriously addressing housing shortages. Singapore's has done so for years while initiatives in the other three are more recent. In a few others, new initiatives have tried to increase government powers although it is not clear whether these powers will actually promote 'public and community' interests. Indeed, they may be used to enforce negative controls which actually make it harder for low-income households to find accommodation. In the rest, there has been little attempt to undertake the first step of an urban land policy—to change the prevailing pattern of landownership and land-use rights. And in so many of the seventeen nations, there are increasingly large commitments to public housing programmes but with little recognition that these are bound to fail or to have only very limited impact if more fundamental land issues are not addressed first.

A Note on Rural Land Policies

For rural land, the *Recommendations* are not very specific about policies governing ownership and use. There is a strong stress on the need to maintain the supply of usable land through, for instance, soil conservation and control of salination and desertification (*Recommendation D6*). There is a mention of public ownership being used to 'implement urban and rural land reform processes' (*Recommendation D4*). And there is a stress on ownership rights being transformed 'to match the changing needs of society' (*Recommendation D5*).

Although this study did not cover rural land policies in much depth—indeed, this would be a major study in itself—we found no evidence of new agrarian reforms in the seventeen nations. The distribution of landownership and the terms under which tenants lease land inevitably influences the pattern of income distribution and thus the settlement pattern in rural areas. A region's poverty and the fact that the economy of its villages is stagnant may result largely from the fact that much of the best agricultural land is owned by absentee landlords and by companies who steer profits out of the region. Examples of this were found in many instances in the seventeen national studies. As we noted earlier, rural land policies are an important part of a comprehensive national settlement policy. Thus, it is discouraging to find few governments paying much attention to the question of transforming ownership rights to match the needs of the rural poor. In all of the nations studied bar Singapore, the rural poor made up a significant portion of both the rural and the national population.

Some national governments have implemented land reforms with tangible results—for instance in Tanzania, Kenya, Mexico, Bolivia and Egypt. Others have passed legislation but to little effect as in, for instance, Colombia, India, Brazil, Nepal and the Philippines. But even in nations such as Kenya, Mexico, Bolivia and Egypt where considerable land redistribution took place, there is a need for further reforms

238

and for policies that support the small farmer and for those who will never receive land because of its scarcity. There was little sign of such initiatives in evidence in the 1970s.

Shelter, Infrastructure and Services

The Habitat *Recommendations*

The overriding objectives of settlement policies should be to make shelter, infrastructure and services available to those who need them, in the sequence in which they are needed and at a monetary or social cost they can afford.

(Preamble)

National Housing Policies must aim at providing adequate shelter and services to the lower income groups, distributing available resources on the basis of greatest needs.

(Recommendation C9)

A major part of housing policy efforts should consist of programmes and instruments which actively assist people in continuing to provide better quality housing for themselves, individually or cooperatively.

(Recommendation C10)

Infrastructure policy should be geared to achieve greater equity in the provision of services and utilities, access to places of work and recreational areas . . .

(Recommendation C11)

Safe water supply and hygienic waste disposal should receive priority with a view to achieving measurable qualitative and quantitative targets serving all the population by a certain date.

(Recommendation C12)

The provision of health, nutrition, education, security, recreation and other essential services in all parts of the country should be geared to the needs of the community and receive an effective priority in national and development planning and in the allocation of resources.

(Recommendation C15)

Governments should concentrate on the provision of services and on the physical and spatial reorganization of spontaneous settlements in ways that encourage community initiative and link 'marginal' groups to the national development process.

(Recommendation C17)

Standards for shelter, infrastructure and services should be compatible with local resources, be evolutionary, realistic, and sufficiently adaptable to local culture and conditions . . .

(Recommendation C3)

The choice of designs and technologies for shelter, infrastructure and services should reflect present demands while being able to adapt to future needs and make the best use of local resources and skills and be capable of incremental improvement.

(Recommendation C4)

The special importance of the construction industry should be recognized by every nation and the industry should be given the political, financial and technical support it requires to attain the national objectives and the production targets required for human settlements.

(Recommendation C7)

The informal section should be supported in its efforts to provide shelter, infrastructure and services, especially for the less advantaged.

(Recommendation C8)

National Action

Although many among the seventeen nations have government sponsored housing programmes dating back to the 1950s or early 1960s, the scale of their operations was generally small. Indeed, it was not uncommon to find most of a government's housing budget going on constructing a few houses for government officials. In actual numbers, these represented a tiny percentage of growing need. Rural housing was generally ignored. So too were inner city slums, except where these were demolished to make way for other developments. The needs of the squatter population were also generally ignored, although many governments did try and eliminate their settlements by bulldozing them (with or without associated resettlement schemes).

Since 1970, there has been a noticeable increase in government support for housing programmes and, in several cases, for a wider provision of basic services. There have been some major changes in the kind of shelter policy implemented. Before assessing government action, which is still very inadequate and often ill directed, we will briefly summarize government policies described in more depth in earlier sections under four headings: urban housing, rural housing; services and infrastructure; and the building industry.[22] The reader should note that most of the figures quoted in this summary are targets from development plans, not units actually constructed. As the Assessment will show, what figures we could find for actual achievements showed that targets are often not met.

Urban Housing

Every one of the seventeen national governments is (or claims to be) increasing its support for urban housing programmes. In eight—Kenya, Nigeria, the Sudan,

Tanzania, Jordan, Tunisia, the Philippines and Indonesia—this is evident through notable contrasts in the scale of proposed government action between the early and the later part of the 1970s. In several other nations—notably India, Singapore, Egypt and Brazil—the scale of government programmes has increased in the 1970s, although the programmes themselves date from the 1960s.

In Kenya, the 1974–8 Development Plan aimed at a four-fold increase in urban housing construction over the previous plan period 1970–4 when some 25 000 urban housing units were completed, around 20 000 funded by the government. The National Housing Corporation was to expand enormously its construction of 'low-cost' units while housing development departments were established in major urban areas such as Nairobi and Mombasa to undertake serviced-site and squatter upgrading schemes. In Nigeria, the government planned a major new initiative. The first evidence of a housing programme aiming to reach lower income groups came in 1973 when the federal government announced it was to build 54 000 units for low and middle-income groups. The National Housing Programme was widened for the 1975–80 Plan, the revised version of the plan setting a target of 202 000 units by 1980, 50 000 in Lagos metropolitan area, the rest built under the direction of the nineteen state governments in their major urban areas. Prior to this, the very little government money that had gone to housing went to support middle and higher-income housing, mostly for civil service or other public employees. And in Tanzania, both the scale and the type of programme changed. Between 1969 and 1974, the National Housing Corporation and other public bodies were only constructing some 2000 units a year. The emphasis switched to squatter upgrading and serviced-site schemes. Between 1974 and 1977, nearly 9000 serviced-sites were provided and 8800 existing houses upgraded. Between 1978 and 1981, the programme's target was for roughly double this. Both Nigeria and Tanzania reformed the financial institutions giving housing loans. In Nigeria, a new Federal Mortgage Bank and in Tanzania, a Housing Bank were set up.[23]

Among the five Arab nations, new initiatives were most evident in the Sudan, Tunisia and Jordan. In the Sudan, the Six-Year Plan 1977–8 to 1982–3 is seen as the first phase of a long-term housing strategy after, by its own admission, the previous plan 'did not address itself in any comprehensive way to the housing problem'.[24] 129 000 serviced sites, 5000 public housing units and 18 000 private sector units were planned with 42 000 units to be upgraded. In Jordan, the government's Housing Corporation has received more support since 1973. For 1973–5, 3900 units were constructed while 7050 were planned for 1976–80. In Tunisia, a new commitment to improving urban housing conditions became apparent in the 1973–6 Plan during which some 72 500 units were built, three-fifths with government aid. The 1977–81 Plan aimed at 125 000 units, more than two-thirds with government aid. Institutions connected to housing programmes were decentralized in all three nations. In Tunisia, the agency in charge of implementing 'social interest' public housing programmes began to work through four regional agencies. In the Sudan, the official housing loan agency, the Estates Bank, opened new branches in towns other than the capital. And in Jordan, the Housing Bank opened new branch offices in several towns.

Among the five Asian nations, we found major new programmes in the Philippines and Indonesia. In the Philippines, a National Housing Authority was set up in 1975 to bring all existing agencies concerned with housing under one organization. This is in charge of a programme to build over 200 000 units between 1978 and 1987 (72 137 in the first five years), mostly for low-income groups. Major slum and squatter upgrading and serviced-site programmes were also proposed. Along with various other housing programmes, the intention is to reach more than half a million households in the first five years and 1.1 million within the decade. This compares with an annual average of just over 10 000 units built or financed by the government between 1968 and 1971.[25] In Indonesia, a National Housing Policy Board was set up to formulate housing policies at the beginning of the 1974–9 Plan while a new National Urban Development Corporation was to be in charge of implementing low-cost housing and serviced-site programmes, and a Housing Mortgage Bank was to provide low-income households with long-term credit. For 1974–9, 90 000 low-cost housing units were planned, 20 000 of which were to be built by the new Corporation. And more than 200 000 serviced sites were planned, this Corporation undertaking 53 000 of them. For the 1979–84 Plan, the target is for 150 000 low-cost houses to be built through this corporation and the Housing Mortgage Bank.

In Singapore, Egypt, Brazil, India and Colombia, urban housing programmes expanded in the 1970s. Singapore's was certainly the largest relative to national population. By 1980, more than two-thirds of the national population lived in units built under the direction of the Housing and Development Board which had only been set up two decades before. In Egypt, targets for public housing programmes were considerably increased in the late 1970s. In 1977, the target was for 34 000 public housing units compared to annual achievements which never exceeded 11 000 units between 1966–7 and 1974,[26] and a new National Housing Fund was set up in 1976. In India, the target for publicly sponsored housing units was 2 million for the 1978–82 Plan to be undertaken by state governments and their agencies, 85 per cent of which were to be for economically weaker sections of the population.

In Colombia, the Institute of Territorial Credit, the government's urban housing agency, has expanded and diversified its operations since 1971. For the five years leading up to this date, it supported an average of some 12 700 units a year. Between 1972 and 1975, 20 000 or more households were reached by its programmes annually, including serviced-site and housing upgrading schemes. In 1975–6, 25 000 units were constructed through its programmes while a major new programme launched in 1976 seeks to raise living standards for the poorest half of the population in 23 major cities (not including the four largest cities). In Brazil, various attempts have been made since 1973 to make the urban housing programme reach lower-income groups with improved housing. The National Housing Bank's programme, set up in 1964, had largely failed to do so. A National Low Cost Housing Plan was launched in 1973 to build some 2 million units in ten years for lower-income groups. Repayment conditions for housing loans were made softer for lower-income groups, and a new programme aimed to provide serviced plots.

We should also recall that among the seventeen nations all the others had some evidence of increased government support for urban housing programmes. In Mexico, a new Institute of the National Housing Fund for Workers was set up in 1972, largely funded by a payroll tax, to give loans to those wishing to buy or enlarge their house. This, along with other public agencies, brought about a marked increase in the number of units constructed with public support. In Iraq, public housing programmes have expanded and it is the government's intention to increasingly take over from the private sector as the major housing supplier. In Nepal, the government was proposing to establish a Housing Corporation during the 1975–80 Plan. In Bolivia, a new Housing and Construction Bank was set up in 1974 to help promote and finance the construction, repair and expansion of houses as well as the construction of infrastructure and the building industry's modernization.

Rural Housing

There are fewer and less coherent government efforts to improve living conditions in rural areas, apart from the extension of basic services which will be looked at in the next subsection. Some nations such as Jordan and Iraq do have rural housing programmes with publicly funded units being built. Although no figures on the breakdown between rural and urban public housing programmes were found, from the information we did gather it seems unlikely that these were making much impact on rural housing conditions. Among the other Arab nations, Egypt and the Sudan had no major rural housing programme. Tunisia's housing policies were unique in that they had a major rural housing component. During the 1977–81 Plan, the government aimed to aid the construction of 40 000 rural units. This means that nearly half the housing units which were to receive government support were in rural areas; and the units built were the most heavily subsidized.

Among the Asian nations, India has the largest and longest-established rural housing programme. A scheme to provide free house sites for landless workers was reported to have produced over 5.8 million sites by the end of 1975. The state of Kerala launched a major rural housing programme in the early 1970s, mobilizing local government committees who, with volunteers and students, built more than 50 000 houses for the landless. Indonesia too is giving more attention to improving rural housing conditions through extension services and demonstration projects that assist and encourage villagers to upgrade their own houses. In the Philippines, there were no major government initiatives to improve rural housing conditions up to 1977 although the 1978–82 Plan had ambitious targets for a new rural housing programme. This includes the promotion of housing improvement through self-help to reach 48 713 households by the end of the Plan.

Among the three SubSaharan nations, only Tanzania has a major programme to improve rural housing conditions. The Tanzanian Housing Bank has extended its lending activities to rural areas. The target for 1981 was for 32 000 permanent village houses. In Kenya, government resources in rural areas concentrate on providing basic services, while in Nigeria little government action is evident in seeking to improve rural living and housing conditions.

Basic Services

The Habitat Conference recommended the establishment of national targets to reach all their population with safe water and hygienic waste disposal by a certain date. The Water Conference held a year later recommended that 1981–90 be designated the 'International Drinking Water Supply and Sanitation Decade' and that national plans should aim to provide safe drinking water and basic sanitation to all by 1990 if possible. A survey of water supply and sanitation services by the World Health

Organization for 1975 revealed that only two people out of five in the Third World had access to safe drinking water and that only one out of three had any kind of sanitary facility. Estimates for 1980 suggest that there has been no significant improvement. For instance, although more people in rural areas have been reached with safe water, the percentage of the Third World's population so served had actually dropped. The statistics for 1980 submitted by national governments show a quarter or less of the rural population with 'reasonable access' to safe water in Kenya, Nigeria, Indonesia, Nepal, Brazil and Iraq with no figures available for Bolivia. Less than a third of the rural population were so served in India, Tanzania and Tunisia. Urban households are generally better served although one does have serious doubts about government claims that 97 or more per cent of the urban population in Egypt, Bolivia and Kenya have reasonable access to safe water.

Table 6 Community water supply and sanitation

Countries	Community water supply		Sanitation	
	Urban (%)	Rural (%)	Urban (%)	Rural (%)
Africa				
Kenya	100	13	50	45 (1970)
Nigeria	92	14	41	—
Tanzania	82	28	93	40
Asia				
India	82	30	47	2
Indonesia	36	15	73	19
Nepal	81	6	18	—
Philippines	73	46	32	27
Singapore	74 (1970)	—	93 (1970)	—
Latin America				
Bolivia	100	2 (1970)	100	4 (1970)
Brazil	75	5	35	25
Colombia	73	46	60	14
Mexico	62	42	50	12
Arab Nations				
Egypt	97	74	70	5
Iraq	97	22	—	—
Jordan	100	55	100	35
Sudan	49	45	80	—
Tunisia	96	29	64	60

Source: Report on the 'International Drinking Water Supply and Sanitation Decade' for the United Nations General Asembly. One should note that these are only approximations supplied by governments and are not directly comparable due to the lack of adequate monitoring systems and lack of standardization in the definitions used. For water supply, the percentage is that proportion of the population with reasonable access which is to say that person(s) in the houshold collecting water do not spend a disproportionate part of their day doing so. For sanitation, the percentage given is that proportion of the population with adequate excreta disposal facilities.

For sanitation, again, urban residents appear better served than their rural counterparts in all the nations for which we have statistics. A quarter or less of the rural population in Brazil, Egypt, Colombia, Mexico, Indonesia and India have any kind of sanitary excreta disposal. Once again, some of the higher figures such as those of Jordan and Bolivia with 100 per cent of urban residents adequately served seem exaggerated. Such statistics were supplied by national governments in response to a request from the United Nations. Our field experience suggests that in many instances, the percentage of the population given by national governments as having reasonable access to potable water and to basic sanitation is grossly exaggerated.

Educational statistics for the mid-1970s also show large sectors of the population excluded from educational programmes. In the Sudan and Nigeria, more than half the primary school age children were not at primary schools. Half or more of the adult population was illiterate in Nepal, India, Kenya, the Sudan and Egypt while a third or more were illiterate in Tunisia, Jordan, Bolivia, Tanzania and Indonesia. And life-expectancy statistics demonstrate the continuing poverty and lack of health care. In 1978, life expectancy remained below 50 in Nigeria, Indonesia, the Sudan and Nepal, and below 55 in Tanzania, India, Kenya, Egypt and Bolivia.

Although programmes to extend basic services to the national population date back many years in all seventeen nations, recently there have been more serious attempts to spread basic services such as potable water, hygienic waste disposal, primary education and basic health care in many of the seventeen nations. The 'basic' or 'minimum needs' approach so stressed throughout the Habitat *Recommendations* is thus receiving more support.

India's Basic Minimum Needs Programme, started in 1972, shows this new commitment with the Sixth Plan, beginning in 1978, further increasing support for this Programme. A rural health programme aims to provide much improved primary health care. The government aims to provide safe drinking water to all India's villages by the early 1980s. Central government's support for water supply and sanitation increased very considerably in 1972 with the Fifth Plan and then again in 1978. And more support was given during the 1970s to slum improvement programmes which included provision of basic services.

All four other Asian nations also show an increased commitment to providing basic services. In Nepal, health and education services have received more support since 1971. The Fifth Plan, 1975–80, gives more support to water supply and sanitation, after the previous plan had initiated water supply and sewerage schemes in several towns and villages. In the Philippines, both the 1978–82 Plan and longer-term strategy point to more support for the provision of safe drinking water, sewerage and flood control. Health and education programmes are to be strengthened, and projections for 1975, 1982, 1987 and 2000 show social infrastructure, health and medical facilities, water supply and sewerage each receiving increased support in terms of percentages of GNP devoted to them. In addition, in the late 1970s, there has been more support for extending basic services to existing slums and squatter communities, whereas before government efforts often tried to relocate squatters.

Such an approach has also received more support in Indonesia. A 'Kampung Improvement Programme', begun in 1969 in Jakarta, aimed to reach some 3.5 million people in that city with minimum basic services by the end of 1979. During the 1979–84 Plan, the aim is to reach all urban low-income residential areas with minimum basic services. In addition, the government is expanding primary health care services throughout the nation.

In two of the three SubSaharan African nations—Kenya and Tanzania—the 'basic needs' approach is embodied in their development plans. In Nigeria it is not, although the new civilian administration may increasingly veer towards such an approach. In Tanzania, the commitment to meeting basic service needs for the whole population dates back to independence in 1961. By 1977, its achivements were impressive. Universal primary education had been achieved. Primary health care facilities were far more widely available in both rural and urban communities. Provision of piped water within less than half a kilometre of all consumers is the target for 1991 with intermediate solutions being devised before then. Adult literacy programmes have raised literacy levels to one of the highest in Africa. And slum improvement programmes with the extension of basic services to slum and squatter areas is now a major part of the housing programme.

Kenya, too, is stressing the basic needs approach. The 1974–8 Plan included a stress on primary health care and on bringing a safe, sufficient and convenient water source to the entire population by 2000. An accelerated public works programme aimed to install sewerage in all major urban areas. Universal primary education and increased adult literacy are major goals. And squatter upgrading programmes are gradually becoming more acceptable to local and national governments.

Among the group of Arab nations, there is less commitment to meeting basic service needs in rural areas and generally less acceptance of slum and squatter upgrading programmes. In Egypt, little attention is given to providing basic services to villages or to households living on illegally occupied or subdivided land. In Iraq, the government's concentration is on expanding public housing construction and replacing slums rather than seeking to extend basic services and help upgrade existing housing. However, the 1975–9 Plan did give strong support to education, social services, sewerage in urban areas, provision of potable water in rural communities and health. In Tunisia, the government's commitment to improving housing and service standards has come to include a new concentration on slum upgrading rather than slum clearance. For water supply, by 1981 the target is for two-thirds of the national population to have access to a fountain or direct connection to a water system while a nationwide sewer construction programme expects to be able to reach all areas now served with water systems by the late 1980s.

Building Industry

When looking at all seventeen nations, it is possible to identify four scales of operation in housing construction. All seventeen have three of these while most have all four. At the top is the large construction company, often part of a multinational corporation, which has large capital assets and uses industrialized building techniques. At the next level, there are smaller national firms with lower labour productivity and less capital assets which utilize industrial building materials (and perhaps some prefabricated components). At the third level, there are small building firms which usually use traditional craft techniques and often rely on traditional building materials. Typically, this scale of operation is only involved in the construction of one or two houses at any one time. Then finally, there is self-help where the household itself—perhaps assisted by friends and, for certain jobs, skilled artisans—build the house.

There is no simple division of these scales of operation between formal and informal sector. The largest two scales of operation operate in the formal sector and tend to get public housing contracts. The third scale may operate in both sectors, building houses to official standards and with official permission for middle or upper-income groups and, when such work is not available, building (say) units on illegal subdivisions. The self-help sector may also build what becomes a unit meeting official standards. But most self-help construction activity remains in the informal sector. Formal sector activities remain heavily concentrated in urban areas while the housing construction activities of the larger companies are usually concentrated in major cities.

Although no national building industry falls into four exclusive categories like these and no simple division can categorize a building enterprise as being in the formal or informal sector (since it may work in both), it is useful to use these distinctions in examining who builds houses for whom. The large construction company using prefabricated building systems or components is evident in virtually all nations with major public housing programmes: Brazil, Mexico, Singapore, India, Kenya, Nigeria, Jordan, Iraq, the Philippines, Indonesia and Egypt. In Iraq, the Philippines and Indonesia, public agencies have established prefabricated housing factories. And in Egypt, the government is working with various foreign firms to greatly expand annual production of prefabricated housing units.

Apart from publicly financed housing units, the scale of formal sector housing construction will obviously depend on the number of households that can afford the kind of units it builds. In Brazil, for instance, this private sector is very large; in Nepal, it hardly exists. Obviously, among the seventeen nations, the size of the formal sector's contribution to total housing activity differs enormously.

In many of the seventeen nations much of the building materials the formal sector uses have to be imported. The result is escalating housing costs as cost of materials rise. There are also interruptions in supplies (and thus shortages which also tend to push up prices). The high price and high-import cost of modern building materials were noted in the Philippines, Bolivia, the Sudan, Jordan, Iraq, Egypt, Kenya and Nigeria. The cost of building materials alone in total construction costs in 1975 (excluding land) was found to be 66 per cent in India, 63.6 per cent in the Philippines, 57.2 per cent in Iraq and 55.8 per cent in Jordan. The average for a survey of eighteen nations for dates between 1965 and 1975 was 55.6 per cent.[27]

Government support for the building industry is almost exclusively directed towards the formal sector. If publicly owned companies do not build public housing units themselves, it is the larger, more modern private construction companies that get the contracts. In addition, there is very little government funding to support the development and production of cheaper building materials based on indigenous resources. Publicly funded housing projects are usually built to designs and standards developed for the industrialized nations and do not seek to use locally produced materials to reduce unit costs.

Thus, the trend seems to be away from developing and improving local building materials and towards more reliance on industrialized building materials and systems. In the Background (page 205), we noted the very low priority that building materials had received in multilateral aid. In fact, virtually all multilateral aid devoted to building materials had gone to cement plants up to 1978. There are a few exceptions. In the Sudan, the Building and Road Research Institute (formerly the National Building Research Station) is seeking to improve the quality and durability of local building materials and a new plant is being constructed to produce mudblocks stabilized with asphalt. In Kenya, research is going on into similar types of stabilized mudbricks and into soil–cement blocks. In Tanzania, the use of locally produced burnt bricks is being encouraged. And the Arab Bank for the Economic Development of Africa has given a loan for a brick, tile and concrete industries integrated project in Dodoma, a major departure from usual multilateral-aid backed projects. In India, mini-cement plants have been developed at a capital cost and capacity to suit the needs of a small group of villages. Despite these and a few other projects, governments have not shown much inclination to encourage the use of local building materials. Nor have they undertaken such basic changes as reformulating building regulations so these allow the use of such materials in legal housing units.

Assessment

The impression one gets from examining national development plans for the seventeen nations is thus one of increasing support for shelter provision and improvement and the extension of basic services to a wider proportion of the population, especially in urban areas. As we noted earlier, there is a notable contrast between proposed government policies in urban shelter provision between the early and the late 1970s. However, the contrast is usually only notable because governments were doing virtually nothing in the late 1960s and early 1970s. The scale of government action usually remains far below anything approaching the scale of needs. And government targets must not be confused with actual achievements. In most of the cases where we found statistics on progress in achieving official targets, the number of units actually built or under construction falls far short of goals. For instance, Kenya's 1979–83 Plan admitted that the previous Plan's targets were not met: 'Over the last plan period, only 8 per cent of the low cost units planned were in fact completed and these cost on average five times the expected cost'.[28] It also seems that the serviced-site programme for the 1974–8 Plan was way behind its ambitious targets. Between 1975 and 1977, only 1031 had been completed in Nairobi and 815 elsewhere.[29] For the whole of Kenya, total urban housing needs were estimated to grow by 160 000 units between 1974 and 1978. Kenya's national report to Habitat claimed that half of these needs would be met through government funded programmes and projects. The final achievement was probably no more than 5 per cent.

Initial reports about other public housing targets—for instance Nigeria's 1975–80 target of over 200 000 public funded units or Indonesia's target of 73 000 low-cost and units and serviced sites built by the National Urban Development Corporation—suggest that final achievements will be well below targets. In the Philippines, although no statistics were found as to progress with its massive public shelter programme, the targets seem far beyond the capabilities of even its expanded institutional base. We recall that between 1948 and 1972, only 13 500 units were constructed by public funds for low-income households and that government-built or financed units averaged just over 10 000 units a year between 1968 and 1971. Government funded 'low-cost' units have usually been too expensive for low-income households. But the government housing programme 1978–82 is aiming at more than quarter of a million units, many of which are claimed to be for lower-income groups, and nearly 200 000 units upgraded, 144 245 of them in urban areas.[30]

Official statistics often provide little clue as to the precise nature of current shelter problems and trends and as to where the major problems are located. As the Background showed (page 204), what statistics and estimates do exist show that all governments bar Singapore's are faced with a massive (and often growing) stock of poor quality and unserviced or badly serviced dwellings. If a government counts (or estimates) the number of legal housing units nationally which meet official standards and then compares this with the number of households, the two figures will bear little relation to each other. Similarly, if the government estimates the number of units needed annually to keep up with rising demands and to gradually replace deteriorating and substandard stock and then compares it to the output of the formal construction sector, again the figures will bear little relation to each other. If the difference between the two figures is used to give a 'housing deficit'—the figure has little meaning; for it would imply that a quarter, a half or even more of the national population—and most of the new households formed every year—are homeless. But they are not. Virtually everyone *is* housed—even if a large and even growing proportion have to endure very poor and often overcrowded living conditions.

We have seen how virtually all the rural houses and a large proportion of the urban houses are built (and have been built) by the informal construction sector in all seventeen nations bar Singapore. Only through such activities are most of their populations housed—and housed at a price within reach of lower-income groups. A concentration on estimating figures for the amount of units needed per year serves little purpose in formulating housing policies. We learn very little from knowing that in Egypt, an average of some 200 000 urban units and 116 000 rural units are needed annually between 1975 and 2000 except that it does contrast sharply with the 1977 target of 100 000 formal sector units. And we learn little from the official estimate that from 1972, 1.5 million units are needed annually in Indonesia although this, too, puts the target of some 60 000 low-cost housing units a year during the 1975–9 Plan into perspective. In neither nation are officially approved units likely to meet more than a small fraction of these needs.

At this point it is important to distinguish between rural and urban housing. National housing targets become very misleading, for housing needs are quantitatively and qualitatively different for rural and urban areas. The *World Housing Survey 1974* estimated that India, the Sudan, Tanzania, Kenya and Nepal (among others) must construct eight or more units annually per 1000 inhabitants to meet housing requirements. For Tanzania, the figure is 13.8 annually.[31] Then we find that official housing targets for both private and public sectors only represent one unit per 1000 inhabitants or less, despite rapidly expanded housing programmes. However, since most of these nations' households are still in rural areas, the new programmes may be making substantial contributions to improving housing conditions in urban areas, although the total appears very inadequate for the national population. And with the level of rural per capita incomes in these nations, nobody could expect the formal construction sector to have a major role in housing the rural population without a level of public subsidy per unit that is far beyond the range of their governments.

In addition, the rate at which new households are being formed differs enormously between rural and urban settlements (and indeed between different urban settlements). Generally, urban settlements have quantitative housing needs growing far faster than rural settlements. Indeed, quantitative needs are not actually growing in many rural settlements. And a rapidly growing urban settlement may have quantitative housing needs growing by fifteen or more units per 1000 population annually.

There are also fundamental qualitative differences between the needs rural and urban houses fulfil. A house gives its occupants access to an income, shelter from the elements, access to basic services, and to family and friends, and some security and privacy. In urban areas, access to an income may be the primary need; it often is for lower-income households. Access to family and friends and water may be the next most important need. These are often more important to the household's health (or indeed survival) than a reasonable quality home. For this reason, the needs of low-income households are often better served by very poor-quality shacks on land subject to flooding or landslides, or even on the local garbage dump, which gives them good access to income-earning possibilities. Higher standard serviced sites or public housing units on the urban periphery may appear to give them better-quality living environments while in fact making them even worse off by lowering their access to income.

By comparison, in rural areas, the site of the house is usually close to (or even in the middle of) the place where the household derives its living. Only rarely is the cost of the site itself a major household expense. Only very rarely would a rural householder consider employing a builder to construct a unit to official housing standards. Generally lower density settlements mean some of the dangers of city dwellings—lack of light and ventilation, overcrowding, contamination of water supply—are lessened.

The fact that basic shelter needs in rural and urban settlements are both qualitatively and quantitatively different makes any concentration on annual national targets for units built by the formal sector or by public funds almost irrelevant for nations with a substantial rural population. The Habitat *Recommendations* recognize the need for new approaches to housing policies. The type of approach they outline is very different from the conventional concentration on annual targets. Indeed, no mention is made of annual targets per 1000 inhabitants. And no explicit mention is made of public housing programmes.

Perhaps the two most fundamental differences between conventional policies and the *Recommendations* is the latter's stress on seeking to reach everyone with improved standards and its acceptance of the informal sector's role in doing this. On this first difference, the priority given to 'meeting basic needs' for all is apparent throughout the *Recommendations for National Action*. The *Preamble* to *Section C* states that the 'over-riding objective of settlement policies should be to make shelter, infrastructure and services available to those who need them in the sequence in which they are needed and at a monetary or social cost they can afford'. *Recommendation C9* states that national housing policies should aim at 'providing adequate shelter and services to the lower income groups, distributing available resources on the basis of greatest needs'. *Recommendation C11* says that 'infrastructure policy should be geared to achieve greater equity in the provision of services and utilities . . .' while *Recommendation C15* states that the provision of health, education and other essential services should receive 'an effective priority in national and development planning and in the allocation of resources'. Safe water supply and hygienic waste disposal should receive special attention 'with a view to achieving measurable qualitative and quantitative targets serving all the population by a certain date' (*Recommendation C12*).

The second difference, the acceptance of the informal sector's major role in housing provision, is also evident in many of the *Recommendations*—*C10* states that 'a major part of a housing policy's efforts should consist of programmes and instruments which actively assist people in continuing to provide better quality housing for themselves, individually or cooperatively. *C8* states that the informal sector be supported 'in its efforts to provide shelter, infrastructure and services, especially for the less advantaged'. *C17* suggests that governments 'concentrate on the provision of services and on the physical and spatial reorganization of spontaneous settlements in ways that encourage community initiative and link 'marginal' groups to the national development process'. Although this is not very specific, it does state that governments should work with the inhabitants of squatter settlements and concentrate on providing them with basic services. *C4* stresses that the choice of designs and technologies for housing should reflect present demands. And with C3, the stress is on ensuring housing standards, designs and technologies are compatible with local skills and resources. In all these one sees the recognition that the informal sector plays a major role in shelter provision —and will continue to do so. For this reason, government policies must be oriented towards helping and assisting this sector. With regard to standards, they recommend that these be revised so they fulfil their primary purpose—of reconciling the population's shelter needs with a reasonable level of safety, health and environmental quality.

In assessing governments' performance in the light of the Habitat *Recommendations*, we shall look briefly at six aspects of government policies: public housing programmes; serviced-site schemes; slum and squatter upgrading; standards; building materials and technology; and housing finance. In each of these, two questions will be asked. Are government policies using their resources to reach as many people as possible with improved housing conditions and basic services? And do their policies recognize (and support) the role the informal sector plays in this?

Public Housing Programmes

The *Preamble* to *Recommendation C9* notes that 'in many parts of the world, the cheapest available contract-built housing is too expensive for the majority of households'. Furthermore, 'publicly provided housing because of the limited available resources can only provide for a small fraction of the real need'. This generalization is true for all seventeen nations except Singapore. Since unit costs are high—considerably more than low-income households can (or are prepared to) pay—each unit has to have a large subsidy if it is to benefit low-income households. Alternatively, if the subsidy is reduced so more units can be built, it puts the cost of the units beyond the range of low-income groups. The result, apparent in most of the seventeen nations, is either relatively few households benefiting from heavily subsidized units or lower-middle and middle-income groups being the main beneficiaries of public housing programmes.

Alternatively, the government may rely on private or semi-public construction firms to build the units with public money going to provide long-term loans for households wanting to purchase such units. But the same problem remains. To reach lower-income groups, a heavily subsidized loan is needed so the number of loans that can be given is limited. Or if loans are not heavily subsidized, lower income groups are excluded.

By 1976, housing policies in Jordan, Egypt, Tunisia, Brazil, Singapore, India, Iraq, Nigeria, Colombia and Bolivia were dominated by public housing programmes (that is, publicly financed housing or public loans to increase demand for housing). Such programmes were also a major part of housing policies in Kenya, Indonesia and the Philippines. In most cases, the scale of government effort fell far short of need. In Jordan, the Housing Corporation's five-year target for 1975–80 actually met less than six months' growth in housing need. In Egypt, the public housing target for 1977 was 34 000 units although urban housing needs grew by some 150 000 units that year. In Bolivia, the combined efforts of various public bodies between 1970 and 1975 supported the construction of some 1300 units a year when annual urban needs were estimated to grow by some 20 000 units a year. In Nigeria, Colombia and India too, public housing efforts were producing only a small proportion of the annual growth in needs.

Tunisia and Brazil had somewhat larger public housing programmes. By the end of 1976, Brazil's National Housing Bank had funded nearly 1.5 million units including around 400 000 loans to low-income households. But estimates put the need for new housing units at between 8 and 11 million for 1960–75, including six million for lower income households. The Tunisian government aimed to construct 120 000 publicly sponsored units between 1973 and 1981, a very considerable number for a nation with 6 million inhabitants in 1978. After Singapore, this is by far the largest public housing programme relative to population size among the seventeen nations. But even so, housing production to official standards falls short of needs. Once again, the deficit will be made up by informal sector activity and by overcrowding in existing dwellings.

In fact, Singapore was the only nation among the seventeen to have a public housing programme that got close to meeting needs. By 1980, some two-thirds of the total population was living in units built by the public housing body, the Housing and Development Board. Elsewhere, programmes usually met only a small proportion of need. Where housing policies concentrated on giving little or no subsidy—as in Brazil—lower-income groups were largely excluded. And the size of the programme was limited by the fact that a substantial proportion of the population could not afford to take part in it. Where government gave sufficient subsidy to bring publicly sponsored units within reach of lower income groups—as in Egypt and India—high unit costs meant the programme could only reach a small percentage of those in need.

Singapore's relatively successful public housing programme has encouraged other governments to embark on similar courses. Thus, it is worth asking why they succeeded while other nations met with far less success. When looking at Singapore's background, we were struck by several unique characteristics which help explain this. Firstly, inmigration to the city was very slow, despite a rapidly growing economic base. Singapore as a nation has very little rural land and thus few poor rural households migrating to the city in search of a better life. Any city in one of the other sixteen nations with an economy growing as fast as Singapore's would have attracted an enormous wave of inmigration.

Secondly, and related to this first point, Singapore's per capita GNP grew at a phenomenal 7.4 per cent a year between 1960 and 1978, far higher than any nation—and probably any city—among the other sixteen nations. With a rapidly growing economic base, relatively few unemployment problems and growing purchasing power among much of the population, public and private funds for housing are more easy to mobilize.

Thirdly, Singapore's government enjoyed one valuable colonial legacy—very extensive amounts of publicly owned land, including public land in or close to the city centre. Thus, public housing estates could be built close to the city centre without involving the government in prohibitively expensive (and lengthy) land expropriation procedures. With low-income households sited close to the major employment opportunities and with good wage-earning prospects (because of the booming economy), some of the often more intractable problems with public housing projects for low-income families are removed. How many other Third World nations can claim rapid and sustained economic growth rates with very little inmigration from other areas? In addition, how many major Third World cities can build on the extensive reserves of well-located public land Singapore had in the early 1960s? Certainly none of the sixteen other nations we included in this study had comparable conditions.

Given the unique circumstances surrounding Singapore's public housing programme, the relevance of its experiences seems to be that effective urban land policies are the only basis for successful urban housing policies. The *type* of housing built in Singapore has far less relevance. Even if other nations could afford to construct similar tower blocks on a scale to get close to meeting rising housing needs, such units do not seem the best way of improving housing conditions. The housing programme demanded a degree of public control that few other societies would have tolerated. As one commentator living in Singapore stated, 'perhaps urban disturbances or riots have not occurred in Singapore only because the present economic prosperity has enough crumbs even for the urban poor'.[32] Many of the thousands of households affected by slum clearance and redevelopment schemes could not afford to stay in public housing despite concessional rates on what were already subsidized rents.

Furthermore, some commentators suggest that the concentration on constructing small flats in large monoblocks has contributed greatly to stress, delinquency and a lessening of traditional, communal aspects of living. Even given Singapore's unique space constraints, residential developments could have achieved sufficiently high density without total reliance on high-rise apartment blocks.

Another serious drawback to public housing policies—and one that Singapore's shares with those of other nations—is the problem of maintenance. As *Recommendation C6* notes, in choosing alternatives for shelter, account should be taken of social, environmental and economic costs and benefits 'including that of future management, maintenance and operations as well as capital costs'. If a government housing programme leases houses or flats to the public and does not provide for broad participation in management and upkeep, then the tenants will feel little incentive to maintain the housing structure since it is not their responsibility. Furthermore, blocks of flats demand maintenance operations beyond the scope and abilities of individual households. There was evidence of maintenance problems in several of the public housing programmes—although the housing authorities are not very ready to admit to such problems. In Singapore, some of the earliest Housing and Development Board's flats have sunk into almost slum-like conditions within 20 years of being built. And every effort is being made by the Housing and Development Board to encourage public housing tenants to buy their own flats so that responsibility for internal maintenance passes from the public authorities to individual households. In fact, generous subsidies are given to encourage this. In Egypt, the Ministry of Housing and Reconstruction is encouraging public housing tenants to become owners by offering generous terms for converting rents into long-term purchase payments. In Indonesia, no doubt the very rapid expansion in the number of people employed by the National

Urban Development Authority relates to the number of areas it has to cover including planning, acquiring land, financing and constructing low-cost housing and being responsible for rent collection and for overseeing maintenance and repair. In December 1977, just three years after its foundation, it had 983 staff and was said to be grossly understaffed.[33] By contrast, the Nigerian government admits that it does not have the professional staff to cope with maintenance and repair of federal housing estates and is proposing to contract the maintenance of estates out to private sector enterprises.[34]

Thus, most public housing programmes do not ensure that government resources devoted to housing reach as many people as possible with improved housing conditions and basic services. Singapore is the exception because of unique circumstances. Besides Singapore, perhaps Tunisia is closest to achieving this, relative to population size. But in Tunisia, recent initiatives suggest less concentration on public housing units and more support for informal sector construction through slum upgrading and serviced-site schemes. It is a policy change that all other governments with large public housing programmes might consider, if they are serious about improving housing conditions.

Serviced-site Schemes

The first sign of governments moving away from exclusive concentration on public housing programmes is usually the support of serviced-site schemes. These bring down unit costs since no house is constructed before the lot is sold or leased. Cost recovery is easier since serviced lots are usually within the price range of a far wider proportion of the population (although very often not the lowest-income groups). Responsibility for maintaining and upgrading the unit is also taken out of the hands of the public authorities. In the Sudan, Tanzania, the Philippines, Kenya, India, Colombia, and Indonesia, such programmes are playing major roles in government shelter policies. In Brazil, Egypt, Tunisia, and Nepal, such programmes—or individual projects—are also in evidence.

Serviced-site schemes do represent a step towards more widely based housing programmes which support informal sector construction activities. But only in the Sudan and Tanzania have they become the central part of urban housing policies. Although serviced-site schemes generally represent less subsidy per unit (indeed, cost recovery may be total) and can reach far more people with improved living conditions, they also suffer from some of the disadvantages of public housing programmes. Firstly, they divert attention away from the real priority—reforming the urban land market so it does not automatically exclude lower-income groups from legal housing. Secondly, they, like public housing programmes, define where lower-income groups can live. This may—and in many cases does—ill match their needs. In seeking to minimize costs, land for such schemes is often purchased on the urban periphery, the lots developed and then sold or leased to low-income households. But the cost in time and money to both primary and secondary wage-earners in getting to work or in lost income-generating activities can nullify much or all of the benefits of the new sites. For this reason, many serviced-site projects have found difficulties in attracting customers and have failed, like the public housing projects which usually preceded them, to improve living conditions for lower-income households.

Furthermore, if serviced-site schemes are to be implemented on a scale which gets close to meeting growing shelter needs, the public authorities will have to have the power and the institutional framework to ensure that land costs for serviced lots are not prohibitively expensive. This they may choose to do with taxes, relying on the private sector to sell the land for serviced lots or by entry into the land market themselves to guarantee an adequate supply of land for serviced-site schemes. As we noted under Land, only a small minority of the seventeen nations have legislation and institutions in place to ensure that this is possible.

One should also note in passing that many government officials still regard serviced-site schemes as no more than officially sponsored slum or squatter settlement construction. There is also a tendency for government agencies to make standards too high—so unit costs are beyond the reach of the lower-income groups—or even to begin constructing core houses or 'low-cost' houses which again defeats the intention of minimizing unit costs. This is particularly noticeable in Indonesia. Their *National Report* to Habitat talked of government efforts focusing 'on stimulating sites and services and low-cost housing for the low and moderate income groups'.[35] But public projects are concentrating on the construction of houses and core units which do not get allocated to the lowest-income groups.

Slum and Squatter Upgrading

In the last ten years, slum and squatter upgrading programmes have generally replaced slum demolition and squatter 'resettlement' (although there are notable exceptions in many of the seventeen nations, including the large squatter eviction programmes in Delhi during 1975–7). In the Philippines, since 1975 public authorities have given more support to slum and squatter upgrading projects which minimize the need to relocate families. We noted that in Indonesia, the Kampung Improvement Programme has successfully improved living conditions in some of Jakarta's poorest living quarters and the programme has been extended to other major cities. India's Central Scheme for Environmental Improvement in Slum Areas has concentrated on bringing basic services to some of the poorest households in major cities. In Tunisia, slum upgrading programmes seem to be replacing the earlier concentration on slum clearance. In Tanzania, slum clearance schemes were abandoned in the late 1960s and replaced with slum and squatter upgrading and serviced-site programmes. In Colombia, since 1972, there has been increasing government support for extending basic services and encouraging housing improvement for lower-income urban households.

However, in some nations, slum and squatter upgrading are not seen as appropriate government policies. In Iraq, the concentration is still on condemning temporary buildings and *sarifas* and seeking to rehouse some of those displaced in new settlements. Little attention is given to improving conditions in older housing stock. The *Arab Report* pointed to the contrast 'between the care devoted to the luxurious, high-technology prestige buildings in Baghdad and the neglect suffered by the debilitated housing within the same neighbourhood'.[36]

Slum and squatter upgrading programmes do seek to reach a large portion of urban households normally bypassed by housing programmes. They also encourage informal sector activity. *Recommendation C8* notes that priority areas for action should include 'ensuring security of land tenure for unplanned settlements where appropriate' while *Recommendation C17* notes that governments should concentrate on providing services and on the 'physical and spatial reorganization of spontaneous settlements in ways that encourage community initiative'. It may be that the relative success of this approach in nations mentioned above (including the relatively low costs per household reached) and the relative failure to date of slum and squatter eradication programmes will encourage the wider use of such upgrading schemes in future.

Standards

Official standards are often entirely inappropriate to what should be the most pressing task; improving living conditions for the widest possible percentage of the population. Infrastructure and service standards aren't related to actual needs and local resources. The result is public works budgets dominated by providing 'western' standards for, say, water supply which benefit only a tiny minority of the population. Similarly, building codes and regulations in most of the seventeen nations make the construction of legal buildings more expensive and more difficult than those needed to meet basic health and safety standards. Official standards usually prohibit the use of local traditional materials and may demand the use of materials or components which have to be imported.

In fact, the standards were often 'imported' too. Many date from colonial times, imposing standards on lot sizes, housing designs and construction standards that happened to be current in the former colonial power's own country, when they were instituted several decades ago. In Latin America, they are frequently based on western models, again introduced many decades ago with little or no attempt since then to modify them. Thus, in the Sudan, building regulations can still demand minimum floor-to-ceiling heights of 3 metres while those in Nigeria can demand a minimum amount of rooms or the use of expensive, imported materials. It is worth noting that public housing units in Singapore built in the beginning of the Housing and Development Board's programme were mainly low standard one-room flats. The public authorities recognized that only with relatively low standards could they reach lower-income groups without unit subsidies severely restricting the size of the programme.

A possible indication of the extent to which inappropriate standards inhibits housing construction is the emphasis given to their revision in the *Recommendations*. We recall that standards for shelter should be 'compatible with local resources, be evolutionary, realistic and sufficiently adaptable to local culture and conditions' (*C3*). *C7* states that special attention should be given to 'establishing performance standards suited to local requirements and capable of being met by local industry' and to 'simplifying formal procedures so that they can be clearly understood and followed by local entrepreneurs'. *C8*, which states that the informal sector's efforts should receive support, mentions that priority areas for action include 'simplifying and adapting building and licensing codes without sacrificing recognized basic health requirements'. *C10* suggests that procedures for acquiring sites, short and long-term finance, building permits and codes and zoning be simplified.

Our survey found that only a few governments were thinking of reformulating building standards and regulations—the Philippines, Iraq, and Kenya being among them. Several others seem to acknowledge that existing standards and regulations are a major block to development since officially sponsored squatter upgrading, slum improvement, and serviced-site projects do not conform to these. In the Sudan, the government simply accepts that households on the cheaper, shorter-term lease plots cannot afford to meet official standards.

assisting an élite. In Brazil, the National Housing Bank's funding base was widened in 1967 by what was essentially a compulsory savings programme. Each employee of both the private and public sector had 8 per cent of his or her salary deposited with the National Housing Bank which could then be used to obtain a housing loan or could be withdrawn on retirement, illness, unemployment or other specified circumstances. Every registered worker thus had to contribute to this fund. But an analysis of the income groups that benefited from the Housing Bank's programmes up to 1974 shows lower-income groups contributing far more to the Bank through the forced savings than they actually received in housing loans. In effect, the whole programme used money drawn from lower-income groups to help fund housing loans for middle and upper-income groups.

Singapore has also used a compulsory savings scheme as one of the bases of its housing programme. All employers and employees earning more than a stated minimum contribute with contributions varying with wage levels. Individuals can withdraw a lump sum after reaching the age of 55. Or they can use it to purchase a unit in public housing projects. It seems that in Singapore this forced savings scheme has not adversely affected the lower-income groups in the same way that it has in Brazil. In Singapore, a far higher percentage of people have benefited from improved living conditions both through economic development and through government's social expenditure.

Tanzania and Tunisia both have payroll taxes that fund low-interest housing loans for low-income groups, and thus a mechanism that redistributes benefits the opposite way to that of Brazil's compulsory savings programme. Mexico has a payroll tax of 5 per cent paid by all employers which goes to help fund the Institute of the National Housing Fund for Workers. This—along with special agencies for the armed forces and government employees—loan funds to those wishing to buy or enlarge their house. Although this fund has reached some lower-income families, when the whole housing finance programme is examined most of the units it supported were only affordable by middle or lower-middle-income groups.

A housing finance policy that aims to encourage far more housing construction or improvement, and includes informal sector activity in this, has to have in place the framework that keeps unit costs low—that is, appropriate standards, land prices that do not make urban housing units prohibitively expensive for low-income groups, readily available, reasonably priced building materials and so on. It will also have to take due note of the needs of rural households and build up the institutional framework so these can be reached. Only then will the policy become effective.

One notes in passing that rent controls have constrained housing construction in the private sector and have discouraged the maintenance of privately let dwellings. Rent controls have contributed to poor and generally deteriorating conditions in privately owned tenement blocks in Cairo, La Paz, Dar es Salaam, Mexico City and many Indian cities. Public authorities are caught between the need to lower housing costs and the need to encourage private sector operations in constructing rental accommodation. Private rental accommodation is open to much abuse by exploitative landlords and yet it can provide valuable accommodation especially for people who need to be able to move at short notice to new job opportunities (and can afford the rent). Once rent control is enforced, it creates a powerful constituency who demand it be kept in place. No mechanism exists in practice to update the rates of controlled rents so as to

But no government seemed to see the true role of standards—whether defining use intensity, technological specifications or criteria for services and community facilities—as that of encouraging better-quality living environments. If the standards are realistic, evolutionary and compatible with local resources, they can fulfil such a role. If the public authorities revise existing regulations so they promote what is desirable (in terms of health and safety) and attainable by both large and small construction operations, then a far higher proportion of the houses constructed in urban areas are likely to be in the now expanded formal sector. More builders can afford to work within it while more households can afford to live in units meeting basic health and safety standards. If existing official standards remain, they will continue to be largely ignored and the informal sector will remain the major housing constructor. In addition, inappropriate standards will be used by public officials to justify inappropriate squatter settlement demolition or forced resettlement and to continue building overexpensive public housing units.

The *Recommendations* point to a new approach to standard setting and enforcing. Indeed, the new regulations become what is essentially an education programme, assisting and advising builders (including self-helpers) to ensure basic health and safety standards are met at least cost to government and to user. Demonstration projects, building advice centres and suggested building designs become part of this process. And it is a process that covers both rural and urban houses—even if different standards and regulations may be used for rural and urban units. Many existing standards such as minimum house size or the precise definition of internal facilities or permanence of structure may have to be waived altogether, at least until most of the population have some hope of affording houses built to such standards.

Such an approach to standard setting gives the only framework through which a poor, predominantly rural-based nation can hope to improve housing conditions. Whereas in urban areas the informal sector plays a major role in housing construction, in rural areas it builds the vast majority of houses. It is encouraging to see more broadly based rural housing improvement programmes in nations such as Tanzania and Indonesia where extension services and demonstration programmes seek to help rural households and builders to improve housing standards. We also found evidence in certain nations of finance institutions decentralizing their operations so that these can also reach rural and small-town households.

Building Materials and Technology

The need to encourage the development and use of local building materials is stated in many of the Habitat *Recommendations*. *C4* states that the choice of designs and technologies should 'make the best use of local resources and skills'. *C8*, under the heading of the need to encourage informal sector construction, states that the system for marketing and distributing building materials be restructured 'to favour purchase in small quantities at irregular intervals and under easy credit terms. *C10*, on aided self-help, suggests that incentives be given 'to the imaginative use of local materials, e.g. through demonstration projects and construction of prototypes suitable to local conditions'. And *C3* suggests, as we have noted already, that standards be compatible with local resources and in particular should 'conserve scarce resources and reduce dependence on foreign technologies, resources and materials'. Thus, throughout the

Recommendations there is a stress on supporting the informal sector, on developing and encouraging the use of local materials and on revising standards and regulations to allow their use in legal housing construction.

In fact, as we noted in an earlier section, government support goes almost exclusively to the formal sector, even though the informal sector is responsible for constructing the households of virtually all low-income families. Only in Singapore has such a policy resulted in improved living conditions for a large portion of the population—and as we noted this was due to unique circumstances not apparent in the other sixteen nations. Yet there are few signs of governments radically changing their policies, except indirectly in increased support to slum and squatter upgrading and in serviced-site schemes. For instance, governments in Nigeria, Iraq, Egypt, the Philippines, Jordan, and Indonesia still have faith in advanced, imported industrial building systems as a key component of housing policies. Other governments—among them the Sudan and Tunisia—are also considering this route. Yet there is little evidence that such systems can meet growing housing needs, as they do not have a very good record to date in the western nations where they were developed. Public housing programmes based on such units have run into extensive—and expensive— maintenance problems. We found no evidence that prefabricated housing units can be built cheaply enough for them to be constructed in sufficient numbers. This is especially true for nations with major balance-of-payments problems since these systems involve heavy import costs for materials, machinery and the right to use techniques developed elsewhere. In addition, an increasing number of blocks built using these techniques are having to be demolished in Europe and North America within 20 years of being constructed because either the design proved to be faulty or because the social problems they generated proved intractable.

Where such systems are transferred with little modification to countries with very different climates and cultures, the design is unlikely to suit the living requirements of the families for whom it is intended. There are also important considerations here, not only regarding physical comfort, but as to the maintenance and support for local values and culture.

Our study does not suggest that all such advanced industrial construction activities are inappropriate. They may well serve the needs of middle and upper-income urban households for apartments. They are also in demand for offices and other commercial buildings. But when viewed only from the need to improve housing conditions, they do not seem to provide a realistic solution. They have met with little success in Nigeria, Brazil and India to date. And governments' support for this type of housing construction, and lack of support for the development and use of other building technologies and materials better suited to the informal sector's capabilities, can only further exacerbate housing probems.

As we noted, there is little government support for developing and promoting the use of local building materials. But apart from access to land and basic services, nothing could more rapidly and effectively improve living conditions than steady, readily available supplies of cheap, durable building materials. It is worth noting that Singapore's Housing and Development Board took steps to ensure a steady supply of building materials for its housing construction programme. It established its own quarries and brickworks, and it used stockpiles and bulk orders placed well in advance of needs to ensure that no bottlenecks in supply hampered construction activities. All

other sixteen nations have the raw materials on which to base indigenous building material industries. If governments are serious about improving housing conditions, they must make far more effort to utilize and develop these.

Housing Finance

Public policies in many of the seventeen nations seek to encourage savings for housing and encourage households to purchase, rent, construct or improve housing units. A housing bank is the central institution of Brazil's public housing programme since 1964. We noted earlier that within the last ten years there are new or much expanded housing finance institutions in Tanzania, Jordan, the Sudan, Tunisia, Indonesia, Egypt, India, Mexico, Bolivia, and Nigeria. In the poorer, less urbanized nations, the lack of financial institutions willing to give long-term loans for housing even to middle and higher-income groups seriously constrained building activity. In many of the seventeen nations, important progress has been made recently in this field. In some—Singapore, Brazil and Colombia among them—major programmes date from the 1960s rather than the 1970s.

However, financial programmes suffer from many of the problems faced by public housing programmes—and these originate in the low and often irregular incomes of much of the population. A large portion of the urban population cannot afford to pay any rent, let alone purchase even the cheapest 'legal' house through a loan with unsubsidized interest rates. Thus, either the housing finance programme caters only for those able to afford market—or close-to-market—rates or it reaches a small proportion of lower-income households with heavily subsidized rates. In Brazil, it was the former. Despite a very considerable increase in housing production generated and supported by the National Housing Bank, unsubsidized loans were too expensive for low-income households. To attract private funds, the housing bank had to rely on generous interest payments (which were index-linked). It also had to draw on a forced savings scheme. But there is a contradiction between attracting private savings and entrepreneurial initiative and building unsubsidized houses for people with very low purchasing power. In addition, if both housing loans and savings deposits are corrected for inflation, this will benefit the depositer and cost the loaner in times of inflation. Not surprisingly, a large proportion of lower-income households that bought housing units on the National Housing Bank's loan fell behind on payments or even abandoned their units.

The alternative is heavy unit subsidies. Egypt's policy of subsidizing loans to private housing cooperatives and subsidized rents in public housing units ensures that government housing money does not go far. In Tunisia, for the 1973–6 and 1977–81 Plans, generous subsidies are given to reduce the price of 'social interest' housing units. Housing loans for lower-income groups are also subsidized. Rural housing units are the most heavily subsidized with rural households paying little more than half the real cost of the unit. Although such policies do show governments trying to bring publicly funded units within reach of low-income groups, they are likely to reach far more people with improved living conditions if subsidies per unit were reduced and standards were set to encourage more informal sector activity. By 1977, it looked as if Tunisian housing policies were changing to do this.

If governments resort to a forced savings programme to guarantee the supply of funds for expanding the provision of housing loans, then the forced savings may simply go to keep up with inflation and increasing maintenance and service costs. Thus, private sector investment in units for rent is discouraged.

Notes

1. Even if the pattern of Nepal's major towns within the national territory is not directly influenced by colonial rule, its longstanding dependence on India both for imports and as an export market is easily seen in the extent to which urban growth and development has been concentrated in towns on the main Nepal–India transport routes.

2. This refers to Khartoum Province as defined prior to the 1974 reform which changes the nine provinces which had been defined under colonial rule into eighteen provinces.

3. The criteria used for each nation to define what constitutes an 'urban' settlement are described in each nation's Background.

4. See the Philippines Background section for the criteria used to define what constitutes an 'urban' settlement.

5. These figures are based on those given in Table 3. For Nepal, around half the nation's urban population lives in Kathmandu, Lalitpur (also known as Patan and separated from Kathmandu only by the river Baghmati) and Bhaktapur (also known as Bhadgaon) which is essentially one urban agglomeration within the Kathmandu Valley.

6. Sources for Table 3 on the Three Largest Urban Agglomerations in each nation.

1950 and 1960 urban agglomeration populations (unless otherwise stated) from Davis, Kingsley (1976), *World Urbanization 1950–1970 Volume 1*, Revised Edition, Greenwood Press, Connecticut, USA, Table E. 1990 Urban Agglomeration projections from United Nations (1976), *Statistical Annex, Global Review of Human Settlements*, Department of Economic and Social Affairs, Table 6.

Kenya: Nairobi (1978), Mombasa (1978 and 1983) and Kisumu (1978 and 1983) from Kenya, Republic of (1979), *Development Plan 1979–83* Part I, table 2.4. Kisumu (1962) from United Nations (1973), *Urban Land Policies and Land Use Control Measures Volume I Africa*, ST/ECA/197, Annex 3.

Nigeria: As we noted in Section IV, note (4), there were no reliable and up-to-date statistics on city size in Nigeria as we went to press. These figures must be taken as rough estimates. Lagos (1975) from United Nations Development Program/Lagos State Masterplan Project (1975). Ibadan (1975) and Kano (1975) from United Nations (1979), *Demographic Yearbook 1978*. Lagos (1952), Ibadan (1952) and Kano (1952) from Table 1, Aradeon, David (1979), *Post Habitat Evaluation Regional Reports on Human Settlements Volume 1 Nigeria*, Faculty of Environmental Design, University of Lagos. Other sources give very different figures. For instance, the Nigerian Report to Habitat put Kano's population in 1972 at 500 000 and that of Ibadan at 895 000 without making it clear whether these were the urban agglomeration or the city populations. And the United Nations Demographic Yearbook 1978 put Ogbomosho as the third largest city with 432 000 inhabitants in 1975.

Tanzania: Figures from the 1978 census were not available as we went to press so these figures are all estimates. Dar es Salaam (1976), Arusha (1976) and Tanga (1976) from Mayao, G. and Kulaba, S. M. (1978), *Post Habitat Evaluation Report on Human Settlements in Tanzania*, Mazingira Institute, Nairobi, table 1.3. Dar es Salaam (1981), Arusha (1981) and Tanga (1981) from Tanzania, United Republic of (1976), *Third Five Year Plan for Economic and Social Development*, table 43. Dar es Salaam (1960) from Kingsley Davis. Different sources give very different estimates for Tanga's population. The Third Five Year Plan gives its estimated population at 85 700 in 1974 while the Post Habitat Evaluation Report on Human Settlements in Tanzania gives an estimate for 1976 at 70 000.

India: Calcutta (1971), Bombay (1971) and Delhi (1971) from census data quoted in United Nations (1979) *Demographic Yearbook 1978*. The figure for Delhi's population includes New Delhi.

Indonesia: Jakarta (1977) from Encyclopaedia Britannica (1978), *Book of the Year 1978*, page 370. Surabaja (1980) and Bandung (1980) are projections from United Nations (1976), *Statistical Annex—Global Review of Human Settlements*, Department of Economic and Social Affairs, Table 6.

Nepal: Kathmandu (1976) from the Economist (1978), *The World in Figures*. This figure of 415 000 inhabitants includes the town of Lalitpur (also called Patan) with a 1976 population of 135 000 and Bhaktapur (also known as Bhadgaon) with 84 000. Encyclopaedia Britannica's *Book of the Year 1978* put Kathmandu City's population at 171 400 in 1976. Biratnagar (1971) and Nepalganj (1971) from census data quoted in Bhooshan, B. S. (1979). *The Development Experience of Nepal*, Concept, India, Appendix C.

Philippines: Manila (1980) and (1990) from Apacible, M. S. and Yaxley, M., *Manila through the eyes of the Manilenos and the Consultant*, PTRC Summer Annual Meeting, 1979. Cebu (1975) and Davao (1975) from United Nations (1979), *Demographic Yearbook 1978*.

Singapore: Population figures for 1947 and 1978 are for whole nation. Singapore (1947) from Yeh, Stephen, H. K. (1975), *Public Housing in Singapore*, University of Singapore Press, page 4. Singapore (1978) from United Nations (1979), *Demographic Yearbook 1978*.

Bolivia: La Paz (1976). Santa Cruz (1976) and Cochabamba (1976) from 1976 census data.

Brazil: São Paulo (1980), Rio de Janeiro (1975) and Belo Horizonte (1980) are projections from United Nations (1976), *Statistical Annex—Global Review of Human Settlements*, Department of Economic and Social Affairs, Table 6.

Colombia: Bogota (1977) Medellin (1977) and Cali (1977) are estimates from Banco de la Republica (1979). *Colombia's Socio-Economic Indicators 1970–78*, Economic Research Department, Table 3, page 13.

Mexico: Mexico City (1978), Guadalajara (1978) and Monterrey (1978) from United Nations (1979), *Demographic Yearbook 1978*.

Egypt: Metropolitan Cairo (1979) from Europe (1980), *The Middle East and North Africa*. The figure includes Giza (whose population was put at 1.25 million in 1976) and Subra-El Khema (whose population was put at 393 700 in 1976). Mahalla al Kubrah (1976) and Alexandria (1976) from United Nations (1979), *Demographic Yearbook 1978*.

Iraq: Baghdad (1977) from census data. Mosul (1974) and Basrah (1974) from Fisher, W. B. (1978), *The Middle East*, seventh edition, Methuen and Co, page 396. This does not state whether these estimates are for the city proper or the urban agglomeration. As we discussed in note (8), Section I, there are enormous differences between the various estimates given by different statistical sources. Many still give figures based on 1965 census data. These were still used by the *United Nations Demographic Yearbook 1978* (printed in 1979) which gives Basrah's population in 1965 as 310 950 and that of Mosul at 264 146. The official statistics based on the 1977 census have not, to date, included individual city populations.

Jordan: Amman (1978), Zerqa (1978) and Irbid (1978) from Europa (1980), *North Africa and the Middle East*. Amman (1948) from Jordan, Hashemite Kingdom of (1975), *National Report to Habitat*. Zerqa (1961) from United Nations (1973), *Urban Land Policies and Land Use Control Measures Volume V, Middle East*, ST/ECA/167/Add 4, page 5.

The Sudan: The figures for Khartoum include Khartoum, Khartoum North and Omdurman. Khartoum (1955–6 and 1978), Port Sudan (1955/6 and 1978) and Wad Medani (1955/6) from Agency for International Development (1978), *Sudan Shelter Sector Assessment*, Office of Housing, USA, Appendices A–4 and A–5. Wad Medani (1973) from Sudan, Democratic Republic of (1975), *National Report to Habitat*.

Tunisia: Tunis (1975 and 1986), Sfax (1975 and 1986) and Sousse (1975 and 1986) from Agency for International Development (1979), *Tunisia: Shelter Sector Survey*, Office of Housing, USA. The figure for Tunis is for the District of Tunis. Sfax's metropolitan area was reported by the above source to have 257 000 inhabitants in 1975.

7. World Bank (1979). *World Development Report, 1979*, page 46.

8. Misra, R. P. and Bhooshan, B. S. (1979). *Human Settlements in Asia*, (New Delhi: Heritage).

9. The percentage of the national population living in rural areas in 1976 was 12.8 per cent (estimated) if 'urban areas' are settlements with more than 5000 inhabitants.

10. Task Force on Human Settlements (1975). *Human Settlements—The Vision of a New Society*, G1/HC/PH1/501.

11. Lu, Martin (1976). 'II PND. Pode O empresario integrar-se?', *Journal Visao*, **19 April**.

12. Tanzania, United Republic of (1976). *Third Five Year Plan for Economic and Social Development, 1976–81* (Dar es Salaam: Government Printers).

13. Blitzer, Silvia and Hardoy, Jorge, E. (1980). *Aid for Human Settlements in Latin America, a Summary of the Activities of Multilateral Agencies during 1977 and 1978*, IIED.
14. Teriba, O. and Kayode, M. O. (1978). 'Industrial location and development policy in developing countries' in Misra, R. P., Urs, D. V., and Natraj, V. K. (editors) *Regional Planning and National Development*, (India: Vikas).
15. Cuenya, B., Gazzoli, R., and Yujnovsky, O. (1979). *Politicas de asentamientos humanos*, (Argentina: Ediciones SIAP).
16. Kulaba, S. M. and Mayao, G. (1978). *Post-Habitat Evaluation Report on Human Settlements in Tanzania* (Mazingira Institute), **July**.
17. Sierra, Pedro Javier Soto (1977). 'Transformacion en el sector urbano', VI Congreso Interamericano de Vivienda, Interhabitat, Medellin.
18. Varma, Rameswari, and Sastry, N. N. (1979), *Habitat Asia: Issues and Responses, Volume III: Japan and Singapore* stated that Singapore's Land Acquisition Act enables the government to acquire land based on the value of the property in November 1973 (page 149). This may well have been changed by now.
19. Darin-Drabkin, H. (1976). *Land Policy and Urban Growth* (Oxford: Pergamon Press).
20. El Agraa, Omer, M. A., and Admad, Adil M. (1979). *Assessment of Human Settlements in Arab Countries*, study sponsored by the International Institute for Environment and Development, London. (A revised version was published by the University of Khartoum Press in 1980).
21. Misra, R. P., and Bhooshan, B. S. (1979). *Habitat Asia: Issues and Responses, Volume I: India* (India: Concept), page 196.
22. Virtually all the figures quoted in this summary are drawn from earlier sections describing in more depth each nation's housing policies. The reader should refer back to these for sources.
23. Nigeria's Federal Mortgage Bank was formed out of the Nigerian Building Society while the Tanzanian Housing Bank took over the assets and liabilities of the Permanent Housing Finance Company of Tanzania which had financed the construction of houses for upper income groups on a commercial basis.
24. Sudan, Democratic Republic of (1975). *National Report on Human Settlements*, Department of Housing Services and Engineering Affairs, Ministry of People's Local Government.
25. De Vera, Jacobo (1974–5). 'Housing needs up to the year 2000 and its financing implications', *NEDA Journal of Development*, **I and II**, page 61, Table 14.
26. Egypt, Arab Republic of, Ministry of Planning with Office of Housing, US AID (1976). *Statistical Appendix—Immediate Action Proposals for Housing in Egypt*, Table IV–1, page 51.
27. United Nations (1976). *World Housing Survey 1974*, Table 28, pages 103–5.
28. Kenya, Republic of (1979). *Development Plan 1979–83 Part I*, page 50.
29. Kenya, Republic of (1979). *Statistical Abstract 1978*, Central Bureau of Statistics, page 163, Table 145(b).
30. Philippines, Republic of (1977). *Five-Year Philippine Development Plan*, National Economic and Development Authority, Table 11.2, pages 225–7.
31. United Nations (1976). *World Housing Survey 1974*, Table VI–3.
32. Lim, William (1975). *Equity and Urban Environment in the Third World*, DP Consultant Service, Singapore.
33. Moochtar, Radinal (1979). 'Urban housing in Indonesia', *Habitat International*, **4**, no. 3.
34. Osobukola, F. O. (1977). 'Socio-economic Problems of Low Cost Housing Schemes in Nigeria', paper presented at the Fourth Conference on Housing in Africa, Tunisia (May 1977), sponsored by US AID.
35. Public Works, Ministry of (1975). *National Interim Report on Human Settlements in Indonesia*, the National Preparatory Committee of Habitat, page 31.
36. El Agraa, Omer, M. A., and Ahmad, Adil M. (1979). *Assessment of Human Settlements in Arab Countries*.

Conclusions and Recommendations

Conclusions and Recommendations

In virtually all the nations studied, most of the population are faced with poor and often deteriorating living conditions. The concentration of much of the public and private investment in a few major urban centres over the last few decades has led to their rapid growth. It has usually meant the exclusion of large portions of the population and much of the national territory from social and economic development. The labour force in the major urban centres has generally grown far faster than the creation of secure employment opportunities there. The population of these urban centres has also grown faster than their stock of housing and the network of basic infrastructure and services. There is generally serious overcrowding in existing houses while the construction of new units to official standards by both private and public sector investment meets only a small proportion of the growth in housing needs every year.

The result is a large and even growing number of the national population with no secure source of livelihood above any reasonable definition of subsistence level, no access to potable water or to basic health case serives, and no adequate arrangements for the sanitary removal of human and household wastes. Access to education is also far from universal. Most housing continues to be built without official permission and without meeting official standards. But only through such building operations are the vast majority of people housed—and housed at a price and in a location they can afford.

Despite widely differing national responses to such problems, each of the seventeen governments was found to be giving more attention to housing problems and to the wider distribution of benefits from social and economic investments. Most are trying to move away from the simple concentration on economic growth and sectoral national development plans that characterize the 1960s and early 1970s. For settlement policies, new institutions are emerging to provide a spatial framework for development investment. In two nations, Mexico and the Philippines, new ministerial-level bodies have emerged. For land policies, many nations including Mexico, Tunisia, Nigeria, Brazil and the Philippines have had major initiatives in the second half of the 1970s. Increased support is being given to more widely based shelter programmes with a new emphasis on slum or squatter upgrading and serviced-site schemes. In the Sudan and Tanzania, such schemes are the central element of urban housing policies. In nations such as Indonesia, the Philippines and Colombia, they are also receiving far more support.

However, despite such promising signs, government action is virtually always inadequate and often ill-directed. Assessments as to the success of government policies are hampered by the lack of accurate and up-to-date social data. But when looking back on the 1970s, only in Singapore, Tanzania and Tunisia does there seem to be a significant proportion of the population whose access to basic services or housing conditions have improved. In Tanzania's case, such progress is threatened by major economic problems which partly relate to its lack of power within the world market. Only a handful of nations show signs of giving serious attention to the Habitat *Recommendations* they officially endorsed at the United Nations Conference on Human Settlements. Most claimed to, but have picked on only those *Recommendations* that serve their political ends. In many nations, urban-based publicly funded housing programmes still dominate government policies even though, to date, these have made little impression on improving living conditions, especially for lower-income groups. As we examined in detail earlier (page 252), Singapore's relative success was due to a series of factors, unique to Singapore, which had little or nothing to do with the actual houses themselves.

It is dangerous to attempt to make any general conclusions about a group of nations that includes Nepal (one of the world's poorest and most rural nations) and Brazil or Mexico (both major economic powers in Latin America and indeed in the world). But some of our conclusions seem of general validity and are backed up by the few examples of successful programmes or policies we came across.

1. Unless there is a firm polititical and financial commitment to the struggle against poverty with such a commitment becoming evident in national development plans and in specific programmes (such as employment creation, technical education and social development) no effective housing or settlement policy can emerge. Several of the nations covered in this volume could solve most of the problems relating to the poor and deteriorating conditions much of their population endures with foresight and with some degree of generosity in the attitude of those social groups who have benefited and indeed are benefiting from the process of development. These nations do not necessarily lack the funds or the technical skills and data for social development. But these resources are not put to adequate use. And even the poorest nations we examined, which did lack such resources, could have a deeper impact on improving the living conditions of their population if they followed suggestions made in (3) below.

2. National development plans must consider their spatial implications. The pattern of economic and social development over the national territory is powerfully influenced by the type and location of social and economic investments (by both private and public sectors). Most national development plans show little sign of having considered the spatial implications of the sectoral investments they propose—and thus of the kind of development they will promote. Despite ambitious social and spatial aims stated in such plans, they rarely contain policies that thave any hope of meeting such aims and all too frequently end up enriching already privileged social groups, regions and large agglomerations. Since such plans outline the sectors to which all public investments are made—and frequently take note of (and try and influence) private investments—such plans must consider the spatial distribution of development funds among cities, towns, villages and regions and the type of development such a distribution will promote. Only by considering such spatial

implications can national development plans seek to spread both social and economic development so they reach a wider proportion of the population and the national territory, *and* recognize their limitations in being able to do so. Many of the national development plans our assessment looked at remain sectoral in nature with no consideration of the pattern of development they were promoting. Several others professed spatial aims which were beyond the scope and power of the plan to achieve. Indeed, the plan's actual distribution of development funds often ran counter to these spatial aims.

3. For housing policies, the government must recognize that a large proportion of households cannot afford even the lowest-cost unit built by private or public contractors. A squatter's shack is often all the household can afford. Given its needs and priorities in the use of a limited and often fluctuating income, this may serve it far better than a heavily subsidized public housing unit elsewhere. Recognizing this, the government's primary task becomes that of encouraging the general improvement of living conditions putting its limited resources where they can have maximum effect. Any attempt by the government to build conventional houses for the population runs into the 'bottomless pit' problem. However much they spend, there are always more units needed. But our analysis of housing problems showed five crucial areas where government action can (and in some instances has) had a major effect on improving living conditions at little (or no) cost.

The government at national and sub-national levels must use its legal powers to ensure there is an adequate supply of land for housing in urban areas. The price of such land should not be so high as to automatically exclude the poor majority. Usually, the National Constitution gives government the constitutional basis on which to formulate needed legislation. Because of the urban land market's peculiar nature (which was discussed earlier) and because of the poverty of so many households, without such action by government, a legal housing site will remain beyond the price range of most families. This is especially true in rapidly urbanizing societies. Without an effective urban land policy which allows a large proportion of urban households to enter it—and choose where to live—no government has any chance of tackling mounting housing deficits and inadequate service provision.

It is also worth noting that taxes on land (whether on the land itself or on the unearned increment in land values) can also provide local governments with valuable revenues. These could help fund the extension of basic services and infrastructure to all the population under their jurisdiction.

The government must revise official standards—building codes minimum plot sizes, building permits, etc. Their purpose is (or should be) to encourage better quality living environments. This was their original intention. They will only do so if they strike a balance between what is *desirable* (in terms of health and safety), *attainable* (by both large and small construction operations) and *affordable* by the majority of households and by the nation as a whole. Otherwise, they will continue to be irrelevant to most housing construction operations.

The new commitment by governments to considering the spatial implications of development plans and to clearly articulating what they intend to do with regard to settlements must be backed up with more comprehensive data collection. In most Third World nations, the quantity and quality of basic social data is very deficient and seriously hinders the task of designing, implementing and continuously evaluating settlement policies and programmes. This lack of data is apparent at national level but even more so at the level of the regions and individual settlements. Each major settlement or region should have basic information about such things as population size, structure and movement, public (and where possible private) expenditures and their spatial distribution, housing conditions and housing production (both formal and informal sectors), land ownership patterns, employment patterns and trends, and building material production. However, lack of such data should not delay decision makers from making preliminary decisions which can be adjusted as more information becomes available. Use can be made of research documents, specialized reports and local statistics (even if they are sketchy and not very precise). Use can also be made of selected local informants in each locality and region to give policy makers information based on their direct experience and observations, if statistical information is not available.

One major area where government action is needed is in the building materials industry. The lack of cheap, readily available, reasonable quality building materials is a major constraint on all construction operations. Government support to the development and widespread use of building materials based on indigenous resources is very inadequate. Again, this will probably demand a revision of urban building codes which often expressly forbid the use of such materials.

Training programmes concerned with settlement policies must receive a lot more support. The institutional changes recommended above need implementation. This cannot be achieved without skilled personnel. Similarly, new initiatives to spread, say, potable water will simply not work unless there is adequate provision for maintenance of new machinery *and* adequate training, education and information programmes to back up new technology or practices the development programme is promoting.

In making these recommendations, however, we do note that for many Third World nations, governments' financial resource base is so weak as to seriously constrain even the modest expenditure entailed by these recommendations. In most of the seventeen nations we looked at, human and material resources are available to tackle the most pressing problems of poverty. But for some—Nepal, Tanzania and the Sudan among them—government resources are limited by these nations' lack of earning power within the world community. For each, the return they receive for the primary produce on which their export earnings depend fluctuates—and has shown a long term trend over the last thirty years of declining in value relative to the manufactured goods and, more recently, the oil they import. Diversifying their exports is constrained by their lack of industrial development and by increasingly competitive markets in this time of economic recession. They are also seriously constrained by rising protectionism in the rich, industrialized nations both for manufactured goods and on processed or semi-processed primary products. Inevitably, development programmes are constrained by lack of capital. Economic imperatives such as increasing export earnings may and often do run against basic development aims—decreasing food imports or a better distribution of social and economic development among their population. The success of such nations in tackling poverty and thus improving living conditions is seriously curtailed by such factors. Only by restructuring the world economic system so it does not constantly turn all economic bargains against the needs of the poorest nations will such basic problems be resolved. Thus, housing problems within nations should be seen as part of a world economic system which must itself be changed if the world community is serious about meeting basic needs for all.

Statistical Annex

Table 7 Physical indicators

Countries	1 Geographical area (1000 km²)	2 Population (millions) 1970	1978	3 Population density (number of people per km²) 1978	4 Average annual population growth (%) 1960–70	1970–8
Africa						
Kenya	583	11.2	14.7	25	3.4	3.3
Nigeria	924	66.2	80.6	87	2.5	2.5
Tanzania	945	13.0	16.9	18	2.7	3.0
Asia						
India	3288	538.1	643.9	196	2.5	2.0
Indonesia	2027	115.6	136.0	67	2.2	1.8
Nepal	141	11.1	13.6	96	2.0	2.2
Philippines	300	36.9	45.6	152	3.0	2.7
Singapore	0.6	2.1	2.3	3833	2.4	1.5
Latin America						
Bolivia	1099	4.9	5.3	5	2.5	2.6
Brazil	8512	92.8	119.5	14	2.9	2.8
Colombia	1139	21.6	25.6	22	3.0	2.3
Mexico	1973	50.7	65.4	33	3.3	3.3
Arab nations						
Egypt	1001	33.3	39.9	40	2.5	2.2
Iraq	435	9.4	12.2	28	3.1	3.3
Jordan	98	2.3	3.0	31	3.0	3.3
Sudan	2506	15.7	17.4	7	2.2	2.6
Tunisia	164	5.1	6.0	37	1.9	2.0

Sources: Columns 1 and 4: from *World Development Report 1980* (World Bank)
Column 2: from *World Development Report 1980* and *World Bank Tables, 1977* (World Bank)
Column 3: Derived

Table 8 Economic indicators

| Countries | GNP per capita | | Distribution of GDP (%) | | | | | |
| | (US$) 1978 | average annual growth (%) 1960–78 | Agriculture | | Industry | | Services | |
			1960	1978	1960	1978	1960	1978
Africa								
Kenya	330	2.2	38	41	18	19	44	40
Nigeria	560	3.6	63	34	11	43	26	23
Tanzania	230	2.7	57	51	11	13	32	36
Asia								
India	180	1.4	50	40	20	26	30	34
Indonesia	360	4.1	54	31	14	33	32	36
Nepal	120	0.8	—	62	—	12	—	26
Philippines	510	2.6	26	27	28	35	46	38
Singapore	3,290	7.4	4	2	18	35	78	63
Latin America								
Bolivia	510	2.2	26	17	25	28	49	55
Brazil	1,570	4.9	16	11	35	37	49	52
Colombia	850	3.0	34	31	26	27	40	42
Mexico	1,290	2.7	16	11	29	37	55	52
Arab nations								
Egypt	390	3.3	30	29	24	30	46	41
Iraq	1,860	4.1	17	—	52	—	31	—
Jordan	1,050	—	—	11	—	29	—	60
Sudan	320	0.1	58	43	15	12	27	45
Tunisia	950	4.8	24	18	18	30	58	52

Source: *World Development Report 1980* (World Bank)
Note: Figures for Tunisia's 1960 Distribution of GDP are for 1961 while figures for Kenya, Nepali, Sudanese and Nigerian 1978 Distribution of GDP are for 1977.

Table 9 Social indicators

Countries	1 Life expectancy at birth (years)		2 Infant mortality (per 1000 live births)	3 Adult literacy (%)		4 Education spending (per capita US$)
	1960	1978		1960	1975	1974
Africa						
Kenya	47	53	114	20	40	7
Nigeria	39	48	157	15	—	13
Tanzania	42	51	163	10	66	5
Asia						
India	43	51	129	28	36	3
Indonesia	41	47	137	39	62	4
Nepal	36	43	152	9	19	1
Philippines	51	60	80	72	87	8
Singapore	64	70	12	—	75	55
Latin America						
Bolivia	43	52	157	39	63	12
Brazil	57	62	109	61	76	33
Colombia	53	62	90	63	81	10
Mexico	58	65	66	65	76	28
Arab nations						
Egypt	46	54	162	26	44	2
Iraq	46	55	104	18	—	38
Jordan	47	56	97	32	70	18
Sudan	39	46	167	13	20	5
Tunisia	48	57	135	16	55	34

Sources: Columns 1 and 3: *World Development Report, 1980* (World Bank)
 Columns 2 and 4: *The United States and World Development Agenda 1979* (Overseas Development Council)
Note: Figures for infant mortality are latest available estimates and some may not reflect current trends. Figures for adult literacy either on or within two years of specified date.

Table 10 Rural/agricultural indicators

Countries	Rural Population as % total population		Arable Land and Land Under Permanent Crops 1977			
	1	2	3	4	5	6
	1960	1980	Area (1000 h)	% under irrigation	Hectares per capita	Hectares per agricultural population
Africa						
Kenya	93	86	2,270	2	0.16	0.20
Nigeria	87	80	23,990	0.1	0.30	0.64
Tanzania	95	88	5,100	1	0.31	0.38
Asia						
India	82	78	169,400	21	0.27	0.40
Indonesia	85	80	17,200	28	0.13	0.20
Nepal	97	95	2,314	9	0.17	0.19
Philippines	70	64	8,100	14	0.18	0.38
Singapore	—	—	—	—	—	—
Latin America						
Bolivia	76	67	3,305	4	0.64	1.34
Brazil	54	35	40,720	2	0.35	0.87
Colombia	52	30	5,505	5	0.22	0.72
Mexico	49	33	23,220	22	0.37	0.95
Arab nations						
Egypt	62	55	2,831	100	0.07	0.15
Iraq	57	28	5,290	22	0.45	1.06
Jordan	57	44	1,365	4	0.47	2.33
Sudan	90	75	7,495	21	0.44	0.59
Tunisia	64	48	4,410	3	0.75	1.69

Sources: Columns 1 and 2 *World Development Report 1980*
Column 3 *FAO Production Yearbook 1978* Most of the figures are FAO estimates
Columns 4, 5 and 6 derived. Area under irrigation (1977) and agriculture population (1977) from *FAO Production Yearbook 1978*; 1977 national populations from *World Development Report 1979*. The agricultural population includes all persons depending on agriculture for their livelihood (including non-working dependents).

Index

Geographical regions listed under country headings; towns, cities and political regions listed on their own. Page numbers printed in bold type indicate page where settlement, region, river or lake is shown on a map

278

284

288